PRAISE FOR...

I0590623

Art & Dotty:
His Diary, Their Letters & Photographs of WWII

"As I read through this text, one word continually flashed through my mind: 'Amazing.' Amazing that this much-in-love couple continued correspondence throughout their long separation brought on by war. Amazing that they were able to resume their storybook life after WWII. Amazing that the letters, cards, pictures, et al, remained intact down through the years. Amazing that we are privileged to follow virtually every aspect of their day-to-day lives— from Dotty's humorous description of squirming into a girdle to Art's visceral depictions of combat. Amazing that their observations from the 1940s parallel many situations in the 21st century, particularly pertaining to (a) the cruelty of racial and ethnic discrimination and (b) the pall of uncertainty for the future —be it war in the Bushings case, or the unknowns about COVID-19 today. Indeed, here is a truly amazing book, on oh-so-many fronts!"

Sam Venable, author and Knoxville News Sentinel columnist

"This book features two parallel stories. One is the enduring romance and love of the featured character and his wife. The other, the guiding story, deals with the service of Art Bushing in the U.S. Army during and after World War II. Following his graduation from college, Bushing entered the Army and, after basic training, received language training. He was deployed to Europe as an infantryman, as part of Patton's 3rd Army, fighting all the way to Austria. This is an enjoyable book, easy to read. The story pulls the reader along, anxious to find out what will happen next, both in Europe and at home in Tennessee. It is an interesting and informative look at one man's journey through the final years of World War II and after."

Michael F. Dilley, Major, U.S. Army (Retired), Military Historian and Author

"Art Bushing had long been a legend at Maryville College when I met him nearly thirty years ago. I had just moved into the President's Office in Anderson Hall, and was looking for advice when some wise staff member suggested: "You should talk to Art Bushing." Art accepted my invitation to go to lunch, and the hour-plus that we spent together was just what I needed. He gave me a crash course in Maryville College history and frank counsel that served me well throughout my presidential watch.

"Those who read *Art & Dotty: His Diary, Their Letters & Photographs of WWII* and/or *Art Bushing: His Diary, Letters, & Photographs of WWII* will be similarly well-served. They will discover a diarist, a philosopher, a photographer, a warrior, a contemporary historian, a teacher, an aficionado of the arts, a travel journalist, and a man of faith. Art was, in sum, a multi-faceted, multi-talented son of Maryville College. Readers of this book, even those who think they knew him, will likely find in its pages the revelation of a breadth and depth of thought beyond their expectations.

"They will also discover a wonderful love story. The affection that Art Bushing and Dotty Barber Bushing had for each other comes through in page after page. Their mutual commitment is there in every letter throughout Art's Army days. Whether in combat in Europe or on furlough in Paris or England, he keeps his pledge to write to Dotty and waits impatiently for her warm letters to find him overseas. The reader comes to share their frustration with the Army's interminable delays when the war has finally ended and Art is waiting anxiously to come home to Dotty.

"On a mild afternoon in November of 2008, I had the sad privilege of conducting Art Bushing's graveside service. Dotty was there, along with their adult children. My heart was heavy for them, and the sadness would surely have been much heavier for me had I read those letters beforehand. Yet I am comforted now by having shared their loving correspondence and knowing that it had survived not only WWII but through more than six decades of marriage. God bless you, Art Bushing!"

Gerald W. Gibson, 10th President Emeritus, Maryville College

"*Art Bushing: His Diary, Letters, & Photographs of WWII (Volumes I and II)* are must-reads to get a behind the scenes look into the lives of the 'Greatest Generation' and the momentous sacrifices that were made to defeat tyranny and preserve freedom. Following the experiences of Art Bushing with his entry into the Army, and his eventual combat deployment into the European Theater of Operations (ETO), and his wife Dotty, this book captures the essence of what soldiers and their loved ones endured both on the Home Front and the Western Front. This is a timely work of one of the most consequential epochs in American History and a must-read for the next generation to understand that indeed freedom is not free."

Doug Mastriano, PhD, Senator (Pennsylvania), Colonel (US Army, Ret), and American military historian

---

"Mahatma Gandhi once said, 'In a gentle way, you can shake the world.' Arthur and Dotty Bushing filled a 24 hour day with 36 hours of life! A smorgasbord of service—to our country, to our community, to our lives, and to our Lord God. This close-up and personal view into their lives, their story, will paint a picture of the 'earthquake' they created in their lifetime proving the difference we can all make in the lives of one another. A national hero serving a local world."

Joanie Latorre, East TN Historian, PBS Antiques Extravaganza

"This is an interesting collection that informs our understanding of the American experience during World War II."

Charles Hubbard, PhDm Professor of History, Lincoln Memorial University & Abraham Lincoln Historian

Art & Dotty

His Diary, Their Letters & Photographs of WWII

Art & Dotty

His Diary, Their Letters & Photographs of

WORLD WAR II

Volume I

Publishing
Angel
Climbing

ART & DOTTY: His Diary, Their Letters & Photographs of WWII (Vol. I)
    Written by Arthur Story Bushing & Dorothy "Dotty" Bushing
Primary letters written by Art and Dorothy "Dotty" Bushing
Other letters from a variety of close family and friends

Art's "Memories of WWII" diary (1945 & 1946) edited by
    Dorothy "Dotty" Bushing and Martha Hess.
Book transcribed, compiled, and edited by Lisa Soland
    Tonya Hobbs, assistant to editor

Published in 2020 by
Climbing Angel Publishing
PO Box 32381
Knoxville, Tennessee 37930
http://www.ClimbingAngel.com

First Edition, August 2020
Printed in the United States of America
Photos contributed by Dorothy "Dotty" Bushing
Cover design by PrintEdge, Knoxville
Interior design by Climbing Angel Publishing

Volume I, ISBN: 978-1-64370-027-4
Library of Congress Control Number: 2020909692

I would like to dedicate this book, written by my deceased husband Arthur Story Bushing, to my children Arthur Stuart Bushing, Barbera Bushing-Rose, Kathy (Bushing) Banfield, and Jennifer (Bushing) Hill, with the fond hope that they will pass it down to the next generation.

Dotty Bushing

CONTENTS

Foreword by Karen Beaty Eldridge   xiii

Introduction by Dorothy "Dotty" Bushing   xix
  My Maryville College Wedding!

Preface by Art S. Bushing   xxiii

Photographs   xxv

Letter dated Dec. 22, 1942   xxxi

1943

1. THIS IS THE ARMY, MR. JONES   1

Diary Entries, Letters & Photographs
  Dated Jan. 1, 1943 to Dec. 31, 1943   7

1944

Diary Entries, Letters & Photographs
  Dated Jan. 1, 1944 to Dec. 31, 1944   307

Editor's Note and Acknowledgments   435
  Lisa Soland

Dotty & Art Bushing with Karen Eldridge's sons,
Robbie and Drew Eldridge.

FOREWORD

"*H*e's such a nice man."

"He's so smart."

When I arrived on the Maryville College campus in the fall of 1990, I found both descriptions of Arthur Bushing, Jr., to be true. They had come from my great aunts, Frances Beaty McDonald and Margaret Beaty Echols, then Nashville residents who remembered "Art" as a dear childhood friend from Jamestown, Tenn., some 50 years earlier.

Frances and Margaret were two of eight children born to Dillard Osborne Beaty and Martha Ellen Smith Beaty. The Beaty siblings' birth years stretched from 1915 until 1932, so Art, born in 1922, fit right in and likely was fascinated by visits to the loud, busy Beaty household that was unlike the home he shared with only a mother and father.

Art was my teacher only once (English 162: Interpreting Literature in the Spring semester of my freshman year), but he always greeted me and my older sister, Ann (also a Maryville College student) like relatives whenever we saw him on campus and frequently asked about Frances and Margaret; their brothers and sister who were still living; our father and mother; our grandmother, aunts and uncles; and Jamestown. It wasn't long after I started at Maryville College that Art proudly proclaimed to me that Ann and I were the fifth generation of the Smith-Beaty family he had known. I was as equally touched that he had bothered to count it as I was impressed that life expectancies allowed such an achievement.

As a student, I experienced Art's generosity and intellect, but it wasn't until I was hired as director of the College's Alumni and Parent Relations Office in 1997 that I began to know and appreciate Art as a devoted alumnus, 50-year employee and campus legend. He seemed to know everyone connected to Maryville College, and he helped his alma mater in any way he possibly could.

This impressive breadth of service began just after his graduation in 1943, when Art, an English major/math and physics minor was hired to teach physics. His appointment was interrupted by service in World War II, but he returned to his beloved Maryville College in 1947 as an assistant professor of English. By that time, he had studied for a summer at the Sorbonne in Paris and had begun work on a master's degree at the University of Tennessee.

Over the next half-century, he would not only earn a master's degree and continue his education at the University of Iowa, Duke, and other universities, he would become a rock in the English Department. His teaching load frequently included courses in 17th and 18th Century British Literature and an upper-level course entitled "The Novel in English." He chaired the department on two separate occasions.

And whether they had him as a professor or not, Maryville College students across the decades knew him for his Manual of Outlining and Research, which taught undergraduates how to organize information and properly cite sources for papers.

In 1957, Art was asked to divide his time between academics and administration when he was tapped to become the College's Dean of Men, a position he held for eight years. He was asked to direct the College's Summer School in 1968, a position he held for nine years. In 1973, he initiated the Continuing Education Program, directing it for five years. And for three years, faculty looked to him to coordinate the Freshman Inquiry Program.

In the early 1990s, Art spent January Terms as a history professor, leading a class on World War II. He supplemented the text with his own stories and invited veterans into the classroom to share their wartime experiences and lessons.

A model for lifelong learning, Art was always studying something. His research subjects included William Shakespeare, Henry Fielding, and World War I hero Alvin C. York, whom Art knew personally in Jamestown.

Art retired in 1996 but walks to campus from his home on nearby Jones Avenue weren't over. For more than a decade after he graded his last final examination, Art was a frequent visitor in the Advancement Offices at Willard House and the Communication Office at Fayerweather Hall, helping with reunions and other gatherings on campus and sharing news from classmates and former students. He kept up with people and often relayed the goings-on of longtime friends like Ted Kidder, Ted Pratt and Ellis Burcaw. He and Dorothy Barber Bushing, his wife of more than a half-century and also a Maryville College alumna, seemed to be present at almost all college functions.

In 2000, Art was recognized with the College's highest honor, the Maryville College Medallion. In presenting the award at the Founder's Day Banquet that year, President Gerald W. Gibson said of the 1943 alumnus: "His devotion is unceasing and his support untiring. He did far more than was asked of him and far more than could have been expected."

————————

I married just months after the 2000 Founder's Day, and as a wedding present, Art and Dotty gave me a blank guest book with a note of advice to begin a tradition of recording all the friends and family members who visit my new home. It might have been an unusual wedding gift from anyone else, but not the Bushings. After getting to know them in those 10 years, I knew that they valued personal relationships and time spent with loved ones above most material possessions. And I knew theirs was a marriage on which I should pattern my own.

One of the last visits I made to the Bushing house was in 2007 to introduce Art and Dotty to the sixth generation of the Smith-Beaty family, my sons Robert Harrison and Andrew Blake. Dotty took our picture, and I took one of her holding Drew while Art and Robbie looked into the camera. In a sweet moment that I'll never forget, Art took Robbie out in the backyard and showed my 3-year-old his garden and water hose. Seeing the water shoot out of the nozzle, Robbie connected the moment to his favorite superhero. He asked Art if he liked Spiderman, and Art replied in the affirmative. A friendship was made.

With this publication of *Art Bushing: His Diary, Letters, & Photographs of WWII*, I am introduced, alongside thousands of members of the Maryville College family, to yet another dimension of Arthur Bushing, Jr.—that of decorated soldier, philosopher, poet, writer, Christian disciple, and devoted son, friend, fiancé, and husband.

Twelve years after his death and 74 years after he penned the last entry in his wartime diary, Art offers a final class in life, love, and the power of words.

He was such a nice man. He was so smart. But Arthur Bushing, Jr., was so much, much more, and I'm thankful for this book—yet another opportunity—to be reminded of that.

Karen Beaty Eldridge
Executive Director for Marketing &
Communications, Maryville College
Maryville, Tennessee
May 2020

Art and Dotty Bushing on their wedding day

INTRODUCTION

My Maryville College Wedding!

I t all started in the Maryville College woods, a beautiful section of the woods with huge trees and a brook running through them. I was a year ahead of Arthur Story Bushing in school, so I was no longer bound by the college rules which would have horrified the matrons if they had known that I went to the college woods at night with a man. That was a "no, no." But I had already graduated.

And so, one summer while "Art" was still a student there, the two of us went for a walk in the college woods, and there among these glorious old trees, we pledged our troth. But alas, the week after he graduated, Art enlisted in the army and was swept off to California to be in what they called the Army Specialized Training Program. His parents ran the local draft board and I'm sure Art did not want to have special exemption so he took responsibility and did his part by signing up. While with the Army Specialized Training Program, he was given training in the Dutch language which was used in the Dutch Islands in the Pacific where he might be called upon to go to help the top brass make decisions.

Art was first sent to camp Roberts. Then after a period of time, he was sent on to Stanford where the unit of the ASTP was held. While there, he decided he would like to send me a special ring. He made a deal with my mom to take the package inside when it arrived, and on Christmas morning, as I was waking up, my mother brought me this package wrapped neatly in Christmas paper. So, Art had sent the ring to me through the mail and I was delighted!

Later when he received a little bit of leave from the program, it was planned that Art would come to Knoxville so we could be married. But, the army cancelled that leave. Then suddenly it was back on again, but now we had less time so I was to travel to him instead. With those last minute changes, I had no berth on the train—nowhere to sleep—and so I traveled from Knoxville to California sitting up. But I was on cloud nine because I was going to be married, so a little inconvenience did not bother me at all!

When I arrived to Chicago, Union Station was a madhouse, so I was unable to get on the train that I had originally scheduled. Instead, I took one that was an hour later because it was the only train available, and after three days of rocking back and forth in the seat, I arrived to San Francisco, California. I disembarked and stood on the platform. All the other passengers took off. And no sign of Art. Help! There I was; I traveled 3,000 miles to California to get married and no spouse in sight.

Finally, I called one of my Maryville College classmates, Helen Pratt Tapp, who lived with her mother nearby. Her husband was already fighting in the war overseas. Helen had been busy making arrangements for our wedding to take place in her church. She said to me on the phone, "Now Dotty, I want you to go to the Greyhound Bus Station to wait for Art. He'll pick you up there." When Art had not found me at the train station at the appointed time, he called Helen as well and she instructed him to do the same.

I went to the station and I waited and I waited, but Art did not appear. It turns out that in San Francisco there were two Greyhound Bus Stations, and he had gone to the wrong one. Finally, after all these mishaps, in walked Art with a bunch of wilted flowers and an explanation of what had happened with him. What a relief! And to finally know that nothing unfortunate had happened to him!

My arrival was on a Wednesday and the wedding was scheduled for a Thursday, the following day. My friend Helen served as my maid-of-honor, and a classmate of Art's, Van Cise, served as his best man. Would it be redundant of me to mention that Phil Evaul, the man who performed most of the ceremony, was also a Maryville College graduate? Phil just happened to be in California studying at the Presbyterian Seminary at San Selmo, so that made every member of the wedding party a Maryville College graduate.

We were married on April 6, 1944, in Helen's church in San Jose on the Maundy Thursday of Easter week. The church was wonderfully decorated with fragrant Calla lilies so we didn't need any other flowers at all. And that's my Maryville College Wedding story.

What you are now holding in your hands is the written and photographic work of the wonderful man that I married in California during World War II.

Art served in the United States Army and was not supposed to keep a diary, but like Sergeant Alvin C. York, he did anyway. My husband's father, Arthur Samuel Bushing, was Alvin York's personal secretary following the Great War. Father Bushing, as we called him, was never fully accepted in Jamestown, Tennessee, because he was a Yankee, having spent his youth growing up in Brooklyn, New York. I don't believe that Art's father was ever fully recognized for the role he played in Sergeant York's life. My father-in-law wrote much of the lectures and speeches York delivered. Father Bushing was a writer too, and because he worked and lived in Jamestown, Tennessee, that is where my husband, Art, spent most of his childhood.

When I think back to those early days when I first met Art at Maryville College, I was charmed by his personality, yes, and his great big smile, as this book's cover gives witness. But it was his concern for others, the fact that he always put other people first that grabbed hold of me and would not let me go. This compassion showed itself primarily in his volunteer work in the church, and in the classroom when he taught.

After World War II, my husband returned to Maryville College, his alma mater, and was hired as an Assistant Professor in the English Department, teaching his beloved subject of writing. He eventually served as chair for that department, and before he retired in 1996, he had greatly impacted the lives of so many students. He even kept up with them after they had graduated, continuing to encourage them in their lives. Following my late husband's death, I'll bet I received close to 200 sympathy cards from former students, writing that Art was the best teacher they ever had.

I hope you enjoy Art's WWII diary, looking at his snapshots, and reading some of the letters we exchanged. Art loved to write. I was only a fair writer myself, but throughout the war we corresponded daily. He never swore, smoke or drank, which were activities that were typical of young men at that time. To me, Art was the most wonderful person in the whole wide world. Simply put, God sent him to me, and together we always felt that God was most significant in our lives.

Dotty Bushing
Maryville, Tennessee
February 2020

Art First Picture in Uniform. Arthur Story Bushing,
Box 245, Jamestown, TN. age 22. Private First Class.14119120
[This was written on the back of the photo.]

PREFACE

The path to progress is littered with the remains of those who have dreamed and yet who have been unable to fulfill their dreams. Appalling figures are given to discourage returning vets from launching out into business ventures of their own. The divorce rate is rising, and literary trends in America seem to point to mass production of trash.

Nevertheless, progress is made only as a result of someone dreaming. Individuals only make individual progress as they dare to dream and make plans by which their dream may be realized. I would sometime like to count up the number of plans which I have dreamed, and which have fallen by the wayside of all dreams. There have been many and yet there have been a few which have been realized. I still believe that one must "hitch one's wagon to a star." We never reach all of the goals which we set, and yet should we fail to set goals as a result, we would accomplish very little.

All of this rambling leads me to my point, of course, that I have another plan in mind. This one just occurred to me this morning while I was writing another letter to you. For some time I have been wondering just how I should attempt to put some of my experiences overseas into writing. I had thought of short stories as being perhaps the best medium for me during the next ten years or so since I will need at least that much time if not longer to develop my own style. The idea which suddenly popped into my head was to rewrite my letters to you—that is the letters written since I came into the Army, perhaps since I came overseas.

My idea would be to comb my letters for pertinent passages from my letters reflecting my experiences, my thoughts, conditions in the Army, etc. Within a letter-medium, I would have more latitude for putting across views and observations, and my novice style would not be so prominent. In additions to my letters to you, I could use my journal, letters to Mother and Dad, and an overflowing journal of notes, I think that I would have a wide choice of source material. The big job would be to choose and delete.

Such a compilation might have more of a chance as a book than anything else I would be likely to produce for some time to come, and yet that is of minor importance. I do hope to find some success in writing—someday, but I know full well that I have absolutely no talent for writing. I have that feeling way down inside of me that I will find myself in writing someday, but I suppose most people experience the same thing at one time or another. To work over our letters and put them in some sort of consolidated form would be to at least provide a source for my own use at some future time....

**Letter from Art Bushing
to wife, Dotty**
Mainburg, Germany
March 30, 1946

Art Bushing in Wagon, Jamestown, TN, 1924

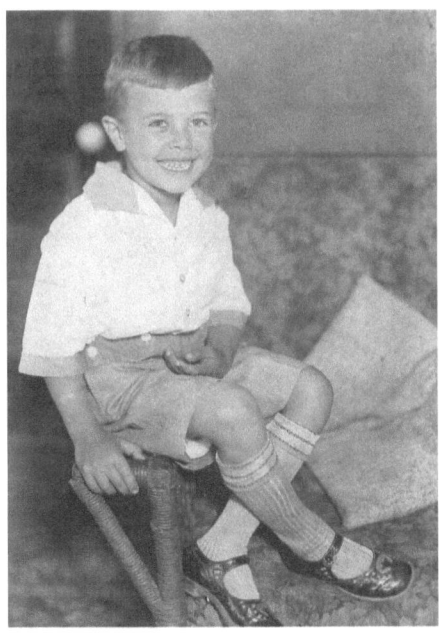

"Young Art Sitting"

Arthur Bushing Sr., Art Bushing Jr. & Mrs. Arza Bushing

Mr. & Mrs. Arthur Bushing & son Art Jr.

Dotty Bushing & Ruth Hoglan 1942,
Holding Diplomas on Graduation Day at Maryville College.

Members of the Fentress County Draft Board, 1940:

Sgt. Alvin C. York, Chairman
Jess Evans
Willie Voils
Dr. Sloan
A.S. Bushing, Clerk [Art's father]

(Photo credit: State of Tennessee Dept. of Conservation)

Treasure Chest

Men in War

THE funny thing was that they were not very much concerned with what was facing them ahead. Each had his own problems, his own desires and wishes. They kept these personal things uppermost in their minds, as they had always done ever since they came into the Army. The war was incidental to a man's thoughts. It entered into them, of course, but it did not take them over bodily. There had been too many years of life, too many memories, before the war had come along. A man could exist on those memories, he could withdraw into them, he could construct them into an unpierceable shell. They were his defense against the violence of the world. Every man in the platoon had his own thoughts as he walked along, and they hovered unseen over the little group, an indefinable armor, a protection against a fate, an indestructible essence.

Harry Brown, in "A Walk in the Sun." (Knopf.)

Published on August 20, 1944, exchanged in their letters, taken from the novel *A Walk in the Sun* by Harry Brown.

"My happy fiancé,"

Your good letter just received, and the joy that you express in it offers one of the principal difficulties that I face in writing this letter. I am glad that I waited until today to write, for with each passing day the gloomy outlook brightens. Darling, during the past week I have been living in a virtual H—-! It has been the feeling that one has when events are taking place over which we have no control. It has been that feeling of utter helplessness that we have at times of crises. A week from now I suppose I can look back on the events of the last few days without the same feeling of despair that I have now, but at present the situation does disturb me greatly.

I must come to the point without further circumloction. I wrote you on the second day I was here. The night before I had had that long and memorable talk with Mother and Dad. Things seemed as bright as I indicated to you because the conversation had been, for the most part, between Dad and me. Dad has been truly wonderful about the whole affair. From the very first he has highly approved of our decisions and has given us his blessing. However, the situation with Mother has been somewhat different.

Mother has and does not disapprove of our engagement, but she has been hurt rather badly. Three things contributed to her feeling it seems. The fact that she was totally unprepared for any such news was perhaps the most important. All the time I have been thinking in terms of Dad's awareness of the relationship between us. He has visited us at Maryville, eaten with us, and seen us together. He was fully aware of your high ideals and your many wonderful qualities; and, I think, saw the inevitability of our mutual love, Mother, on the other hand, has met you only once, and has never realized how far we had progressed in three years. In part, she had no opportunity to see; in part, she perhaps did not want to see. At any rate, she was taken completely by surprise. In the second place, I was brutally blunt in telling the news as I did. It was my first evening at home; I had talked with Mother and Dad only a short time on arriving before going on home and to bed; we had just settled down for the evening when I blurted out our engagement. A third and equally important reason for Mother's reaction to the news was the fact that she was secretly visualizing a different scheme of things when the war is over. A careful analysis of Mother's nature and personality seem necessary for either of us to understand the latter point. She is by nature a person accustomed to sacrifice. As I think I have told you, she took the responsibility of keeping house for her father and three younger brothers at the early age of twelve, in addition to continuing in school. At the age of seventeen she was teaching school. With the little money she could save from teaching, she went through college, washing , dishes for 7¢ an hour. When she and Dad were married they moved to New York City to live for two years. She who had loved the country, the wide-open spaces; she who loved fresh, clean air and kind, friendly country people, now living on the eighth floor of a New York apartment house. We prospered during the gay, late twenties. The country was spending, spending, spending! Dad, making money easily, was bitten by the same bug. Only Mother remained calm and level-headed. She had not forgotten the worth of a dollar made, and she knew still how to save. We crashed, not as hard as many, but still we knew the feeling of being out of work, interest and taxes due, and no income. Nother made no complaint, but continued to go without things essential for convenient living in order that we might hold our heads above water.

When I started in at Maryville, Dad was making the remarkable sum of $25 per month, with an added income of $12.50 for a house that we rented. Our debts still amounted to about $1600 and interest and taxes still came due. Mother continued to sacrifice those things that she would like to have in order that I might have an education. She rejoiced in my joys and successes at school, and as she saw me growing into manhood she felt a deep glow of pride. All that she had given up for me was worth while. She dreamed of the day after the war when I would be working, Dad would have a job, and then we three could enjoy the new car, the new improvements around the home, the many things that we had gone so long without. Our debts have been paid up in their entirety and the future does hold hope.

Then, like a flash from the proverbial blue, I walk in to say that I do not plan to return home after the war, that I plan to begin life anew on an independent basis. I think you understand, darling, how she might feel. If, and God forbid it, we should have only one child, one child in whom we put all our hope, how would we feel if he came in long before we expected him to tell us of a new anchorage?

Mother freely admits that her feeling arises out of pure, human jealously. She does not want to give me up. She wishes for us all the happiness that the future holds for us, yet she cannot help the feeling that she would have liked to have had me with her a little longer. In a

Art Bushing and his parents, Dec. 1940

small way I can faintly conceive of her feeling, but it has not prevented the torment that I have suffered during the last few days. There has sprung up a barrier between us that I cannot explain or surmount. Mother cannot help the matter for the present, although she has tried desperately hard. I seem to have hands that are tied in the matter.

As the days go by, I can see and feel a gradual change. Last night Dad went to the show and Mother and I put up Christmas decorations. Tonight Mother and I are going to the show. She is trying very hard to overcome her feeling, and her resilience is such that she cannot be so unhappy for any length. However, the interim is torture for me. Be assured, darling, that Mother's feeling is in no way directed against you. She has every respect and admiration and love for you that is possible, knowing you as indirectly as she does. However, the fact remains that she is having great difficulty in conditioning herself to the new situation. Please do not worry or fret about all this. It is simply a crisis that I must face, and one that your prayers may aid. Among the other things that it has given me, I have learned in a new way the depth of parental love that a Mother has for a son. We shall never forget the responsibilities we have to our parents.

I am planting to visit my grandmother before I return to school, and may go down tomorrow. I perhaps could come over on Sunday or Monday in order to see Pete before he leaves. Would like to make it Saturday, but that seems too close to Christmas, and travel will be very bad any time next week. Will let you know more shortly, but Monday night seems the best night for us to plan something with Pete.

My dearest, there are so many things I would like to say, but I must finish this. Yes, our spirits will be united on Christmas Day as never before. Try to forget all that I have said in the letter, except that both Mother and Dad are very happy for our futures. May you have the merriest of Christmases and may the New Year hold for all of us a brighter vision of the Brotherhood of Man as was seen so many centuries ago by Him whose birth we commemorate at this glad season. My prayers are always for your happiness and joy.

      Your own,
      Bushy

P.S. Very much interested in clipping which I had not seen. Maybe yes!

Young Art Bushing portrait,
Maryville College Days

1943

1

THIS IS THE ARMY, MR. JONES

Basic Training

*O*n the 6th of August 1942, I enlisted in the United States Army. When I had investigated various programs with the Navy, the Army Air Corps, even the Marine Corps, I discovered that poor eyesight and/or color blindness were enough to keep me out. My enlistment with the Army provided an opportunity to complete my college work and earn my degree at Maryville College in TN.

In early 1943, when Dr. Lloyd asked me to teach college physics to the newly arrived Army Air Force Cadets, he hoped that the Army would release me from my enlistment or postpone my active duty in order to continue with the teaching. After some correspondence, the Army denied the request, and so on 1 June 1943, I reported to Fort Oglethorpe, Georgia, for active duty. About two dozen of us from Maryville reported at the same time. During the processing, I saw written on my papers the word "Meteorology," a program for which I had earlier applied. It happened, however, that the Army was setting up the Army Specialized Training Program (ASTP), a requirement for which was to be college trained. The minimum was two years of college or university experience. Apparently, ASTP had priority over meteorology because I and sixteen others were shipped to California.

We were loaded on a special car with private rooms and an observation section at one end—by all means the most luxurious travel conditions that I was to have during the next three years. On the way

West we sometimes passed troop trains with officers and other soldiers of rank who looked with wonder and envy at our quarters. Other times, we were put on a side track for priority trains. With a corporal as our leader, we stopped in St. Louis, Kansas City, Salt Lake City, and San Francisco, each time being able to get off the train to eat and often to wander a bit waiting for the next move. I have a vivid memory of crossing the Great Salt Lake with a full moon reflecting on the waters. Our destination was Camp Roberts, a basic training camp near Paso Robles and roughly half was between Los Angeles and San Francisco.

With a bit of the confusion that we learned to expect—the GI slang was SNAFU, situation normal, all fouled up—we soon discovered that a full complement of men had not arrived. To begin a training cycle, we needed 1,000 men; we had perhaps 700. Those in charge knew of nothing to do but to start basic training. After six weeks the remainder came, and so we began right and left face by the numbers, repeating everything that we had already covered. Late in this cycle of training, I was hospitalized for three or four days, returned to the unit, made up everything that I had missed. Nevertheless, I was sent to another group that was a few weeks behind mine, "This is the Army, Mister Jones...."

On the positive side, I was with a number of friends from College including Ken Cooper, Ted Kidder (both classmates, Bob Hunter (older son of Dr. Hunter, English Dept. Head), Dean Stone, Ken Talbot, and Peter Van Blarcom. All of the trainees were college men, and for the most part we had army career officers in charge of training. The drill sergeant was a very strict German, for whom there was nothing but intense discipline. Morale was high, a fact that I appreciated even more when I found a relaxed and demoralized group when I went to my second unit.

Camp Roberts was located in a desert area. In the hot summer sun, the parade ground temperature often reached 120 degrees. Even so, at night the temperature cooled quickly so that we needed all the cover available. Sometimes the early morning fog that rolled in from the Pacific did not burn off for two or three hours. In light of the fighting going on in North Africa, we were on strict water rationing, often being restricted to one canteen per day. We trained hard, ate like horses, slept like logs. After six months of training, I was probably the healthiest I had ever been.

Basic training was intended to put army recruits into top physical condition. We were on a rigorous daily routine involving calisthenics, close order drill, marches, obstacle courses, field operations in which we simulated a combat problem. By all odds the worst part of all for me was the bayonet drill. We had to run through a course in which dummies were posted with grotesque faces, almost always Oriental. With yells and inflammatory words, those in charge tried to arouse our adrenalin as we ran the course and slashed our bayonets through our opponent. Hand-to-hand combat was included. The psychological conditioning was far worse than any physical demands. We had training films and lectures, again part of the mental conditioning. We had experience with firing most of the small weapons of combat: large and small machine guns, two sizes of mortars, bazookas, hand grenades, and the M-1 rifle. At one point we crawled through a barbed wire entanglement with live machine gun fire a few inches above our heads. Some of the training did simulate combat, but nothing can be compared to the real experience. Night projects were dangerous, in part because the ground in the areas where we trained often had long cracks wide enough to sprain or break an ankle or leg.

We lived in two-story barracks, sleeping on double bunks with forty men making up one platoon and occupying one building. I slept on a top bunk with a bare light bulb shining in my face and giving me a lifetime habit of sleeping with a pillow over my head. We were aroused at an early hour to fall out for reveille and then marched to the dining hall. At least once when we were slow to line up in the allotted time, all passes were revoked and we spent all day Saturday scouring the barracks. That process involved moving all bunks and footlockers out of the building and, on our knees, scrubbing the floor with hand brushes. The Army had many methods to condition green recruits. Every hour was scheduled, but a ten-minute break came at the end of every fifty minutes. I thought that was one of the smartest things the Army did. I learned to sleep for most of that break. When we had nothing else to do, we were lined up to "police the area," i.e., picking up cigarette butts and all other trash in our area.

We did have movies and an occasional USO entertainment group came through, which included Bob Hope and his troupe. Each area had a chapel and weekend worship services. I came to know a fellow GI who had majored in philosophy at Notre Dame and another who was a devout Jew. We had many ten-minute discussions about our faiths, and I occasionally went with the Catholic friend to mass. He, however, could not attend Protestant services with me.

For the first few weeks, we were not allowed weekend passes. I recall that my first one was to go with Ken Cooper, a Maryville classmate, to Santa Cruz, a resort town on the coast. My habits were such that I recall feeling guilty when we went to a movie on Sunday afternoon—I think it was one starring Bob Hope. Another pass was with Ted Kidder going to to visit one of his aunts, who took precious gasoline to drive us around to see some of the sights. Civilians were very kind to us, and usually we could hitchhike and beat the bus schedule.

Army Scheduling

Although I never fully adjusted to the condition, I soon discovered that Army life involves constant rumor and thus constant uncertainty. Since our training at Camp Roberts began, we were told that we were destined for special assignments. Upon completing my basic training I was sent to Santa Rosa Junior college, a few miles north of San Francisco. We were put in classes to occupy our time and held there until early January. My friend Ken Cooper and I were invited to a home for Christmas dinner. I recall that a son from the family was overseas, and they gave us an opportunity for a festive meal. They took us for a drive through the Valley of the Moon, made famous in Jack London's writings. The area is famous for its wine production. I was also near San Anselmo Seminary, where my college friend Phil Evaul was enrolled. Ken and I were able to visit with Phil and wife Peggy and enjoy Phyllis, their new baby.

During this period Cooper was shipped back East to enroll in medical school, and after the holiday I was sent to Leland Stanford University in Palo Alto, south of San Francisco. After V-E Day (Victory in Europe), I was selected to attend the Sorbonne (the University of Paris) for summer courses. I describe that experience in later journal notes from that period.

Stanford University

Many thousands of men and women in uniform received special training in a wide variety of fields. Since I was among a few chosen for language study, I was diverted from meteorology to Dutch studies at Leland Stanford University in Palo Alto, south of San Francisco. Opening in early January, 1944, the program was headed by a lady who had escaped the German invasion of Holland. Her staff was made up of people from different parts of the world with varying degrees of competence in teaching. One male came from the South Pacific who had learned English from missionaries from the southern part of the United States. His accent revealed his training.

4

I don't recall the numbers, but I estimate that the enrollment was about sixty, all college graduates from a variety of fields. One of my roommates was trained as an engineer from Cornell. We were housed, of course in the school's dormitories. For my last quarter I was with a man of Jewish faith from Brooklyn and a Greek Orthodox believer from Chicago. The program was designed for three quarters of intense study of conversational Dutch. In addition to mornings filled with instruction, we spent additional time in practicing our conversational skills.

At the end of the first term, we decided that my fiancé, Dotty Bushing, would come out from Tennessee for our wedding, an event planned mainly by the efforts of Helen Pratt Tapp, a classmate of Dotty's at Maryville. The date was set for Maundy Thursday of Easter Week at Helen's church in San Jose. Phil Evaul (another Maryville grad.), who was studying for the ministry at nearby San Anselmo, performed the ritual except for pronouncing us husband and wife, which only an ordained minister could do. With Helen acting as Matron of Honor, and Oliver Van Cise (still another Maryville classmate stationed nearby) serving as Best Man, all members of the wedding party were Maryville College graduates! Most unusual for a wartime wedding three thousand miles from home.

The schedule at Stanford was rigorous. Classes, physical education, and movies (which I don't remember) filled the days and hours to the brim. Except for weekends, I was not allowed off campus during the week, which was a little tough for newly-weds. But finally, during the last quarter, I had some small duty (exchanging sheets and towels once a week) which gave me the privilege of going home each night. My classmates joked constantly that I didn't have enough energy for the calisthenics. In reaction, I redoubled my efforts and was rewarded in the third term with my choices for exercise—swimming, tennis, etc. After one strenuous afternoon of the latter, I developed intense pain, which was first mis-diagnosed. After attending classes the next day, I reported to the clinic and was found to have a very high level of white corpuscles. Thus I had an emergency appendectomy, was in bed for a week and in the hospital for thirty days. I was given a chance to make up my classes, obviously an impossible task. At any rate, at the end of the third term all of us were graduated and then shipped to various army units.

I was sent to the 71st Infantry division stationed at Fort Benning, outside of Columbus, Georgia. Dotty came down from Knoxville, where she had been living with her parents. She joined newly married

Cordelia Kidder; both girls found jobs at Tom's Toasted Peanuts factory along with other transient army wives. After three months of maneuvers in very cold, snowy weather, the 71st Division was sent to Fort Dix, N.J. for shipment overseas, still lowly PFC's, having been given no credit nor ranking for their months of training in the Army specialized Training Program.

Jan. 1, 1943

In recent weeks I have worked over what is usually called a New Year's Resolution. The result was

TO LIVE MORE EFFICIENTLY

I. Mentally -
    1. Daily improvement, by
        a. reading,
        b. writing,
        c. thinking;
    2. Develop discipline of the mind by exercising
        a. mental control,
        b. power of concentration;

II. Physically, by
    1. Proper sleep
        a. regular hours,
        b. seven-hour minimum;
    2. Care in eating
        a. regular habits,
        b. moderation;
    3. Daily exercise, to develop
        a. versatility of skills,
        b. muscular power;

III. Spiritually -
    1. Daily Bible reading,
        a. as literature,
        b. as guide-book for living;
    2. Daily meditation
        ("as a man thinketh...")
    3. Constant touch with spiritual ideals, through
        a. fellowship,
        b. books;
    4. By following more closely the Leadership of Christ;
    5. By living more helpfully
        a. going second mile,
        b. thinking of others
            1) attempting always to be unselfish in action,
            2) making conscious effort to discover the
               needs of others.

Art Bushing's New Year's Resolutions, January 1, 1943

Friday, January 1, 1943, Diary

As I enter upon the New Year—a year to be filled with many important history-making events—I consider perhaps more seriously than never before the business of a New Year's Resolution on a group of Resolutions. After giving the matter some thought, I found myself evolving some of a code of ethics or a series of standards. I put these standards under one head—My New Year's Resolution:

[original document on the left]

Letter from Art to Dotty

[Art lived at Box 245, Jamestown, Tenn.
Dotty lived at 607 W. Glenwood Ave. Knoxville, TN]
Jamestown, Tennessee
January 2, 1943

Dearest Heart,

'Tis Saturday afternoon and work is slowing down in the Draft Office for the week-end. I must soon go home and do several odd jobs that must be finished, but first I want to write though it be a mere note.

With a bit of old Bushing luck returning, I found the bus on which I was to come home loaded with only twelve passengers. Oh Happy Day! Finding myself near the back of the bus, with no one either in the seat next to me or across the aisle, I stretched from one side of the bus to the other and snoozed quietly, I arrived home in good order, and felt so good that I spent a couple of hours in the office doing a big typing job. Mother was well-pleased with her pocket-book, and would seem to recommend me as one able to shop for ladies. We-l-l—l?

My trip to Knoxville was most refreshing, not only from the standpoint of the excellent food, but from the mental and spiritual aspect. As we tend to become one, as all who love do, our thoughts and our reactions tend to be thoughts and reactions of the two. When I faced the crises of the past few weeks, I felt the need of your presence more than ever before. Darling, it was wonderful to see you and be with you again!

This morning I had to turn down a chance to see Tom over the week-end. He is staying with a friend of ours in Nashville tonight, and I was offered a ride down to see both of them. I declined because of the work here and also because the trip to my grandmother's that I intend to take next week. I will probably leave Tuesday morning and return sometime Wednesday. It would have been a nice trip, but I do want to spend a little time with Mother and Dad.

For the past couple of days I have done little but write letters. I think I have written more in the last two days than in any other two-week period during the last year. Last night I read a book on the Human Machine and one on Marriage. Both interesting. The New Year's Resolutions that I am still working on include under "Living Efficiently in a Spiritual Manner" the items Daily Bible reading, and Daily Meditation. I will try to send you a copy of my Resolutions when I put them in the final form.

My prayer is that we may have a joyous and successful New Year. Let us both pray that in the coming months men everywhere may see and feel a new vision of the World Brotherhood that Christ saw almost two thousand years ago. Peace will come, and with it new hope for Man!

> Your own,
> Bushy

P.S. I think I left my checkbook on the table. It would come in an envelope for 3¢. Thanks!

Letter from Dotty to Art
[January 3, 1943]
Sunday, P.M.

Dearly Beloved,

It seems as if I spend half my time seeing you for the last time for a long time. It is wonderful experience as long as it lasts, but ah, me—the time in between. But you know, don't you?

It seems that in the rush (do I mean <u>crush</u>) you left your check-book behind, so I am sending it on to you.

Set your mind at rest about the day after the night before, darling. I was only a <u>little</u> bit sleepy, and besides, our party fell through, because only one little girl appeared for the skating, and I knew that a number of others would be unable to attend the rest of the party, so I called the party off entirely and then fell into bed. When the New Year actually showed its face I was fast asleep. I really should have watched it in, for it is an important year for us, dearest. It is the first one we have faced together, and I feel that it holds great things for us. There may be dark things in store, but all will be overlaid with the exquisite gold of our love. I thank God that with each day that love grows.

Did you get a seat on the bus on the way home? How are your father and mother, especially your Mom? Don't let her work too hard.

I thought I wouldn't mind working all day on Saturday, but I do. It will mean that I may have to cut out trips to Maryville and such. I worked all day yesterday, and somehow it didn't seem like Saturday. Don't worry—I'm not griping—I realize that I'm doing it for a cause—the biggest cause there is right now, and I want to do everything I can to help that cause <u>win</u>. I hereby resolve to discontinue "minding" little sacrifices—otherwise, sacrifice is not the term to be applied.

I thought of you last night when I saw the evening sky. It was so unusual; there were a host of very white clouds in a very blue sky—these covered the entire dome, clear down to the horizon—but right on this horizon was a huge orange-red sun, and the funny part was that this sun looked out of place in that sky—it just didn't belong in that blue and white sky.

Communion this morning in church. I prayed for us. It meant a great deal, but would have meant more with you beside me.

Enclosed please find one (1) check book, one (1) picture, and all the love (xxxxxxxxxxxx) you can stand in one dose. And then some.

       Forever your
        Dotty.
P.S. Remind me to give you yet another picture when I see you.

Letter from Dotty to Art
[January 4, 1943]
Monday night

Darling,

That letterhead comes in so handy. Nearly all the starting-off-words start with a "D." Isn't that peculiar? And, ah, even more peculiar that I right (write) to you two days in a row? Ha. You didn't know I had reformed, did you? Well? How do you know? And besides, what does that have with my reformed personality? Oh you can't love two for that wouldn't do, oh darling you can't love two. (Sung to the tune "Darling, You Can't Love One")

Well, I've caught up on my sleep now, so I'm rarin' to go again. Oh, anywhere, so long as it's with you. That is, I'll be caught up if I don't spend too much time writing to you. Yes, yes, you have guessed one of my resolutions—to keep up with you in a fashion more suitable to engaged couples. If I don't hurry, I won't get enough letters to fill my hope chest with. What hope chest? Well, I can dream, can't I?

Here I sit, like a love sick something or other, gazing into your eyes. Did you know how directly you were looking into the camera from the picture you gave me for Christmas? Oh, darling, next to you in person it is just like having you here to look at that picture. Your eyes keep talking—they say "I love you" just as plain. Gosh, you must have an awful crush on the person who took the picture! I do hope you'll be happy with each other. Superfluous statement. The person that gets you is bound to be happy. How did I know? Why by means of a bit of expert espionage and amazing dedication I found out for myself. That's where I get my artistic streak—drawing so many conclusions.

I'm glad your mom liked her purse. Did you tell her that you had picked our silver, too? Why?

Here's to our love—long may it grow and prosper and enrich the lives of others.

> Thine own,
> Dotty.

Letter from Art to Dotty
At Home
Jan. 4, 1943

My Own Dearest Darling,

"Twas midnight by the castle clock," or there abouts. It is very late, darling, and I can find no paper suitable to write you on. However, I feel as tho I must write in spite of the absence of time, paper, and a typewriter. After all, darling, the army doesn't furnish typewriters for a mere lover-lorn private to write his dearly beloved. You perhaps will grow accustomed to this scribble that lends itself to neither beauty nor speed.

Mother and I saw "Mrs. Miniver" tonight. I thought the warmth and beauty of that remarkable picture would touch her heart as it did ours last summer. She was touched but hardly as I had expected. She takes a pessimistic view of almost everything these days, and perhaps she took their decision (Vin's and Carol's, I mean) as one that we might take—to marry before the war ends.

Perhaps she fears being left alone as life wanes for her. She saw Vin leave his parents' pew and go to that of the grandmother's. Perhaps she saw me leaving her alone to go to you and your parents. Mother says almost nothing, yet I read her thoughts too well.

She once wrote to me on the edge of a letter from Dad. "Weather is terrible, but Spring will come." [Dotty's underlining]. That was so typical of her spirit. She always saw the brighter side of things, but it is all changed. She's more thoughtful now; there are new lines on her face and her hair seems a little grayer now; her manner is less sure. Dearest, I feel so helpless! My hands seem tied and I know not what to say or do. I try to be cheerful and smile. I try to reassure her of my love and devotion to her, but it seems to no avail. I pray nightly that she may come to a new understanding of our love for each other. I pray that she may feel she has gained a daughter rather than lost a son.

Darling, you think of faith and so do I. I do believe that Mother will come to a new understanding of the entire situation. It has been a great shock to her, but her brave spirit of faith and hope for the future will return. Such a spirit is unconquerable, and hers will return to hold sway in her heart. Meanwhile, let us pray that we may both be a strength and a comfort to her in the days to come.

I write of these things because it helps to tell you of them, to talk with you of them. I know your thoughts are of Mother and her feelings and I know you pray for her. Pray constantly, dear heart, and may we come to a new understanding of the parent's love and affection through these experiences.

I have many things to write about tonight, but I must stop now. I leave tomorrow morning early to visit my grandmother. I return Wed. morning.

As the days swiftly pass, I feel an ever-increasing nearness to God and to you, my dearest. May we three ever draw closer until would become one in Him.

Good-night and sweetest dreams,
Your Own,
Bushy

Darling,
I am almost ashamed to mail this letter this morning, but I have no time to re-copy it. Your letter, love, checkbook, and picture just received. Thanks loads for all. I thought my bus left at nine, however, it's nine-thirty. So, I have a half an hour to wait. I had hoped yesterday afternoon to make a copy of my New Year's Resolutions. I have only one—To live more efficiently—but it has many parts. I will send it to you, for it well may be worked out as our creed for living. I love you, dearest, and think of you always.

January 5, 1943, Diary

Down to Grandma's today by mail. It seems to me that the people of the world can be roughly divided into two classes—those who are optimists and those who are pessimists. In the latter group I am thinking not only of those morose individuals who wear the long face but also of those who see, usually, the darker side of events or situation. The weather is always uncomfortable for them—too hot, too cold, too wet, too dry; the new rationing laws are particularly hard on them, for they just can't walk everywhere they need to go. For them, the current administration is always going "Red," and young people are always going to the dog. Another type of pessimist, and one far more dangerous to society, is the person who feels himself the center for the mudslinging contests of all his fellowmen. It is this type that so readily gloats over the story that the local draft board has held so-and-so out of the Army because of such-and-such. A story of this kind, when once heard, is taken out again and again with miser-like joy and intense satisfaction is gained there from. It would seem that this is the highest point that these people reach in the joy of living—the joy, such as it is, of seeing a failure or finding a smattering of proofs for their pessimistic predictions and views.

That broad category does not, however, include all people. I would like to think it includes only a small majority. There are those who see the silver lining, who see in every situation some good and always hope. These God-Gifted optimists are the ones who encourage the weak to grow strong, and uncover hidden talents in others for joyous living. With Christ, they come not to condemn, but to save. There can be no greater or truer happiness than the continual joy of seeing the brighter side of our environment.

Letter from Art to Dotty
Jamestown, Tennessee
January 6, 1943

Dearest Heart,

I arrived at home this morning at nine o'clock, after a lovely visit to my grandmother's. I showed her the picture that I am carrying with me of you, and she agreed that you are quite beautiful. She sensed the situation, and promised to make a quilt for us. (And tell me that I don't have pull!) You're two epistles received; and I, of course, am overjoyed to hear of your new intentions. I think I can stand a few letters, and I know that I long to write more often. (Your mother will say we are shifting into high gear.)

Your mention of the importance of the New Year brought a flood of thoughts to my mind. Yes, dear, it does hold many history-making events, not only for us, but for millions of individuals like us all over the world. One of the most important spots where the destiny of the future will be planned is Washington, where the Seventy-Eight Congress convenes tomorrow. Not only will they, in a large measure, decide our problems on the home front and our foreign policies; but, more important, the Congressman in office today will determine the world history of tomorrow. Mistakes are unavoidable, but Mr. Roosevelt has certainly bungled important issues during the past year at home. Although we have startled the world—particularly Hitler—with our production records, there has been a lack of over-all planning, which has seriously hampered our war effort. The President has also been indecisive concerning India and China, but I do think that he has a world-vision for the peace terms and for the post-war period. Willkie, Wallace, and others have such an international view, but I fear the growing influence of the Old Guard Republican element in Congress. It was such a situation that prevented Wilson from carrying through his famous Fourteen Points; and, if a nationalistic outlook is pursued by this Congress, peace terms and post-war planning would be seriously encumbered.

You may easily see why I am watching, along with the rest of the country and Britain, our new Congress. But, there are other, many other, phases of the war to watch. Russia is doing a remarkable job on the Western Front, and the signs that are beginning to emerge concerning her plans for the post-war world will have a far-reaching influence at the peace table. Churchill's plans are not entirely clear, but these three leading powers will have to work out a compromise most certainly.

Halsey in the Pacific area has predicted complete victory within the year. That is, of course, an optimistic view that may or may not be justified. Hitler is with little doubt cracking up, and, although it will be at terrible sacrifice, it seems likely that he can be defeated by the end of the year. Russia's great drive now will be supplemented by a great reservoir of reserves when the Allies invade Europe. After that, however, there is still Japan to defeat; and that will not be easy.

Dear heart, there will be many important decisions and problems arising in the days immediately ahead. In the month just ahead I will graduate, enter the service, make the adjustments, and begin my record there. There will be adjustments and changes for you at home. We can find our place in the ever-changing world of tomorrow. Our love will over-shadow all storms, and a quieter sea lies beyond. Peace will come!

Living for you alone,
Bushy

Letter from Dotty to Art

Late
Dec. 7, 1943
[The post date on the envelope is January 8,
so Dotty could have written this letter on January 7, 1943.]

Dearest,

I must try out all my new paper, just as one has to wear all one's new things on Easter.

How odd—I've just been to a show also, and it is late and I have a slight headache, but I feel that I must write you. The show had a very strange effect on me—I feel so peculiar. The picture was "Now, Voyager," starring Bette Davis, and showed some of the smothering effects of mother-love. The mother made all the decisions for herself and her daughter. The girl became an ugly, old-maidish person, introverted and terribly unhappy under the tyranny of her mother. And she nears a nervous breakdown, a psychiatrist steps in and changes things. The girl emerges like a butterfly, and has many interesting experiences testing her wings. I would like to see your mother's reaction to this picture, also. Now, don't jump at conclusions—I merely think her reaction would be interesting. No inferences intended. By the way—while we are on the subject—I wonder if your mother has red "Spring Comes on Forever" by Bess Streeter Aldrich, I think. No matter what happens, or how many things change, Spring comes on forever, nor does it change.

I do have faith, darling. I do believe that a new understanding will come to your (our) mother. I pray that the day may be not too far off.

"My heart is so full of a number of things" - - - - - I hardly know which to write of, nor could I express it if I tried. It grows later and later, so I must start making this letter shorter and shorter. "I want to dream so I can be with you."

Glad to see that checkbook, etc., arrive safely, with the exception of the love—I know that love—our love—can never be lost.

B-r-r-r-r. I am also getting sleepy and cold. It snowed here this afternoon—looked beautiful coming down, but it didn't stick. Now it rains.

Goodnight, dearest.

Love Dotty.

P.S. "Love that blooms in violet—time finds no wintry ending." [This quote is from "Chorus of Homage" by Louis C. Elson.]

Letter from Dotty to Art
[Art now at Maryville College, January 14, 1943]
Record-Breaking
Night.
Or
The night after.

(Darlinckal)

How!

You seem to know! So you still don't believe my good intentions? Guess this will show you.

Even if you had to be at Sunday School over there, you could come over here for church, or in the afternoon. Here I go again—influencing you to do things you don't really have time to do. Just refuse to pay me any mind when I do things I ortn't. You have the privilege of turning me over your knee at any time and——well, what do you usually do?

Luck is against me—my pen ran out of ink, and this borrowed one is doing the same. Ah—Elaine saved the day—somehow my thoughts won't come out so well when the ink doesn't flow well.

This record-breaker's has degenerated into dance music and such. That is the sort of effect caused by the absence Uncle West and Carl. They won't tolerate any but the best. Yeah—and I'm his neice!

Another change of pen, and of scene, this time. The pen—my desk pen. The scene—the bathroom, where I can shut the door, and make a little noise and turn on a light without disturbing anyone.

Tell me, Father Confessor, how can I come out of my shell a little? People frequently take me for a quiet, shy retiring person, and I don't feel that way at all. It always surprises me when someone asks me why I am so quiet. Yes, dear, I realize that I can't sit and dream of you all the time—I must work to make you come true, according to the books.

15

Query: Am I being shy and retiring, or merely reserved? Answer comes there none. Perhaps you, with your superior psychological intuitiveness could shed some light on my plight. (Pome!) But on the other hand, Prof., I do not wish to become as obtrusive as some girls I know.

My slight cold seems to have cleared up entirely. I never shook one off this easily before. I guess you are just downright good for all my afflictions.

Tomorrow (Friday) night I go skating—instead of the usual affair at the church there will be a skating party for the young people. Its really a belated New Year's party for my gang. How I wish you could be here—so I would have someone to skate with! Dean will be there. Incidentally, Dean is the nicest substitute around. You'd better watch that guy—I could fall for him without half trying.

How are Muriel and Jane and Hal and Jack and all the rest of the gang if any? Tell Hal I enjoyed his note very much. I want to see them all. It still doesn't seem as if they were back.

Well, I am growing slightly chill, and since I have not my love (in person) to keep me warm, bed seems the only solution. Hoping you can read not only this poor excuse for a scribble, but also my miserable between-the-lines,
I remain

> Forever <u>yours</u>,
> Dotty.

Letter from Dotty to Art
[January 19, 1943]
Tuesday
Night

Darling,

> Spring-warm weather
> Wind
> High wind
> Winter again runs in its own groove.
> The wind blew the mist away
> from the moon, and polished it.
> Now it
> shines like a
> diamond
> on black velvet.

Very poorly done, but the cold night is as beautiful as the warm one, except that it lacks your presence.

See if you can make the poem look any better by rearranging it.

Did you make your bus, huh? I don't see how you could have, Superman, but you must have.

The song on the radio says, "Would you rather be a colonel with an eagle on your shoulder, or a private with a chicken on your knee?" Well, would you?

So I have the current events schedule straight—play and Jones in the same week, and two weeks later the three concerts in a row? How! How are things shaping up for Mary Ruth and Joe? Mary Ruth looks as cute in her bangs as a pickled plum-gudgeon, I'm telling you!

Is Muriel any happier these days? I am. Every day I am happier as it draws closer and closer to "Oh, happy, happy wedding day." (from "My Hero" from the "Chocolate Soldier") from now till then.

Do I seem disconnected and flighty? Charge it up to the fact that nothing of any importance or note-worthiness has occurred, so I just put down little thoughts as they come into my head. Proof enough of the type of mind I have. You'll be sorry, I'm warning you———!

Mother just now placed some silver patterns in my lap. Very interesting. Wish you were here to help me pick and choose and cast aside and indecision. You always did help me indecision things. But one eternally definite thing about which there is no indecision, if the fact that

> I love you.
> Dotty

Letter from Dotty to Art
[January 22, 1943]
Fri. Nite

My Own True One,

I am never going to trust anyone but the mailman again. Elaine was on campus Wednesday morning, so I sent my letter over by her, but she wasn't there as long as she had expected to be, and so forgot all about the letter until she got back to town (Knoxville), at which time she put a stamp on it and stuck it in the mail. So you didn't get the letter probably 'till late Thursday when you should have gotten it Wednesday.

Please forgive my writing in pencil. All the pens are downstairs, and I am too tired to go down and get one. What I mean is lazy, not tired. I ran the whole show down at the church tonight. Aunt Carol didn't come at all, and Dean is in the hospital with a strep. infection in his leg. We made him a card out of a paper bag, a piece of dirty string, and the remains of supper. The string was made into a bow. Mary Ruth wrote a silly verse (?) to go on it, and we all signed our names to it. More fun!

Sorry Joe is booked up for the play. Mary Ruth says you don't have to get her a date unless you <u>want</u> to.

Be sure you are getting into what you want in the Army. You are well prepared for a number of things. Please be careful which choice you make—you want to be satisfied.

As I get to know the people in the office better and better, I like them more and more. There are several highly colored personalities, so there's hardly ever a dull moment. I just found that one boy is a consist [consistent] punner [one who makes puns]. He doesn't inspire me like you do, though.

It is dream-time, and I want to dream. Will you dream with me?

Your Dotty

P.S. One more thing — I LOVE YOU darling.

Letter from Dotty to Art
[January 24, 1943]
The Sabbath
While listening to Brahms' "Requiem."
A lovely thing.

Dearest Heart,

It hardly seems possible that in a little over a week Harriet will be here! If she should want to go to the concert in Maryville, would it be possible for you to get her a ticket without too much trouble and expense, such as by borrowing somebody's activity card who will not be using it? Or are such things done? Yeah, I thought they were. That is, I hope we can keep her here that long. She has such a peculiar attachment for her husband that she just can't bear being away from him for long at a time. Isn't that funny?

Is the play this week? Let me know so I or we can make plans. Mary Ruth and I will not try to stay over night. If she is with me I'll have someone to come back with. The play would be over in time for us to catch the 10:00 bus, yes—no?

The war news has been so overwhelmingly good lately that I am beginning to have wild hopes. If it continues as it is now going, I don't see how the end of the war could be so terribly far away. What is the latest dope on the meteorology stuff? Know anything more than you put in your letter? I see by today's paper that our Dr. McClelland is a captain in the Marines! [note: Dr. Frank McClelland was a Marine and Veteran of both World Wars.]

Gee whiz!

I missed you today. (Superfluous statement) The weather was scrumptious. Also superfluous. I lovelious very much.

Please, darling, remind me next time you are here that I still have that picture of Christ to give you. You still want it, do you not?

Does the bicycle work? Does it put you in two places at once like you thought it would? We have never been cycling together, have week. We must try it sometime, Bud. One should try everything with one's fiancée before the fatal step, they say. O.K., it's a date!

We went over to see Dean this afternoon. He is better, but still not ready to come home. I rubbed his head. Hmmmm. Don't you have an ache I could rub, hmm don't you, hmm don't you, hmm don't you?

I'll mail or male appreciated. Please address to the gal that's so in love with that Bushing guy. You know where she lives, don't you?

I love you,
Dotty.

Monday, January 25, 1943, Diary

After a week and a half in this last semester, I found myself unable to settle down to my new schedule. For one thing it was a light schedule and I wasn't accustomed to that sort of thing. Practice Teaching—time-consuming but certainly requiring no concentration; Physics—rather simple; Shakespeare—highly interesting but not demanding; statistics–almost a farce it seemed after the first few class meetings. My honors work, of course, was the big thing; but, weighing all of my work, I still felt that I was not working at full capacity. Living as I felt on borrowed time, I should be wasting no time that could be put to an advantage.

Dr. McClelland had called me into the office during my first days back and explained a new Army-sponsored Meteorology Training Program. This, however, called for two semesters of calculus and I only had the one. I talked at some length with Dr. Hunter about my feeling that I was not doing as much as I could or should. I thought eighteen hours of education was necessary even for teaching on the college level, and this war the reason for the statistics in my schedule. When I found that no education is necessary for college work, I saw the chance to drop my statistics and spend my time on something more important. In an amazing short time I found myself formally enrolled in calculus class (seven class meetings late) with statistics dropped entirely. Other shifts in my program were made with a minimum of difficulty.

I knew that now I would have to work at top notch pace to keep up with my work. However, I love to be under pressure, for then I work at maximum capacity. The men before Stalingrad had no spare time nor did the boys at Bataan. They are holding the line until the rest of us arrive.

Letter from Art to Dotty
Maryville College
Jan. 26, 1943
(Tuesday night)

Dearest and only,

Events of the past two days have been so unexpected and so far reaching in their results to come that I hasten to write a short note to keep you informed.

As a result of several factors, I have been feeling just a little low concerning the importance of my work during this semester. What good is a study of Restoration Comedy to the war effort? Isn't a course in statistics under Dr. Briggs a rather useless way of spending my time? If we are going "all out" for war, am I not a slacker to stay in school, studying subjects which seem well-nigh useless for the time? Of course, I realized the answer was in my favor for most of these.

....

As I was saying before I was so rudely interrupted just a week ago today—well, you know the story by this time. I changed my courses, I entered calculus class seven meetings late, and I am now working my head off to keep up with the new load. I do think it was a wise move, and it may have far-reaching effects on our future. Reading last night in a book on Aviation Careers, I found the statement that meteorology is a more recent field than aviation itself; and that it has excellent opportunities for research and advancement. If, after the war, I do have a thorough training in the field, and find that I can step into a three or four thousand dollar a year job, I think we would take it temporarily. By doing that, we would have the chance to become adjusted to our life together and to the post-war world. At the same time, we would be able to see the future of the liberal arts college and the opportunities there.

Darling, there are questions and problems that confront us today. We cannot say without reservation what we will be doing after the war. There is one thing which we do know, however. At the earliest practical moment, when a semblance of peace is declared, we shall face that unpredictable future together.

The more I think about Harriet and her radiant vivacity, the more I realize that I must see that girl more. To think that three girls as wonderful as the Barber children are could be in one family always amazes me. You know, I think I might try to marry one of them someday. Who knows? (I do!)

I enclose a note which I received from our good prince Hal this morning. [below] A great guy that!

Give my love to all, but take this g-r-e-a-t l-o-o-n – n – g kiss for your own.

Ever thine,
Bushy

Letter from Art to Dotty

[February 1, 1943]
Maryville College
Monday afternoon

Dearest,

I have just one hundred and twenty seconds to tell you how much I love you, and to say how much I love our wonderful sister. She tops on any list! I must see more of that gal.

Here's is the note Bob gave me Sat. night to bring over. I hope you can get the tickets for him, without difficulty.

Trip home made in good order. Arrived in time for first of the Feb. Prayer Meetings in our room.

I love you more, but 100 of those precious seconds are gone.

Yours,
Bushy

Letter from Art to Dotty

Maryville College
Feb. 4, 1943 (Thur. night)

Dearest darling,

'Tis four minutes past time for the lights to go out. Another one of my rush messages............. (The lights caught me!)

Friday afternoon it is, and I still have only a few brief minutes for a long letter. For two or three reasons I want to come over this week-end, but it seems almost impossible. (Grieg's Norwegian Dance No. 2 in progress—there you go!) However, I am going to make a business trip to Knoxville by the middle of next week, I fear. As soon as I can gather my papers, I am applying for Meteorology Training; and I need to come over to get a photostatic copy of birth certificate.

February Meetings are wonderful and I wish you were here. The minister is very fine—powerful in speech, witty in words, pleasing in dramatic ability, and thoroughly sound in theology. When are you and Harriet coming over to hear him? Sunday, perhaps?

Remind me sometime to recount a conversation I had with Dr. McClelland yesterday. Very encouraging as to our future. Yes, dear, we have a wonderful future ahead. Remind me also to tell you of that sometime.

The steady rains, so characteristic of this variegated paradise, continue. But far more constant and steady than this rain is my eternal devotion to my own dearest heart. Until I can express my feeling far better than these feeble words can ever do. I am

    Faithfully your own.
    Bushy

Letter from Dotty to Art
[February 5, 1943]
Friday Night
Very late

Darling,

I don't know what to tell you to do about this weekend. As far as I know now, we will not be invited out for Sunday dinner, so you could come over any time you please. Harriot will probably go over to see Mary Jo Saturday afternoon. Now, where does that leave us? I don't know either, so I'll look for you when I see you coming.

I received your regards from Dave. Wasn't he looking good? He said he was embarrassed when the girls on the campus whistled at him. He hadn't seen me since my facial disturbance, at which time he had a similar affliction in his neck. P.S. We both got well. His neck will rubber and my face will shine. Well, is looked as if it would!

Pardon me while I snooze between paragraphs. When I get to this pain, it is high time I was abed.

    I love you
    Dotty.

Dearest,

I can hardly wait to see you—more on general principles than anything special I have to tell you. You know what I mean? What day are you coming over? Are you going to try see Stockdale personally when you are here? Dean says that you should have an appointment if you wish to see him because he is usually out of his office and difficult to contact.

I received a letter from our mutual friend J.A. Hawkins yesterday. He wrote at length on what a wonderful guy you were. As if I didn't know, already! Yes, you are, too. He hardly mentioned himself in the letter, but I inferred from everything in general that he is quite lovely, so far away from the friends he really cares for. He said it took him from Jan. 22 to Feb. 2 to write the letter, so you can imagine the proportions.

The symphony is delicious. I have to take time out every now and then to just let the mood of Wagner soak into my ears. (Would that you were here to enjoy it with me)

Harriet is having the Maryville gang over for Saturday night—Dan, the Myneers, Mary Jo, etc. She wants you to come also, and asked me to put the invitation in my letter, since I was writing anyway. She didn't mention it to you yesterday because she hadn't then decided what night to have it on. Since Harriet is going to sing Sunday morning, you could stay over with Carl and be here for that (Mother piped up and said naturally you would breakfast with us.)

I like your rush messages. Much better than no message at all! I am afraid I can't get over at all for the February meetings, much to my sorrow. I certainly would like to hear him. You listen good and tell me about it, hmmm? I don't know why I keep skipping words. My mind must be a little bit faster than my pen. Huh.

My thumb nail finally came off last night! It caught in the bed clothes last night—I felt it catch, but didn't know it came all the way off until I saw it this morning.

I'll see you sometime this week.
        Ever your
        Dotty.

Letter from Art to Dotty
Maryville College
February 9, 1943
Tuesday afternoon

Dearest Heart,

I'm afraid that I didn't explain very fully the reason for my intended trip to Knoxville this week. I do not need to see Stockwell, as I have all the necessaries. The trip was to secure a photostatic copy of my birth certificate to send along with my other papers. The Meetings, honors work, and other studies seem to fill my schedule, particularly since I am to be in Knoxville, not only this week-end, but most of the following week. I enclose my birth certificate and the address where another photostatic copy can be made. The cost is a quarter, and I will reimburse you with interest. I hope it will be convenient for you to do this right away, since as soon as it comes back I will make my application. To explain the reason for another copy, the one I enclose is the only one I have. Since it was secured from the State of Wash., it takes weeks to secure another from there, with much red tape.

Will write a long letter by tomorrow—I hope! Meetings continue very inspirational. Wish you were here. Addresses of two places for copy:

Sehorn and Kennedy
715 Market Street,

Real Estate Title Insurance Co.
612 S. Gay St.
(This one has moved across the St., says Jimmy Smith.)

I love you, darling, and think of you constantly.
Your own,
Bushy

Saturday, February 13, 1943, Diary

The Army is in need of a large number of men for technical training in Meteorology. Calculus and physics are required for the Advanced Course; these I will have at the end of the current semester.

Today I forwarded via Special Delivery Air Mail my application for the course beginning June 21st. Can only hope for a favorable consideration.

Letter from Dotty to Art
[February 25, 1943]
Thursday

Dear Bushy,

Always when the salutation seems a bit lacking I am writing where people may see what I write. If you noted the day you know where I am. Or do you? No, I haven't broken any yet.

Are you coming over this weekend? It is very important that you do, for Carl's sake as well as for mine. He wants you to bring his diploma to him. The college is unable to get tubes in which to mail them, it seems, so Carl would like for you to bring it to him. And of course he is anxious to get. And of course I am anxious to see you. You just don't know how much, darling. I had determined to settle down and catch up on my correspondence the rest of this week. So far I have written a letter to Jenks (I went sound to sleep in the middle of it Tuesday night) and this to you. But I ain't through! Last night I spent on odds and ends. Dishes, fingernails, shoes, mending, cleaning room, and presto—bedtime.

Oh—another reason you must come this weekend—you must meet Mary while she is here. (The Japanese girl)

I felt so futile on the bus Monday morning. Ruth and Johnny Sue didn't hear me when I spoke to them as they got on the bus. Neither did they see me any of the numerous times I turned around in my seat to grin at them. I finally gave up in despair. They didn't know I was on the bus until they met me getting off. Oh yes, I bawled them out proper. Have the cadets come in yet? Or do they not supposed to get here till March? That isn't very far off how time flies. I always say that don't I where were we anyway?

I shall look for you when I see you coming, I hope.
Carl is playing a very beautiful piece by Brahms. I don't know when he finds time to practice, but he is forever memorizing something new.

Goodbye for now—I'll see you Sunday—or Sat.—or both as the case may be.

> All my
> Love,
> > Dotty.

Letter from Dotty to Art

[March 1, 1943]
Monday Night

Darling,

Yep, tis I. Don't forget that this is one of my various writings. Can you read it? If not, just shout and I will read the rest of this to you myself. I will be over Friday, if you can wait that long (to get the letter read). That is the night of the party for Hal, isn't it? Really you should be glad I am writing like this—I get much more on the page.

Bushy darling—I was so sorry to hear you got hurt. What time I wasn't thinking of you I was wishing I was with you, after I got your letter (Sat. Night). I was so relieved to get your card tonight, informing me that you are much better. Please take it as easy as possible (could it be, with your schedule?) Till you are completely o.k.

Cal was very disappointed that you did not come over this weekend, not only on account of his diploma, but also because I think he wanted to talk to you. But Carl's disappointment was not half as great as mine. I don't think he loves you like I do. I'd be awful jealous if he did!

Tonight I went to the National Missions Regional Institute of the Synod of Mid-South. Sounds most impressive. I got quite a hit out of it, even I did only get to attend two meetings and supper. I went and re-met a number of interesting people, including the young people's director from New Providence, and Doctor Davies, and Jim Huff, etc. The churches in this region really have a challenge before them, and it is a challenge that will be adequately met if the spirit prevailing among those present tonight is infused throughout the churches of the region.

Have the cadets created as much of a sensation in Maryville as they have here? Probably, if I know Maryville. Will they be quarantined for thirty days? Do they march around singing? Has the "Double Rule" caused any conflicts yet? On second thought, have they arrived at all?

You really should have been here yesterday. Mother was under the weather somewhat, so I got breakfast, dinner, and supper, ably assisted by Beulah II. And dearest, I hope you heard the symphony play Rachmaninov's Piano Concerto No. 2. Mary Ruth and I just sat and listened to it all the way through before we even started on the dishes. It was excruciatingly beautiful, and touched me to the very core of my being. I would like to add it to our collection. Or am I assuming that you are highly intrigued by it, merely because I am?

When I write this way, there is a strong tendency for it to develop into a mere scribble utterly unworthy of being termed "writing." I do hope you have been able to read this. Especially the last half of this sentence—I love you always.

Forever your
Dotty

P.S. What about my coming over Friday?
P.P.S. What about Carl's diploma?
P.P.P.S. What about your meeting Mary?
P.P.P.P.S What about? Me?

Letter from Art to Dotty
Maryville College
March 3, 1943
Wed. afternoon

Dearest Heart,

Another letter that is destined to be a short one. I just returned from H.S., and the mail goes out in fifteen minutes. Your letter came last night, and I was happy to hear all the news. Particularly was I glad to hear of you attending the N.M.R.I.S.M.S. It sounds something like my address in the Army.

One reason for my haste in writing concerns the week-end. The party for Hal is on Saturday as I think I explained in my letter which should reach you today. I will have to be on the campus for part of the program that the Senior Class is sponsoring, but we will be able to be at the Hut for most of the evening. Bob and Arlene would like to have us for lunch on Sunday if you can stay over. I explained to Bob this morning that you perhaps could not stay. Let me know as soon as possible about Sunday so Arlene can make plans accordingly. If you do have to return, they are inviting me out for lunch.

The soldiers arrived at seven o'clock this morning, but there has not been enough time elapse to see how conflicts will work out. So far, everything is going smoothly. The weather was true to form and greeted them with one of its original ideas. I went to school yesterday with only my suit coat on, this morning when the soldiers arrived the temperature was 19 degrees above, with an inch of snow. (Pardon all the mistakes, but time draws nigh.)

Will get Carl's diploma, and you can take it over to him when you come. Do want to meet Mary. (Trying to pan me off on someone else, huh?) As to "what about? you?". Will tell you that later. This machine does not have type enough in it for me to put down my thoughts, nor is there paper enough to hold the expression of

My love,
Bushy

Letter from Dotty to Art
[March 4, 1943]
Thurs. Night

Dearest,

Already it is ten-thirty, here I am just beginning. I fear I copy you with a "rush" message.

I shall arrive Saturday at the usual time, prepared to stay over for Sunday. The dinner invitation sounds thrilling—I"m all for it!

Hey, Bud—give, why don't you? What do you mean, the N.M.R.I.S.M.S. "sounds something like my address in the army"? You mean everything is all settled? You have heard from your papers and stuff? Why don't you tell me all these little (big) things? If I don't show up Saturday at the appointment time, you will know that I have perished of suspense.

I forgot to explain in the first paragraph that only because I helped with dishes, washed and set my hair, and filled out my income tax return ready to mail was this a rush message. After then you come first!

The pictures (remember) were all quite good, especially those of you. I shall bring a set with me when I come. And that look emanating from your eyes whenever I gave upon your picture rises from a deep and endless

Love,
Dotty

Letter from Dotty to Art
[March 9, 1943]
Tues. Night

Dearest One,

I am tired to point of dropping, and I have a host of letters to write and a multitude of things to do, so I write to you. I love you.

Darling, I am so ashamed of myself. I was so absorbed in having a good time that I forgot all about asking you if you had completely recovered from your kick in the ribs. Pure, unadulterated self-centeredness. That's me. Are you? I mean, is it?

Are you aware of all the things that are going on here next week? The concert is on Wednesday, the 17th, the party on the 19th, and the wedding on the 20th. Can you really get here for all of that? Is Wed. your busy day, or could you and Bob & Arlene get here for supper? Let me know, so I can plan. If you can't come I won't ask them.

Sunday was so wonderful. I didn't want to come home. And Sunday night after Christian Endeavor I wanted to stay at the church. Such initiative. My, my. The funniest thing happened Sunday night.

You recall, I presume, how habitual if its for my little (?) girls to get tickled at each other of nothing and to giggle? Well, the leader called upon one girl to pray, and she started out bravely enough, but after a few moments she suspended her prayer with "and_____"
Everyone remained with bowed heads waiting on her to at least complete her sentence But she seemed unable to, either because she was tickled or because she couldn't think of anything else to say. The silence was becoming more and more embarrassing, and I could sense that suppressed giggles would begin to blossom any moment, so I pretended it was a planned affair and completed it as a directed silent prayer asking God to speak to us in the silence. We were all relieved when I pronounced the "Amen."

  Goodnight, darling. A constant and constantly growing thing is

     My love,
     Dotty

P.S. I had to order the book. It cost $5.00 and takes about 2 weeks to get here. Is that soon enough?

March 9, 1943, Tuesday, Diary

Today at noon Dad called me from home to tell me of receipt of orders from Fourth Corp Hdg. for me to report for active duty at the University of North Carolina by tomorrow Mar. 10, for Pre-Meteorology training. Taken completely by surprise, I was a little disturbed. I said goodbye to many of my friends, and made arrangements to have my things packed for Dad to come after. I found that to get to Chapel Hill on time I would have to leave Knoxville tonight. At Dr. Lloyd's suggestion, Dr. McClelland called Atlanta to find out if I could possibly have any extra time. He was told that since it was an appointment, I could decline the invitation. However, there was no assurance that I would get another chance at Meteorology. I went out to see Dr. Hunter and helped him plant onions as we talked. He advised me to stay in school. After trying to weigh the decision carefully and look at it from all angles, I decided to stay.

HEADQUARTERS FOURTH SERVICE COMMAND
ERC - 373   Office of the Commanding General   -ES/fm

Special Orders   EXTRACT   Post Office Building
No.   57   Atlanta, Georgia
                                                      8 March 1943.

22.   Pursuant to authority contained in letter, AG 221.99 Aviation
Cadets (2-27-43)PE-R, War Department, February 27, 1943, subject: "Transfer
from ERC to ACER and assignment to active duty", and 2nd Indorsement,
War Department, March 4, 1943, each of the following-named enlisted reservists (ACER) is ordered to active duty, effective March 9, 1943, in grade
of private, and will proceed on that date from the address shown after his
name to the Air Force Training Detachment, University of North Carolina,
Chapel Hill, N. C., reporting not later than March 10, 1943, to the Commanding Officer thereat, for assignment to class "B" Premeteorology training:

NAME	SERIAL NO.	ADDRESS
BEASLEY, William M.	14199978	Lebanon Road, Murfreesboro, Tennessee
BUSHING, Arthur S.	14119120	Box 245, Jamestown, Tennessee
LYNCH, Kenneth W.	14071847	Route 2, Maynardville, Tennessee
RAGSDALE, Keener B. Jr.	14184350	Holly Springs, Mississippi
TEAS, William C.	14183358	Presbyterian College, Clinton, S. C.
WORKMAN, James M. Jr.	14117387	2309 Crescent Ave.,Ext.,Charlotte, N. C.
WRIGHT, John P.	14101344	Lookout Mountain, Tennessee
WHEELER, Fernie J.	14147446	Route #2, Clayton, North Carolina

Each reservist will be reimbursed for travel from the address shown after
his name to Chapel Hill, N. C., at the rate of five cents (5¢) per mile,
computed over the shortest usually traveled route. Travel directed is
necessary in the military service and payment, when made, is chargeable
to FD 31 P 431-02 A 0425-23. (AG 326.22 ERC)

23.   So much of Paragraph 56, Special Orders 55, this Headquarters,
March 5, 1943, placing RUSSELL W. PARK, JR., (ACER) 14183361, General
Delivery, Lake City, S. C., on active duty, effective March 25, 1943, at
Army Air Forces Technical Training Command Basic Training Center, Atlantic
City, N. J., is revoked. (AG 326.22 ERC)

24.   So much of Paragraph 9, Special Orders 55, this Headquarters,
March 5, 1943, placing RUTH A. IRWIN, (WAAC) A-401808, Box 234, Gloster,
Mississippi, on active duty, effective March 14, 1943, at Second Women's
Army Auxiliary Corps Training Center, Daytona Beach, Florida, is revoked.
(AG 324.4 WAAC)

"Office of the Commanding General"
Special Orders dated March 8, 1943, pg. 1

SO 57 Hq   Serv.C X (Extract) 1943   con't   RESTRICTED - 2 -

25.   Pursuant to authority contained in letter, AG 221.99 Aviation Cadets (2-26-43)PE-R, War Department, February 26, 1943, subject: "Assignment to Active Duty of Air Corps Enlisted Reservists", and 1st Indorsement, War Department, March 3, 1943, each of the following-named enlisted reservists (ACER) is appointed Aviation Cadet, and ordered to active duty, effective March 25, 1943, and will proceed on that date from the address shown after his name to Air Force Technical School, Boca Raton, Florida, reporting not later than March 26, 1943, to the Commanding Officer, thereat for assignment to nine weeks basic military training in Aviation Cadet Engineering, Class No. 13-43-EB, scheduled to commence March 29, 1943.

NAME	SERIAL NO.	ADDRESS
KLUTTS, Milton J. Jr.	14202251	1408 Canterbury Road, Raleigh, N. C.
LUTON, Horace D. Jr.	14199909	2401 Hillsboro Road, Nashville, Tenn.
SPAIN, Kenneth C.	14199916	Glendale Road, Nashville, Tennessee
WINCHESTER, Dewey R.	14157114	604 Andesboro Avenue, Monroe, N. C.

Transportation Corps will furnish the necessary rail transportation. Reimbursement to cover the necessary expense actually incurred, not to exceed five dollars ($5.00) per day is authorized for the time required to perform the travel by common carrier in accordance with 2nd Indorsement, The Adjutant General, AG 221.99 Aviation Cadets (12-28-41)EA, March 8, 1942. Travel directed is necessary in the military service and payment, when made, is chargeable to FD 31 P 431-02 A 0425-23. (AG 342.1 Aviation Cadet)

26.   Paragraph 7, Special Orders 53, this Headquarters, March 3, 1943, placing WOODROW J. DAWSON, (ACER) 14191354, Bridgeport, Alabama, on active duty, effective March 9, 1943, at Fort McPherson, Georgia, for processing and assignment, is revoked. (AG 201 DAWSON, Woodrow J.)

By command of Major General BRYDEN:

W. R. NICHOLS
Colonel, General Staff Corps
Chief of Staff

OFFICIAL:

GEO. R. SHEDGE
Colonel, A. G. D.
Chief, Adjutant General Branch

- 2 -

"Office of the Commanding General"
Special Orders dated March 8, 1943, pg. 2

Maryville College
Maryville, Tennessee
March 10, 1943

My Dearest Heart,

How impossible it would be for me to forget the significance of the anniversary which this day commemorates! How carefully will I cherish the vivid memories I have of this memorable day three years ago! It does seem impossible, doesn't it, that we should have known each other only three short years. It seems more a life-time; and truly it has been a life-time, for it was three years ago today that I began to live.

Before I met you, dearest, I knew a longing for something that I knew not. It was a longing akin to the feeling that the tiny seeds must have in the spring-ground as it longs for the life-filling light of the warming sun. It was a longing akin to the feeling that ships of old felt as they sought a guiding star to compass for them a safe journey. It was a longing akin to the feeling that the man-bird has today as he searches the airwaves for the homing beam.

But then I found you, dear heart, and that feeling of longing was gone. It was replaced by a new feeling of exultation in discovery: the thrill of discovery such as Columbus must have felt when he kissed the soil of a New World, or the thrill that Edison felt when he saw the first flicker of light emanate from his first successful electric bulb. I knew then that there was a real pot of gold at the end of the beautiful, multifarious rainbow which I had discovered.

It was then that I began the long climb to the top of that rainbow, for I knew that at the top would I be able to gain some minute conception of the boundless vista lying on and beyond. I watched the development of our love as a Mother watches the growth and development of her own dear child. As a lover of flowers waits patiently the completed formation of the tiny rose within the bud, so waited I until our love would blossom in full bloom. As the gardener comes forth at the break of each new day to observe the growth of the past night, so came I fourth to note daily germination of our love. At last he is rewarded when, upon entering the garden, he blinks his sleep-forgotten eyes as the first rays of morning rush with youthful vigor across the horizon to halt and gently stroke the soft petals of the rose that have at last burst forth in all their splendor. I too blinked my eyes and lifted them to Heaven to give thanks. The bud at last opened into the full bloom of our love.

And so, my Heaven, my Haven of Love, I recall with a heart filled with thanksgiving the day in my life which is three years young today. As the years wax and wane, other days will take on new significance for us. Days of joy as well as days of sorrow will make their imprint on the walls of our memory. There will be the day when we become man and wife, the day when the first major crisis or decision comes; there will be the day when our first child is born, the day when Death first knocks at the door of our heart. These days that will live in our memory must come, and yet none will be more meaningful and memorable to me than the 10th day of the month of March, for it was on that day I met the angel with whom I plan my future.

As the world looks forward with happy anticipation to peace and the brotherhood of man, may we look forward to the part that we, as a unit in Christ, can play in spreading Love that passeth all understanding among the men and women of the world. In doing so, we shall find the approaching perfection of our strong love.

> Thy loving,
> Bushy

Letter from Dotty to Art
March 24 [1943]

My Own,

This is a happy day in my life. It commemorates the day on which the person who means the most to me in this world came into it (the world).

I don't suppose he ever realized that he was destined to be the nicest guy in the world—but he is, whether he realizes it or not. So therefore I am happy, because he was born, and because he belongs to me. And my writing is going to the dogs and gets worse all the time and I am sitting on the bathroom floor (warm spot) writing and no wonder I can't write well what a sentence no punctuation poor grammar and no point to it anyway so why am I writing the answer is I love you so there too now is that clear I love you I love you hah another record for our collection and a broken one at that it just says I love you I love you all the time do you like it or should I exchange it for another Mary Ruth and I are coming over Saturday but not until the six o'clock bus since Mary Ruth doesn't get off till six so we will see you then have you found a date for her yet I hope we will be over anyway here goes that record again I love you I love you I

> Love You Darling.
> Dotty
> HAPPY BIRTHDAY

Letter from Art to Dotty
[Art now in Jamestown]
Jamestown, Tenn.
March 30, 1943

Dearest,

Just a line to let you know my plans. Will leave here tomorrow afternoon (Wed.) about five-thirty. Should arrive Knoxville about eleven P.M. Will call you as soon as I get intown. Since I cannot get on to Maryville, would like to park on your doorstep. A number of things to tell you, and I may not get back over for some time if assignment comes through. Will on to Maryville seven o'clock bus Thursday A.M.

Arrived here after good trip 5:30 Sunday. Mother and Dad completely surprised. Am enjoying a good rest, and delightful change. So far, have done little along a constructive line except listen to Grieg and write to Bill.

Hope to see you Wednesday night, and promise to not to keep you too long away from the Sandman.

> Ever thine,
> Bushy

Letter from Art to Dotty
"The Hut"
April 3, 1943

Dearest,

The flames leap up with a new burst of cigar, the clock on the mantle ticks merrily the seconds by, and Hal's pencil makes a spasmodic scratching, as it hurries across the page. With almost all the comforts of home. Hal and I are spending a glorious Sat. evening of study at "The Hut."

We came out in the middle of the afternoon to devote ourselves to a few hours intensive study. Hal is speaking in Vespers tomorrow evening, and he needed to spend more time in preparation. I can always spend a few more hours in study to no little profit.

'Tis truly wonderful here: the cozy fire making the difference. Since the middle of the afternoon we have been here studying, talking at odd moments, but studying primarily. The heart warming glow that comes from such a fellowship adds immeasurably to my treasury of memories here at Maryville.

Letter from Dotty to Art

[April 4, 1943]
Sunday

Darling,

I have been sitting here feeling so incomplete. True, I have beautiful music. Granted that I am at home. But something is lacking. I must learn to keep my mind from dwelling too much on such a feeling.

Think how many other girls there are who have the same feeling right now, with much less hope for doing anything about it than I. Oh, dearest one, I am extremely fortunate in having you only 16 miles away instead of 1600 or 16,000. It humbles me to consider my very good fortune.

I'll be thinking of you tomorrow as you begin your new task, and praying for your success. Give it all you've got, Bud! Have you heard from Washington yet about your release? Silly question of course you haven't, or you would have let me know.

How is the Jack-Annie situation, and the Boyd-Hal situation, and the Boyd-Cain situation? Have the new cadets arrived? Will you be able to stay on in the dorm? Will you get your degree right away, and if so can you be a part of the graduation with your class? Will you be able to complete Honor's Work? When will I see you again soon I hope it won't be too long maybe?

Thursday night I conducted the party for the Intermediates, suffered slightly from appendicitis and missed you. Friday night I went out to see Ruth Duggan and missed you. Last night I studied my Sunday school lesson, rested, and missed you. Tonight I shall go to C.E., write up a report for the congregational meeting and miss you. Tomorrow night—but this could go on and on ad infinitum, as does

My love for you,
Dotty

P.S. Mary Ruth says "Hello"
P.P.S. I say "Hello"
P.P.S.S. I say "Hello, darling."
P.P.P.S.S. I say "Hello, darling— smack smack m-m-m." Quote "And also Auf Wiedersehen." Unquote.

Letters from Art to Dotty

Maryville College
April 5, 1943

Dearest,

I have just enough time to dash off a note t the end of my first day of teaching. It's wonderful, darling! I may have a different story tomorrow for I have four hours of lecture in the morning. Today I had only two.

There is as yet no word from Washington concerning my status. I am not alarmed over the matter as far as the time element is concerned for the mills of the gods—in Washington—grind slowly. However, I will be relieved to find out something definite.

Almost all of the hundred and twenty men that I have are college bred and many have had physics before. One fellow has had fifteen semester hours plus a year in high school. Such small details make my job doubly challenging. I intend to make good!

April 6, 1943
Tues. Night

Darling,

This is my third attempt to write you. I hope to finish this attempt. Your letter of Sunday arrived tonight, and it gave me new inspiration for my work.

Four hours of lecture today left me feeling as though teaching is more than roses. I love it—thorns and all. After an extend talk with Dr. Lloyd yesterday, I came away knowing a little more concerning my status. At this point I am hanging between three points—the M.C. faculty, student body, and Army. Whata feeling! I am to receive $110 per month until school closes. Then my salary will be $125, with a possible raise in the Fall. I will probably be able to live in Carnegie and eat in Pearsons. That will make my living expenses much lower and should enable me to save a good deal. The Scotch blood will flow with renewed vigor as I save my pennies!

April 7
Wed. Afternoon

Dearest,

Mail loving.

Have been writing this for five days now. Intended to recopy other side. No time!

Love, Bushy

Dearest Heart,

As I begin this letter I am reminded of the other four letters I wrote this week, and the conditions under which I composed them. I trust I will have more success with this one. In fact, I better get this off in the afternoon mail if I expect to get any dinner Sunday. Yes, darling, I'm afraid that I can't stay away any longer. Unless something drastic comes from the Army this afternoon or tomorrow, I'll try to get over for Church, and perhaps Sunday school.

Teaching is a wonderful experience, particularly when the men I am trying to teach have degrees in engineering—one fellow with fifteen hours of college physics and a year of the stuff in high school. Almost all of my students (one hundred and twenty in all) are within a few months of graduation or already have their degree. One fellow that I met last night has had five years of university work in music, and is looking for a hundred and ten piece band for which he can orchestrate. This second group to come to our campus is made up of Army Reservist from northern universities.

As to my situation, there has been no word whatever from the Army. I did get a letter yesterday from Meteorology saying that the quotas for "A" have been filled, and that my case was closed. We are still hoping to get favorable word from the Man Power Commission as to my future; but, as I think I told you, the mills of Washington grind slowly. If the request is granted, I will be allowed to remain in the dorm for the remainder of the semester, and perhaps longer. I will not get my degree now, but will continue in a state of suspended animation until May 17. My honors work will have to be completed at a later date—I hardly know when. Dr. Hunter is already planning to give me four more hours per week during the summer if I stay. However, this will not be so bad, since it will be the college class which is largely lab. We are unable to take the cadets into the lab, and thus the work is increased greatly.

Jack, as you may have heard, was elected the new Y Prexy last Tuesday. The other situations that you mentioned are progressing in a wonderful fashion. However, Jane is torn up over the fact that Joe Suitor hasn't continued to date her. Poor girl, she had her hopes high.

There is little more of the news that I have time for, except that Dad has had a relapse and was in bed at the last writing. I hope to hear today or tomorrow that his condition is improving.
my dearests something

Unless something unforseen occurs, will see you Sunday, my dearest.

> I love you,
> Bushy

Letters from Dotty to Art
[April 8, 1943]
Thursday Night

Dearest One,

I was <u>so</u> glad to hear from you, darling. I didn't know whether you were sinking or swimming, or merely floating along on top. I'm so thankful to know that it is not only on top but swimming vigorously.

Tonight I spent a quiet evening at home, for a change. Tomorrow I shall try it again, and Saturday night also, unless you come poking your handsome pan around, in which case I might be persuaded to make whoopee. Are you as busy as all get-out? Well then, you could come see me. Nicht wahr? [Is it not?] That's what I thought.

There are some interesting letters from Carl floating around. He is now in Louisiana, being trained in radio work, on account if he made high aptitude on ear and rhythm tests, which he claimed are very similar to the Seashore musical exams. He also gets to play the organ for the camp and direct a choir—I'm so glad he has the opportunity to use his music while in the Army.

[April 9, 1943]
Friday night

And it is too far downstairs to go after ink on a cold dark night. What I need is someone to protect me and keep me warm. Do you know anyone who might be in the market for such a position?

Out of the 12 deacons and 12 elders who were invited to our shuffleboard affair we had <u>one</u> deacon (Uncle West) and six elders. We had a good time, anyway, and those who did come appeared to enjoy himself immensely. And Dean didn't act at all as if that were his last night at home, or way from home, as the case may be.

I have something to show you next time you come—several somethings, in fact, so you'd better come.

The time drawers nigh, so good night, and <u>happy lecturing</u>! My love is all

> Yours,
> Dotty

Maryville College
Maryville, Tennessee
April 14, 1943

Dearest One,

Today most of the seniors are deep in the heart of comprehensives. I thank my guiding stars that I took mine last December, rather than wait until now. It would have been tragic for me to have tried to take them along with my teaching.

As you have probably guessed, there is still no word as to my status with the Army. I hardly know what to think about it. Dr. Lloyd wrote me a very nice letter this week confirming our conversation concerning salary, etc. The work does not grow easier, and I see no let up for the first five months. After that time, it should be less difficult to keep up with. Every day I realize more and more what I am facing. For me to be attempting to teach men who have actually been engineers seems more than ironic.

It was a wonderful relaxation to get away from work last Sunday, and to spend the time as we did. The tension that my mind works up during heavy work is always relaxed when we are together. I love you, darling. May God hasten the day when we begin our lives together. My reason for hesitation Sunday as we talked was due to the dawning realization of the futility of planning very far ahead in these times. A month ago who would have thought that I might be stationed here for the duration? On March 9, I thought I was going directly into Meteorology with no opportunity to finish my college work. Within the month that situation had cleared, and I was in a classroom teaching Cadets. A month from today circumstance may alter again our outlook.

I had a long letter from Hargrave this morning. He asked about you as usual. He is doing well, it seems: is singing in a big choir, playing in a dance band, seeing all the movies that come, and studying on the side. At least, so it would seem.

Bob and Dick wanted to bring the girls to Knoxville for dinner and a show after comprehensives Thursday. I wanted to plan it very much, but I can't possibly get away. My papers are still behind, and I haven't a minute to spare. Perhaps we can plan something like that toward the last of the year.

Dearest, I will try to write more often, if only to write one of my rush messages. However, tempus fugit [time flies]. Write me when you have a spare moment, and always remember

I'm yours,
Bushy
P.S. Dad still weak but improving

Letter from Dotty to Art
[April 15, 1943]
Later Thurs.
Night or
"After the call is over"

Darling,
Just in case you should decide to go to the mts. I am not really expecting you, but I never can keep down that faint glimmer of hope when there is the slightest possibility. You know what I mean? Well, just in case you should decide to go with us, here is what you had better do: 1) Call me so I'll be expecting you—at work is O.K., extension 603 in case you've forgotten—and we will arrange where to meet; 2) Bring your papers along and I'll help you grade them—there's nothing like the peaceful mountains for such concentrated work, I always said—and besides four hands and two heads are better as one or two as the case may be. And as for the cold—there's nothing like a trip to the mountains to cure things like that. It's really miraculous. Remind me to write an essay on the subject sometime.
Good night, my love,
Dotty

P.S. Really though, <u>I'm not expecting you</u>—you should go to Retreat if at all possible. On the other hand, why did I compose such explicit directions? Huh?

Letter from Dotty to Art
[April 20, 1943]
Tuesday

Dearest Bushy,
I am ready for one of your rush messages. Just any time. (Only except now would be the best time) How are you? Have you heard? Are you keeping up with your papers and ahead of your brilliant class? Did you go on Retreat? Did you catch all the mental telepathy floating out from the hillside in the moonlight Saturday night? I <u>share</u> missed you, me darlin'. There I was , walking up to Addison's cabin with Flo and Add. And Mary and Johnny Sue, when think how much more wonderful it would have been if your presence had graced the

40

company. I had a good time and a nice rest. Nothing unusual happened except we had fudge sundaes. Remind me to tell you. Mmmmm.

I haven't found out yet whether I will be over Sat. night or early Sunday morning. If I come over Sat. it will be late—the 7 or 8 o'clock bus. I'll write you later in the week—also Muriel and Jane if I plan to come Sat. night.

How is your Dad? Not working to hard, I hope.

Snuff said now.

I love you,
Dotty

Letter from Art to Dotty
Maryville College
April 22, 1943, Thursday afternoon

Dearest,

Your letter just received. By this time, I am sure that you have my letter covering most of the questions that you asked. Still nothing new from Washington. It is rumored that the Army Reserves will not be called until July 1. If that be true, I will probably continue here until sometime in June. We are still hopeful that the answer will be in the affirmative.

Had hoped that you would be able to get over early Saturday evening in order that we might have supper with Bob and Arlene in town, and go out to their house to hear a certain Concerto later on. However, if you can't get over sooner that eight or nine; I still hope you can get over then.

My roommate is back from the hospital, and I have only fourteen more days in which to catch the measles. Woe is me! Am spending twelve and fourteen hours on physics and dream about it most of the night. No stuff, I work problems in my dreams. Don't worry though, I still. have time to dream about things more wonderful,—namely, my own dear heart.

Anne may come to summer school here. Bill wants Nettie Rose Spraker to come up to Notre Dame for his graduation. Jane is still terribly hurt over Joe Suitor. Muriel is happy with Hal, but worried about Jane. Jack is happy. No word from Dad this week. Easter Services very fine. I love you!

If you can plan to stay over Sunday, we can plan to eat Sunday dinner in town with Bob and Arlene. Anyway you plan will be all right, as long as you come, darling.

Ever thine, Bushy
P.S. Still no paper on Church by Dr. Orr.

Bushy Darling,

Don't you dare get the measles! Are you broke out yet? Is your throat still sore? Haven't you had the measles before? Well, why didn't you?

Here are the colors in my Easter outfit: green, tan, and rusty brown. I was going to compose a wild tale about a green satin dress with a yellow sash and straw hat with a ribbon hanging down my back, but decided you wouldn't quite choke it down.

I guess I'll be over Sat. night on the 7:00 bus, if nothing happens to prevent it. When I'm going to eat supper, I don't know, nor do I know what I'll do with my knitting after I get through it. But why do I tell you all these little things—they're my worries, not yours. Perhaps it is because I love you, and enjoy thinking out loud to you. There were several bad newest concerning my musical education and career. No, I haven't lost my voice nor gone suddenly deaf—I'll tell you about it Sunday.

Speaking of Sunday, I've been looking forward to it for a long time, with an absurd eagerness. By the way, I finally heard from girls today. Where are we going to eat breakfast Sunday—here or there? I'll be seein' of you

Always your
Dotty.

Friday P. M. 4/30/43

Dear sonnie boy:

I left Monday A. M. by Bus to Crossville and took train at 1.55 P.M.
for Nashville. Nice trip. Was at a nice little Hotel near the
Courthouse where I was scheduled to appear Tuesday at 10.00 A. M.
Had to wait all day, that is until about 4.00 P. M. They never got
to our case - U. S. vs Oliver Edmond Smith. I was finally called
before Federal Grand Jury at 1.20 P. M. Wednesday and was before
the Court less than 15 minutes. After the Judge charged the Jury
(Of course, I learned this from the FBI man after Court adjourned)
Smith was indicted. He will have his trial in Cookeville before a
jury about June 10. Pinckley and Guy Jordon will be witnessess with
me for the Government. It looks as if it will go pretty hard with
my assailant and perhaps stop these threats. Got back home Wednesday
night about 9 as I was fortunate to meet up with with the Sheriff
of Cumberland County and he for small sum got me into Crossville
in time to meet (7.00 P. M.) Louis Delk driving back to Jamestown.

Well, dear boy, so sorry that it is impossible for wither
Mother or me to get over tomorrow to see you crown the queen.
I will buy the Knoxville Sunday paper hoping to see some ac-
count of the event. Time is short now for your graduation. And

then will come the departure, maybe, from Maryville and getting
your things home. I'll let you know at once about getting the
books over by Express - which I assume would be the best way to
ship them. I have in mind that you could send them to Crossville
letting me know by card when you shipped same. You could address
the package "Crossville" and in addition mark package somewhere
in brackets, Home or mail address Jamestown, Tenn." In the meantime it might be well to pack them for expressage. If you should
get sudden call to be inducted and there was time, I would of
course, come right over with car or pick-up and get all of your belongings. But we hope with you that you can finish up your work
and come home for short time before leaving.

Are you short of funds ? Just write me and I will deposit to cover
your needs. Tell Dot that I did appreciate the lovely card. So
sorry not to have her address or be able to find it. Send it to me
in your next and I will be delighted to drop word of appreciation.

Must close dear son. God bless you. I am feeling a little weak in
my legs for what cause I don't know. Medicine maybe. But expect
to get on the mend or go to Nashville soon for entire check up.

                                        Dad

Letter from Art to Dotty
Maryville College
April 28, 1943

Dearest,

Spring blossoms anew on the campus, and 'tis lovely now. The trees fill out in all their splendor, and the grass is shooting up. Maryville is a wonderful place to be when spring comes round.

I have little of news to relate except that I love you, and that is a story that is ever new. Sunday was a wonderful day for me. The rest and relaxation from my daily round of work was most refreshing, and I think that I made the most of it.

Dr. Hunter gave me my tentative teaching schedule for the summer. As it stands, I would have my regular cunntiles that I am teaching now; inaddition, the college class in trig. During the second half of the summer, I will have the second semester of the College course in physics. I am beginning to wonder if there is any limit to the amount of work to be done. I am spending twelve and fourteen hours on the stuff now, but I love it, darling. Success now means success for us later on. I'll work sixteen hours per day if it takes it.

Am looking forward to seeing you Sat. I have four hours of lecture Sat. morning and may not be able to meet the bus. When do you expect to get here? What did Addison have to say? I haven't seen Bob since Sat. night.

Forever yours.
Bushy

Letter from Dotty to Art
[May 3, 1943]
Monday

Dearest Darling,

Our prayers are answered. The Lord takes care of his own. I am amazed and humbled when I think how things nearly always work out right for me and for us. Our ride has come through! Isn't that wonderful!! Addison called me this morning and said that he would be able to take us after all. I am overcome with happiness—I've been walking on air all day. Oh, joy. Bliss. Hurry, Saturday.

Here are the details, as far as I have worked them out. We'll leave from here right after work, or about 5:00. You contact Bob and Arlene, and come over when you want to. Bring a blanket and some sheets if you want them. There will be six in the crowd, for Addison said he was taking a friend. I am going to let Mother buy all the food, and we will split the cash. Bring you your bathing suit if you think it is warm enough to swim.

I had such a nice time last night. I felt so exhilarated. I got the records home O.K., and can hardly wait to play them.

Brinnnggg! Hello, darling! Note to all who are interested! The better part of this letter was written after aforementioned phone call.

Mother shouts from the bedroom to tell me that it is high time for all girls, good & otherwise, to be in bed. Then how come I'm still up? Because I love you. Minutes between now and that certain time are precious—we won't be together nearly enough—so we can only stretch out those minutes, cherish them and make the utmost of them, and finally pray as never before—pray that God will bless your footsteps and be nearer to you than ever before. I know He will.

> Love always,
> through whatever
> comes to you. Dotty

Postcard from Dotty to Art
[May 11, 1943]
Tues.

Dear Bushy,

I'll see you Thurs. night, Bud! Miss Lee thinks it will be all right for me to take off—Yippee!! I'm looking forward to a swell time.

Did you all get home o.k. Sunday night? Have you found a place, I hope? Start packing as soon as possible so we'll have more time.

> Yours,
> Dotty

Letter from Dotty to Art
[Art now lives in Jamestown, Tennessee]
[May 19, 1943]
Wed. Night

Darling,

My beautiful desk pen spreads a little too much ink, doesn't it? A little writing seems to clear up the trouble, however, so much writing would—Oh, it would, would it? Well, we shall see.

Did you, your bag and baggage arrive safely home? I hope you got something to eat before you got home—you looked as if you were about to break down, or something, as you left Monday afternoon. I realize that the look in your eyes that haunted me the rest of the day was not due to heat and hunger alone, but more to leaving all the dear things that are college. We'll come back to those things, darling—perhaps not soon, but some day.

I wonder if you felt me grip your hand as I listened to the painfully gorgeous music on the Telephone and Firestone programs Monday night, or heard me speak to you as I walked down the hill in the moonlight to meet Mary Ruth? I thought you would. You're psychic that way.

You have an appointment with Dr. Edgar Grubb for an eye check-up on Monday, May 31st, at 2:00 P.M. You also have an appointment with Miss Dorothy Louise Barber (but not for always) for Sunday and Monday nights, May 30 and 31, and maybe you think that young lady isn't aware of that exciting fact!!

I was quite taken with your Mother—I was scared at first, but as soon as I found out how much like you she was, or vice versa, I felt quite natural with her. You are an amazing combination of your parents—when I first saw you with your dad, I thought "how much alike they are." Then I saw you with your mother and I thought "how much alike they are." I see a great deal of both your ma & pa in you, and also a lot of just you. It's amazing. I repeat. And my Mom likes your Mom and so I guess everyone will be happy, no?

How is your Dad? Please make him go to the hospital and make him stay long enough to do some good—if you can and have that much time. Give my regards to both your parents.

As for the room at Proffit's, I still don't know. She was not there when I went after my bag, so I wrote her a note, in which I asked her to let me know how much it was, etc. I haven't heard yet, but as soon as I do I'll let you know.

Here is the poem I'm forever trying to quote, without success. Get a picture of water chasing itself over stones before you read.

> "I have known a sound so full of music
> It echoes through the high peaks of my mind—
> The clear, cold sound of running mountain water
> Taking its swift way seaward, there to find
> A deeper music in the ocean's vastness.
> But oh, the lovely solos that it plays,
> Moving across wet rocks down spruce-dark canyons,
> Flute to its lips and piping its sweet lays!
>
> Often I hear it over miles of distance.
> Often it sounds across wide leagues of air—

The rippling music, the high silver fluting
Of water stepping among wet stones, somewhere.
And on the high peaks of my mind are echoes
Clear and sweet as the flute notes strike them there."

by Grace Noll Crowell

The title is derived from the first five words. I hope you like this little number as well as I—it's so descriptive.

> Good night, darling.
> My love to you
> Dotty.

Letter from Art to Dotty
Jamestown, Tennessee
May 21, 1943
Friday afternoon

Dearest Heart,

The wonderful change that has taken place in your letters, namely the lengthened size, was welcomed with opened eyes and arms. I trust that it is not a chronic ailment, and I also assure you that it is catching. Just wait and see! You are still going to see what a long letter really looks like: patience is a virtue!

Mother too enjoyed meeting you very, very much, and was quite well impressed by her future d.i.l. She also enjoyed meeting your mother a great deal. I hope we can arrange other meetings soon. Your comments on the resemblance of sons to fathers and mothers is also amazing. Jack told me Monday that he would have recognized Mother if he had seen her alone. I only hope that I have inherited a few of the virtues of my parents. I owe a great deal to both of them. By the way, I am happy to report that Dad seems much improved since I have been here. The pain in his side has disappeared, and he feels much like his old self. Today he began running up and down the hall outside the office as he did of yore when he had to leave the office. What a man!

Ten hours sleep each night, along with plenty of good food, is doing wonders for me. However, my eyes have not reverted to their 20/20 status. I am trying to read as little as possible, but you know me. After all, I do have to study calculus and write letters. Thanks very much for getting that appointment with the optician. (One friend of mine called him the "Optimist". I hope so!) From the reports I get from friends in the Service, I better get my teeth looked over before going in. I understand the doctors are not particularly interested in the welfare of the soldiers. An appointment for about nine or ten o'clock on Monday (31st) would be the best, I believe.

All of which reminds me: you're wonderful! I'll never be able to return to civilian life for long without you. The efficiency you showed last week-end as we struggled through physics papers proved again how remarkably lucky I am in getting the most wonderful girl in the world.

(Put down those eyebrows!)

I have a bit of news that isn't so good for us, and yet perhaps it is very good. I am told that the Induction Center has a daily quota for all branches of the service. When these quotas are filled, no more can be taken that day. Since all the breaks I can get will be to our advantage, I think it wise to plan to get to Ft. Oglethorpe as early on Tuesday morning, June 1, as possible. I am writing to get the bus and train schedules, but I may find that I should leave Knoxville Monday afternoon or Monday night. I will then be able to get to the Fort from Chattanooga very early Tuesday morning. I have written notes to Ted Kidder and the others with whom I plan to go down, and I will hear in a few days what they have to say about the idea. As you well know, it is going to be extremely hard for those of us going in this late to get a chance at OCS or the other choice positions. Every break that we get or can make will help. As a result of the tentative alteration in plans, I will plan to leave here on Sunday morning rather than Sunday afternoon. That will mean that I get in Knoxville in the middle of the afternoon of the 30th, rather than late that night. The whole thing isn't definite as yet, but it may be wise if I plan it that way.

As you will probably read in the paper, Sgt's. mother died last night. She has been very low for sometime, and her death was not unexpected. The service will be held tomorrow afternoon.

I have spent the whole day writing letters that have been long since overdue. I just finished a long one to Carl, giving him all the latest scandal. I hope to keep in touch with him after I get in the Service. Pessimist that he is, he signed his last letter "your friend and future cousin-in-law". Takes one to recognize..... Oh yes, and another bit of news I heard today was to the effect that one group of Army Reservists has been down at Oglethorpe for almost four weeks now. Surely the Army has something in mind for us—dopes. A handsome picture from "ex-roomy" Bill materialized out of the Post Office today. In full dress uniform, he looks as though he was in command of the Pacific Fleet,...Flight....Float... or something. I can't wait to see what a uniform will do for your headache. That reminds me of a surprise I have for you, but I will save that until I see you, or you see me.

'Tis truly amazing how anxious I am to get into the Service. I was able to concentrate on my work at school, and avoid thoughts of Army life; but now that the time draws near I can hardly wait. If I do nothing but dig trenches, I am going to dig the best trenches the Army ever had. I'll show them that a soft, pantiewaist from college can do something besides study Shakespeare. (I can't find anyone in the dict, or otherwise that will confirm some of the words I use; but if there wasn't, there is.)

Thanks a lot for the lovely poem: it is very nice to remember. Also remember,

> I love you, darling,
> Bushy

Letter from Dotty to Art
[May 23, 1943]
Sunday Afternoon
May 23, 1943

My Own True one,

The wonderful change that has taken place in your letters, namely the lengthened size, was welcomed with open eyes and arms. End quote, ditto, etc. I surely am glad that it is catching, and shall try to make it a permanent fixture.

All your Dad needed was for you to come home. Mother tells me that most of Mary Ruth's ailments disappear when I come home. Nice to be a doctor, eh what? Which reminds me—I may take up nurse aid in the near future. Then when you get sick I'll know just how to bring you a glass of water! Oh, life of joy, come thou soon! No, darling, I don't mean the day you are sick, I mean when you're mine to care for all the time. Fortunate indeed am I, to have the privilege!

By the way, what could a headache have to do with the surprise you have for me? You must have had a haircut—that would indeed surprise me. I can hardly wait for it—(your visit my adorable dope, not the surprise—any surprise could only be purely incidental to that.) My writing does want to go uphill this afternoon. Serves me right for having hiking instincts, I suppose.

It pays to say nice things about people. Friday night I went with Flo to the spring concert of a women's choral club. As the women filed onto the stage, I recognized only one face, and in pointing her out to Flo used a number of complimentary terms, for really she was the most attractive person there in regard to face and figure; I speak without prejudice. After the program was over and we rose to go out, the woman who was sitting in the seat ahead turned around to me, introduced herself as the mother of the girl in question, and thanked me profusely for all the nice things she had overheard me say about her daughter. Made me feel kinda funny.

Last night I went to the show with Mary Alice to see "Keeper of the Flame," starring Spencer Tracy and K. Hepburn. I found it extremely interesting and a bit unusual. It attempted to show that the people of America want the truth, even if that truth hurts; sometimes that truth destroys belief in something we used to think was fine and beautiful, or rather that appeared to be thus. Oh Bushy darling, hold fast to all that is fine and high and beautiful within you—don't let it be crowded out or replaced by any phase of army life—keep the flame of truth and beauty burning as high as ever!

I'll see what I can do for you in the line of dentistry—it may be a bit difficult at this late date, but I'll try.

Just think—next week this time you'll be here—I hope. But alas, when my thinking (?) goes a bit further and I realize that it may be the lasted time for—but let's not get started on that.

I love letters like that last.

> Also
> I love you—
> Dotty

Letter from Art to Dotty
Jamestown, Tennessee
May 24, 1943
(Monday afternoon)

Dearest Heart,

One week from this afternoon I will be winding up my last few hours as a civilian preparatory to getting a new suit of clothing from my favorite uncle. Yes, darling, one week from tomorrow I become one among eight and a half million. Oh joy! Why, with a B. A. tucked under my arm and the letter of recommendation under my ego, I can look any Pfc. in the Army in the eye without stuttering. It will be so much more fun to lick Japs rather than stamps.

I received the train schedule from Chattanooga to Knoxville (or rather vice-versa), and it seems that the best schedule for us to make will be on the train leaving Knoxville 8:05 P.M. Monday. In that way, we will have a chance to get a good sleep before going to the Fort on Tuesday for examination, etc. I haven't heard from all of the others as yet, but I am sure that they will feel as I do that the sooner we get there the more likelihood of getting a break.

As I think I mentioned in my last letter, I plan to leave Jamestown Sunday morning, 10 A.M. I should arrive in Knoxville about 2:30 I believe. The music for next Sunday afternoon sounds quite wonderful, and perhaps I can get out to Glenwood before Debussy's work is finished. I certainly hope so.

Speaking of music, I heard "Through the Years" last night on the Hour of Charm. You better plan to have that on our Hour of Charm next Sunday. I have been trying to save my eyes as much as possible during the last few days, and I have spent much my time listening to records. Grieg is still more wonderful each time I hear him. Wish you could hear some of the other records I have.

I am slowly getting caught up with my letter writing, but it seems that it is a very slow process. I hope to write Jenks a short note before I leave, and I have already written a long letter to Pete and Marianna. Have spent the day today in the Draft Office and will probably work here several other days this week. Rain has prevented me doing very much outside at home.

Mail leaving. More later concerning
                    Our Love,
                        Bushy
P.S. We will need at least $2,000 to go to Chicago for a Masters. Hmn. I can't stay a buck private very long.

Letter from Dotty to Art
[May 25, 1943]
Tues. Night
Blackout

Darling,

Don't you think I write well in the dark? I fooled 'em—I have every light in my room burning, but it doesn't show from the outside.

You are going to be a busy man Monday—you have an appointment with the dentist (Dr. H.M.A. Smith) for ten o'clock in the morning and one with the eye doctor for 2:00 in the afternoon, and a date with me for lunch at 12:00 and a date with the choo-choo at 8:00 pm. But Sunday, as of week before last, is OUR DAY.

Florence leaves tomorrow morning for Shreveport, La., there to meet her beloved for a couple of days. She is so excited. Can't say that I blame her. She plans to visit Dean on her way back. Some trip, eh.

I hear Mom and Dad downstairs in the unlit living room, talking like a couple of young things. Gee, I love 'em! Which reminds me—is your Dad still improving? I guess he didn't go to the hospital, did he?

He'd better not work too hard, or he'll be in the same condition again. But I suppose I might as well tell the wind not to blow. Your mother is apt to overwork too, if she doesn't watch out—but don't they all? There seems to be no stopping them.

Have I ever mentioned to you before the fact that I once had my portrait done in oils? Remind me to show it to you Sunday—I want to see what you think of it. (Came across it while cleaning house and was glad to discover its hiding place.)

Sooo—we will have to acquire $2,000 for Chicago, huh? We shall see what we can do. If you were only a two thousand-buck private y(our) worries would be over. When my forty a month goes into savings instead of loan, it won't take long to develop a nice little nest egg for us. Yessiree bobtail, it is so a common fund. "What is mine I'll always share" from "Through the Years."

Greater and greater grows my anticipation of the weekend, because
>   I love you,
>   Dotty
P.S. "Character is that which can do without success." — Emerson

Letter from Dotty to Art
[May 27, 1943]
Thurs-late.

My dearest,

Why do I sit here and look at your picture and think lots of fluent thoughts to you instead of writing them down on paper? You'll bite— why don't I? Perhaps it is because I am not inspired by a letter from you. Yes, perhaps that is it. Or perhaps I am just built that way. I always think a lot of things that I never say, especially when I write.

Speaking of pictures—Mary Ruth wishes to return T.L.—she doesn't feel that she knows him well enough to keep his picture, and is apparently not interested enough to want to dream. We sort of built her up to an awful let-down on that proposition, didn't we.

Also enclosed please find the note from Mrs. Proffitt which I didn't receive until yesterday. I thought you would want to attend to it right away, nicht wahr ["is not it," in German]?

I never known a coiffure [an elaborate hairstyle] of mine to cause such a sensation as the one I wore yesterday and today. Almost every single person (some were married) I saw during the day that I knew or even slightly knew made some comments. Compliments by the gallon, trade lasts, and assurances that if only they could wear their hair like that and have it do for their personality what my hair-do did for me—it was all quite bolstering to my morale and ego. My head is now twice as big ads it should be. You'd better come quickly and take me down a notch or three.

I love you,
Dotty.

P.S. If I made $2,433 per annual I could save more, couldn't I?

May 28, 1943, Diary

History making event today occurred when Howell Thomas made the first long-wave broadcast from the air. He gave his daily news report from a helicopter which remained virtually stationary while he spoke. These dream birds as destined to revolutionize transportation after the war. Within ten years after peace is resumed, private helicopters will be almost as common as cars. We are living in a fast-changing world.

Postcard from Art to Dotty, dated June 1, 1943

Letter from Art to Dotty
Ft. Oglethorpe, Ga.
June 2, 1943
"On Vacation"

Dearest,

Oh the joy of the soldier life! Here it is Tues.—or rather Wed. (the day of the week has lost much of its old meaning) and another day of inactivity. It's really blissful so far, even more rosy than I had expected.

Our train-ride, down was just about as smooth as any ride could be on the ground. Four of the Maryville gang were together within a few seats of each other, and we made the most of our time. We backed into the Chattanooga station on time; and, after walking for half a mile, we arrived at the station. Tom, bless his heart, was there with a grin scattered all over his countenance. Eight of us piled in to the car and we drove to the "Y." (Tell Mary Ruth I still think it is wonderful stuff 'n things.) Eight excited and somewhat-wondering college men walked from the Y to the corner of Market St. to catch the bus for their last civilian ride. We arrived in front of the Fort about eleven and found that we still had about half a mile to walk before arriving at our Reception Center. As we passed through the WAAC Camp, we were greeted by "You'll be sorry!" On all sides. I still can't figure out what they meant.

When we at last found the proper building we were greeted by none other than Carl Wells—a Maryville lad. I never knew him very well, but he knew some of the group and it was a friendly greeting we received. Soon we were assigned to bunks, and the Army promptly forgot our existence. We found out this morning that our orders have not yet arrived from Atlanta. Nothing can happen to us until those papers arrive, although we may get our uniforms tomorrow. There is every possibility that nothing will happen to us until the end of the week. What a life!

"We arise at the inspiring hour of 4:45 when all the world is sleepily waiting for the sun rise. To compensate for this, if it requires compensation, we go to bed in the middle of the afternoon at nine P.M. My bed is better than the one I had at Maryville, and the food is better in both quality and quantity. Altogether this Army life is like one gigantic vacation with pay—so far. Of course, it will soon change and perhaps not for the better, but certainly these first few days are going to be lovely.

I think it makes all the difference in the world to have these eighteen here together from Maryville. All of us are in the same

54

barracks, and the eight that came down together are in a single group. This morning we played softball and one would think the game was being played on the practice field on the "Hill."

We have no chance to enjoy such entertainment as Bing etc. as yet, but we can receive visitors between six and eight each evening. I hope that Tom can come out before he leaves.

I expect to be here at least another week at the minimum, and all mail will be welcomed, darling.

This Army life is swell, and only life with you can beat it. However, this is my job now and I'm going to love it. I must go to Retreat now, but I think and dream of
> Our love,
> Bushy

Letter from Dotty to Art
[Addressed to "Pvt. Arthur S. Bushing,
Area 'D' Reception Center, Fort Oglethorpe, GA"]
[June 3, 1943]
Thursday Night
Dear Mr. Jones—
I mean

Darling,

We too are suffering from the heat, and I do mean WARMTH! I'll let you go around leaving little puddles of perspiration in your work. (Dotty—how romantic!) Question: how are a very hot day and the inside of a circus tent similar? Answer: see page two (3) #4.

A number of amusing things happened during or following your departure. I stood talking to Dotty Buchanan for a few moments, and as we talked she took me by the hand. After a while she looked down at my hand and exclaimed "Why Dotty, where is your ring—what happened to it—why aren't you wearing it?" Fortunately I was able to not-too-obviously change the subject without answering her questions. (Editor's note: This is not a hint to the wise, or anything—I just thought how funny it is the way people take our engagement so far granted.) After the train pulled out, I started back toward the bus stop, accompanied by Arling Kressler. Do you know what he had the effrontery to do? He asked me to go to the show with him instead of going on home as I had planned. Maybe he was just trying to cheer me up, or something, but it seems to me that he could plainly have observed that I had lips and heart for you only that night. Nicht wahr? I declined politely, but again was highly amused.

Darling, my watch is beautiful. You have such good taste. As soon as possible I showed it to Mother, who later accused me of holding my wrist out in a prominent position, so that al would take notice. (She wasn't far wrong!) It keeps perfect time. I haven't needed to adjust it one iota, jot, or tittle thus far.

Mother and I went to a cousin (one of the four perfect children to whom I constantly refer) was one of the commencement speakers. He made a fine speech, using much poise and well-bearing—in short, carrying on in the well known (?) family tradition. Har-r-r-umph.

Florence had a wonderful time seeing Carl. She reports that he had had his hair very cut, and that it looked most peculiar when he didn't have his cap on. Has your hair been cut any more? Have you received your uniforms yet? Have you heard anything about what you will be getting into or where you'll be sent? I am so anxious to receive the letter which the card states is following.

Every day in every way I am more in
   Love,
    Dotty.
Answer to Question: The heat is (in tents / intense) in both.

P.S. #3—I'll bite—where was number two?
P.S.#4—My new watch (it is such a comfort to have) looks me straight in its face and says that it is past bedtime. Wel-l-l-l-l—late, anyway.

Letter from Art to Dotty
Ft. Oglethorpe, Ga.
June 4, 1943
(Vacation over)

Dearest Heart,

Yes, my vacation is rapidly coming to a close. Yesterday we spent our morning again avoiding the corporals. After breakfast all men in civilian clothes were ordered to the theatre building where the chaplain makes his daily welcome to new men, and other instructions are given. We listened again to the same jokes and the same routine. As had happened the first morning, we were dealt with last because of the small number in our group. Some colonel down in Atlanta is still on vacation, or else has a personal interest in eighteen men from Maryville continuing their vacation at the expense of Uncle Sam. We were marched to another office to find out if perchance our records had arrived. The answer was, of course, "no"; and we were told to return to our barracks. (Second day same as the first.)

Having learned the ropes, we thought better of the matter. As half a dozen of our number were picked up ahead of us to pick us paper, we —that is, Ted, Bob Hunter, and four others off us—lined up and began marching in the opposite direction as if under orders. That is a system that we have found to work quite well. We marched to a recreation area and pitched horseshoes.

Yesterday afternoon we were told to report for uniforms. Several of us had been wearing the same clothing for three or four days, and to maintain their standards the Army had to do something. In a very short time for the usual procedure, we found ourselves toiling back to the barracks with the sweat pouring off in rivulets and eighty-five dollars worth of clothing on our back. I was pleasantly shocked to find everything fitting as well. My shoes (10-C) fit better than any civilian shoes—except perhaps those old brogans I wore in AAA work. We were issued five suits plus overcoat, dress coat, field jacket, extra shoes, etc. etc. What living!

This morning our day began in the same manner as the two preceding. The same greeting by the chaplain, the same jokes, the same health talk by the doctor. However, when we began to play softball after not returning to our barracks, we were told by a young lieutenant that we couldn't play ball while there was work do be done.

Actually there was no important work to be done, but there is a definite tradition in the Army that men must be kept busy. That is the reason that I feel perfectly justified in staying away from work when possible. Even some of the corporals told the fellows this morning to sit down and work only when anyone appeared. The "details" as they are called consist of scrubbing walls that have been scrubbed until they shine, picking up imaginary bits of paper around camp, and adjusting blankets within a half an inch of a line on the bed. The Maryville gang remains together, and it is a wonderful feeling of fellowship that we have.

Tom was here one night, Thursday I guess, and is coming back tonight. (It is now Sat. and I received your wonderful moral-building [morale] letter this morning!) He promises to spend a week-end in Knoxville some time while at Carson-Newman and promises to spend part of his time at 607 W. Glenwood—if a Sunday meal is thrown in. By the way, he will be there for a year he thinks. Why don't you three plan to see at least one concert together?

To get around to your questions concerning my status here: status quo. We were put on detail again this morning but most of the gang has taken up quarters in the reading room for the afternoon. (The temperature was 96 yesterday and seems that or more today.) Our orders are not here yet, and we have no way of knowing how long we are likely to be stuck.

I was told this morning that E.R.C. [Enlisted Reserve Corps] men have a good chance of getting in the branch which they request. I feel sure that we will get a chance for something good, and I remain hopeful that I will rate meteorology.

Tomorrow I spend my first Sunday in Camp, and if I am here another week I will probably get a pass for next Sunday. It will be nice to get out, and yet I do not have the feeling of being confined. I repeat again that it has made a world of difference being here with the Maryville gang. We have a short service here in camp tomorrow morning, but it would be wonderful to go to a real church. We have to clean up before Church tomorrow, but our afternoon will be free I believe. Another wonderful thing about Sunday will be that we get to sleep until 6 o'clock. That is a rare privilege here for we continue to arise at 4:45 each bright morning.

You made no mention of my glasses, but I presume that you took my address around to the optical company. Think it was very wise for me to get fixed up as I did before entering the service.

You spoke something concerning when I will be shipped and where. I will not know when until shortly before leaving, and even then I will not know where. If I made any attempt to call or write the fact that I was leaving, the order would likely be cancelled. There is too much danger of a train wreck resulting from information leaking out in such a manner. There is a chance that some of us might be here for three or four weeks, and yet we might be shipped by this time next week. One never knows what tomorrow brings.

Nights were made for dreaming, and I find myself using them to full advantage. However, my days are not wasted in that respect for I have plenty of time to think and plan for the future. Every day brings us a day closer to victory and a return to a time when our dreams can be realized. I fight for the hastening of that happy day; I fight for our love.

> Eternally thine,
> Bushy

P.S. #1

> Build Morale!
> Write
> Your Doughboy
> Today and Everyday

P.S. #2. Dr. Hunter wonders if I have "drummed up an acquaintance with the camp Barber." I wonder what he means.

P.S. #3 Give my regards to the family.

Letter from Art's parents to Art
[June 5, 1943]
Saturday

Dear Pvt. Bushing:

So it's great to be in the Army. What you mean is: it's great to have plenty to eat, good clothes, plenty of time to sleep and nothing to do. Well we surely hope you continue to be pleased with Army life. We had a three page Release this morning about the Army Specialized Training Courses. Sounds very fine and states that those who passed the April 2 test are "ear marked" for further investigation and training. Says trainees are to be placed where best fitted in the Army program and are to be trained for post war work.

We are O.K. Things going about as usual. "Believe it or not" we plowed and hoed the potatoes and tomatoes Thursday afternoon. I saw Mrs. King using a plow like ours, so decided that I could do anything in way of work that she could. Your Dad came along and found by experience that he can plow and likes it.

The Frogge girls are home and so is Gertrude, but I haven't seen any one of them. I understand that Chesterlene plans to go to Summer School. Seems that Glenn got into Radio Service and is in Mo. or somewhere in the middle west.

Mrs. York is going to see Edd [George Edward Buxton York] tonight. She plans to take the 5:30 bus. He is to be moved in a day or so.

Charles Taylor is here from Mass. Is looking good and is in a Diesel Engine training camp. He is Sgt. Taylor when in camp.

Sorry that you failed to take the extra shirt, but glad Tommy could help you out. Maudene Wright will be at Carson Newman by the time he gets there. I understand he goes for the summer. Barbra Lyons enters Peabody next week.

The Smiths from Nashville are here, and Edna wants to be remembered to you. She's the only one I've seen.

Am sending the only letters rec'd for you. Your grade card came but you know what's on it. Have had no word from home or Uldene.

We will be anxious to hear about your processing, etc. Hope you can stay with a few of the Maryville bunch. Am sure it would help a lot.

Your Dad is working hard trying to get the work up for the time he will be out next week. Lots of love from us both. Mother

[In red at top of this letter, a note from Art's father.]
Howdy Sonny Boy! Thinking of you a lot. Glad to hear all well. Dad

---

June 6, 1943, Diary
Ft. Ohlethorpe, GA,

Spent third day on K.P. washing dishes. Very few men here, and work not too heavy. Tonight I asked the Sgt. about the possibility of getting a pass tomorrow night to hear "Carmen" in Chattanooga. "Buddy, you get the short-arm tomorrow," he said. Seven of the gang from Maryville are leaving at 8:30 tomorrow night. (Ted Kidder, Gordon Stone, Peter Van Blarcom, Bill Wagner, Kenneth Talbut, Dean Stone, and myself.) Needless to say I was overjoyed that we were to go together. It looks like A.S.T.P. [Army Specialized Training Program] for all in the group have qualified.

Letter from Dotty to Art
[June 6, 1943]
Sunday

Dearest,

Here I sit, giving Mary Ruth suggestions on how to write you instead of doing it myself. Ain't I awful? (I hope you don't really think I am)

Oh, darling, I am so glad you like everything so well. It must be rather nice if it is all as you describe it. Vacation with pay, indeed! Have you heard from Atlanta yet? Are you wearing a uniform by now? Do you get to play ball every day? Do the other fellows like it as much as you do? Oh, dear. I want to know everything. Every little detail. Even gruesome ones. I am also glad you got to see Tom and talk to him—I know it did your heart a world of good.

O-o-o-o-h. Mary Ruth may get you yet, what with making you candy and writing you illustrated letters. I'd better watch me step. At least you'll have a clear picture of what Mary Ruth and I do almost every night.

The heat continues to be terrific. Home is usually cool, but in the office we all gasp for breath and just sort of endure the place till the day's work is done. I hope we become immuned to it before the summer is over.

Mary Alice came home with me Friday night and spent the night. We had a good time playing badminton and rook. She claimed that it was about the only card game she ever enjoyed. It seems that she mostly plays bridge which she plays poorly and has always lived in terror lest she play the wrong card.

Last night I finally buckled down to the task of cleaning out my desk drawers. Threw away more correspondence and junk and stuff—it took me all evening (past your present bedtime) to clear out just one drawer. Remind us never to let too much junk accumulate in <u>our</u> house.

Are there any radios in the barracks? Did you by any chance hear the symphony, then? Gee, what a juicy program they did have. Franck's D-minor symphony, Prelude to Lokevgrint, and Clouds and Festival by Debussy. And before the symphony, John Charles Thomas singing "Abide with Me" gave me goose pimples and also a deep worship experience, during which I didn't get a single dish washed. I felt as if I were holding your hand all the while.

The funniest thing happened at Christian Endeavor tonight. I went into our Intermediate room and there sat a fellow who has been to church only a few times. A queer-looking duck with lots of pimples and a deformed looking hand which he usually holds new his chest. I told him where to go to be with the group his age (he looks several years older than I). It seems that he just came mostly to see me—he wanted to take me out dancing next week. I was so completely flabbergasted that I stammeringly declined and then quickly changed the subject. Outside of you, Darling, the queerest people pick on me.

I have two quotations to quote—one I heard over the radio, the other a poem that seems to be meant especially for us. First the quote (author not known by me) "We are inclined to judge ourselves by our ideals; others by their acts." Next—

"Words Against The Wedge of Time"

Let us accept this moment as the sea
Accepts the sunlight of a summer's day;
Let us not look beyond this hour or be
Concerned that it shall pass. Let us not say—
As others say who are unworthy of

The greatest moment love shall ever know—
Tomorrow shall see the ending of our love:
How shall we bear to see each other go?
Let love be as the cove of some bright beach
That holds day-long the sun, its tireless lover,
Each giving back the warmth each gives to each;
Let us so love that when these hours are over,
Our hearts, like saturate seas when day is done,
Shall hold their warmth until tomorrow's sun."

Anderson M. Scruggs

Perhaps that explains why my heart has not lain very heavily within me since you left—it is holding the warmth of our last hours together. Nevertheless, it also explains why I'll be waiting for the sunrise!
        Your Own
          Dotty

June 7, 1943, Diary

"Short-arm" this morning at 8:30. A kind corporal put us on detail at the theatre building where another very kind corporal let us sleep on the benches most of the morning. At noon he told us to come back in the afternoon, at which time he gave us nothing to do again. At 8:30 pm we left Ft. Oglethorpe for what was to prove to be a rather long and interesting trip.

Letter from Dotty to Art
[June 7, 1943]
Monday night

Dearest Doughboy,
    I received your "moral building" letter today and it surely was a sight for sore eyes. You'll get your glasses in a day or so—I'm sorry I didn't see about that sooner. Are you able to go without any any?
    And now for tonight's bedtime story. Anne was sick Saturday, so she was a little late getting in this morning—(we are required to check through "Medical" after taking sick leave, before returning to duty). I noticed that she spent quite a few minutes talking to the supervisor before she started working. A little later she came over to me with her

face just glowing and informed me that she is leaving a week from Friday for California—to be with her husband who is stationed there for part of his training. (The lucky gal.) All this leads up to the fact that when Anne leaves, someone will have to take her job—and that someone will be <u>this little chicken</u>!

A promotion, at last! Do you know what that means, Darling? It means I will be able to put a little bit more in the bank—for us, and I'll be able to put a few more things in my hope chest. And the fuller I fill my hope chest, the less it will cost us to get married! Oh joy, bliss, etc! No, darling—I'm not money-mad—I'm just "for" anything that brings me closer to you faster, or something. And so endeth the bedtime story. Good night dearest—

Always yours
Dotty.

Letters from
Mr. and Mrs. Bushing Sr. to Art Jr.

[June 8 & 9, 1943]
June '43
Tuesday P.M.

Dear Son,

Your Sunday letter came this a.m. and I was glad to hear that even a waiting existence can be interesting. Jean Cravens is on furlough and told me today that he waited 10 days for orders from Atlanta. Your 10 days will soon have gone by, so perhaps you won't have to wait much longer. Am so glad that your Maryville friends are there. Mrs. York went down last night and wondering if you will see her. She did have difficulty in getting to go, and I wouldn't want to pay their phone bill but talked with Edd [George Edward Buxton York] yesterday and couldn't get a message [unreadable] to 19.12. so called her.

Nothing new has come up here. Your Dad is in Cookeville today on the Angie Pierce Case, and if they call it today he'll come home tonight and go back Thursday on the Smith Case. He might have to stay the three days. Should he not come home, I will get the 57 boys off tomorrow. As you know Fay will be in with the bunch, but the chances are that you won't ever see them or will you?

Your Dad is feeling fairly well and I think on the road to recovery. He is looking more like himself before getting sick, and I believe he is beginning to gain weight.

We had a good rain yesterday and last night, so we will have a nice job finishing up our plowing and hoeing. We lost two or three hours work waiting for the Smith's to visit us, as Edna said they would, but they didn't come.

You didn't tell us about ordering regulation towels. Have you gotten your wires crossed? We will be glad to send whatever you need. I've gotten all your things put away—socks handkerchiefs etc. and will add the things you send home.

The Salesman, Oweno, was here last week (asked to be remembered to you) and your [unreadable] bought a new suit, so I guess he won't need [unreadable] any of your things—shirts maybe.

I really believe you will get some interesting branch of the service. If only we had gotten two copies of the "Release" which I mentioned in Sat. letter, you could have had one.

We were told that your mail would only stack up if we wrote soon as you got there. Seems that Glenn didn't get mail until they had written 5 letters and he got them all at once.

- INTERRUPTION -

Just got your cards: one of Sat. and one of Tues. so we will get off towels to you, and will send any papers about Meterology we can find. We hope you get what you want in that line.

This is Wed. afternoon and I just gotten off ike 56 boys. [unreadable] restless to leave, the poor things—they have never scrubbed floors nor made beds. They have a lot to learn.

Mrs. York had a nice trip but didn't see you. She called from Crossville this a.m. to say that she would be here on the 5:30 bus.

Your Dad came home last night, and is going back tomorrow, and has to go again next Monday. The Pierce case was put off until then, because some smart guy forgot to have him brought from Nashville jail for the trial.

Philip Livingston mowed the yard for us yesterday and it looks real good. You would be surprised how much our garden has grown since you plowed it. You remember plowing it, don't you?

Wed P.M.
Dear Sonnieboy!

Better say right off the bat that I'm not feeling very well. Poor nights and old recurring trouble. Next week I'll be able to give some attention to matters. Perhaps trip to Nashville. By the way, Miss Lenny is coming back. There seems some chance, so says Prof. Davis for Jr. College this Fall. As mother stated, I am driving K Jo back to Cookeville tomorrow (Smith Case) Sgt. York is also summoned as a witness. I'll go in car, will try to find copy first Army/Order, a little recollection of having destroyed it but will look and send right on. Mother would have gotten towels etc for you today (She needs-wants to buy ones perfectly white) but all stores close now on Wednesday afternoons—so slight delay.

Join mother in trusting that get along nicely while you wait—& thereafter loving wishes—a heart full and my prayers go up for you daily. God bless you abundantly. Dad.

[original letter below]

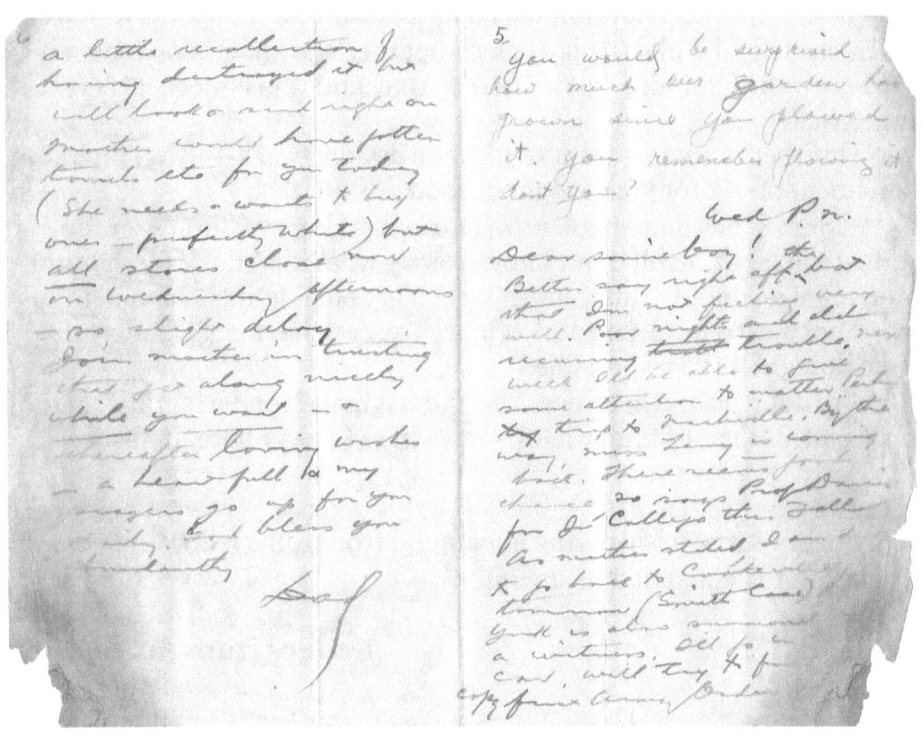

Art Bushing Sr.'s letter to Art, June 9, 1943

Letter from Dotty to Art
June 9, 1943

Dearest Soldier,

The neck, it goes this way, and then that way, and I wish it could go the other way, but you're too far away. (Elastic, ain't it?) First I cleaned the ceiling in my room, and now I bend it the other way writing to you, by way of explanation. I long to hear from you, but know that you are either too busy to write, or else have started on your way somewhere, or else the mail has been held up. I can think of many reasons why letters don't come, but more reasons why they should. Now how did I get off on that subject——thought it was closed.

Last night at the church, I got four games going and played some of each—ping-pong, shuffleboard, badminton, and croquet. More fun on a hot night! I can take almost all corners at ping-pong. (now that Dean has left). I'd like to play you sometime. The affair is no longer a Friday evening shindig, but a Tuesday one, and it just meets every other week.

Our thermometers went to 98° one day last week——that tops your statement of 96° for your neighborhood.

Florence has quite a job now, and is working at Fulton's on the 3:00-11:00 shift. I still don't know exactly what it is she does—her only statement is, quote, "different things." Very elucidating. Or something.

I got a card from Bob and Arlene. They are having a wonderful time doing as little as possible.

I'm doing as much as possible and having a wonderful time, and on top of all that, or under it, or somewhere (everywhere, in fact)

I love you,
Dotty.

P.S. Peggy Murrian is wearing a diamond from some fellow in Miss. They plan to be married next winter.

Letters from Art to Dotty
Ft. Oglethorpe, Ga.
June 9, 1943

Dearest Moral-Builder,

Although there are half a hundred things I want to write about, there are two or three details that I want to mention before I go on K.P. or some such detail.

After waiting—just waiting —for seven whole days, we began to get busy yesterday—taking three tests and a physical. Today we got our shot and will probably finish up processing this afternoon. (I'm sitting on the floor in my barracks trying to write on my knee—I believe you can do a better job there than I.)

Two important things I want to mention concern my work and the way it may effect our future; and, of secondary importance, the fact that you may not get my letters for several days.

In regard to the first,—I have found out that this Army Specialized Training which I have qualified for involves post war work in a foreign country, possibly for as much as five years. The training I understand is for about fifteen months and is equivalent to a college education. Upon successful completion of this training, we would get a commission I believe. I am not at all sure whether or not I care to take if and when it is offered, but I think it wise to consider. It might be a wonderful opportunity for us, darling, for I do think if would be possible for you to go with me. Since you are involved or would be, I want to get your opinion—that is, would you consider spending our first years abroad? Take plenty of time to think about. I may have to go ahead on the assumption that you would approve, but my decision may be asked for much later. The more I think of the idea, the better it seems, although it might cause some delay in my M.A. That is one of the big reasons that I would hesitate.

In regard to the second point, my letters may be held here for several days. We will probably go to the shipping area tomorrow and may be shipped out any time. We cannot tell anyone by letter or phone of the time of our departure, and I believe that our letters are just held until we get away.

Thursday afternoon

Dearest,

Again delayed in getting this written. Finished up processing this morning and moved to shipping area this afternoon. Found out this morning that I made 142 on Gen. Aptitude Test (similar to I.Q.) I am slated for the Air Corp and that may mean meteorology. 110 is required for O.C.S. and 115 for Army Specialized Training so I passed with plenty of margin for everything. Difficult to say what will happen but I will go to school after basic for sure. I intent to make good, darling, whatever I get.

Some of the fellows are on K.P. this afternoon. I will get it shortly very likely.

I enclose program from last Sunday morning service. [program below] Very nice. Much to say about that later. Also a poem I found. (Answer, "yes"!!!) I love to hear from you.

With all my love,
Bushy
P.S. Thanks for letter, Mary Ruth. Will answer as soon as possible.

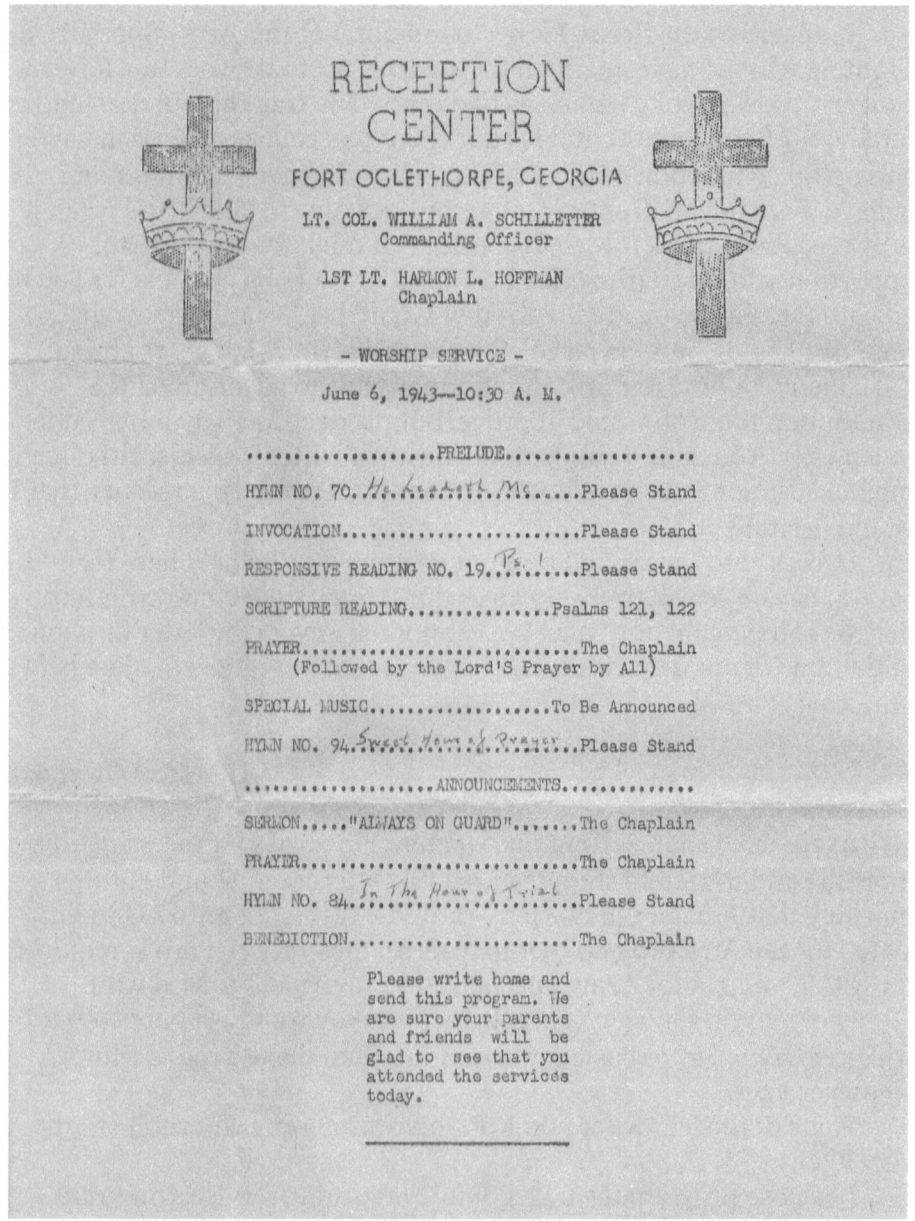

Worship service - June 6, 1943 - Fort Oglethorpe

Letter from Dotty to Art
June 10, 1943

Darling,

From now on you can call me <u>Aunt</u> Dotty. We received a telegram from Sam stating that the new member of the Blizzard household is James McMurry Blizzard, age 5 hours, wt. 7 and a fraction pounds! Since telegrams of congratulations are frowned upon, we composed the following telegram:

> "Received your wire of the 10th—Hope
> merchandise is satisfactory—Delay
> further shipment until you hear from
> us—Letter follows.
> Signed,
> Barber Incorporated"

Aren't we <u>awful</u>? And oh so excited. I'll bet Mother won't sleep a wink all night. She is going up there about a week from today. Then I shall indeed be lonesome.

Have you received your glasses yet? If not, let me know past-haste, so I can see about it again if necessary.

Went to Record Breakers tonight—we played "our" Rachmaninoff all the way through. It is beautiful, nicht wahr?

When my eyes get to the point that they stay shut all the time, then bedtime must be here. Please write, Darling.

> I love <u>you</u>
> Xxx
> Dotty

Letter from Art to Dotty
Ft. Oglethorpe, Ga.
June 11, 1943
First Day of K.P.

Dearest Heart,

Your letter containing wonderful news about promotions received. Our knack for getting lucky breaks seems to continue, and I'm so proud of you. I'm afraid I don't know much concerning Anne's job, so tell me all the details. It's wonderful in more ways than one that she is going to be able to be with her husband. Patience is still a wonderful virtue, darling. I think we may find new opportunities opening that we never expected. Do tell me all about your new job as soon as you can.

Today I rolled out at 4:30 for thirteen hours of K.P. That is supposed to be the worst the Army puts out, but it wasn't bad at all. I washed about five to six hundred dishes during the day, and you should have seen me sweating. Never in such quantity in my life. We will probably have K.P. almost everyday until we are shipped which may be any time. I hope you will not stop writing for I may be here a week or a day.

General Somerville (spelling uncertain) was expected here today, but he failed to show up. May be around tomorrow. He's in charge of all supplies for the Army and has done a grand job. (This letter is being written under very adverse conditions in the barracks, on my knee, with a great deal of noise.)

The sunsets are lovely here, and in my fancy I hold you tight as we gaze at the fading sky. I read and reread your letters and their poetry they contain. I hope to get a chance to write at length very soon, but while K.P. lasts I will have little time.

The more I hear about Army Specialized Training the better it sounds. It will be technical training in some college or university. Our day may be dawning as our love grows on into the years.

Ever thine on,
Bushy

P.S. Note change in address: Area "C"
Tell folks hello, will write to all.

Letter from Art to Dotty
Ft. Oglethorpe, Ga.
June 14, 1943

Dearest Darling,

By the Time you get this, it will be past your birthday, and I have had no chance to properly congratulate you. However, many, many happy returns, sweetheart; I trust that the coming year may bring you close to the realization of the dream which we both cherish.

I wish I could predict what the next twenty-four hours holds for us: I leave here at 8:30 tonight. Seven of us from Maryville leave at the same time, but we do not know that we will go to the same place. Ted Kidder, Pete Van Blancon, Gordon Stone, and three others. I think that all of us are lined up for Special Training, but we know little about that except that it seems to be a good thing.

I got your letter about our little nephew. Will write a note to the "Storm Center" as soon as I get the chance. Also appreciated letters from Mother. Will write everyone when I get settled.

Letter from home today saying that Dad is much improved. Mother's lilies are just beginning to open and I wish I could present you with a bouquet tomorrow.

I think I mentioned the fact that I had K.P. for three days—Friday, Saturday, and Sunday. I had hoped to get a pass to go to Chattanooga last evening, but I was washing dishes at a furious rate all day. K.P. really isn't bad: we arose at 4:30 a.m. and worked until 6:00 p.m. I washed trays for the nine meals, averaging about four hundred per meal. Suds fun! There was some rest but variety in work provided the principle relaxation.

"Carmen" is being presented in Chattanooga tonight, and several of us wanted to go. However, when I asked for a pass last night, I learned that we were leaving today.

I must admit that it is rather exciting to be leaving with no idea what part of the U.S. we may land in. I found it rather difficult to drift into dreams last night after hearing the news, as did Ted K. and several others. We have heard that we travel Pullman [a railroad passenger car made into a mobile barracks to transport troops] which means not only style, but also a long trip. I'm looking forward to anything and everything.

The moon will probably be full by the all important day of the eighteenth. It hardly seems possible that it was a year ago Friday that I found myself at a new stage of ultimate happiness. [Art proposed to Dotty on June 18, 1942.] Now, more than ever before, I am realizing how much it means to know that someone is more than a little interested in ones welfare, and to know that there is a wonderful helpmate awaiting my return. It gives a fellow a great deal more to fight for and to live for. I will be thinking off you in a very special way on Friday.

The hour approaches when we leave the dear Fort of Oglethorpe. I must begin to pack my belongings and prepare for travel. I will write just as soon as it is possible to do so. As I have this section of the country, I leave my prayer that you will be safe and secure while I am away. Meanwhile remember

Thine own,
Bushy

June 15!, 1943

Darling,

I've had a happy birthday, but I'm fearfully tired, and the hands on that wonderful new watch insist on painting out the correct time (very late) so this letter may be short. To continue with the happy birthday—it started out at the breakfast table when Mother presented me with a wonderful contribution for my hope chest—a pair of unmade, uncut, unembroidered pillow cases for me to work on and finish. More fun! I came upstairs to dress, and was at the point of digging into my drawer for a pair of pants when Mary Ruth (who was supposed to be sleeping) opened one eye and said, "Why don't you use those on the back of the chair?" I looked, and there hung two bright new pairs of pants! (Step-ins, drawers, what have you—no, no—I mean etc.) Also at the breakfast table Daddy informed me that he wouldn't even tell me what my gift was to be until tonight, and even then that it might not be ready for months. But he didn't have to tell me—I smelled it as soon as I got into the house. It is the cedar with which to build a chest, a chest to be used first by me as a hope chest, and later for us as it is needed. We all went to the show tonight, and saw "Once Upon a Honeymoon." (The way all good stories start.)

There is very little that is "new" in my new job—I'm just in charge of the "B" files is about the only change—the same work still has to be done—it's just that I have to see that it all gets done and that everything is in good order.

I enclose a clipping from the funnies. Good philosophy, nicht wahr? Another good thing is

Our Love,
Dotty

"Clipping from the Funnies" in letter dated June 15, 1943

Dear Heart,

I begin a series of letters that may not reach you for more than a week, but things are happening so quickly that I can't wait to begin writing you. This day is not only important and meaningful to me because it commemorates the birth of the most wonderful girl in the world, but it is the day on which I began my trek into the unknown.

As I wrote my last letter from Ft. Oglethorpe, I found Sunday night that we were to ship Monday. Seven of us from Maryville found that we were leaving together. By the grace of a friendly corporal Ted Kidder and I were able to get off with a light day of details. Two or three of the poor fellows had K.P. most of the day. We had no idea whatever of our destination and speculation was wide and varied as to our destination and branch. We wondered about the Post in our last hour before leaving with all thoughts crowded out of our mind except questions concerning our future during the next twenty-four hours.

Promptly at eight-thirty we were lined up in front of our barracks with our packs ready for any and everything. The night was clear, the moon past the half as it waxed in the blue, and our not-so-lucky friends gathered on the barrack's steps to give us a hearty send-off. (I am writing on a moving train. I hope you can make out what I intend to write.) After the minimum of delay, we were given orders for forward march and we were off or a long trek. In another part of the camp we boarded trucks and were driven into Chattanooga.

It was on those trucks that we found several new men had been taken into our group. As the wind blew through our hair, I found myself talking with a thirty-year old man with a B.S. from an engineering school in Wis. (He, by the way, is the first college graduate that I have met so far with the exception of the three of us from Maryville.) Other that I know in the group were of a high calibre and all had qualified for Army Specialized Training. We felt sure that our mission had something to do with ASTP, and we knew that we were going to the same place. More than that, we knew nothing.

It seemed that we took almost all of the back streets to the Station but we arrived to find a swanky car awaiting us. We had heard the rumor that were traveling Pullman, and that in itself indicated to us that a long trip was in store. When we saw the car we were to travel in, we looked forward to a trip anywhere. The car is a Pullman with private compartments: that is, we have wash basin and everything right here in this private room. To the rear is an observation section with plush seats, a rear platform, and all the comforts of a living room. Our individual rooms are intended for two-upper and lower berths; but we have to ride three to the section. The place is so compact that we don't even mind that. Ted. K. [Kidder], Gordon Stone and myself are sharing one compartment, and it is proving great sport.

    (To be cont.)

[Art continues on the back of this letter through his letter of June 19, 1943, from Oakland, California, which follows below.]

Letter from Art to Dotty
June 16, 1943
Vol. I, Book II

Dearest,

    I am writing as you see from the Service Men's Club in Kansas City, Mo. The letter that I began yesterday had us on the train at Chattanooga, so I continue from there with Book II. (We are delayed here from about 8:30 this morning until 5:30 this afternoon, or perhaps 11:30 tonight.)

    When we got on the train in Chattanooga we found ourselves in a stylish car fit for high class travel. I think I described its features in the previous installment. We were scheduled to leave about 11, but the train was late—a thing unusual in this modern age—and we pulled out about midnight. Soon after we began to move, the kind Corporal who is traveling with us told us our destination. We had guest almost every section of the country—North-East, South, South-West, North-West— but no one imagined that we were headed for California! It was a real surprise. Camp Roberts is supposed to be about 15 miles from St. Miguel which is half way between San Francisco and Los Angeles.

    After the first excitement had passed away, we had last fell asleep on the first leg of our long journey. All of us were tired and sleep came without difficulty. We arose about eight-thirty Tues. morning to find ourselves rolling Northward through Kentucky. The car behind us was overflowing with WAACs and many of them overflowed into our car. By the way, darling, remind me to warn you never to join a branch of the Service. I am thoroughly against it.

    As soon as we had crossed the Ohio River, we found a decided change in the general typography. We found southern Indiana and Illinois flat as a very flat floor. For miles we could see farm land stretching out field after field. It is unusual to the eye of a Tenn. Hillbilly and I like it. There is a decided change also in the quality of the soil in those states. Real farming must go on there.

At Evansville, Ind. (located in the Southern tip of the state), we picked up a new train and also two cars of Navy Cadets headed for St. Louis. They too came into our car to take advantage of our deluxe accommodations. From that point, we turned West with St. Louis as our next big town.

As we traveled farther into Ill. We found more and more water collected on the surface of the ground. One of the great problems would seem to be that of drainage. As we came to streams and rivers, we found them swollen and overflowing the banks.

We spent part of our time sleeping, reading, and writing as best we could. Our train was late but about 4:45 we arrived in St. Louis. Just as we started to cross the river, the rain began to pour down in torrents. This guy hung low over the city, and we certainly did not get the best impression of the city.

After eating a very nice meal at a service men's room, we begin a short tour of the city's inside train did not leave until midnight. The buildings were beautiful, the streets wide, and the amazing thing was to find no lights after street corners. It seemed to work too. We soon found the lovely theater building and spent the next three hours seeing a double feature. The pictures were not the best, but they were relaxing. More than once Ted and I punched each other to remind us of the fact that we were on our way to California.

Still June 16, 43
Vol. I, Bk 3

We have spent our afternoon at the USO in town—a really swell affair. Was just told that we do not leave until 11:45 tonight—I wonder when we will get to California.

After getting home, that is, to our Pullman home, we played rummy until sleepy and finally got to bed about one. What hours for the Army!

By the time we arose this morning, we had almost crossed the state of Missouri. Rain was beating steadily on our windows, and the low flat country around us was covered with an endless expanse of water. We ran parallel to the Missouri River for some time, and its overflow came within a few feet of the tracks.

(To be Cont.)

My Own True One,

It seems so queer to be writing you without having the faintest idea where you are. It is impossible for me to think of you as far away, darling, for your letters bring you so very close to me.
June 17, 1943

Forgive me. All the pens up here were out of ink last night, and midnight was no time to be traipsing downstairs after more. By the time I got Mother all packed ready to leave, and had cleared off a place on the desk (tsk, tsk.) big enough on which to write you , it was nearly midnight. Mother finally got a reservation for today because someone cancelled their's at the last minute. I guess she is there by now. It was more fun cooking supper tonight, stretching the meat and dressing up the cake. It should be even more fun if you were around to appreciate (?) It. (Oh happy day!)

The new nephew has long black hair (a musician, no less) and the dimples which it inharrieted from his mother. Oh, gee. Wish I could go see it, too. Dad is going up on the 1st of July. He doesn't know it yet, but he is. Mary Ruth and I are going in together and putting up the money for his tickets as a Father's Day gift. I talked with the powers that be and arranged his vacation to begin at that time. I can hardly wait to dump all the tin his lap and let him smoke it. Or something.

Tonight is Florence's birthday, and I am going up to spend the night. Her party must progress without her, for the most part, because she works from 3:00 - 11:00 P.M. Too bad. I'll catch up on my sleep some day.

Precisely why I am heat. I have found - - - a poem! Are you reminded of anyone in particular?

Maternity

I have a child at my house
With very naughty habits.
He will not touch his spinach.
He says it grows for rabbits.

He mows me down with arguments
When I hold forth his rubbers,

76

But at the slightest sniffle
He runs to me and blubbers.

Once immersed in water
The soap he's sure to lack;
And after I have fetched it
I must stay and scrub his back.

When it's time for him to dress
You aught to hear him squall.
He couldn't find his underwear
If I hung it on the wall.

Caring for this child of mine
Completely fills my life.
I wonder how he lived at all
Till I became his wife!

— Virginia Conroy

It remains to be seen whether or not my husband will be like that. Why? 'Cause I haven't got one yet.

Hope to hear from you soon—at your new headquarters.

All my love,

Dotty

Letters from Art to Dotty
Vol. I, Br 4
June 17, 1943
Cheyenne, Wy.

My Darling,

I'm having some difficulty keeping up with my daily writing, but perhaps I can catch up tonight. We are having a short layover here in Cheyenne, a town of about 20,000 and almost 6,000 ft. above sea-level.

I see that yesterday I had events up to our arrival at Kansas City. We ate breakfast in the station and made our way from there through the rain to a Service Men's Club where I wrote you.

At the Club we found almost all the comforts of home. A radio, piano, games of all kinds, and soft lounges. As we were to find true in the afternoon at the Canteen, the ladies in charge were perfectly lovely.

In each place they seemed anxious to satisfy our every need, and spared no pains to make our stay a pleasant one.

We were still near the Station and plan to go uptown for lunch. However, we decided to take a look at a beautiful War Memorial directly in front of the Train Terminal. It was situated on a high hill overlooking the city and was surrounded by a well-kept lawn. The edifice was more than four hundred feet long and build of granite. It was something of a plaza on top with a two hundred foot tower in the middle. We saw it at a distance last night; and then top of the tower, built in the shape of a bowl, emitted a bright flame. It was truly a beautiful sight both by night and by night.

We walked down town in time for dinner and spent the afternoon in the K.C. Canteen.

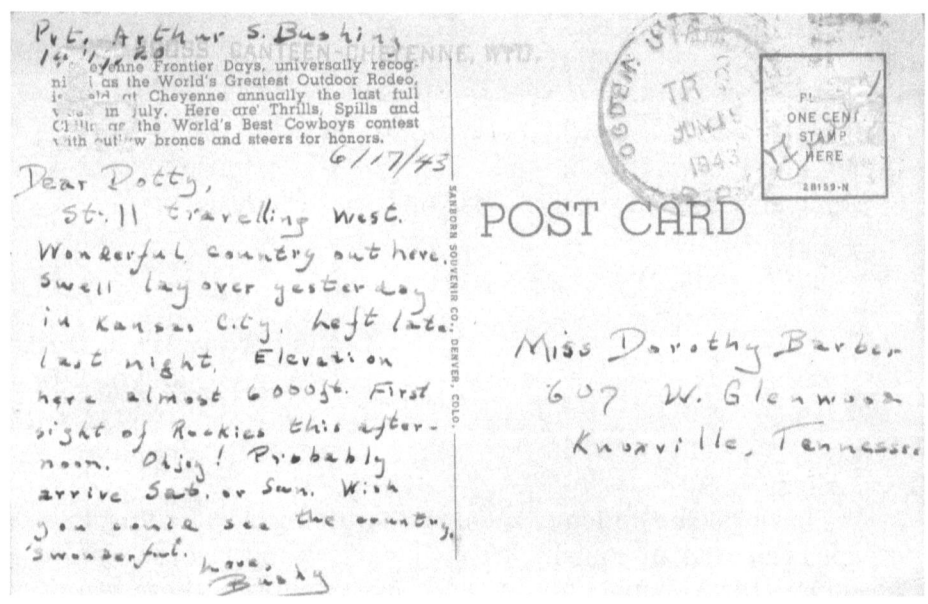

Postcard from Art to Dotty, June 17, 1943

(As I write this morning I am looking at the snow-capped Rockies and long to have you here.)

The Canteen that I was speaking of consisted of six floors and contained everything. I immediately thought of the chance to listen to good music. They had plenty of excellent records but the only thing they did not have was a record room. It was being worked on then. However, the ladies began rushing around and soon found a crank model in excellent condition. Ted K. Gordon and I played for the better part of the afternoon.

After leaving there we saw "Five Graves to Cairo," [a 1943 war film directed by Billy Wilder] a very good picture. We left Kansas City about midnight, and as the full moon shone on the rolling plains I thought lovely thoughts of my darling many miles away.

Before we left, Ted and I managed to slip off from the rest of the crowd and go for a few minutes up on the enormous lawn before the beautiful War Memorial. The Memorial itself was lit up by spotlights in addition to a beautiful moon bathing it in a soft glow. At the top of the tower, as I mentioned before was a yellow flame burning bright against the sky. We sat there and silently dreamed of that which would make the moment complete—the presence of the one we love. Thank God we can always dream!

Yesterday morning (Thur.) we awoke to find the rolling plains of Kansas stretched out before us. As I pictured them, they stretched out in a gentle roll for miles and miles unending it seemed. For the most part it seems that there is about four miles from the crest of one hill to the next. For many miles we rode in the center of the valley with that crest on either side dotted with farm houses. The immense fields seem very rich and certainly productive. If we ever get to the place that we want to forget everything, let's come West. It is forsaken except for God and the prairie stars. I love it!

Late yesterday afternoon we rolled into Cheyenne Wyo., a town of about 20,000. We had a few moments there to stretch our legs and enjoy the air at that new height.

After we had started on into the night and into the West, we spent our evening as usual playing Rummy. Four Maryville College students on a train bound for California—it still seems like a dream. None of us can realize it is true.

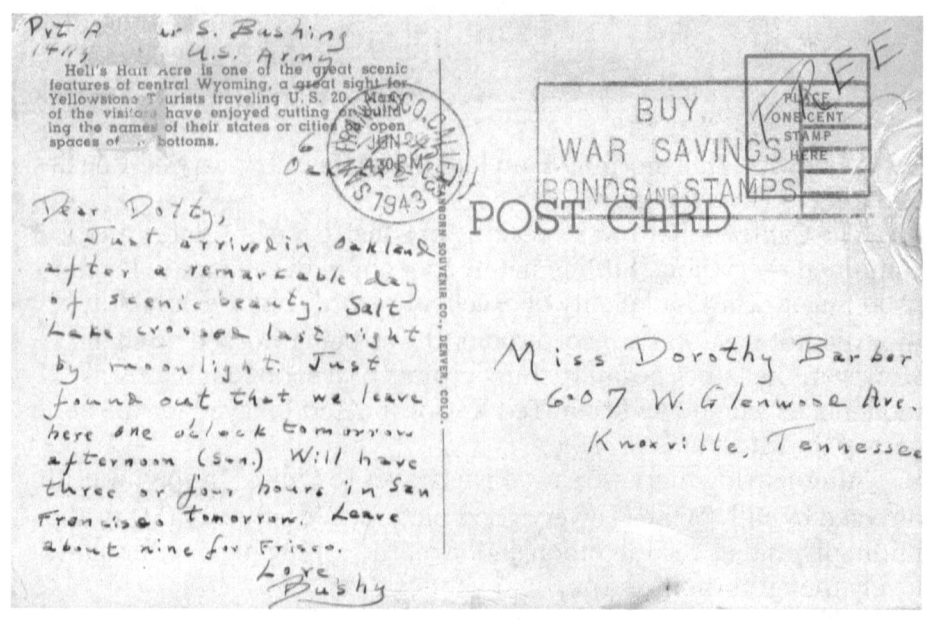

Postcard from Art to Dotty, June 19, 1943

Romantic souls, all of us, we turned off the lights at frequently to ostensibly to look at the scenery—actually to look at the beautiful full moon shining down on the flowing prairies. As I looked at the moon, I whispered my love and I felt your hand in mine. Your answer came clear and soft across the plains and I fell asleep to dream of you, dearest and fairest of them all. I love you.

(To be cont.)

P.S. Also the letter.

Bushy

6-19-43

I do not have my mailing address, [Art's underline] but will get that to you as soon as possible. Hope to mail this in Oakland.

Dearest Heart,

I awoke this morning in Green River, Wy, more than a thousand miles from you and from Maryville College. Nonetheless, I felt myself very close to you, bound by a tie that cannot be stretched by many thousands of miles. No, darling, I have not forgotten that it was just a year ago today (almost to the hour at which I am writing) that we promised each other our eternal love as we sat beneath the tress at the Picnic Grounds. So many things have happened in that year, and so many things are to come during the next twelve months. But each passing day brings us closer together. I love you more than words can say, and want to spend a lifetime proving my love.

I am getting somewhat ahead of my story, for I have not told you yet of the rolling plains of Kansas. However, I will try to go back and write of that in the last book volume I. We arrived in Ogden (north of Salt Lake City) about 3:30 and will not leave until 7:30 tonight. Meanwhile, we spend our time at the U.S.O. Tonight we cross the Great Salt Lake.

As I mentioned , we found ourselves in Green River, Wy. (remember Walgreens?) when we opened our eyes this morning. Although we had caught glimpses of the Rockies in the far distance yesterday, we actually had reached a portion of them this morning.

It is almost impossible to paint a picture of the beauties we have seen today. The desert has a grandeur all its own—long, sweeping hills, almost bare of vegetation except for a short stubble; sharp hills that stand out like giant memorials to a desert race long since gone. These pinnacles with the shadows that they form on the rocks and sands make up one of the outstanding marvels of the West. Occasionally we travelled for miles looking at hills in the distance, perfectly flat on top with sharp breaks at intervals reminding me of the peak we commented on so much from Addison's Cabin—Bob thought it Chinese in effect.

The altitudes are amazing on this trip west via the Union Pacific. One is conscious of traveling up grade, but the rise is so slight that there is no idea of the tremendous height which one gains. The land around seems always relatively flat, but we climbed from about 6,000 ft this morning to about 8,800 and then began to descend. It was rather evident when we crossed the Great Divide for one minute we saw the streams flowing East, as they had been doing for hundreds of miles, and the next minute we saw them flowing toward the West, as they will continue to do for the remainder of the trip.

At intervals all day long we were able to see the beautiful snow covered Rockies in the distance. They appear as soft white clouds just above the horizon but soon the clear outline of the mountains is unmistakeable.

The picture that I had preconceived of the West was not far wrong. Of course, it was a little vague in many respects; but the general conception of the flat farm land of Ind. and Ill., the rolling plains of Kansas, the desert and bad lands of Wy. was basically sound. However, it is far more wonderful in its grandeur than one could ever imagine.

This afternoon we came to perhaps the most beautiful place of our trip thus far. As we neared Ogden, we found ourselves passing through a narrow pass with high peaks on either side. Our elevation was about 4500 feet and some of the peaks were as much as 8,000 feet. Just behind the town, where we have spent three or four hours, lies Mt. Ogden rising 10,000 feet above sea level. Oh darling if you would only be here to see the breath-taking beauty of it all! There are almost no trees whatsoever on the mountains here, but there is a short stuffy growth that covers almost everything. As beautiful as they are, I have seen few scenes that exceed the wondrous awesomeness of Le Conte and the view from our Cove [Art is referring to Mt. Le Conte and Cades Cove which are located in the Great Smoky Mountains National Park.]

(To be Cont.)

Friday [June 18, 1943, Vol. III, Bk 1.]

Our train had quite a delay in getting started, but finally we pulled out about eleven o'clock. I had hoped to be able to see the sunset on the Great Salt Lake, but instead we were rewarded by seeing a moon just past the full glow in all its splendor on that beautiful body of water. The lake is far larger than I had ever imagined, although I was surprised to find a railroad track built almost directly across it. Moon light on the water at any time is an experience not soon to be forgotten, and especially is that true if one is entirely out of sight of land. As we rode along, there was a wide path-strewn with moon glow and extending for quite a distant out into the blue. Before we had gotten across, clouds scattered through the sky, and at times it seemed as though there was a giant spot-light on the water. I thanked God for such beauty and for the faculty for appreciating it. How I longed to have you there!

This twenty-four hour period, beginning at Ogden and ending with the sunset in the Golden Gate, was without question the most wonderful of our entire trip. When we arose Saturday morning we were racing through the beautiful valley more than two hundred miles long, sixty or seventy miles wide, and bounded on the sides by a chain of mountains. The valley was absolutely flat, and is located about 4500 feet above sea level. Lovelock was the first big town we saw in the morning, and Reno was at the other end just before we began climbing again. In the early part of the morning we passed through cultivated areas, but later the valley was nothing but desert sand and a short stubbly grass that spots the landscape. During one interval we rode for miles along a lake that extended it seemed to the foot of the mountains far in the distance.

We merely passed through Reno but it impressed me little. Perhaps I'm hardly ready for that—yet.

Vol. III Bk. 2

After Reno, we began an upward climb which was to take us many thousands of feet into the blue. The vegetation on these mountain slopes was not quiet [quite] so plentiful as to be found in the incomparable Smokies, but tall pines did claim respect as they towered skyward. We were pulled by a special engine for such steep grades and the climb lasted for several hours.

At one point we saw a vast mountain lake (I wish I could recall the name) stretching a couple of thousand feet below us. The clean blue waters reflected the beauty and majesty of the surroundings. At more than one place we could look from the platform of our car, down, down —shear drops extending far into the canyon below. The vastness of everything in the West is the thing the [that] overwhelms one.

As I recall, we found Sacramento at the foot of the range of mountains. I remember little of the city, but it must have been here that we began to enter the fruit and vegetable belt. Row upon row, mile upon mile of fruit groves, of vineyards. Flat country lay on both sides of the railroad and far in the receding distance we could see the Eastern range of mountains. We circled around the San Francisco Bay as we road into Oakland (just across the Oakland (?) River from Frisco); and, as we came in the Golden sun sank behind the Golden Gate. I well knew from whence the name came. Clouds were there, water, everything. The sight was one no words can aptly describe. I hope to show you someday.

It was at Oakland that we were to leave our car which had carried us all the way across the continent. We were parked in a corner of the station and prepared to spend our last night aboard here. The following morning we boarded a Ferry after breakfast and crossed to Frisco. Here we saw the sights through the courtesy of a couple of nurses and an Army truck. A drive along the coast and return through Golden Gate Park high-lighted our tour. At one o'clock we boarded a train for Camp Roberts and a new life.

       Love,
          Bushy

                         Oakland, Calif.
                         June 19, 1943
                         Sat. Night

Dearest,

This is written much later than the regular sequence of my letter, but we have just arrived in Oakland, across the bay from Frisco. We leave here for Frisco early in the morning and will have three or four hours there before leaving for Camp Roberts. We leave at one o'clock.

I will write in some detail concerning the last twenty-four hours for they have been the most wonderful of the trip. We crossed Salt Lake last night by the light of a full moon; it was a marvelous experience. Today we rode through a valley fifty miles wide and more than two hundred miles long without a change in our elevation—absolutely flat! We rose to a height of seven thousand feet, saw beautiful lakes tucked among the gigantic crags, rode along the snow line and almost to the timberline, dropped to salt flats, passed through Reno, Truckee, Sacramento, the beautiful Sacramento Valley, and finally San Fransisco Bay. The latter in time to see the beautiful sunset. Darling, this has been an outstanding inspiration. I say good-night to dream of you and of the time when we shall see such beauty together.

       Your own,
          Bushy

June 20, 1943, Diary

This morning we spent our last night aboard "Louis Frontenac." After breakfast in Oakland we crossed by ferry to Frisco. The day perfectly clear and the views perfect. By chance we were taken on a two or three hour tour by a couple of nice nurses. Rode up twin peaks and out through a beautiful residential section to Ocean Drive. Return trip through Golden Gate Park. Took one o'clock train for Camp Roberts. Travelled through a rather narrow valley all afternoon arriving San Miguel about seven-thirty. By truck to camp. After short-arm assigned to C.C. 81st.

Letter from Art to Dotty
Camp Roberts
June 21, 1943
Monday Morning

My Darling,

We are here! About seven-thirty last night (nine-thirty Knoxville time), a little group of sixteen men rolled into San Miguel, three miles south of Camp Roberts. We were due here on Friday night, and there was some delay in getting from San Miguel. However, we soon had the red tape cleared , and we loaded into a truck. By the time we reached Camp and had been assigned barracks, it was almost nine o'clock (the time for lights out). We had just enough time to make our beds and take a good hot shower—few have felt better to me. We slept until 5:45 this morning and arose, raring to go. Eight and a half hours sleep can do wonders to a tired body. This morning we are waiting to be interviewed for further classification.

Our first taste of California weather came Saturday night when we rolled into Oakland (just across the bay from San Francisco). As we walked out on the observation platform of our car we found a very cool breeze blowing. Our sun tans (summer outfits) seemed uncomfortable and we welcomed the chance to stay inside. Here at Roberts the nights are cold—wonderful for sleeping—and the days are warm. So warm in fact that we are told it gets up to 145° on the parade grounds. Oh the joy of the solders' life!

We have had little chance to see anything here, but I think I am going to like it a great deal. All across the country we heard that this is one of the nicest camps anywhere.

I have no idea what to expect during the next few days in relation to getting a chance to get air mail stamps, etc. Perhaps you could send me a few until I get a chance to buy some myself. We are not allowed off the area for some time. I wanted to send you a telegram upon my arrival, but there seems to be no chance. The address I put on here will only be for a few days in all probability, but I think your letters will be forwarded to any part of the camp that I happen to be in. Write as soon as possible, darling, I long to hear from you.

Always your,

Bushy

Pvt. Arthur S. Bushing

Co. C, 81st Inf. Bat.

Camp Roberts, Calif.

P.S. Send me the Blizzard address

Letters from Dotty to Art

June 20, 1943

The Sabbath

Dearest Soldier in the world,

I still don't know where you are, except in a general direction. I hate to keep sending letters to a place where I know you ain't. I keep feeling that they won't ever reach you. So may I just save it all up, and send you a volume as soon as I receive your new address?

The 18th came and went, but proved to be as uneventful a day as I have spent in a long time. It was a hot day, and I worked so hard I hardly had time to realize that there was something special about the day. After work I came home and got supper, then helped with the dishes; finally, after a short visit with Elaine (she is here for her vacation, and believe me, she knows every bone and muscle in your body by name) and a bath, I flopped into bed and slept like everything. But I thought about you as I do every day, paying special attention to the following thinks:

1. I am a lucky girl (very fortunate indeed)
2. I love you. (exceedingly and excruciatingly)
3. You're wonderful. (did anyone ever tell you?)
4. I love you (I want you more and more, but it looks as if I had you less and less).
5. Can something be done?

Five points is enough for any sermon. End quote. (?)

I got your card mailed from Kansas City, so I presume you are going west, young man! I can hardly wait to find out where and when and why and how and how long and do you love me, too?

I bought a new hat to go with my hairdress. It looks like so.

I bought a new hat to go with my hairdress. It looks like so.

Hat →
Hair →
← Neck (oh, Boy)
Looking down, on top
from back.

Disregard.
No good.
Very poor
likeness.

Dad was very pleased and somewhat overcome by our gift (money for tickets to Maryland) for Father's Day. I wrote your Dad a note today. Aren't fathers wonderful? So are you, and (so shall you be, Bud!) The hour grows late, so I'll see you in the next chapter, darling. Nothing was ever quite so wonderful as

Our love,
Dotty

June 22, 1943

The letter ended for a while, but I didn't. I kept right on going. You're extensive, wonderful, exciting, adventurous, amazing, delightful, and much looked for letter arrived today! Oh darling, I'm so thankful that you are there at last, safely, that I know <u>where</u> you are, even if it is California, and besides, it surely was <u>good</u> to hear from you. Even my (?) patience was beginning to wear thin. Somehow, California doesn't seem any farther away then Ft. Oglethorpe, even though there is a heap of difference. As soon as I get the card I mailed from Kansas City I knew that you were on your way there and California was the first place I thought of as a destination. How true, how true. That is a powerful long way for an East Tenn. hick like me to come and pay you a visit. Perhaps I could fly across. Yes, no? The fact that you haven't mentioned anything about the baby and other things I have said in my letters leads me to believe that you have not yet received a number of my letters. Did you or didn't you? Mother sends glowing reports of the baby—it has long black (turning brown) hair almost to its shoulders (according to Harriet), very dark eyes, and two luscious dimples. Which he inherited, no doubt. Dad plans to spend his vacation, which starts July 1st, up there. Mary Ruth and I will then be truly alone; however, we plan to ask some girls to stay with us that week. The house work continues to be fun, but rather difficult to accomplish "after hours." I am so tired tonight that my mind is almost blank, and words fail to come to me. After a hot day at the office I came home, read your letter, set table and got supper, went to the church immediately after supper to supervise the games, came home and sprinkled some clothes and then ironed them. I hate to leave you till the very last, like this, but there doesn't seem any other way to work it right now. Things will be changed when Mother gets back.

No wonder you heard me answer you as you looked at the moon that night on the prairies—at the very time you mentioned, I too was looking at it and thinking of you! It continues to amaze me the way we telepathize (?) each other. Get set—I am now sending you a huge kiss by telepathy. Got it? (I love you so very much.

        Dotty.

P.S. Have you heard "My little cousin eats flies by the dozen; When you say "what's buzzin'" — it's just my cousin"?

P.S. No. 2—When you come pounding down the home stretch, the score will be "no Hitlers, no ruins, no terrors."

P.S. #3—Sorry my epistle isn't quite as long as yours—I don't have quite as much to tell.

June 24, 1943

Dearest,

Picture to yourself one of the wilder, tree-filled spots on Le Conte; trees, and rocks, and moss, and moonlight sifting down through a soft, fairylike mist; add to this a chorus singing "Love is a Song that Never Dies," their voices sort of echoing, as if in a deep, huge chamber. Such is the setting for Walt Disney's incredibly beautiful picture, "Bambi," the story of a deer. Very dear. Please see it if you have an opportunity—and think of me in all the breathtaking spots (you won't be able to take a really deep breath until it is all over).

This is just a short note because I am late as usual. I saw our friend Gabriel today, and he asked about you. He knew you were on your way west, because Pete V.B. had sent him a card from Ogden, Utah.

Yesterday I received a statement on the balance of the loan—just $28.68, Bud!! I can wipe it out completely with my next paycheck. You don't know how thrilled I'll be. Or do you?

Also in yesterday's mail I received a note from Marianna. She had heard that you were at Oglethorpe, so she was going to invite you up and me down to their house in Benton, which is sort of half-way between here and Chattanooga. Had we been able to accept it, had we had most wonderful time, no? (Answer—<u>yes</u>!!)

I love you always.

Dotty.

P.S. Marguerite Harrison says that there are just "stacks" of Knoxville and Maryville boys at Camp Roberts. She especially wants you to look up Rex Cole.

Dear sonnie boy: We do indeed miis you a lot and don't feel just right about not being able to have written you after receipt of your good newsy letters en route West. Once you are settled we are going to write you very regularly. I just bought $1.00 of special delivery stamps and air-mail ones for future use in reaching you as early as possible.
We will have the things you have been writing for all ready to shoot right out when permanent address arrives.
Now for the news. Work going along better. My several trips to Cookeville put us behind for I made three trips along on the Angie Pierce case (delinquent) having on two trips ~~having~~ been forced to leave home at 5.00 P. M. (Crossville Bus) spend the night in Cross-ville, then catch a 6 A. M. Bus to Cookeville and return late in the late afternoon over same route. You see, the case was put off several times but always for the day after; this made me return home to be able to help in the office. However, these cases-Smith and Pierce are now out of the way with both registrants getting 3 years in the pen.
Dorothy or "Dot" sent me the Jefferson Bible on "Daddy's Day". Pleased to get the little book. I immediately answered enclosing $1.00 the cost of the book. I recall that I asked you to request Dorothy to pick up a copy for me. She is very well but Mrs. Barber is visiting one of the other girls.
As mother states in her letter, we are expecting a let down in the calls for August and September at least as the Army is reluctant to go in full swing about inducting married men with children. By the way, Joe Ligon is the proud father of a fine bouncing boy.
This is Saturday in the old town with people galore visting the stores, etc. Did we tell you that Miss Terry is coming back to YAI next year. She resigned but reconsidered the matter. Sgt. and Davis working on possibility of opening up the School next year (next Fall) as a Junior College. Mr. Davis says everything moving along nicely and he believes he will be able to get the program in operation at school opening.

Well, dear boy, you will have lots to write us about when your program gets under way. We shall not fail you with all the news and to help drive any blues away for you must a bit lonesome but always remember that that same West called me and you are a son of the West for I loved those wild open spaces at one time and do still. It was a re-freshing change from the stuffy East. God be with you, dear precious boy. You can always count on Dad - come what may. Mother too thinks and speaks of your being so far away and looks forward to every word from you. Will chase this along and be writing you very very soon again

Always - lovingly, prayerfully
DAD

Letter from Art Sr. to Art Jr., dated June 23, 1943.

THE ALVIN C. YORK FOUNDATION

To Foster Christian Education
In The
Cumberland Mountains

JAMESTOWN, TENNESSEE

June 24, 1943

Miss Dorothy Barber
Knoxville, Tennessee

Dear Dorothy:

It was real nice of you to send the little book just received, as also your little intimate note. I enclose my check for the former.

Our mutual concern, one familiarly known to all his pals as "Art", has written us several notes enroute Calif. He is expecting to be stationed at Camp Roberts. We await his address and details of his assignment.

As you refer to the state of my health, might mention I am "mending up asight", and when I can find the time will take myself in hand and see if the process of improving more rapidly can be speeded up. Need new glasses; much dental work and some out-of-doors.

Mrs. Bushing and I are incidently very busy in office but expect a slowing down of the Selective Service program during the coming few months.

I trust you are getting along nicely at home and downtown. Arthur will, no doubt, keep in closest touch with you pointing out the wonders of the great West, and eventually, all those glorious plans you have worked out together will become realities with a new world confronting two very determined and ambitious youngsters. A little prayer goes up each day for a happy consumation of Arthur's and your dream of the wonderful future which lies ahead.

Junior's mother and I join in loving wishes. Also kind remembrances to the family.

Very sincerely

Arthur the elder.
(That sounds a bit presbyterian)

Thanks again for Book

June 24, 1943, Letter from Art Sr. to Dotty
[Note the letterhead with A.S. Bushing listed as
Alvin C. York's Secretary.]

91

Camp Roberts, Calif.
June 24, 1943

My Own

I see now that my letters of necessity must be written at odd intervals as best I can. My schedule already is crowding my time; and, as time goes on, it will be an increasingly heavy one.

June 25

Oh darling, your letter written on the 18th arrived last night, and you will never know how wonderful it was to get it. You must have been inspired to have been able to write such a M.B. (moral-builder). Ted Gordon Stone, and myself got away from Army life long enough last night to see "Coney Island" and we returned to our barracks with no thoughts of mail for several days. When someone yelled out the window that I had mail, I almost tore the stairway down getting on the second floor. The fact that I had heard nothing from you in two weeks (lacking only one day) had something to do with my feeling of course.

June 26

Progress has been slow on this letter so far, but 'tis now the early part of Saturday afternoon and we have the time off. I think I never knew how wonderful it could be to have free time, knowing that there is no danger of being called to "fall in" ten minutes from now. I have Vol. III, describing why tour from Ogden on, in the making, I hope to finish it also before I report for duty Monday morning. One thing I fear about my writing in general is that I will probably be forced to confine it to the week-ends. Lights are out in the barracks at nine each evening. There will be almost no free time during the day and any time that we have will probably be needed in resting. Rifles, clothing, and self must be cleaned up for the most part after supper. However, I feel sure that I can make up on Saturday and Sunday for all that I fail to write at other times.

And now for a few details about where I am and what's cooking. Camp Roberts is located about thirty miles from the coast, about two hundred miles from Frisco, and something like two hundred and fifty miles from Los Angeles. We are in a desert valley running south from San Francisco. The Camp itself contains mere sixty thousand men, and is reported to have the largest parade grounds in the country: it is more than a mile long and one spends almost ten minutes walking across the thing at a regular pace. Around this giant rectangle and standing seven or eight buildings deep, lie the barracks, mess halls, and supply houses for this little Army.

One of the amazing things about the place seems to be that there will be no feeling of being lost in the "madding crowd." I am not at all clear on the subject, but it seems that there are about sixty men in each platoon, four platoons in each company, and four companies in each battalion. Each platoon is headed by a second lieutenant and four or five non-coms (non-commissioned officers). These non-coms live with the sixty or so men in one barrack, and I can see already that the relation may be very worth while as the weeks go by. We share the same food, the same schedule, except they are responsible for teaching us the fundamentals of Army lore. We have already received name-tags to sew on our work clothing in order that we may learn to know each other the sooner.

Although we have been here a week now, our thirteen weeks have not actually begun. We drill daily, we have started our physical conditioning, and our daily schedule is much like it will be later on; but the regular basic training seems to await the arrival of more men. I think I mentioned the fact that we are a part of an A.S.J.B. Battalion, and a large number of men are yet to arrive.

Oh yes, that leads up to another thing: "Tell me more about this Army Specialized Training," you ask. Darlink, I wish I knew; I wish anyone knew! Our company commander knows less than we about it. About the most that we know is that at the end of our basic we will be tested and classified for specialized training, with the probability that most of us go to a college or university for study varying in length of time from six months to two years. It seems only logical that this training can be for nothing less than post-war work. I was overjoyed to get your reaction and assent to my taking part in this reconstruction program, but I am of the opinion now that there will be little choice in the matter. Uncle Sam is giving the orders now, and he will probably tell me where and when he wants my services. As I say, the details are obscure to everyone; but I know that our future will work out for the best. A couple of years on the Rhine might prove very pleasant as we begin our lives together, and I would take a great deal of pride in being a part of the forces that are to mold a new and better world for all mankind.

The traditional Bushing luck continues as I find myself, not only with seven Maryville men, but also in an entire Battalion of college men. There are a few high school graduates, but the vast majority have had one or two years of college work. A surprising few (I know of only two others) have graduated, but the caliber on the whole is of a high type.

June 27
The Sabbath

You see, I do write everyday, but today I have a great many things to write about, first and foremost of which is the fact that I just received another wonderful letter from the dearest girl in the whole, wide world. Darling, I wish it were possible to express an infinitesimal part of my love for you. That job is one that can only be begun in a lifetime of concentrated effort; I intend to apply myself, diligently to that delightful task at the earliest possible moment. The thing that I can do now is to attempt to make myself worthy of the faith and trust that you have in me.

I feel the warmth of your soft lips brushing mine as I see the multi-colored canvas of the western sky record the passing of each day or see the distant hills around the camp turn baby pink as the twilight slips silently down. I feel the understanding pressure of your hand as I sit in the beautiful little chapel, as I did this morning, and listen to two Church Services. When I read my Bible at night and say my prayers, I know that the Father of all good and truth-loving men and women is guarding our lives and our destinies and our love. Do I love you? I love you as constantly as the stars that carry our messages of love, I love you as truly as the values of truth and beauty themselves exist. As long as those values continue supreme in the order of our ordered universe, our love will continue to grow in beauty and strength until at last in some far distant eternity we reach the ultimate unity with our Guide and Father. Yes dearest, I do love you.

You wondered about the possibility of coming west. Remember, it took me six days traveling with all the priority that the Army can muster. A round trip ticket even by day-coach is sixty to seventy dollars, and by plane would probably be around one hundred and fifty. From those discouraging facts, you can well see the problem to be faced. There is every possibility that I will be shipped east after I complete basic training here. Even if I didn't get a furlough at that time, it seems that there would be definite possibilities of you visiting me then, nicht wahr?

Yes I finally got the letter concerning the blessed baby up Maryland way. I want to write them as soon as I get the address from you: for the life of me I can't be sure that is is Long Green, Md. I also want to write Mother up there. I know she is very proud.

Only as you know how excited I can become and as you recall how much I love a good library can you imagine any feeling yesterday when I found a wonderful little library here in Camp with 3,000 volumes, all good selections. I like many things here (there are few things I don't like), but my joy was complete (as it could be here) when I found good books available.

Our regular schedule of training begins tomorrow morning and I look forward to every day of it. However, starting tomorrow, my day will be filled to the overflowing. I do long to hear from you as frequently as possible. I will write at every opportunity. Meanwhile, "love endureth long."

My love is boundless
Bushy

P.S. Heard from Muriel. She sends love—to you.

Letter from Dotty to Art
Sunday night
June 27, 43

My Dearest,

Now don't you go falling for any of them Hollywood dames. I hear tell you are not far from Hollywood, etc.

I hope I get this written before I fall asleep. Last night Aunt Mary, who has been slightly sick for serval days, wanted one of us to come up there to spend the night, so that if she needed something we'd be there handy. (Uncle Tom sleeps downstairs and is slightly deaf, Aunt Mary upstairs) Sooo—I was elected. It was sticky, relentlessly hot, I slept on a hard cot, and something kept biting me all night long. I was never so miserable—it was terrible then, but funny now. When I wasn't panting or hunting for a cool spot, I was scratching for dear life. Sleep was impossible, and yet I was dead tired and way behind on sleep. And to top it off, Aunt Mary didn't need a thing all night! Hell must be something like that.

Got a note from your Dad yesterday. Do you know what he did? He sent me a check for the Jeffersonian Bible which I sent him as a gift! What shall I do? Will he be greatly offended if I return the check and explain that it was intended for a gift? What would his reaction be?

Haven't you gotten any of my letters? You still talk as if you hadn't heard from me. I am enclosing four airmail stamps. Is airmail not free? Not even part of it?

I have no startling news to tell—my days are humdrum without you in them. Darlingcal.

All the love you can take in one dose, Dotty.
P.S. Blizzard address—Rev. S. N. Blizzard, Lang Green, Md.

Letter from Art's Mother, Arza, to Art Jr.

June 26 [1943]

Dear Son:

We received our cards and letters enroute West and have gotten your Tuesday's letter written from Camp, but the Monday letter hasn't arrived as yet. We are extremely interested in all you have told us about the trip and all that is happening to you in the Service. We wrote buy Special Delivery on Sat. before you left the Fort, but didn't hear that you received it. In the letter we reported that Smith got 3 yrs in Federal Prison for his interfering with Selective Service work. He is now in service (behind 4 walls) some where in Ky.

Things are going along about as usual with us. We keep busy here all day, go home and do some work in garden and are managing to keep pretty well up with both work and weeds. Phil Livingston is mowing for us and is keeping the yard in good order.

We are having some warm weather, but plenty of rain and the garden is coming along with a bang. We have potatoes larger than eggs, turning galore and our radishes are grown & gone. The early corn is waist high. Your Dad is getting a kick out of plowing and I'm wondering why he didn't begin farming years ago.

Edd York [George Edward Buxton York] is still at the Fort. Sgt. & Mrs. York went down on Thursday after you left and I was planning to go with them until we got a letter saying that you were leaving. Fay left Friday and Clarence is worrying an awful lot. Too bad that he only recently realized that he had a son.

Gertrude, the Frogge girls and Chesterlene are home, but I seldom see any one of them. I saw Mrs. Wheeler few days ago and she told me that Joe is in India. He wrote that "The teeming millions of India" means just that. He is well located and very comfortable.

When you say "barren hills" I know just what you mean. I looked at barren hills in Washington for two years and in all that time saw rain twice. In time one longs for "The hills of Tenn." and when one is away long enough, home means hills.

Soon as we get an address which can be counted on, will send a package. Sorry I didn't get the towels to you but just about the time I bought them you wrote and said that you could get them down there. I didn't know how they would handle a package if you had been shipped out, so just have to wait. Have a couple of letters to send on, and will send them immediately upon receipt of correct address.

Manza came out and spent the day and night with us since you left. She is going to Muncie [Indiana] first of July to spend the fall and winter with Uldene. She has a sister living there and will no doubt visit some with her. Fred is getting on O.K. it seems. He has directed $15.00 be sent directly to her each month by the War Dept. Guess he didn't want to have the trouble sending it himself. He asked about you in one of his recent letters to her. I hope to write him sometime.

We were led to believe that I work would lighten up to some extent by two fellows (Major Butler & "Someone") from State Headquarters. They say that our calls are going to be lighter—which means less work of course.

It's going to be hard getting accustomed to hearing irregularly from you, since for so long we've known when to expect your letters.

Our daily prayer is for your health, safety and success, and we send love & best wishes to you.

Mother

Letter from Art's parents to Art
July 1, 1943

Dear Son:

Last night we received your Sun. June 27 letter and are so glad that you continue to get on good. Glad that you are sign to have the opportunity to enter the A.S.T.P. which seems very wonderful, and may prove to be more wonderful than being Prof. For 18 to 24 hrs. per week at Maryville. We have always known that you had ability and could make good, and our hope has been that you would let nothing interfere with your becoming equipped for a useful life. Now that Uncle Sam has you in charge, give him all that you've got and let him continue from where we had to leave off. When I compare your opportunity with so many of the other Fentress boys, I wonder how it all came about. We have the booklet of 50 questions about A.S.P.2. and wondered if you would want it sent on. It came to you but its nice to keep in office if you don't want it.

Today we sent package containing bathing suit, sweat shirt, 2 polo shirts, sewing kit, testament and Abundant Living. I sent also about 5 letters, Hargrave, Pratt, Boyd and two without names on outside. The letters went in two large envelopes. You might mention receipt of all the above. If you get our letters we would like to know, so that we wouldn't need to repeat any news. We are particularly anxious to know that a report of the "Cookeville Case" reached you.

Frank Baesd is home looking brown as a berry and says he likes Navy life very much.

Eston has bene sent to Fort Benjamin Harrison, Ind. Glen is in Missouri in Signal Corps. Edd York [George Edward Buxton York] has been sent to Camp Campbell, Ky. in the Infantry. He still calls home every few days. I would have enjoyed the trip to Oglethorpe if you had stayed another week. Fay is still down there, say he likes the Army fine, but called & wanted the folks to come and see him, so they are going Sun.

We are rocking along so usual, with plenty of work but with the satisfaction of knowing that we are keeping things up to date. We are supposed to attend a zone meeting of Selective Service in Cookeville July 9, 8:00 P.M. Hope we get to go. You should see our garden, and see us working it after supper evenings. Your Dad is an awfully good "Plow Boy" and with his help we are keeping the weeds down in a way that I never expected to do. We have potatoes, cabbage, turnips, greens and when the tomatoes get a bit more color we will be eating those.

Things in general are just as dead as ever. 50 more go to camp in just a week, then we begin on married men without children for our calls. It won't take long to finish those.

By the way Bes. Smith is at March Field, Cal. but I find that it is some way South of Los Angeles.

Lots of love
Mother

Letter from Art to Dotty
Camp Roberts, Calif.
July 1, 1943

My Dearest Heart,

Tonight at this very moment your are no doubt curled up in a chair at Flo's house writing to me—I hope—and listening to an a beautiful symphony. Well, you can't put one over on me. I too am listening to wonderful music, writing to you, and longing to be near you. I found out just a few days ago that the Service Men's Club here (where the Library is located) holds Thursday evening open for the playing of classical music for the men. Probably fifty or more of us are here tonight enjoying at the moment Brahm's Concerto No. 2 The program has just begun, but I know that I am in for a very wonderful evening.

The longing that I constantly feel for you reaches a new height as I enjoy these rare moments of pleasure.

Another of these rare moments came last Monday evening. Ted, Gordon, and myself were seeing "Stage Door Canteen" (a picture which seems only fair to me). We had gotten to the theater after the picture had started and we therefore stayed to see the first. There is always a break for the building to empty and fill; and, during that intermission, I walked out a side door to enjoy a bit of fresh air. I was struck completely breathless by the site before me. A wide band of cloud was stretched across the western sky and the sun was just dipping into the distance sea. The western sky was a blaze of pure gold, fleece clouds covered the rest of the sky, and the surrounding hills were tinted in multi-colored shades. In all my life I have never seen a sunset so beautiful. I hate to admit it, but that sunset exceeded anything that I have ever seen including those sunsets that were so beautiful at Maryville. There was only one thing to do; I pressed your hand tightly and prayed a prayer of thanksgiving that such beauty could still exist in the world lost it seems in chaos. I promise that you are going to see the West in all its glory, it's vastness, and its beauty. This is a good place to quote a delightful passage from Dad's letter of a few days ago: in reference to my trip West, he says, "....always remember that the same West called me, and you are a son of the West for I loved those wild open spaces at one time and do still. It was a refreshing change from the stuffy East." Yes, I too am learning to love the "wide open spaces" though I am not seeing them under ideal conditions.

I must move on to other things as tempus fugit again. Please give Pete and Marianna my address in the fond hope that they may write. I wish they could send me Phil Evaul's address. I tried to look him up or rather call him in Frisco but had no luck. Will write to that happy couple as soon as I get the chance. Yes, I got the news about the glorious event for Samarriet. I wrote them last night. Will write Mother this week-end—I hope. 'Tis wonderful to hear that your debt is almost gone. I know you are thrilled as am I. I finished one month of training yesterday, so I can begin saving a little now.

In regard to the "stacks" of Maryville and Knoxville boys. I will almost have to have at least the battalion which they are in. Remember that, Camp Roberts has almost half as many men ad does the city of Knoxville. I do want to look them up, but who and where is Rex Cole?

Oh yes, about Dad's book: I think the reason he did that was because he ask me one to ask you to get it for him. Since he didn't understand it as a gift, he sent the money. You need have no fear as to his reaction if you wish to send it back. However, it isn't necessary to do so.

The music continues to be very wonderful though after nine any evening I begin to yawn a wee bit. My habits have certainly altered since I entered the Service.

I love to get your wonderful letters. Please write as often as you have time for "I belong to you, you belong to me," and, my darling,
"You are always in my heart."
Bushy
P.S. Thanks so much for airmail stamps. I am now able to secure them here.

Letter from Dotty to Art
July 1, 1943

Dearest,

I got your wonderful, wonderful letter of the 24th, 25th, 26th, and 27th, and my morale zoomed to a new high. I thought at first that California seemed no farther away than Ga., but now that letters are slower, the distance looms greater.

Now sit very still—control your eyebrows and try not to look very surprised and I'll let you in on the ground floor of a deep dark secret. Even some members of the family don't know it yet. Florence and Carl are going to be married! But soon—some time in August. The exact date hasn't been definitely decided; she wants me to be her maid of honor; the wedding will be in Louisiana. She is so excited and happy and thrilled. I am glad they are able to go ahead with their plans. They can say with Farragut, "Damn the torpedoes, full steam ahead!" I am very happy for them, but a wee bit anxious at the same time.

Mary Ruth and I have the house to ourselves now—Daddy left this morning for Maryland, to stay for a week. Dad and Mother call this trip their "second honeymoon."

The weather here has been beautiful and cold and rainy and clammy. If I look somewhat mildewed the next time you see me, you'll know the reason why.

And now—whether my letters are short or long—
I love you,
Dotty.

Darling,

How are you, my love? I dreamed a wonderful dream last night—I was in your arms again, and it gave me an indescribably delicious feeling to be there, and seemed so very real. Now, lean a little closer and shut your eyes and I'll—mmmm. How was that? And now for a big —whuff—hug. Oh, I was not trying to tickle you—just 'cause I hug you in a funny place is no reason—. Well anyway, I love you.

If Carl gets a furlough, the wedding will be on the 1st of August, here; if no furlough, it will be there in the middle of the month. Oh, dearest, I dare not think long on the fact of their wedding, for it stirs up within me that which I can hardly put or push down—an urgent desire to be going through the same process myself. Please forgive my impatience. I am fully aware of the impossibility of such a thing right now, but sometimes my hopes and desires break through the wall of patience which I have so carefully built around them. I repair the holes with faith—faith in an extraordinary and wonderful future which I know lies ahead of us.

All of which reminds me—I was reading in Song of Solomon this afternoon, and was struck anew with the beauty and symbolism of its passages. Do you think perhaps we might use some of it in our ceremony? On second thought, it wouldn't be suitable at all, unless something from the 4th chapter.

The rain pours heavily down; the thunder rumbles incessantly, and the lightning flickers almost without ceasing. This has been going on for almost five hours without a break. Very unusual for Tennessee, don't you think? It has been rainy and cloudy for about two weeks—I've almost forgotten that there is such a thing as a sun. (But not son!)

I was very bad today. I skipped church (communion today, too) to go see our Ensign Ruth E. Duggan, who has been home en route to New Orleans. She and Johnny Sue both left early this afternoon for Missippi; Johnny Sue is going to Keesler Field to work. [Keesler Field in Biloxi, Mississippi, was activated by the War Department in June of 1941.]

Received a letter from Muriel, who also mentioned that she had written to you, but was afraid it hadn't reached you. Ha—she needn't have worried!

When it gets to the paint where I am sitting here in my chair with my eyes closed in sleep, then perhaps I'd better give in, and continue in the next chapter. Loves and kisses & hugs, a Daring Dottie

My Dearest Own,

Among the last several Fourth of Julys that I remember, there have been nothing quite like this one. It is just four o'clock now (six your time), and I can just imagine you eating a typical Sunday evening Barber meal preparatory to going to C.E. Here I lie, taking my first sun bath in the California sun. For two weeks I have baked in its heat, but little sun has reached my body. Now is my chance to build resistance so I won't have any cold to prevent—next winter when I pay my respects. This morning I attended a very nice communion service here in the chapel (one of nine on the post.) The service was simple but very impressive and it held a great deal of meaning for me.

In a few preliminary sentences the Chaplain recounted the story of the Last Supper. Three things he gave us to remember as we partook: the bread as the broken body of Christ; the wine as the blood of Christ shed for the remission of our sins, and the towel representing service to others. The last point was a new twist which I liked very much.

We talked to our Chaplain for more than an hour last Sunday after the Vesper Service and found him to be a very interesting man. He was in the last war as an enlisted man and returned to attend seminary in Chicago. He attended Cumberland University at Lebanon, Tenn, and his mother was born within thirty miles of Jamestown. He knows Dr. McAfee and others friends.

Further proof of the global shrinkage came yesterday afternoon when I was rudely awaken from my bunk to find Jim Walker laughing in my face. In case you have forgotten him, he was in my class for four years at Maryville. He's been here ten or twelve days now, living within a hundred yards of my barracks and neither of us knew the other was within a thousand miles of the place. Whata life!

Jim is starting tonight to form a glee club in our company, and I think he may make a go of it. Pete Van Blancon and Gordon Stone are two others from the M.C. choir and a number of good voices are to be found. The Church Service tonight consists of a half hour of singing of hymns and a half hour of Bible study. Few are usually present, but the program is very nice.

On both Sunday Services that I have attended I have been impressed by one outstanding fact: In a very real sense, the Army set up is diametrically opposed to the principles of Christianity. We are being drilled constantly on military courtesy and the way we should act in the presence of officers. That is very fine and is certainly necessary, but the fellowship that one feels when he sees a second lieutenant in the pew is not in keeping with the tradition of the Army. I like many things about Army life; I like strict order, I like the hard physical training, I like the demands for co-operative effort on the part of the individual. However, there are some things that are irreconcilable; there are some things about Army life that I must always hate. I will not and I must not allow basic changes to take place.

We have been here two weeks already and the time is speeding by very swiftly. The disappointing thing about our program is that it has actually not begun as yet. We still await more men before we begin regular training. Our work now is practically the same thing as what we go into when basic actually starts, but it just doesn't count on our fourteen weeks. We are not likely to begin until July 11th. That means we finish basic in the middle of Oct. Nevertheless it will pass quickly, and then I hope to be sent East. Oh Joy!

I think I mentioned the fact that I am going to read up on my psychology in the hope that I can get in that branch of Specialized Training. The library has a number of good books on the subject and I have just completed Link's <u>Rediscovery of Man</u>. He has a number of very good points and I want to read his book, <u>The Return to Religion</u>. I picked up Shaw's <u>Pygmalion</u> and read it last night, but I did not feel that I had missed a classic by passing it up before. I have a book already to begin on by J.H. Robinson called <u>The Mind In The Making</u> and I have my name on a waiting list for Ruch's <u>Psychology</u>, the text we used at Maryville. I feel more and more that psychology can and will play an important part in winning the peace. To quote Link, "Just as our civilization has codified the habits of science and given man control over his physical environment, so the next step will give man greater control over himself and his social institutions." That must be the next step, and this A.S.T.P. program may be golden opportunity to carry out that ideal.

As I continue to see sunsets out here, I understand the name "Golden West." Just now (about eight o'clock) the western horizon is filled with a golden glow that has filled the hearts of men with hope and promise through many decades. That same promise lies just over the hill for us, darling. Our days and years together are to be happy because we are apart now. Our golden day together is coming.

I got your letter written last Sunday and hope that more are on the way. I look forward to every word and I read and reread every paragraph. Look up at the stars and know that every one brings a thousand kisses from the one you love.

Thine own,
Bushy

July 5, 1943, Diary

Still the other A.S.T.P. candidates have not shown up, but it was rumored tonight that our basic has begun. I hope so for the program that we are carrying on is the same as the regular basic and every day is one less. Typhoid, Tetanus, and Small Pox vaccination today.

Letters from Dotty to Art

Wednesday, July 7 [1943]

Dearest,

No, I wasn't! ("Wasn't what, you say?") I wasn't curled up in a chair at Flo's house listening to music because Record Breakers is this Thursday, not last. I started you a letter that night, but didn't finish it, probably because I was getting Daddy ready for his trip and because Mary Alice spent the night with us that night. Mary Ruth and I have had a lot of fun bringing home various people to spend the night with us while both Mom and Dad are gone. They left orders for us not to stay alone (just us two, but we did for one night. Aunt Mary nearly had a duck fit, or something. Stop me if you have heard all this before. I vaguely seem to remember telling you part of this before.

What a night tomorrow night will be! I am going blackberry picking right after work, and will get back in time for Record Breakers – I am the hostess! Mother and Dad get in about 8:30 and will want to meet then. I still intend to try them all.

July 8

The above paragraph was written while in the process of going to sleep. When I get to the place where what I say doesn't make good sense and where I consistently write "trye" when I am striving to pen "try", then you know that I am truly sleepy! (As I was this morning at 1:00 A.M. Mary Ruth & I ate at Aunt Carol's, then went to the show with two other girls, who also spent the night with us. By the time we got our guests and selves ready for the night it was morning. Or something.

"All things work together for good to them that love the Lord." And I do mean <u>all</u> things. Today, every single one of my troubles vanished. Mother and Dad don't get home till tomorrow, the berry picking has been post-poned and Record Breakers is now over. Nothing to worry about now but you.

Are all the chapels for different religions, or what? Is the evening service well attended? About what percent of all the boys go to a service on Sunday?

It is going to be so good to see Mom and Dad again and hear everything. In less than twenty-four hours they will be here—Oh Joy! Bliss! Ecstasy! Rapture! Contentmentbeyondcompare!

Oh, Happy Day!

> I love you
> X X X
> I love you
> X X X
> Dotty

July 11 – Sabbath.

Darling,

I have thought of you so much today. I do every day, but I have a little bit more time to on Sundays, I guess.

I should write you of bright cheery uplifting things, but tonight my mind is so full of my failures and inadequacies that all else seems sort of blotted out. You said you wanted to hear the bad as well as the good, so I am taking advantage of the privilege—I won't do it often, darling.

Sundayschoolclasswasamessiwenttotheywtohelpentertainthesoldiers thisafternoonandnoneofthemcameandchristianendeavorwasafarceinste adofaprogramandmystomachhurtsandimissyousomuchyouinspiremen owtherearemytroubles. But I also had a long talk with my Savior, so things look much better now. I am going to spank them all and tell them that they (Primaries & Intermediates) that they <u>cannot</u> act so in the house of the Lord. I have often wondered why some people bother to come to church—it seems to bring out the worst in them rather than the best. The little boys in my class sort of defy me to interest them in anything. Antagonism seems their only accomplishment. My intermediates hid from me when I went in tonight. Then they breezed in and informed me that they had already had their meeting (in 5 minutes). I asked for a repeat performance, and then sat in frozen horror while they gave it. The hymns were sung half-way through the first verse and then ended with a gusty "amen." The scripture was Genesis 1:1, period. (No relation to anything else on the program) The talk consisted of two short paragraphs read from a little book. Quick the benediction and then out the door they ran, and I do mean ran. Me —still sitting in frozen horror.

Now. That's off my chest. Gee it surely are nice to have Dad and Mom back at home. They had a good time, and came back so full of THE BABY. It has developed quite a personality already. Harriet and Mother were pleased to get your letter and card respectively. Oddly enough, I too appreciated all the letters that came from California. Wonder why? Wonder why I read them through and through and through, avidly? Wonder why I can hardly wait to find out what the postman leaves on his daily visit? Wonder why I feel so good on the days I do get a letter? Do you know? I do, I do, I do!

I was surprised that you didn't care much for Pygmalion. I saw the picture years ago and was quite impressed by it. I don't know how the picture compares with pure Shaw. I still haven't decided which was exalted the most—the man for making the girl, or the girl for making herself.

Here is something to think about. "Not in doing what you like, but in liking what you do lies the secret of happiness."—J.M. Barrie. How very, very so. For often we crave doing anything else besides what we <u>are</u> doing at the moment.

I have started embroidering my new pillow-cases. (<u>Our</u> new pillowcases). It will be a long job, but I love every stitch.
I love every you, too.
        Your own,
          Dotty.

* Letter from Art's mother, Arza, to Art Jr.
July 8 [1943]
Thursday

Dear Son:

Your July 4 letter received, and it is evident that our letters haven't gotten to you. Since none have come back you no doubt will get them.

So glad you are getting on O.K. and that you like the "Wide open Spaces of the Wild & Wooly West," and that you have Maryville friends with you. It seems that Ted Pratt got there before his letter reached you. We had to hold the letters until we got an address which would surely reach you. A letter was forwarded a few days ago by just re-addressing same. Hope it reaches you.

Seems that its taking a long time to get the A.S.2.P's together , but you will soon begin work in earnest I suppose, and in the meantime you can practice being patient.

Things go on as usual with us. We got off 51 this morning and in one month Aug. 9 we send another 25. I wonder when Uncle Sam will feel that they have as many as they need. We had a form letter from headquarters this a.m. saying that they expected the work to lighten to a great extent, and that Boards should cut down on their paid personal —"which doesn't mean us." We go with Sgt. Mrs. Y. [Alvin York and his wife Gracie York] and board members to Cookeville tomorrow night to a District Conference. I don't expect to get a big lot of information, but will enjoy getting away just for the trip.

Edd [George Edward Buxton York] seems to be getting on O.K. and Fay is still at the Fort. Seems that they plan to make an orderly of him. When you get to be an officer you might requisition him. Shelby Turner came up to see us few days ago. Says he is working hard, and that Texas Rattlesnakes are thick where he is. He wasn't looking up to par and said he has lost weight. How are your eats coming and do you get plenty? I could give you plenty of fresh vegetables from the garden. We are having lots of rain and everything is coming along nicely. Biggest trouble is finding time to cook. We have beens, tomatoes, cabbage cucumbers, potatoes and turnips in plenty.

I now know that my magnolia is going to live—the new leaves coming out look awfully good after watching the brown buds so long.

I knew you would find army expenses high, but if I were you I would see some of the big cities of the West if you get a chance for a trip. I will send on the towels and enclose the dictionary you want. I am sending some pictures in this and will send more next time I write. I take it all back about a picture "with no smile." It just isn't you. Some of both films were no good.

There is absolutely nothing new in way of news to tell you.

Mr. Cross asked about you yesterday and wanted to be remembered to you. Said he knew you would make good because you're so much like your grandfather. I was pleased when he said that he thought my Dad was the best man he ever saw, and that he always did everything the best he could and did it cheerfully. I guess that is a pretty good slogan: "Do what we do the best we can, and do it cheerfully." You might try that on K.P. duty.

I appreciate your mentioning the insurance policy. Fred took a $5,000 policy which Manza got just before she came out to see us. I learned yesterday from some Pickett people that Manza went to Muncie last Sunday. She is going to spend the fall and winter up there. Uldene only has a two room doll house, but Manza may stay with her sister most of the time.

Write when you have time for we anxiously await your letters. All good wishes and lots of love from us both
          Mother

Your Dad wrote yesterday airmail and sent $10. money order. Sgt.'s phone bill was just $75 for the mo. Edd [George Edward Buxton York] was at the Fort. He has called home from Camp Campbell. Phone calls & $99,000 tax runs into money.

Letter from Art to Dotty
Camp Roberts, Calif.
Co C 81st Inf Tr. Bn.
July 9, 1943

My dearest,
I have only a few minutes in which to begin this letter, but I do want to write. In fact I always want to write everyday but the schedule here gives me no time. I am so happy that Carl and Flo are going ahead with plans though I disfavor war marriage under present conditions. Darling, when you become my wife I do not want twenty-five hundred miles between us. I too am more than a little torn up when I think of the wait ahead. As never before I feel the need of your presence, and I pray daily for the hastening of that blessed day when we walked down the aisle as man and wife. However, I am thankful for the strength of faith and patience which God has granted to us in order that we may await that time with the knowledge that "an extraordinary and wonderful future... lies ahead of us."

July 10, 1943

As I feared the whistle blew yesterday and I had to run. 'Tis Saturday afternoon again and we have the afternoon free. Week-ends are so wonderful! Our training has not officially begun yet, but we have certainly begun something. Thursday we began our first hike when we marched out to one of the ranges for instruction and practical work. Marching in rank is not exactly like a "Y" Hike but both involve walking and I love it. It really felt swell to get out and away from the camp area even though we went only about a mile and a half.

I think I haven't said much about our daily program, and I might outline it for it certainly isn't as I expected it. When we get started, we fall out for our daily drill at 7:20. We arise at 5:50 and line up for revillé. Immediately after that we have breakfast and then clean up barracks. We have four periods in the morning and four in the afternoon with a ten minute break every fifty minutes. Usually we spend about half of our time listening to lectures and the rest of the time in actual practice. There are a thousand and one things that we must learn and this makes for a great variety. I think that no one subject will ever get tiresome. We have orders not to write anyone as to what part of our training we are going through, so I'll have to be careful just what I write. Our fourteen weeks will include the use of the rifle, machine gun, entrenching tools (constructing fox holes, prone shelters, etc.), field equipment (pup tents, etc.), compass, bayonet, and the solving of many tactical problems. We will have 10 days of bivouac in which we live in the rough and I do mean rough. All during our training we will have physical education and close order drill. We will have frequent lectures on such subjects as personal hygiene, military courtesy, the use of the gas mask, and similar subjects and when the weather gets warm in Knoxville, think of me sweating as we double time through a drill with the temperature up to 135° or 145°. It's wonderful, darling.

We have just heard the latest news on the invasion of Sicily. The first report came late last night, but the details are just now coming through. This is the beginning of a gigantic operation involving the loss of millions of men, but victory will be ours and peace will come again. I am beginning to see how important the individual becomes as we seek to preserve the right of the individual. I think I discussed last week ways in which the Army is opposed to the basic ideals of Christianity. I find again and again that this is true. However, war as we see it now is the choice of the lesser of two evils.

July 11,
Sunday

I spent a wonderful afternoon today listening with you to the Grieg concert. It was wonderful, my darling, and I held you very close. Amazing as it seems, most of us in the barracks this afternoon wanted classical music, so we listened to the Grieg program. (If part of this seems incoherent, I blame it in part on the fact that an Army barracks is no place to write and concentrate.) This morning, of course, I attended church and plan to return tonight. I must rave again about how wonderful it is to be able to relax on the week-end. We finished inspection yesterday about 11:30 and had the rest of the day to ourselves. I did a big washing under the warming California sun in the afternoon and saw a show last night. "Once Upon a Honeymoon" is coming next week and perhaps I can see it.

I too have been dreaming of late. In fact, I dream often of being with you and holding you in my arms. A new moon is growing rapidly out here, and I kiss you gently each evening before closing my eyes. The sky is truly a heavenly stage out here, and the stars appear as the glorious colors of twilight fade and are gone. You are always present as I see these beauties and these moments make life very real and very wonderful.

The second thing that keeps me strong in the daily round is the habit of reading my Bible at some length. My Abundant Living (by E. Stanley Jones) arrived from home yesterday and I am already reading "Today" and "The Upper Room". I read from the little testament you gave me constantly and I gain new power. The faith that we have built up together is a Power higher than ourselves, the strength that we find from the Book of Life, the growth and stabilizing power of prayer, and the Living Example of higher living that we have in Christ will carry us through this crisis and through all trials that we face in the future. In the Army we know our activity only from day to day—we never know what the morrow brings. I do not know how I could continue on an even keel if I had to worry about my fate. Each day I place our future in the hands of our Guide. That is sufficient!

I got a letter from Hargrave last week that was written just a month ago. He is going to Harvard studying the new marvel radar. The lucky guy was one of a group of a hundred selected out of eight-hundred at Notre Dame for this special training. He is getting along well and asked about you. Today I had a long letter from Carl and he had a lengthy argument for the coming event. I think the Army has done a great deal for him. I hope their plans work out completely.

Another break: Ted and I just returned from the evening service at the Chapel. As I think I have mentioned, the first half hour is devoted to singing and the second half to Bible study. Tonight the entire hour was conducted by a new chaplain—new as far as we were concerned. The entire thing was very well handled, and we studied the first chapter of John. It is truly inspiring to sit in a Chapel in the middle of an Army camp and hear men from all parts of the country pray and sing together.

I want you to tell Aunt Carol this fact which the Chaplain told me some time ago: The Recreation Hall has found a decided drop in the sale of beer since this new increment arrived. As I have told you, our group is made up largely of college men and it is good news to know that they are asking for soft drinks rather than something else.

It sounds wonderful to hear reports of rain. There hasn't been a cloud in the sky since we arrived. On our march the other day we dug fox holes beneath real trees. It really was like walking in a dream to be able smell something green again. Oh to see the Smokies again!

Darling, please write as often as you possibly can. I love to get your letters; and, when I went for more than a week with no letter, I was very much disturbed. I doubt that I will have the chance to write more than once each week on Saturday and Sunday, but I will try to make these letters long enough to compensate. To come in from the field to find a letter—even if only a note—from the girl I'm fighting for and the one who means all the world to me is a remarkable refresher.

The hour grows late and I must arise at five o'clock in the morning to go out with full field pack (forty pounds) for a little walk. Oh joy! Give my hearty congratulation to Flo; my loving regards to the family. I still promise to write Mary Ruth and Mother.

Thinking, dreaming, living and fighting for

Our love,

Bushy

Letters from Dotty to Art
July 13, 1943

My Own,

I talked to you in the sunset last night. Did you hear me? I was saying the sunset here was beautiful, but in such a different way from those you describe in the west. There is nothing spectacular about it, just a very delicately tinted rose glow in the entire western portion of the sky, which changes imperceptibility and fades under your gaze. But a sensation of quiet beauty lingers. Somehow it seemed symbolic of the difference between my life and yours at the present time. Yours is bold and spectacular, swiftly moving, containing quick change. Mine is quiet and unexciting, with little of change in it except that time goes by. It takes a little of both to make a full life. Yes, no?

Speaking of time going by, you would have accused me of trying to turn the calendar back if you could have seen me tonight. Everybody (mostly my Intermediates, bless their hearts) wanted to have the recreation night at the church tonight rather than next Tuesday for which it was planned, so I slipped into some cooler duds, and then made myself some pigtails, complete with a yellow bow on one and a blue bow on the other. I felt so childish—must have looked as though I were trying to be an Intermediate myself—but I had such fun!

Last night I sewed and sewed and sewed on <u>our</u> pillow cases (the ones Mother gave me for my birthday)—I can hardly wait to see what the finished product will be like.

We are quite excited over the pictures that arrived today—pictures Dad took of The Baby while he was there. He is precious, and not just because he is my nephew either. See if you don't think so, too, when I send you the pictures, which I shall do as soon as copies are made. I can hardly wait to see him <u>in person</u>.

Carl is getting into Specialized Training, too, I hear, and is very happy about it. But then, he's happy about everything nowadays. Did I tell you that the wedding will most likely be here—that Carl's furlough seems a pretty sure thing? We are going to have quite a gang in A.S.T.P., nicht wahr? Confidential (very confidential) note: Harriet and Sam are "in waiting" as missionaries to India as soon as the war is over. The thing apparently sought them more than they have sought it, but if called they will go. It is in the hands of the Lord. I know that Mother will have a terribly hard time "taking it" if two of us are abroad at the same time. She won't try to keep us from "flying the nest," but just the same, it will hurt her deeply. Are all Mother's that way? Will I be?

No letter so far this week. Your training must have really started in earnest. And also Bushing.

Goodnight, darling.
I love you,
Dotty.

July 15, 1943

Dearest,

Your wonderful letter received tonight. I read it while standing out on the street corner waiting for a streetcar that was about twenty minutes late. A rather public place in which to review my most private and precious mail, but I just couldn't wait. We went out to the park tonight straight from work (we = church gang); Mary met us halfway, and she brought my letter to me. Otherwise I wouldn't have seen it until about 9:30 tonight. And speaking of letters—it helps me just as much to get frequent little notes as it does you, even if it is just a little "rush message" like you used to send me from school. Nothing does me more good than to get some sort of message from you. When was the week you didn't hear from me? (Pardon me while I flaunt my righteous indignation) I've written you twice every week and sometimes more, except for the week you were traveling. I still have the feeling that a few of my letters didn't reach you. The letters are definitely being sent out from this end—if you don't receive them, please let me know. I'll write as often as I can, Darling.

Listen, you. <u>Flo and Carl are not going to be 2500 miles apart</u>— they are going to be together—Flo is going down there to live with him, and will go wherever he goes from here on out. Or in, as the case may be. If they can do it, <u>so can we</u>. I don't mean now—I mean when you get settled for your specialized training, which, as you say, may last for two years. I have heard, by the way, that during this specialized training you have every evening and weekend free. What more could we want? (Don't say it.) Carl by the way has also been approved for A.S.T.P., which stands for Army Specialized Training Program. If I am wrong, please correct me.

Got a card from Schwartzwander today. As he expressed it: "a card from a card to a card." He is at Parris Island.

My eyes just won't stay open any longer. Goodnight, darling.
        I love you.

Sunday again. July 18, 1943

Dearest,

Since I plan to write part of this on this machine, I might as well go the whole hog. Or something. You know, I almost have to write you every day to keep you informed on the latest news about Carl and Florence! There may not be a wedding at all is the latest- -soon, I mean. There is a rumor going around that numbers of men are going to be called into Specialized Training August 1. If Carl is among those thus called, and is sent to who knows where, then the furlough or any leave he would have gotten at the end of his basic would also be off, as well as the wedding, I guess. And by the way, lots of the information I glean from anyone who professes to know anything about it about Spec. Tr. is probably all wrong, notably that about conditions of living and leaving (see letter of the 15th). In fact, it will be just opposite from the way I described it, I think. And speaking of the letter of the 15th, just kind of forget it or something--- I raved at such length that I got myself (and you if you took me seriously) way off the track. Please forgive? Tell me, Mr. Bushing, what brand of lipstick do you use? M-m-m-m-m-m it tasted <u>wonderful</u>!

I talked to Dean a little while ago. We were up at Aunt Carol's when the call came. But only Mary, Mary Ruth, and I were there, so we all talked to him. Oh Darling, if ever you want to call here some night maybe, I'll pay all charges and hangthecostanyway-itwouldsureputmewaytherefora longtimetocome i'llbe listening!

Hught – oh. Somehow this is Monday night, and also somehow this ain't a type-writer too also. Now I wonder what happened? We have been having stuffy, humid, relentless heat here. Sometimes I get to thinking that I can't <u>bear</u> it, and then I think of you and what you must be doing, and how much greater heat you are compelled to endure, and I get at least two degrees cooler!

The sermon yesterday was very helpful to me, in view of the way I felt last Sunday. It dealt with the implications of feeling worthless, insignificant, inefficient—a failure in comparison with the high qualities of Christ. It was as if Mr. Hamilton knew my every thought, and was preaching directly for my benefit. No matter how low we get, we can always feel a sense of personal worth when we consider that Christ would not have given his life for us if we hadn't been worth it. I was singing for you yesterday in church—did you hear me? Florence, Mary Ruth and I sang a trio. Call it Barber-shop harmony, then, if you insist!

I clipped the clipping of "Clippy" from yesterdays paper. Thought you might be just a little interested. Very good picture, no?

Today was what might be called a red-letter day. I wiped out the very lastest last of my loan, got my insurance policy back into my hands again, and got a bond all in one breath (I mean day). And bought a new dress and material for a blouse. I really blew myself. For a change!

Sweetheart, when I think of the happiness that lies ahead of us, I nearly shout for joy! (Quiet Dotty—you'll wake up the neighbors) Day by day the thoughts of our love give me greater insight into many things, lift me above all that is commonplace, and provide a sense of deep, abiding happiness. In short—I Love You.

Mary Ruth is sleeping, but a few moments ago she opened her eyes, held her hand out in front of her (the way girls <u>will</u> do) and said, "Beautiful, isn't it?" As if she were admiring a new coat of nail polish or a new ring. But there wasn't a thing in or on her hand. I wonder. The hour is very late, and I, too, must get in a little sleep at least. Goodnight, darling.

       Love,

          Dotty.

P.S. XXXX to you!

My Dearest Heart,

It is already past bedtime for good little soldiers but I slipped away to the Recreation Hall where the lights are on a little longer. I wish the powers that be would give us just a little time now and then to have a minute to ourselves, but it seems that that is out for the duration.

For four weeks now we have been training with an incomplete battalion. For this reason we have not been heretofore assigned permanently to barracks. No more men have arrived, but tonight we were assigned to barracks in alphabetical order. I might note in passing that we have the toughest lieutenant in the company. He is extremely particular about every little detail and really puts the guys through the mill. However, the tougher he is the better soldier I'll be so I'm glad I have him. (He is also considered the best instructor in the company so I'm doubly lucky.)

We have heard all sorts of rumors concerning our training, but it seems that there is a bare possibility that we have begun. As I say, we still have had no definite word. We are still waiting more men, but we may get at least part credit for these past weeks.

Your quotation from Barrie was perfect as a description of the Army: "Not in doing what you like, but in liking what you do lies the secret of happiness." I believe that with all my heart and I'm practicing it more than ever before. I do like what I'm doing very much; and, when I have to do things that are not pleasant, I like to do them just to prove to myself that I can do them and like them. Crazy maybe, but it works!

Darling, I was so glad that you wrote me of your difficulties. Please do so again whenever things go wrong, as they so often will. It's all right to get down in the dumps once in awhile, for after we take time out then to check up on ourselves. The important thing is to bounce back all the harder because we have bit ebb tide. You know that we couldn't have Le Conte [a mountain in the Great Smoky Mountains National Park] if he had no cove or valley around. After living here in this desert sand for three or four months where trees hardly exist, I will appreciate our mountains as never before. Your little angels with dirty faces have great potential power in the Fourth Church and in other churches. You are training them for the jobs that they will take over when I take you away and others go elsewhere. You are doing a swell job and you are going to "keep on keeping on."

Art Bushing and Ted Kidder

Tempus Fugit and I am just now getting a chance to continue, my sweet. Thursday night when I began this letter I thought that I was getting a pass this week-end. Ted Kidder and I planned to go to the beach and get away from it all. However, instead of a pass I got K.P. for tomorrow. Just a few days ago they began taking K.P. in alphabetical order so Bushing fits right into the picture. As Tom and I used to say, "it's a great life if you don't weaken, and sometimes it's better if you do!" I don't mind the work—it will be nothing compared with K.P. at Ogelthorpe. However I do regret missing church tomorrow and the general day of relaxation that is always so welcomed.

Whether our training has started or not, we are definitely getting down to business around Company C. During the past one week, I did not have a single free night in which I could do what I wanted. Our week officially ends at 11:30 each Saturday. But I spent the entire afternoon right up until the whistle blew for chow scrubbing clothing and equipment. Laundry Service is very slow at best taking at least ten days to get back. Thus we must do all of our small things including socks, underwear, handkerchiefs, and in addition we do our work clothes which are extremely dirty—always. I addition to this weekly job, I had to wash my rifle belt and haversack [a small bag with a single strap]. (Darling, if everything else fails, I can always take in laundry and support you by scrubbing.) Every Friday night after supper we use a G.I. brush and soap on the floor of our barracks and clean it generally. After that is done, we must prepare for inspection which comes Saturday morning. Rifle must be cleaned, shoes shined, and foot lockers (a small wooden trunk) put in order.

I fear that I must confess, darling, I feel myself a very mediocre soldier. Pardon me for telling my woes, but time about is fair play and it will do me good to get it off my chest. There is so little encouragement from those in charge; one always feels that he is doing a poor job. I suppose the mass psychology of that is necessary to get the maximum results, but it makes for a growing feeling of inferiority. The trouble, of course, is that I have always worked under conditions where earnest effort was at least approved. I must get accustomed to this way of doing things, and all of it is a part of the invaluable training that I am getting. Men who graduate from this Camp after basic are considered among the best trained in the country. I'm out for the top and I have no intention of failing!

During the last few days we have had the Commander of the Post, General Fales following us around like a dog, or better, an inspector. There are twenty-two battalions here on the post and General Fales came out to look us over on the range four times this week.

Sunday Night
Lights out in 15 min.

My Dearest Own,

I got through K.P tonight just in time to clean up and roll my pack for tomorrow. I didn't even get a chance to go to church which I missed very much. K.P. was steady work but not hard and I actually enjoyed it. I ate more than I have eaten since I have been in the Army, but it felt wonderful.

I heard you last night and the night before as I watched a full California moon come over the hills—I heard you whisper our love as I covered your lips with warm, long kisses. I felt your arms around me and I held you tight.

Monday Night

Again I rush to attempt to finish my letter. Again we were out all day on the range and got in just in time to rush to Retreat, supper and clean our rifles, prepare for inspection and clean up. It is now eight o'clock and I go on duty at 8:30. I will finish just in time to get fed before lights out. It's a great life!

One thing is clear, the C.O. (Commanding Officer) doesn't know what to do with us! No more men have arrived and the grape-vine has it that wires have gone to Washington and other hdq's [headquarters] to find what is to happen to us. Rumor has it that there is a possibility that we will be moved to another camp but that does not seem likely. I don't know what to think or expect. Our regimental commander confirmed the fact this morning that we are to be a part of the Army of Occupation. Where? when? how? etc.? remains unanswered.

Ran into Allan Rock Sat night at Service Club. He's been here since April. Probably you don't remember him, but he was Les' brother. Jim Walker's Gleeman are doing well and appear on a program with "Red' Skelton to be given from the Camp in August.

I have absolutely no time now for reading or relaxation of any sort. I have been unable to answer letters from John, Dick, Tom, Carl, etc. but I still promise a letter to Mother and Mary Ruth whenever possible. Give them my love.

Meanwhile, my darling, know that a great day is coming. Time flies here—I have been here more than a month now. I have complete faith and trust in what tomorrow and tomorrow will bring, for our Love grows on into Eternity.

                        With all my love,
                        Bushy.

Letter from Art to Dotty
Camp Roberts, Calif.
July 20, 1943
Tues. Noon

Darling,

Your letter of the 15th arrived just a few moments ago and here I go with a rush message. I must hasten to explain the system whereby it is so frequently impossible to even write a rush message. Five days last week we were out on the range: that is, we left early in the morning from the camp area and returned very late in the afternoon. We carry our mess kits with us, and eat right in the field. Every night last week we had some job to do; and, as I mentioned in my week-end letter, I had to laundry all Sat. afternoon and do K.P. Sunday.

Tues. Night

Just to continue my illustrations of how we are kept busy: a whistle blew as I began at noon and something else will break in here. As soon as we got through the regular day this afternoon we were told to wash our work clothing by tomorrow. In addition, we have to stamp clothing tonight. I have had one free night in nine and Ted and I plan to see a show tonight even though it be a late one. Enough of my troubles, however, I know you write as often as you can and you may know that I will do the same.

Yesterday I had a long letter from Dad. He is vitally interested in our future. He was in Nashville when he wrote where he was getting fixed up with new glasses, teeth, etc. From his letters, I think that he is regaining his old vigor. I am very happy for I was really worried about his condition.

Wednesday Night

Dear Heart,

I have been thinking very seriously along the same line as you suggested in your letter yesterday. It seems that there is a definite possibility, and yet I'm almost afraid to think that it might come true. What I mean is that I am learning how uncertain everything is in the Army, and, when I speculate as to where I might be a year from now, I grow globe dizzy. As we have been told here, we are scheduled for specialized training; but we could be called for further infantry training as soon as we finish basic. I don't mean to be a pessimist, but that is what I mean when I speak of the uncertainty of our future. If and when I go on to school, the training may last from six to eighteen months. Classes are held twenty-four hours a week in addition to twenty-four hours per week of supervised study, six hours a week of physical training, and five hours a week of drill. I fear that evenings and week-ends would hardly be free.

The thing that is so confusing about the whole situation is that almost nothing is known even by General Fales (Commander of the Post) as to the plans for this bunch. No new men have arrived and we still are waiting to officially start according to our officers. This indecision seems to become more and more confusing. Can't you see why I am afraid to build up my hopes too high as yet? I think there is a definite possibility, and I only hope and pray that our Guide will hasten the blessed day.

Today we spent the entire eight hours on the light machine gun and tomorrow we spend our day on the mortar—a heavier type of weapon. I spend an hour and a half tonight getting instruction so that I can assist tomorrow. It is no particular distinction since most of my platoon volunteered for the work. However, it will be lots of fun.

Under separate cover by regular mail I am sending a booklet on Camp Roberts. I enclose in this letter pictures (3) that you may like to see. Mother wanted to see me in a picture without a smile, but she says never again. I agree! Keep them as long as you like, but I would like to have them back sometime. I have so few pictures to bring you near to me.

As so often happens, the sands of time run swiftly. I must hasten this to a close. I promise to write "rush notes" as often as possible. Have faith in what tomorrow brings, my love
    Ever Thine,
    Bushy

Letter from Dotty to Art
July 21, 1943

Dearest,

Now what happened to all the deep, profound things I had in mind saying to you? Gone they are, and only the shallow, everyday, commonplaces remain.

You'll be sorry someday that you chose such an one (shallow, etc.) as me. You'll think to yourself "Why didn't I choose someone less beautiful (?) and with more of a mind on her, someone whose thoughts could keep pace with mine? (Harrumph!)

Last night I worked overtime, then came home a [and] started making a skirt. Tonight I went to choir practice and almost finished said skirt. Tomorrow night I go to Record Breakers, work overtime, and a few other odds and ends. Working overtime is not a bit like it was in the old days. It is fun now, and not so tiring. Last night I took off my shoes and a hot belt and really went to work. There were people working on the other side of the files, but no one to bother me on my side, and I really put out the mark.

Got a letter from Muriel today. She mentioned you. She can hardly wait to get back to school. Do you blame her? O.K. Let's do. For the day at least. But come dressed for chiggers—you know those woods.

The night is far spent; for spent. Therefore, I must leave you for the nonce.

Love,
Dotty
Much love,
Dotty.
Scads of it, in fact.

Letter from Art to Dotty
Camp Roberts Calif.
July 24, 1943

My Dearest Own,

Oh joy and bliss! I do believe that telepathy works and how. For several days I had been wondering if perhaps you could possibly find time to make a little candy or a few cookies for me. The other guys had been getting food from home and from the girls and then—oh joy! It was absolutely the most wonderful candy I ever ate, darling. It's sweetness and goodness could only be surpassed by the sweet little cook who made it. Here's a great big, loving kiss—whe-e-e-w-w. Your wonderful!

Also wonderful was your letter of Sunday and Monday nights. I was terribly sorry to hear that the plans for the coming wedding have been delayed. I'm afraid the let-down would be terrific, but their plans may materialize soon anyway. I hope so. Just that situation is typical of what I was trying to say in one of my last letters when I spoke of the uncertainty of Army life. We know not from day to day what is coming tomorrow. I think you understand.

I know how much it must have meant to you to get your debt paid off, insurance back, etc. Last week I had my first chance to sign up for the purchase of bonds. Upon the advice of the Service Officer, I am starting out with only $6.25 per month. That isn't enough but I already have insurance ($6.50) and laundry coming out each month. I intend to buy extra as often as I can. I still have had no pay at all from the Army, but I think we will get a check within the next ten days.

We have just finished a good week of training. In three days we took up the light machine, the 60 mm mortar, and the '03 Rifle. We covered a lot of information in a short time, but it is nothing like a rush season at dear old Maryville. One thing that Ted and I have noted is the fact that we are rapidly being whipped into top physical shape. Nothing that we have had so far has been too difficult, for Coach Honaker had given us good training. However, the usual physical routine seems likes a picnic now. This Army life is great, and I still think it is rounding out my education that could hardly be found elsewhere.

Sunday Afternoon

'Tis Sunday afternoon and through your ears I hear the wonderful music that you are listening to. If I could only be there with you! However, I can sit and talk with you which is also wonderful.

Ted and I attending a couple of Church Services this morning since both of us missed last week. Both services were very fine and I got a great deal from them. The first, on "The Changeless Christ" treated an old subject in an interesting fashion. The second was given by the Chaplain I have come to know rather well. He, by the way, is leaving tomorrow for another camp. The topic he discussed was "Four Roads to Jerusalem:" (1) Damascus Road – awakening; (2) Jericho Road – service; (3) Jerusalem – commitment (the "must" in Christian Living); and the Road to Amais—the road of fellowship. These ministers are by no means second rate, and it is wonderfully refreshing to be able to hear them. This morning in the first service we sat with a capacity crowd of about three hundred men. To repeat with them the Lord's Prayer is a real experience.

You know, darling, you may get a preacher after all. There is nothing I would rather do more than return after our service abroad to attend seminary and then spend the rest of my life in His Service. I know that rather than being weaker, my spiritual life is growing daily here in the Army. I find new needs and new strength in prayer and Bible reading. The least that we can do is to place ourselves in His hands to be directed completely by His will. Time will provide the answers to our quest.

As time goes on, I find out more and more about the boys in my platoon. As I think I have explained, there are forty-four of us in the first barrack making up the first platoon. Most of the fellows are eighteen and nineteen years old, but I was somewhat taken aback when one guy asked me if I wasn't a good deal older than the others. It must be my gray hairs! For the most part the group is O.K., although the vocabulary of a few is extremely limited. I am making no effort to form any bosom friends until I get to know them better. I don't mean to be snooty and I don't think that I give that impression for I like all of them. However, Ted and I were close friends all four years at Maryville and we find it convenient to see a great deal of each other now. He is only two buildings away and we frequently manage to see each other at ten minute breaks during the day's work. He has an invitation from an Aunt in L.A. for us to come down any week-end. If we can manage a pass at the same time, we may go down within a few weeks. I do want to see some of the West Coast while I am out here.

I am amazed at the interest the Army takes in the welfare of its men. Every battalion has its own recreation hall with a stage, piano, books, magazines, movie facilities, etc. A new feature that was introduced last week is the daily reading of the news bulletin to the entire company. These bulletins are not propaganda sheets but are taken directly from the government news releases. It is certainly a help for I see a paper only irregularly. Speaking of papers, I do get to see the Knoxville News-Sentinel every day, although it is almost a week old when I get it. A fellow from Knoxville who came with us from Oglethorpe bunks next to me and he has a subscription. It is always with a great deal of pleasure that I snatch up the paper and pour over it for the news. I have heard about nothing concerning Maryville and what is going on there. In case you get any gossip, be sure and tell me.

I am keeping up my dialing readings in E. Stanley Jones' book Abundant Living, Darling. I wish we could work out a program where if we read the same thing each day. At the first opportunity I plan to get a copy for you and then perhaps we can work out such a plan. The thought is very fine, and Jones has an effective style of writing.

By the way, I'm all for this idea of calling you up sometime. I wonder if we should plan for you to talk from Aunt Carol's. You know what a time we used to have with that phone even to Jamestown. I would like to call some night when you were not expecting it; but, because of the distance, it might be wise to plan ahead. It will have to be after pay day for I will not have you paying the bill. Gee, it would be wonderful to hear your voice over the phone again! Oh joy!

Yesterday I received a very nice letter from Samarriet—mostly the latter. She sounds extremely happy with her new bundle of charms. Can't say that I blame her. "All things come to him who learns to labor and to wait!" I can wait although it is hard.

Speaking of letter, I am at last in the process of writing Tom. As I told you, he is at Carson-Newman with about twelve M.C. [Maryville College] boys. I think it would be interesting to get him down to see you before Sis leaves for school. As soon as I get an address, I will let you know and you can write. I still think that those two should hit it off together. I've been counting on that match for a very long time.

Do you ever hear from Maxianmart? I have written them a card asking for Phil Evaul's address, but have heard nothing. Perhaps you could call Agnes or Mrs. Peterson and find out something from them. If you do get a chance to call, give them my regards.

As you have no doubt noticed, the war news is looking very bright these days. I don't want to build up undue optimism in my own mind, but it seems to me that the end may well be in sight as far as actual fighting is concerned. The big job will then have its beginning. I do hope and pray that I can play some small part in that vast reconstruction to come. It will be a superhuman job, but that is the sort of thing I love.

I hope you received the four pictures in my mid-week letters. Also the little booklet on Camp Roberts. The letter may give you a clearer picture of the place.

I close for this time as I listen to the strains of the "All Girl Orchestra." As the strings of those instruments blend in perfect harmony, so will our love blend and harmonize to sound perfect notes into the future.

> Goodnight, my Love,
> Bushy

Letter from Mary Ruth to Art
[Dotty's sister Mary Ruth is going to be attending their Alma Mater, Maryville College, in the fall.]

July 25, 1943

Hello, Bushy,

When I asked my sister (Dotty) what to say to Bushy, she began to dictate. I got a musical "Hello Bushy" written down, and then she wouldn't let me write the rest of the things she said. I guess she decided either that they weren't fit to say, or that I wasn't the one to do it. Take your pick.

Well, are you a very busy little man? I believe you must not be, or you wouldn't have time to sit down and write as many letters (big joke).

This is one of those peaceful Sunday afternoons, with beautiful music furnishing the proper background for a day of rest. The object of your affections is studying her Christian Endeavor lesson, and I, who have no lesson to study, am writing to the object of her affections. (Bet you can't guess who that is!) We took some pictures a little while ago, in the front yard. If they are any good, I presume you will be receiving at least one of them before very long. We hope they will be good, because we take so few, and films are so precious.

Just think—only about five or six weeks now, and I will have my first real taste of college. I have been smelling it for some time now, and my mouth is beginning to water. Also, I'm getting a little hungry. Just the same, it's new food, and I will probably have to get used to it.

The beautiful music is gone, I have no more to say, and I am fast running out of paper, so I think I shall say goodbye.

Sincerely,
Mary Ruth

P.S. – x x x x x x x x x x x x x x x x x x x x x x x x x x x x x (for Dotty)

July 27, 1943, Diary

Temp. up to 142° today.

July 28, 1943, Diary

Nomenclature and functioning of machine gun today in temp of 138°. Not conducive to concentration.

Letters from Dotty to Art
July 26, 1943
Monday

My Own,

I am still kicking myself for that somewhat nasty letter I wrote you. Again I beg your forgiveness—it must have rankled a little. Darling, the more I see of Flo's wedding, the more I hope ours won't have to be like that. Here it is, not more than a week from the originally selected date, and Florence still doesn't know whether it will come off when planned, or whether the wedding will be here or there. (Don't let me fool you—I'd marry you anytime, anywhere, under almost any circumstances) Darling, I wish you could be here for it—really here. In spirit I will feel you grab my hand and squeeze it into numbness as the beautiful ceremony proceeds. Florence is going to wear a long dress, made of white satin (she is making it herself), and I shall wear my blue net dress that was worn in Harriet's wedding, and which you saw numerous times at school. Those two facts are about the only definite ones, to date. I am sending you the picture she had put into the newspaper. You may keep it. And speaking of pictures—I am returning the snapshots. Your mother is the only one who shows up well in all of them. Me—horrors—do I really look like that? Mother—not so good. You—I love, by my you look ferocious in the pictures. Your Dad—a little thin, bless his heart.

We got a letter from Harriet today, in which she broke "The News." She and Sam start in missionary training school Sept. 9, after which they will be sent to India as missionaries. Isn't that wonderful? Mother, of course, is having quite a time becoming adjusted to the idea. Her mother's heart can hardly stand the thoughts of her child being as far removed, I suppose. Reasons why "they'll be sorry" keep occurring to her. As for me, I am proud of them. It seems odd that Harriet should be actually doing all the things of which I dreamed as a child, but things she never pictured herself as doing; so queer that <u>she</u> carries out <u>my</u> former ambitions. What do you think of the situation, dearest?

I put in 6 ½ hours overtime last week, which will account for any scarcity of mail you may have noticed. The work has been very heavy lately, not only for me but for the entire office. I haven't been working overtime by myself! My work, at least, looks better this week, so I don't think I'll have to continue working overtime this week also.

What is all this about your assisting the instructor? You said nearly all of them volunteered, but only mentioned yourself as getting to do it. Am I correct in assuming that you were the only one to be used in that capacity out of all those who volunteered? Tell me more, tell me more!

I am in an "up" period now, after being down in the dumps for a while. Little unexpected compliments and events keep cropping up to holster my ego to a new high. I feel <u>much</u> better about my church work; not only have my Intermediates reformed, but I met the mother of one of my little boys, and she told me that I was exerting a great influence (good according to her) over her son! Now that came right on the heels of my feeling very strongly that I couldn't do a thing with those little boys. Darling, I realize more and more that God brings us out of adversity into new comfort and freshened courage. He knows our every up and down.

Don't you dare send me letters until you get good and ready! I won't have it. Just forget what I said about rush messages.

Well. What about Mussolini. To me the news of his resignation was just about the most startling news of the war, outside of Pearl Harbor. His guiltation can lead to a number of things, and I hope for the best. One is tempted to jump at conclusions, but there is only one conclusion I would really like to jump at, and that is the conclusion of this war!

Also, this letter should be conclusioned. But one thing will never be concluded, and that is

Our Love,
Dotty.

P.S. I love you, too.

Wed. July 28

Darling,

Talk of intuition, telepathy, or what have you! Today I received two letters in the mail—one from Bob and one from Arlene! Bob is at Parris Is., you know, and Arlene is in Pa. Do you not think it odd that letters from each should arrive in the same mail? About all Bob said in his letter was that he wanted your address. His address is

Platoon 507 Battalion 8
Parris Island, S.C.

Arlene's address is

350 Fitzwatertown Road
Willow Grove, Pa.
c/o H. M. Higgins.

I'll send you her letter as soon as I read it some more and answer it.

This afternoon I got off from work an hour early, went to the beauty shop, and had my hair cut but short and then had a permanent. Talk about being hot—phew, I'm still fanning. (But ah, how nice to have my hair fixed and shortened and stuff).

I must hurry and finish this because my eyes are getting heavier and heavier.

Roblene (cute, huh) both want to write you and no doubt would be glad to hear from you. If I go North on my vacation I might get to see Arlene. Samarriet will be in Connecticut by that time, so I won't get to see them as I had planned. (Unless the wedding knocks my entire vacation in the head.)

Goodnight my dearest. Psalm 46:1

I love you,

Dotty.

Thurs, July 29

My Own True One!

Oh, joy, oh bless!! What a wonderful, exhilarating, morale building, etc. etc. letter, darling. Mother brought it to me while I was at work, and I just went around in a happy glow from then on. I worked an hour extra tonight to make up the hour I spent yesterday having my hair fixed.

Whoa, hold on here. I am going to have to watch what I say very carefully, or you will get the wrong impression. The wedding plans have not been delayed, rather they are going on apace, and I do mean full force. The only thing is, the date still hasn't been definitely set, and won't be until Carl finds out a few things. Florence has her dress almost finished, and I have started work on mine. I have to make a new one after all, because the old one has a spot on it that can't be removed.

I am afraid that I am not doing so well with my exercise and physical trim as you. I just don't have time enough to spend on it. About the only real exercise I get is down at the church every other week. No, indeed that isn't enough. Oh, I get some exercise at the office —sitting down & standing up, walking around, stooping, reaching, lifting, etc. But it isn't the same. And of course I dance very flighty dances around the house, whenever I hear certain kinds of music.

I am deeply thrilled about the prospects of being a preachers wife! I purposely never mention the subject to you, because if the call does come to you, I want you to feel that it came from God only, and not from me. Be utterly sure before you decide, darling.

Ted's aunt must be Mrs. Tootell (Tutelle?), who was a classmate of Mother's. I hope you and Ted get to go.

Thanks for the little booklet on Camp Roberts. I read it from cover to cover, and found it very interesting. The diagram I studied for a long time. At least I'll know my way around when I get there. I can now visualize where you when and what you are doing a little better than before. I noticed a number of telephone buildings. Hmmmm. Just name the date and the hour and I'll be at Aunt Carol's, come _____ or high water. If payday doesn't come soon, why go ahead and call anyway. You can pay me back later if you <u>insist</u>. I can hardly wait to hear that Bushing voice!

I am enclosing a picture of that "bundle of charm." Please return sometime. Daddy—I want one, too. Where can I get one, and what store would you recommend? Speaking of pictures—when are you going to send me a picture of you in your uniform, Buddy? Make that snapshot snappy, Soon.

I like the idea of reading the same thing you do each night. Perhaps I can get a copy of the book myself, then we can start at an earlier date.

Reconstruction is such a vast enterprise. I am so afraid that the U.S. will muddle things. We can't set up our way of thinking and doing and gov't with any more justification than Germany can say that her "master-race" should rule the world. We have made some promises to other countries (past-war) that we can't hope to fulfill. Our friends can so easily be turned into enemies. I hope not. Goodnight.

I Love You,
Dotty.

Letter from Art to Dotty
July 27, 1943
Tuesday Night

My Dearest Own,

Many things fill my mind, and I must write you if it be only a note. Last night I spent a long time after lights out just thinking and talking with God.

You know how I have played with the idea for years of entering the ministry. I think in my sophmore year at Maryville I just felt the urge, and the feeling waxed and waned throughout college. As you know, I have always wanted to feel that I belonged in the pulpit, and yet I have been sure that that was His plan for me. During the last three days, I have been filled with a new longing to help others by teaching and preaching. I have a habit of allowing such ideas to simmer in the recesses of my mind, until they appear of their own accord complete and certain. It is thus with this newly intensified thought. Our immediate plans would be altered little by whatever choice I should make for I will be under the management of Uncle Sam for several years. I do not intend to rush such a decision, but I eagerly watch the trend of my own thoughts.

Rather than drawing me away from the ideals that I have built up over the years, life in the Army has caused me to draw closer to those ideals and strengthen them. When I look at the other men around, (college men at that) I see unhappiness and discontent abounding merely because so many of these men are not aware of the vast storehouse of strength and comfort to be found in Christ (I over state the case when I speak of "unhappiness and discontent abounding." It isn't that bad, but there is a certain amount of grumbling at general conditions.) I know that I have the "Living Water" that they have failed to discover, and I want to tell them.

Wednesday Night

As my thought trend continues, I will write more on the subject I discussed last night.

Today we spent the full time on the machine gun again. Next week we spend at least part of the time firing it. I notice in the paper tonight that three soldiers died as a result of the heat in a camp just south of here. The temperature there was 124° in the shade. For the last two days we have spent the entire day out in the sun where the thermometer registered 140°. Both days it has been about 123° or 124° in the shade. Tonight at nine o'clock the temperature in the barrack was 92°. Don't worry, darling. I think I will survive the heat. I think of what our buddies went through in N. Africa and I forget the heat. As long as we do not exercise violently, it isn't so bad. The officers like the heat less than we, so we get by with less work than formerly.

I wish I knew something concerning our training, but we are still in the dark. It seems almost certain now that we will get some credit on our fourteen weeks for the last few weeks of work. How much I don't know.

The war is breaking fast now and the events of the next few weeks are going to be of major importance for the future. Watch the boiling Balkans.

Inform Carl via Floty that I hope to write him soon. Meanwhile I would like to have any information he has on A.S.T.P.

I may go on pass this week-end but will write as early next week as possible.

> Ever thine with all my love,
> Bushy.

August 2, 1943, Diary

Out to P.R.I. this morning after arising at 4:45.

Dearest Heart,

Your letter of Monday and Thursday were more than welcomed, and as usual I continue to read them over and over. Please think nothing more of the letter which you seem to regret having written. It is often good to give vent to our feelings and we can always think more clearly on the subject afterward. As I mentioned before, I think there is the bare possibility that we can go ahead before the war ends, but it is too early to plan right now. Never hesitate, darling, to tell me exactly how you feel about such matters. We know of old that that is the only way.

You ask what I think of Samarriet's decision and plans. I am both happy and proud. Happy that they are doing the thing that they believe God has for them; proud of the prospects of such a brother and sister. You can never know just how much it means to me to think of having brothers and sisters. More than once I have seen little affections pass between children in a family group and I have felt an intense yearning. I am going to gain many, many wonderful things the day I first call you Mrs. Bushing. Please tell the lucky couple that I am extremely happy for them, and that my prayers will go with them in the work that they do. By the way, what is the length of the missionary training school?

Before I go further, I want to explain the confusion concerning my helping the instructor. I shouldn't have mentioned it in the first place, for it was a very minor thing. There were probably twenty of us who spent a couple of hours one night studying the 60 m.m. mortar in order that we might help in the regular instruction the following day. All that we did then was to sit at a gun with four or five trainees and explain the details of the gun as the officer lectured on it. The Army has adopted the "coach, pupil method" in which we assist and correct each other. The system usually operates with pairs, but in some cases the plan is used as described above. It has proven of considerable value and is certainly a step forward in educational procedure. (By the way, I saw an article the other day on O.C.S at Fort Benning. Methods used there for training officers have been called tops by the educational leaders of the country).

The weather continues warm and our routine training schedule routines with variations. I think I mentioned in my last letter that we were studying the machine gun which we fire soon. We may get a chance to fire the rifle next week. Monday we fall out at 6:45, half an hour earlier than formerly. For the next two weeks our battalion is responsible for fighting all fires that occur in the surrounding hills. I think I have failed to mention that as barren as the country is, there is a short grass that covers the ground. As you could guess from my description of the weather, this "grass" is as dry as the sand we eat as we march. With men smoking during the ten minute breaks, fires occur often. For example, the other day a spot a hundred feet in diameter was burned off when an officer threw a fire cracker down. Once started, such fires are difficult to control. So if I write that I have been fighting a California desert fire for two days, you will know what I mean.

August 1
Sunday Night

Today I received a copy of the The Atlantic Monthly which I suppose Dad has been thoughtful enough to subscribe to for me. By the way, we have a couple of wonderful fathers in case anyone asks. I am learning by necessity new ways to get my reading done. I carry a Reader's Digest with me during days on the range in addition to a "Gospel of John." These I read during our ten minute breaks and during the lunch hour. Almost the only time I have for reading in the barracks is while I occupy the seat in the latrine. Nevertheless, I am getting some things read.

I reached a new understanding of myself last week when I read "What We Can Learn From Children" in the August Reader's Digest. I hope you can look it over. You see, darling, I'm still a kid at heart. As the article says, I still look at my world through the eyes of a child. I get a great kick out of going all day with only a little water at noon when I have a full, quart canteen on my belt. The Army refers to that as "water discipline" but some of the men have trouble getting by after drinking the whole canteen they carry. My heart skips a beat when I hear that we are going to march twenty miles with full field packs before we are through, or to hear that we get up at 4:30 in the morning. I make a game of such things, and I take pride in proving to myself that I can do them. Yes, dearest, you have a child on your hands, but my childlike philosophy is proving of incalculable worth here in the Army.

New men are coming at frequent intervals. I don't know what that means. One bit of news that appeared in the Camp paper is that a Star Unit is to be set up here at Roberts. This Star Unit classifies A.S.T.P. men and finds out what sort of training they are to get. Men from here formally went to Stanford University, but now we will be selected and classified right here. Shucks! I wanted to go to Stanford.

Letter from our dear sister came today. I love to hear from her, but not half so much as to get your letters. I know how anxious she must be to get started in at Maryville.

By the way, I just remembered what you said about going North on a vacation. When, where, etc.? Don't forget, I may be East by November, and I would consider seeing visitors. I may not get a furlough until three months after I start school. Really, my sweet, I can't wait that long to see you. Also let me here your news on the telephone situation as I mentioned in my last letter. I long to hear "thy sweet voice."

The hour is late and I must arise very early on the morrow. Under separate cover I am sending folders of the camp. Did you get the booklet?

Give my loving wishes to the family and take a great, big, long
— x
You're my very dearest own, darling,
        I love you
           Bushy,

P.S. I received my first Army pay yesterday—$80.58 I am sending $80.00 home to add to <u>our</u> savings. That, dear heart, is the beginning of our earthly treasure. May we always have enough to eat and enough to wear and enough to help those in need.
        Bushy

Letter from Art to Dotty
Camp Roberts, Calif.
August 4, 1943

My Dearest Heart,

Your wonderful letter and my wonderful ration book arrived tonight. I can assure you that I will begin to take up those stamps at the earliest possible moment. Oh joy!

Time is short, but there are a couple of important things that I must tell you. Your question concerning basic was answered at 1:45 this afternoon. We begin tomorrow a training to last seventeen weeks. Don't faint or do anything drastic, darling. The gang here really had a let-down feeling. Most of us felt certain that some credit for the past seven weeks would be forthcoming. Not only are we failing to get credit but the length of time has been extended. Some fun! I am sorry that it happened this way, but it could be much worse. I could be leaving for a combat zone as soon as I finish here, rather than have the prospect of going to school. In the long run, it may be by far the best, for it will certainly be strenuous training for six entire months. I think that we can reasonably hope for a furlough around Christmas, by which time I should be somewhere East—I earnestly hope.

The second thing that I must write about in haste concerns that little call I intend to make. Please remember that it is often impossible to get calls through at all, so if something goes wrong don't be too disappointed. Unless something goes wrong, I will make my attempt to call you at Aunt Carol's Sunday night (Aug. 8.) around six o'clock Pacific time or 8 o'clock Knoxville time. Because of supper, etc, here I will not be able to get to phone before that time. In case of difficulties, I will continue to try until eleven o'clock your time. I do hope I can make connections for it is very difficult to be sure of getting to a phone during the week, and the following week-end I hope to go to Los Angeles.

Darling, I can hardly wait to hear your voice again. I have so much to say and so little chance to say it. But even an eternity would not afford time to tell of our love. Don't forget: Sunday night at eight o'clock your time. I so hope it will go through.

Thine own,
Bushy

P.S. No time to write of my feelings concerning the ministery. That later!

***

August 5, 1943, Diary

On R.R.I. today Lt. Teague made the much-looked-for announcement that basic was to begin tomorrow with opening exercises. These weeks of "blood, sweat, and tears" to go for naught as far as our thirteen weeks are concerned. Everyone happy however that at last we are to get down to work with a definite goal set. Later today told that credit will begin as of last Mon.

Letters from Art's parents to Art

Friday Aug. 6, 1943

Dear Son:

I feel that I've neglected to write and I can't give any reason without seeming to complain about so much work and I don't want to do that. Sufficient to say that after weeks of patiently plugging, I have a big report in the final stage of completion for "Old brother Elliott" of State Headquarters. I feel somewhat elated when I think, and firmly believe I am right, that he can't ask for a report of any kind which I can't make.

Your Dad is in Nashville yesterday and today and I've had two very quiet days in office. I am hoping that he gets fixed up with glasses for he's been having a bit of trouble with his eyes.

The past few weeks have been extremely busy ones for canning. Sat. afternoon I went home about 1:30 and by Sun. night I had put up 30 jars of Soup mixture, 24 jars of corn and 1 ½ gal tomato juice. I plan a similar weekend this week. By this time next week I'll be working up the grapes. I dislike Sunday work but if poor old Fred and a million other Freds can work 7 days per week. I guess it won't hurt if I do all I can to enable them to have plenty to eat. Your Sunday letter came yesterday and we are always interested in your progress. I wouldn't carry that water experiment too far. Today's paper tells of four soldiers in Calif. dying from thirst. It must be interesting as well as encouraging from your standpoint to compare yourself with the other college men, who, no doubt, had many more opportunities for advancement in every way than you had. This period of training is probably the hardest you will have, and it can't last forever, and one can stand anything for a while, so every week brings you nearer the end of this phase of Army life.

Several of the home boys have been here on leave of late. Fay was home 3 days, Edd York [George Edward Buxton York] was home 5 days to be ordained as a minister during the Camp Meeting, Rollan Case, Noel Jones and Oakley Pennycuff have been here. Daily Bales is here now and I saw Denton Beerden & Ella Jean F. on the street this morning.

Waymon's boy is training as an aviation Cadet at New Port News, Va. He's in the shipping area but doesn't know where he will be sent. Ward Story is home on an extended furlough from State of Washington. The DuPont Co. is building a plant in state of Wash. and Edith Case's husband has been sent out there. Edith and the two

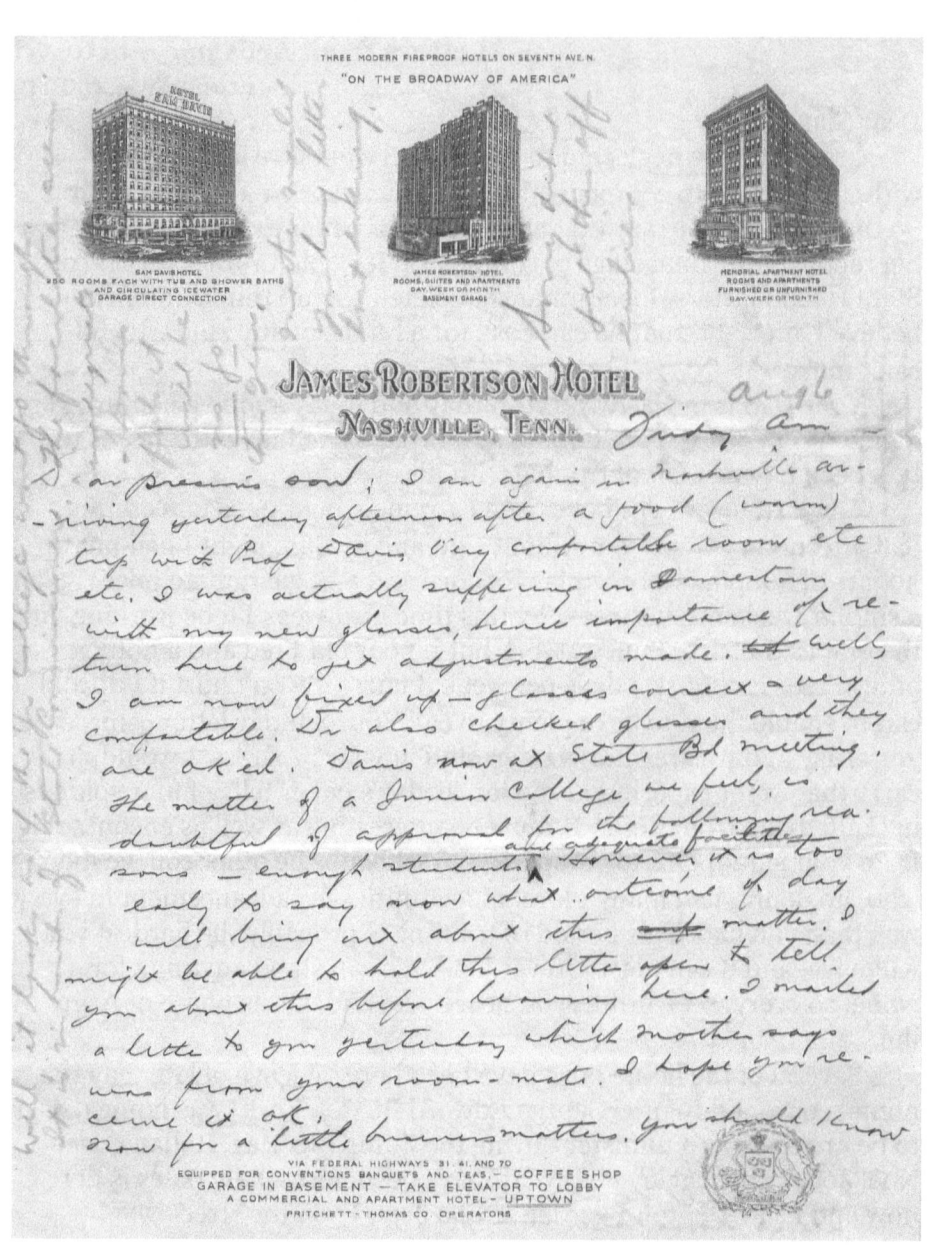

Letter from Art's Dad to Art, Aug. 6, 1943, page 1

that we have two (2) of your Bank Statements (Bank did not make up your June account. Do you want your statements mailed to you? I assume you should have them. The July balance should about $30.00 balance. Of course, you need only write me if you wish me to deposit any money for you anytime. I appreciate you will be getting your Army pay right along, but I am writing about any emergency which may arise, & you should know that you can always bank on Dad. Mother now has some $400.00 worth of war Bonds in her name. I intend to open up a checking account now for her by depositing $50.00 cash each month for her to fall back upon — just in case. Mother has had a wonderful garden this year & canning has gone ahead fine.

Dear boy, you should know and make allowance for how busy mother & I are in the office. I have to finish up & get out 1095 new questionnaires to all married men of our regiment — these must be out by September 1. Mother has her big Report for August 16 in good shape & she will have it ready, but it has been a big job. So glad that when I get back home there will probably be a good letter awaiting me from you. I hope you are very well and getting along nicely. Shapero Jr is now a Corporal, he jumped from Pvt. to Cpl — in other words he jumped 1st class Pvt. Hope you got copy my letter to Tommie Jones. God bless you dear boy. I will be leaving here about 2 or 3 P.M. & get home late tonight. Will try to locate

[left margin, vertical:] the Bible you want. I will see if our Chaplain here has any I hope. Good bye, dear boy, & may the Lord be with you.

children are here until houses can be built for workers of the Co. Our home people are seeing the U.S. for once.

I heard from Uldene. She and her husband are both working 6 days per week. She says Manza is enjoying here stay up there. She asked for your address and I'm going to suggest that she send you some cookies. She can make them on Sunday.

Your Dad will take care of your deposits when he comes. I think it wise to not carry a big lot of money. We can always send what you need.

We are taking a $20.00 bond per month beginning with the August salary. We thought that would be our share. Seems that we've never had as much rain or as many electrical storms as during the past few months. Mrs. Case's barn burned from lightening about two weeks ago. As luck would have it neither his nor Doris' car was up for the night.

We got the Moons for neighbors again, so I'll probably not have any Martin's next year. The Baptist minister has resigned and as yet they don't know who will be here. Bes. Parker initials are B.H. We are curious to know if he will come back. I was surprised on reading what you said about being a minister. It's a very wonderful profession of course, but if you should make the decision in favor of the ministry I hope you'll be a different minister than any I've known. To me it's a lazy man's job and I've never considered you lazy. You will, I believe, be a success in whatever field you choose.

Tenn. may not be like Calif but it was 90° in the shade yesterday afternoon. Today is some cooler.

Lots of love Mother

[Written in the margin of paper...] Wiley Bell been in office. Asked about you. Going to start paper here says Edd Bell is Capt. of an air squadron en route China. Today we had a letter from Typewriter Co. about Edd. Debts should be paid.

Letter from Art to Dotty
Camp Roberts, Calif.
August 9, 1943
Monday afternoon

My Dearest Heart,

Yesterday was the most wonderful day that I have had since I entered the service and for the glorious reason that I heard your voice once again. Even though the minutes passed with the flashing speed of light, it was a marvelous thrill just to hear you say just three little words. Darling, I wanted to talk for an hour; but, at the rate Mr. Bell's income was increasing, I could hardly continue. As I promised in my telegram, I began trying to call at one o'clock your time. With you, I waited for almost three hours and a half, but I would have waited twenty-four hours if necessary. We will have to try again sometime.

Ted, Ken, and I went to Church yesterday morning and it seemed as if we were dreaming. It still seems utterly impossible that we three, having been such close friends at school, should be together here. As I think I mentioned last week, Van Cise is just outside of Frisco now, and the four of us are going to try to get a pass and spend a week-end at the beach or in Frisco. Ken can't get a pass for several weeks, so Ted and I still hope to go to L.A. next Sat. if we can find someone going. It is almost impossible to go by train or bus and still have any time to see the sights.

I am very happy to hear that Carl and Floty are now Mr. and Mrs. However, I await details. Be sure and tell me all you can find out about A.S.T.P. and Carl's entery into school. When he gets settle, I would like to get his address. After all, I hope to be going through the same procedure soon. As I told you by phone, there has been another change and we are told now that our training is to last only thirteen weeks with one week gone. That means that if I do get to come East to school, it will be a full month earlier than before. Of course, as you see, Army plans may change hourly! However, it seems now that I may get away from here by the middle of November. There has been a Star Unit established here and we will be classified after basic. That should take one to two weeks. I'm dreaming of a white Christmas, dearest, and I'm only praying that we can see each other during that season.

Our work just at this time is not too strenuous although some days we are pulling in seventeen hours of it. The forty-five new men are getting oriented and we are repeating a great deal of the material already covered. We know now that what we are learning is a part of our actual training and that gives certain satisfaction. Wednesday we are to go through the gas chamber with gas masks. Bayonet training comes up frequently and I am at last getting adjusted to the idea of using the thing. At first I was repulsed by the idea, but now I am able to go through the drill with something of a detached attitude. It is not that I am becoming hard, but I am learning to get away from the practical use of my practice. We have never hiked more than five or six miles in a day, but soon we will begin to do more. Before we're through we do thirty miles in a day carrying our forty pound pack, nine pound rifle, and a few other incidentals. Darling, this training is marvelous. I am inclined to think it might have been tragic if I had stayed at Maryville and failed to extend my education via U.S. Army. War is still "hell," as Sherman said, and there are many things here that I must hate if I am true to myself. I do hate them and I could never compromise with forces that are at work here. However, the training itself in adjustment and discipline have a life-time value.

I have not written more concerning my thought and plans for the ministry, because I am still trying to find the final answer. A week ago last Sunday I knelt at the altar in the little Chapel which I attended and offered myself without reservation to Christ and His Service. I felt that it was a step closer to the certain knowledge of His plan, but I know too that I can see only a step at a time. With patience I await the answer to this, _our_ problem. I say "our" for it is our future I am considering. Meanwhile, let us pray for guidance.

A letter from Mother tonight indicates continued heavy work in the office. However, she tells of canning "30 jams of soup mixture, 24 jars of corn, and 1 ½ gal. of tomato juice" after working hours. What a woman! I think Dad was quite flattered by your letter concerning the Jefferson Bible. He is planning to write if he has not already done so.

Tomorrow I have K.P. again. Thank goodness it isn't Sunday work. Tomorrow night I will have to make up training missed while in the kitchen, and Wednesday night I will have to work. If I am lucky I will have time Thursday night to dash off a note. During the last few days, we have been getting up at 4:30; and, by the time the sun peeps over the rim of the eastern hills, we are out exercising.

I rarely get a chance to have good music now. The show last night with Jim Walker's Gleeman, the I.R.J.C. band, and Judy Garland was swell. At least that much of it was. The variety show featured these, but the joke and variety acts were extremely crude—disgusting in fact. I was proud of the job Jim has done. Judy was nice, but I know another songbird far sweeter.

Dearest, whether it be a soft note of music that filters through the other sounds, or a star lit sky in the early morning hours, or a half moon filling sky with its golden glow, I think of you constantly. Without our love I would be like a ship without ballast. Let us thank God that Love exists to fill our lives.

> Thine own,
> Bushy

Judy Garland, Soldier's Bowl, Camp Roberts, 8.8.43
(Mentioned in 8.9.43 letter.)

Letters from Dotty to Art
[August 4, 1943]
Wed. Night

Hi, Kindred Spirit!

Record Breakers, hence the informal salutation, darling. This is the first chance I've had to breath since Sunday night, and it is too hot to do that now that I have a chance! Sunday night I sat up till 12:30 working on a game for my party. Monday night I went to a party, came home and sat up again till 1:00 working on the same thing again. Wellmp, last night was my party and one of the girls stayed all night with me (and of course we caught up on lost time in our talking—too hot to sleep, anyhow). And tonight R.B. I went to a luncheon at noon,— Miss Lee was perfectly willing to let me off for an hour. If I would work late and make it up! At this rate I am going to feel more like a bride than the bride. You know—worn out with gadding? Ah me—it's a great life!

They are now playing Tchaikovsky ballet music, and as usual I feel the urge. Darling, I am afraid I wouldn't make a good preachers wife—I

141

am too fond of the art, the drama and the dance, the unconventional. Mostly the art (here).

Which reminds me. I talked (over the phone) to Marrianna last night, and said "Boo" to Pete. They are in town just long enough to be in and officiate at a couple of weddings. Phil Evaul has no street number—the name of the town is Centerville (I think). Try that, anyway. Must run now.

Love always,
Dotty

8.8.43 Camp Roberts, CA

My Light and Life,

Oh, darling, darling, darling! Just hearing your voice took my breath away so that I mostly just listened to you instead of saying all the things I had planned to tell you. So I'll tell you now. But the call wasn't long enough—we hardly got started—are you sure we talked three minutes? They surely did fly. On wings of song.

The wedding was utterly and simply beautiful. It was held at the Parmelee's house of Flo's grandparents. You've met the old couple haven't you? There was no best man. Carl and Rev. Hamilton came in from downstairs. Florence and I descended the stairs and transversed the length of the room to an improvised altar. Florence (who glowed from within and without) looked lovely in her long dress of white satin; long sleeves, slight train, short but pretty veil. My dress was blue, made by the very same pattern as Flo's except for short sleeves and no train. Florence carried white flowers—with roses, tube roses, and composite flowers made of white gladiolus petals wired together. My bouquet was of talisman roses and composite flowers of a deep peach gladiolus petals. It went with the dress like a vivid sunset contrasts with a patch of bright blue sky. But these little details are things you can read in the newspaper. As the triumphant-sounding strains of the wedding march sprang up after the last words of the ceremony. Mr. & Mrs. Alette turned and kissed very tenderly, and then stood beaming expectantly at the guests and family. Then everybody started greeting and kissing everybody. You know how it goes. I aided Flo as much as possible in escaping her grandmother's house, but turned traitor and filled their baggage full of rice before they left their own house for the honeymoon trip (to the cabin, naturally) itself!

Monday Night.

Whee. I just finished working eleven hours straight (thirteen hours away from home)! Nothing like it, eh, Bud? Only not very conducive to leisurely letter writing. My work just keeps piling up on all sides. Miss Lee said today that she was going to "order" me another helper. That would greatly relieve the congestion—after he, she, or it gets broken in. About 400 "employed cards" poured into to my box in about three days. That means over a hundred new employees per day! My average rate of filing the cards is 40 to 50 per hour, and with all the other things I have to do in addition to that I can't spend more than an hour or two out of eight for filing them; but they must be kept up to date. You see why I have to work overtime. The funny part is that I don't mind working overtime at all; nevertheless, I don't want to make a habit of it.

Colbert's death was quite a shock to me—I didn't even know he had been sick, but it seems that he had a heart attack about a month ago, and hadn't been very far out of bed since. He somehow symbolized Music-at-Maryville because he dominated it so, and as he was to me, so he must have been to others. In this way he will live for a long time to come.

Carl tells me that they have cut out the field of psychology in A.S.T.P., so what will you take instead, darling? He says he is going to Baton Rouge for classification, and will probably remain there for his training. Flo will join him there as soon as possible.

I think it is <u>terrible</u> that the army refuses to give you credit for you seven weeks of training—after all, you haven't been exactly paying around all the time! But as you say, worse things could have happened, and I am glad that it will be thirteen weeks instead of seventeen. Hmmm—that will put you through (if all goes well) sometime around the first week in November. You will, in all probability, get a furlough at that time. Oh, my dearest, I've thought and thought and thought about things lately, and the more I chase those thinks up one side of my brain and down the other, the more I come to the conclusion that we should start making plans right away for the greatest and most wonderful event in our lives. To me it no longer seems the thing to do to wait until the war is over. At first I thought it wise; now I think foolish and utterly useless to waste so much time. The war may last for several years longer, and when it ends you may be abroad and have to remain there for several more years. I would be in my thirties by then. It is worth waiting for, but what is the point in waiting? Why lose these precious productive years—the years of greatest vitality, vivaciousness, and spontaneity? I know that army life is very uncertain; that conditions would be far from ideal. <u>Conditions cannot be ideal in wartime</u>; since we cannot adjust the war to fit our plans, we must adjust our plans to fit the war. Darling, what is to hinder us from planning our marriage for November? What if it will be uncertain? Carl and Flo managed beautifully, despite the fact that their plans remained uncertain up until the very last moment, even to postponing the wedding two days after all the guests had been invited and everything. I realize that this should be the other way around—you urging me rather than me urging you—but these thoughts have been consuming my mind like a forest fire lately, and I must show you what is on my heart. I'll be waiting breathlessly and somewhat tremorously for the answer to this letter.

The night is far spent and so am I, and I am afraid I'll have to save my discussion on "Bushy, the Preacher" (that I had planned to put in this letter) till the next volume, and I do mean <u>tome</u>!

My love for you grows apace,

Dotty.

P.S. Clippings, etc. about wedding will be sent you as soon as I can gather them up.

Aug. 8, 43, Camp Roberts CA.
"This experience of dipping into the cross current of American life, being just one in eight million, is of lasting value for me." ASB Jr.

August 11, 1943, Diary

Gas chamber today.

———

Letter from Art to Dotty
Camp Roberts Calif.
August 11, 1943
Thursday

My Dearest,

Last night I was out until ten-thirty on a night problem after putting in a full day. The hour is late now and I must dash off a mere note. Tomorrow we have a very heavy day again, and I need sleep.

During the past week we haven't had a single free night and I will have no chance to write before Monday—if then. Sat. Ted and I are planning to get a pass and go somewhere—just to get away from camp and see what civilian life is like. I haven't been out of here in eight weeks now. We will probably go south toward L. A., but no chance to go all the way. Just some small town where we can relax and see some new scenery...

Field Selection Board working on battalion interviewing A.S.T.P. candidates. Accepting almost everyone. I may have to take engineering, but I know I would enjoy it very much.

If at all possible will write over the week-end. No letter from you yet, but expect one tomorrow.

News continues good on all fronts. I hold to my conjecture made last October that the war in Europe may be over by the new year. I fear it will be a tragedy if FDR re-elected.

You were very close to me as I looked at the beautiful moon and stars from the hills surrounding the Camp last night. I love you, dearest heart. I think of you constantly; I am working and living for our future.

Goodnight My Own,
Bushy.

———

August 12, 1943, Diary

Bayonet range for second time. Terribly hot but not quite as bad the second time. Grenade course this afternoon.

146

August 13, 1943, Diary

Morning tossing grenades for record. I couldn't even qualify. This afternoon to the bayonet course. After a strenuous workout in intense heat I felt devoid of energy. Recuperation comes quickly however. Am going entire day with no water, except that given us at lunch (2/3 of a cup) just to prove to myself that I can do it.

Letters from Art's parents to Art
[August 12 & 13, 1943]
Jamestown, Tenn
Friday afternoon
Awfully hot

Dear boy: Mother and I went to a show last evening and she was so tired today that she left for home early. Said she was going to pick the grapes. There are not many-due to early and late frosts. Seemed to have dropped off a sight.

So sorry I did not get the attached letter off to you from Nashville. We got home 1.00 A. M. Saturday, and I jumped into the work and been busy all week but seem to be a little ahead now.
Found your good letter and read same with pleasure and sympathy with you about delay of credit for the basic training these past few months. So sorry to say that after visiting several book stores and Bible houses in Nashville I could not find a zipper Bible. The demand has been very great so I was told, and stocks out of this article. Hope you can find one later or that I may be able to get one on next trip to city.

I deposited all your $80.00 to your account. I prefer that you let me supply you with the little spending money extra that you may want each month-as you feel you have need to write for such extra sums.
Here is money order for the $15.00 you will need after or even before you take off the week-end. Hope you have a nice time and will be glad to get the report of trip when you send us your regular letter. By the way, the souvenir cards of the Camp are very nice. We enjoyed your thought to send them on.

We are getting the clothes together you want sent out and I had the slippers fixed today. Hope to get the package off tomorrow morning.

Well, dear boy, I must get a little personal message off to you in this. I pray God may lead you into His will and work for you after the welter of the war is over. The ministry is a wonderful and scholarly calling. I hope that your decision may be made after an understanding of first, your ability to render a good service and appreciating as you should the sacrifice to be made in entering upon the work. I know you will pray over this matter a great deal and that God will make plain to you His will about it.

I must close as it is near mail time. Loving wishes go out to you constantly and be assured that you are in our thought always.
                    Dad

Encl Money Order

Mother is sending all the heavy socks she found and if this is the kind you need and more of them she can get them here. Package getting off this Sat Am
                    Dad

                                        Thursday, Aug. 12 '43
Dear Son,
        Your Sunday letter came today and we notice from recent letters that we can't expect to hear from you before Thursday of each week. We are anxious always to hear how things are going, but that having to go on to Nov. 1 isn't as easy as it might be. However, you can't tell how things will plan out. By the time new classes are being started in colleges for the Fall term, you may have new regulations or orders. Anyway Army rules are rules and must be obeyed. By the time you fellows get all fixed up and trained for whatever they give you, the war may be over and you will have had the training for nothing. I am enclosing clipping from last Sunday's Times which says your ASTP will be used after the war. You may get to go to China, India or somewhere. Any plans they have for you may work out to be for your best development and we hope that it will.
        Things are going along with us in the usual manner. Your Dad feels quite well at times and at other times not so good. However he keeps working away at over a 1000 forms to get out in addition to the regular

work. Yesterday I finished the big report which I've worked on for weeks, and since its not due to be finished until Sat. I feel pretty good about it.

We continue to have rain and regular Fall nights. Our garden has finished active growth and begun the curing up process. All the corn will be too hard to cook within a week's time, and my early beans are all gone. The tomatoes are practically gone. I've just about finished my canning with a considerable supply on the shelves: 64 jars beans, 62 corn, 52 soup mixture, 40 tomato with smaller numbers of cabbage, turnips, turnip greens and pickles. I also have over a bu. of beans of this year dried, and quite a few cans of fruit left over from last year's canning. I'll put up grapes over this week end and call it a day for this season. There is no fruit to be gotten for canning this year. Looper's got one basket of peaches which sold out for over $5.00 per Bu.

Our yard is looking best that its ever looked. We've gotten it mowed regularly and the rain has kept the grass in good condition. My gladiolas were simply gorgeous. I had about 200 of the Picardy and was able to give away a lot of bouquets to my flower loving friends. My late bulbs are now in full bloom and are really pretty. The magnolia is coming on fine and each branch has a nice cluster of fine big leaves. I am real proud of it. I'll need to cut the hedge again before Fall, but it too has been in good shape all summer.

Did I tell you that Leonard (Sprig) Story passed all his exams for Aviation Cadet. He is ready for training and thinks he is going from Ft. Eustis Va. To Florida for a 14 mo. Course. Waymon and Mary Ann met him at Knoxville yesterday. He gets only a 3 day leave, and they planned to spend the time at Pag's in Maryville.

Fay left Ft. Oglethorpe Monday but we haven't heard yet where he went. The folks went down to see him Sunday. Clarence is still out of Looper's Store. We went to Clark range two days this week to help pick green beans.

We don't hear about the Mulinix boys since the Red Cross has a paid worker (Lola Gaudin) who has taken over the work and with it got the Red Cross Directory about camp etc so Dr. M. has no occasion to come to office.

We read in today's paper where the Selective Service System is to help with the reemployment of returning soldiers, so I guess we are in for a nice sweet job.

A group of 25 left here Mon. and 13 were turned down. Luther Beaty accepted, Tom Wheeler Jr. rejected (eyes).

Aug. '43

Bought the underwear this a.m. and will get off package tomorrow. Your Dad will write tomorrow and send money order. He deposited your money.

Glad you got fixed up with glasses. I hope to get new ones at first opportunity to get away.

We send all good wishes and lots of love.
Mother

(Written in margin of letter)
No York College this year. A survey showed that we don't have the facilities

Wed. Night. [Aug. 11]

Dearest,

I have picked up so many odd bits of news about people and stuff that this will be a very conglomerate letter, I am afraid. But I hope you like it.

Kittie (Bennett) Chandler showed me a letter from Kay Estes (something or other), and it contained quite a bit of news about Maryvillites. Cherie Curtis is a dietician in St. Luke's Hospital in N.Y. Roger Graham and Lorraine Adkins (remember them) finally got hitched. Joan Humann married a 4-F guy from her home town. Wonder how many other fellows were on the string when it happened? Joe Dickenson and Spike Tinley washed out of O.C.S.. Incidentally, Pieper and Mc Clelland are both stationed as officers in the place where it happened. Hmmmm. Does that strike you as odd, too?

I am enclosing clippings about the wedding. Will send more as soon as I can obtain the papers from which to cut them. (Guess they didn't like my picture—it didn't appear in either paper).

David was supposed to arrive home tonight (today sometime), but has not yet put in his appearance.

Heard from Janice today. She loves her new job as D. Rel. Ed. in a Detroit church, and sends her regards to you.

Joey (The little black dog next door) got killed the other day. Poor dog—it was right cute.

Good night, my darling.

[Dotty drew music scale with notes.]

P.S. Can you read it? And do you know what words go with it? You could guess.

August 14, 1943 - Diary

Left camp about one o'clock with Pete Van Blancon on first pass. Had planned to go with Ted Kidder but our plans were again thwarted. This time he had K.P. on Sunday. We hitch hiked to Santa Cruz, about one hundred and twenty miles up the coast. It is amazing to find so much range in temperature within fifty miles of Roberts. Soon after leaving this vicinity we found trees growing, vegetables in abundance, and cool breezes.

My Dearest Own,

Sundays are wonderful, 'cause they are days when I have time to write you. This one was very hot, but very nice. I got to S. School "on-timer" than usual, showed my youngsters who was boss (for once), then got into my nice (?) hot robe and settled down in my seat for Dr. Lloyd's sermon. For once he didn't have an extremely outlineable, thoroughly followable speech as is his usual work. He based his speech on psalm #29, centering the talk around the last part of verse nine. The main thought was that since all was created by God, that all things were temples at all times, and that all things and peoples in the universe bespoke the glory of God in some way. He quoted a whole flock of figures and facts about atoms and molecules and the universe and how fast things travel and things that make you dizzy to think of them. You know. I had a nice chat with him afterwards. Hal graduates this week, darling—did you know that?

Carl left today, due to command to return to duty; it cut his leave short by about three days, but even at that he and Flo had a whole weeks' honeymoon in the mountains, and that is pretty good for times like these—yes, no? Flo spent the afternoon down here with Mary Ruth and me—we put on our bathing suits and had not only a sunbath, but also more fun. Flo and I had a silly dancing spree. She is to join Carl in two or three weeks.

Say, guess what! Kitty Bennet—Chandler's husband is now in specialized training (engineering) at Columbus Ohio, and he writes her that he will be able to <u>live off-campus with</u> her all the time during the specialized training. Carl expects to be granted the same privilege. Does that mean anything to you, Bud?

You mentioned on one of your letters that you had received a check for $80.50, and that you sent $80.00 of it home to be put in the bank. Now that puzzles me greatly. How could you buy new stationary, call me long distance from Calif., and have enough money for incidentals until the next check arrives <u>All</u> out of the fifty cents you kept? That just doesn't add up—which of us is goofy? Tell me, what is the secret of your economy, Master McBushing?

I mentioned David's being home, didn't I? Well, he is, and looks swell. Darling, do you mind if I have a cousinly "date" with him? Speaking of cousinly goings-on—Mary Ruth and I kissed Carl goodbye today. He is our cousin now, you know. Wellll—cousin-in-law, anyway.

I have been thinking and praying daily about your call to the ministry, my dearest. I, too feel that a final and definite answer to the question has not yet come to me. I think perhaps God will make His Will known to us as a unit rather than to you and then to me.

I felt you with me tonight, as I gazed at that gorgeously bright, full moon. I felt your arms around me, your lips upon my hair; I heard you whisper sweet nothings into my ear, heard you relate again the wondrousness of our great love, of the infinite promise of our life together. Then said I unto you, I love you—with my whole heart and mind and body I love you—from the depths of my soul, I love you.

Eternally yours
Dotty.

August 17, 1943, Letter from Art to Dotty

Santa Cruz, Calif.
Aug. 14, 1943
Saturday Night 11:30

My Dearest,

In a cozy room within a half mile of the blue-clear Pacific, I sit. The fog rolled in from the sea two hours ago and the full moon is hidden now from view, but before it hid its face it whispered a message of love from and to you.

With luck that was doubly disappointing, Ted drew K.P. for tomorrow just as I had done for four weeks earlier when we planned to take a pass. There was no recourse; I came away and left him behind. Luckily, Pete Van Blarcom asked for a pass also this week, and we decided to come together. Although Ted and I had planned to go South to see the scenery there, Pete and I ended up a hundred and twenty-five miles North of dear old Camp Roberts. Ted came to Santa Cruz and we had heard glowing accounts of the place.

Our trip today was made in a leisurely fashion and proved quite educational. We rode on a truck with fifty or more fellow soldiers for eight-five miles to Salinas, the "salad bowl" of the world. The truck bed provided a capital view of the beautiful Salinas, which is beautiful as soon as one leaves the vicinity of Camp Roberts. We had almost forgotten in the past eight weeks that trees still grew green. The fields of beans, lettuce, sugar beets, etc. were often a mile long and three or four hundred yards wide. All of them were watered by irrigation. Of interest also was a government rubber farm where things seemed to be bouncing right along. [ha!]

At Salinas we enjoyed a refreshing bite and did a bit of shopping. With almost no delay we were picked up by four consecutive cars to arrive in Santa Cruz about six-thirty.

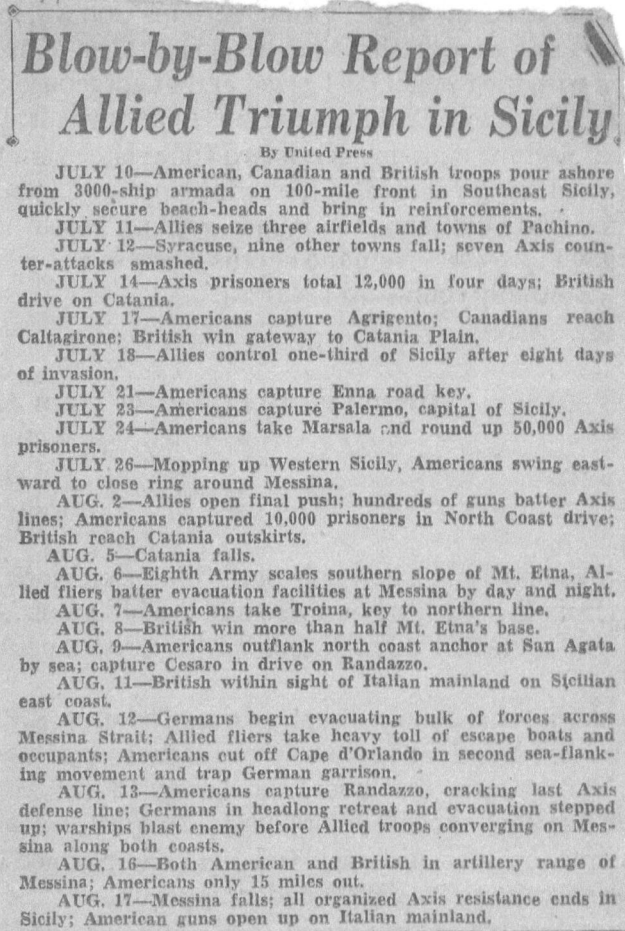

Blow-by-Blow Report of Allied Triumph in Sicily

By United Press

JULY 10—American, Canadian and British troops pour ashore from 3000-ship armada on 100-mile front in Southeast Sicily, quickly secure beach-heads and bring in reinforcements.

JULY 11—Allies seize three airfields and towns of Pachino.

JULY 12—Syracuse, nine other towns fall; seven Axis counter-attacks smashed.

JULY 14—Axis prisoners total 12,000 in four days; British drive on Catania.

JULY 17—Americans capture Agrigento; Canadians reach Caltagirone; British win gateway to Catania Plain.

JULY 18—Allies control one-third of Sicily after eight days of invasion.

JULY 21—Americans capture Enna road key.

JULY 23—Americans capture Palermo, capital of Sicily.

JULY 24—Americans take Marsala and round up 50,000 Axis prisoners.

JULY 26—Mopping up Western Sicily, Americans swing eastward to close ring around Messina.

AUG. 2—Allies open final push; hundreds of guns batter Axis lines; Americans captured 10,000 prisoners in North Coast drive; British reach Catania outskirts.

AUG. 5—Catania falls.

AUG. 6—Eighth Army scales southern slope of Mt. Etna, Allied fliers batter evacuation facilities at Messina by day and night.

AUG. 7—Americans take Troina, key to northern line.

AUG. 8—British win more than half Mt. Etna's base.

AUG. 9—Americans outflank north coast anchor at San Agata by sea; capture Cesaro in drive on Randazzo.

AUG. 11—British within sight of Italian mainland on Sicilian east coast.

AUG. 12—Germans begin evacuating bulk of forces across Messina Strait; Allied fliers take heavy toll of escape boats and occupants; Americans cut off Cape d'Orlando in second sea-flanking movement and trap German garrison.

AUG. 13—Americans capture Randazzo, cracking last Axis defense line; Germans in headlong retreat and evacuation stepped up; warships blast enemy before Allied troops converging on Messina along both coasts.

AUG. 16—Both American and British in artillery range of Messina; Americans only 15 miles out.

AUG. 17—Messina falls; all organized Axis resistance ends in Sicily; American guns open up on Italian mainland.

"Blow by Blow Report of Allied Triumph in Sicily,"
July 10 to Aug. 17, 1943

Sunday Morning

Immediately upon arrival we went to the USO to inquire about a hotel room. All hotels were filled, but a number of private homes were recommended. After making a reservation we began a tour of the city. Our first destination was to the best restaurant in town. We found a deluxe coffee shop in a large hotel which reminded me of the Farragut where we ate a few times. It is difficult for you to realize how wonderful it is to get back to civilian life.

(Continuing the above) For eight weeks now we have seen hundreds of uniforms and nothing else. It was most pleasant to sit in a quiet dining room and spend an hour in leisurely eating delicious food. After our meal we walked down to the beach under the light of a full California moon. What we found was a deserted beach with breakers rolling in and a great fog bank coming in from the sea. As we listened to the waters roll over the sand, the moon was snatched from our view and behind the curtain.

We continued along the beach sand and found the reasons for the absence of people on the beach. In the amusement area we found a miniature Coney Island. Every amusement that one might imagine— and many that you couldn't imagine. We merely passed through and returned to find our room and bed.

We awoke this morning (about nine) to find a heavy fog still over the city and a dampness in the air that was most welcomed. (The atmosphere at Roberts is always dry.) It was with a great deal of luxurious feeling that we remained in bed and laughed at the visionary Sgt. who couldn't get us out of bed. After a light breakfast we found the Presbyterian Church on a high hill in the town. The minister, Rev. Seigle, is a former missionary to China; and I seem to recall the name from some past incident. The church was small, but well-filled, and the sermon was good. It is a real experience to get back to a real church for worship. After church, we again enjoyed an excellent meal at our deluxe coffee shop.

From our talks with various people who picked us up, we gathered that Santa Cruz is very popular resort in this section. It is a town of about fourteen thousand population, many of whom seem to be older couples who have retired. One kind lady who picked us up told us of coming to this country from England twenty-five years ago. Another interesting character was the father of one of the eight surviving officers of the "Arizona" at Pearl Harbor.

In the afternoon we returned to the beach and enjoyed a forty minute boat ride on the Pacific waters. Now I have dipped my feet in both oceans, but I would love to enjoy them more.

We arrived in Salinas (forty miles from Santa Cruz and eight-five miles from Roberts) at six-thirty last night via the thumb. From there we decided to bus or train our way home. After a couple of misunderstandings and mis-directions by the station agent we found ourselves on a home bound train at 10:30. The train lost two hours between Salinas and Camp arriving here at 2:30 this morning. Since we arose at 4:45, I did not get an over-abundance of shut-eye. Nevertheless, it was a wonderful weekend.

Today I was accepted by the Field Selection Board for A.S.T.P. I will probably be placed in engineering. Your letters of the 10th & 12th just received tonight. No time to talk over the points that you mention, but I wish it could be an unquestionable "yes." More as soon as possible.

> Thine Own,
> Bushy

Letter from Dotty to Art
Thurs. Aug. 19

Darling,

How charming! I was sitting at the table eating (stuffing it in) my supper when up drove a man on his motorcycle. And he stopped at our door. I knew it was for me, so I started to jump up, but Mother beat me to it. Mmmm. Best dessert I can think of! Charming also is the pin that fell out of the letter. I'll wear it proudly, my dearest. What are you trying to do—"give her the gun?"

The weather here is wonderful, absolutely great. I wish you were here to enjoy it with me. It has turned deliciously cool, the sort of cool that makes the life in you spring way up—energizing, enervating, and quite invigorating, the sort of cool that makes you dream of going back to school, buying fall clothes, and of just starting things in general. I feel good!

I am so glad you got away from camp for the weekend. Morale-building, what? The trip sounded quite exciting, and I know the change did you a world of good. For your information—the tree and grass here are such are such a glowing green that it takes my breath away to look. This is not meant to make your mouth (or is it eyes) water, but merely to holster your faith in humanity or something.

This is the first night this week that I have spent at home. Had more <u>fun</u>. May I tell you about it? O.K., I'll tell you anyway. Monday was my date with David. Aunt Carol had planned a picnic supper and it was at Uncle Charlie's place (on the bluffs, just off the new Maryville highway). Since there wasn't room for nine people to ride all the way in Uncle West's car, David and I took the trackless trolley out from town, disboarded at the University Farm, and started hoofing it from there on out (about 2 miles, they say). Uncle West and company picked us up and stuffed us in just a little ways before we got there. "And company" included Aunt Carol's family, our family, Aunt Carol's sister, and Mary. We had fun together, as always. When we got back to town, David and I (walking most of the way from U.T. farm) we went to see "China." Slightly propogandous as are all war pictures, but otherwise very fine.

Tuesday night I gather up my Intermediates and took them out to the Park. We took a picnic supper, and after eating we went riding on all the gadgets. I felt just as if I were one of them. There were nine of us; I didn't have a bit of trouble keeping them together, because we all rode the same things at the same time, and what was even more amazing was the lack of dissension over what we were going to ride next—everybody agreed with everybody else. Thus we had a lot of fun <u>together</u>, creating a sense of unity that was very beneficial to all of us. I wonder why we never went to the park, dearest? It is scads of fun. Along with the kids I rode the merry-go-round, the swings, the airplanes, the "dodge-em" cars, and went fishing. I was lucky fishing and won a gadget that is fun to play with—a ball to be thrown into a cup on a stick—Dad and Mother even have fun playing with it. All in all, it was a highly successful evening. You were especially with me as I rode the ferris wheel, and gazed upon the broad expanse of evening sky.

Last night "T" (Theresa) and I went to the show at her theater (her father owns one of the smaller theaters on Market St.) right after work. From there we came on out to David's house where there were a number of the old hiking club gang (whats left of it) gathered to see David. We talked, joked, played "Pit," and ate cookies & ice-cream, and had genuine fun. Again. You know hiking club gangs. Or don't you?

My own true one, no matter how many things I do, how many places I go, I think of you constantly, and am continually making plans for <u>Our</u> Future. Which I hope ain't too far away. Good night, darling. I love you, oh, so <u>much</u>.

      Your
        Dotty.

My Dearest Own,

At last I find a chance to sit down with a little time to write at some length in answer to your letter suggesting the possibility of Heaven being closer than we had formally thought. There are many things to consider in our all-important decision and I think I have gone over almost every side to the question during the last few days for I have thought of little else. (In fact, I have even been dreaming that we were already settled down.) There is one thing about which there is absolutely no question: both of us are very much in love and both of us anxiously await the day when we can unite our lives. The sooner that is possible, the better. However, there are a number of points to reflect upon.

As I pointed out in a brief note I wrote a few days ago, I have almost given up hope of being S.T.A.R. Unit (where we are finally classified in A.S.T.P) is to be set up here—having formerly been at Stanford University. That will take up two to four weeks after our thirteenth week and in all probability we will be sent directly to school from there. I'm still keeping my fingers crossed but I fear that it will be no soap. This is merely a matter of circumstance. There is another reason to weigh against our desire to go ahead with November plans.

Along with everything else connected with A.S.T.P., our rating at the end of training is uncertain. However, there is a definite chance that we will get a commission if we make the grade. Darling, I am going to work my fingers to the bone, if it takes it, to make a good record for us while in the Army. Psychology is closed as a branch of specialized training now and I cannot qualify for language. I will be placed in the engineering branch with a bunch of engineering students. The competition will be stiff and the schedule tough. I am trying to say that the adjustment to Army school life while I was at the same time adjusting to married life might prove a big job. I wonder if we can afford to take any chances for the difference of a few months.

On the other side of the picture, there are a number of forces favoring a green light on our planning. Your suggestion is absolutely valid that we are not growing younger and that the best time of our lives to begin life together is right now. I think it would be out of the question to consider putting it off until I got out of the Army now. Another thing favoring our planning is the fact that experiencing these chaotic times together will do much to weld our lives into a single unit.

In former paragraphs I made no mention whatever of the financial end of marriage. That must not be forgotten. I do have a job, 'tis true, but $50 per month isn't a great deal to offer a bride. To delay immediate plans would give me a chance to save up enough to get started in some semblance of comfort.

My suggestion is this: let us practice our overworked patience just a bit further, sweetest heart. By Spring I should know something more definite concerning my future with the Army. I am supposed to get a week off every three months while going to school. My first furlough should come about March 1st. Who knows but that we might be able to hesitate no longer by that time. Meanwhile, I want you to plan to see me as soon as I get East whether it be in Knoxville or at some university. I am going going to have a little trinket for you (size 5). Again--------Time catches me behind! 'Tis now Sunday night, late, and I have just returned from a very fine Vesper Service with Ken and Ted. We heard two sermons this morning. I promise another long letter at the earliest possible moment. The glorious dawning of _our_ day will come. When it does "Heaven can wait." (which I saw last night.) Good show. Anxious to hear of Carl's plans. Plan to write soon. Also will write Mary Ruth when she gets to school.

Darling, patience! Our love is Eternal.
Thine own,
Bushy
P.S. Mailed 3 copies of Camp Paper. Hope they arrive O.K.

Letter from Dotty to Art
[August 22, 1943]
Sunday Night

My Dearest Darling,

I'm still hungry. I had a sandwich, a glass of milk, and a small piece of watermelon, yet I am unsatisfied. Perhaps it isn't food I crave. Really, I've had plenty to eat, more than plenty to wear (it's getting warm again), and plenty of spiritual nourishment; even almost plenty of music for once, but there is still something lacking. I am fully aware of the fact that I can't have that certain something yet for a while, but you can't stop me from dreaming. They say if your writing goes up, that's a sign of optimism. I must be very optimistic tonight, if so, _for_ I have been having trouble all afternoon with my lines slanting upward. Which reminds me, Soldier, did you know how irrepressible and a lot of other peculiar things I am? Huh. You'll find out.

This has been a lovely Sabbath. The Sunday school class situation gets better and better. Reason—I have been depending more and more on the power of God rather than my own highly adequate resources. I find that I fail when I do not ask God's help. Another factor contributing to the build-up of my morale was that the piano in the primary room now plays all its keys instead of only six or seven as it was in its previous sticky condition. Then I went upstairs to get ready for choir and there sat Al Cole, the good tenor—remember? He has been in Alabama for some time. Oh, joy. He sang in church. Our sermon today was by Rev. Chas. Marston (Maryville grad. 50 years ago —also remember?), and I didn't once wish he would hurry up and finish it—I could have listened quite a spell longer. He spoke of the certainty we have in Christ Jesus, a certainty we must hang onto, for it is easy to lose if we do not use it. See Acts 1:1-4 for text. Add to all these things a good dinner, some good symphonies, some letter writing, some singing at Flo's, some Christian Endeavor, and you have my day. I am sure you must have heard me singing "Because" and "Gipsey Sweetheart" and "Hills of Home," because I sang them directly to you. I've had music pent up in my soul for a long time—I had to let it out this afternoon, at least a little of it.

Mary (Japanese Mary) called me just now to a come-as-you-are-now party for Thursday night. Hah—I am dressed in my brown & white striped seersucker dress (garnished with an inkspot), long stockings rolled to the ankles, and Mary Ruth's white shoes. I have been running my fingers through my hair and it is sort of standing out from my head like a something or other. That promises to be a good party.

Monday P.M.   —

Guess what—I've already bought my ticket and made my reservation on the streamliner for my trip for the 5th of Sept. I have written Harriet and Jenks, etc. to start dreading my arrival. This will be my first long trip—and will I be green! But I know I'll love every minute of it.

I went to the show tonight with Mary Alice and Mary Ruth (my last time with M.R. for quite a spell); we saw "Cabin in the Sky," starring only colored people (Rochester was the hero)—there wasn't a white person in it—and I was surprised at how very good it was.

Here are some address if you want them:

Pvt. R.W. Schwarzwalder
Platoon 507, Battalion 8
Parris Island, S. Carolina

Mrs. Arlene H. Schw.
350 Fitszwatertown Rod.
Willow Gove, Pa.
of H.M. Higgins

Pvt. Carl Alette 33593124
Co. A. ASTP (STAR) Unit #3880
Arkansas State College
Jonesboro, Arkansas.

Carl is just there for classification—he may be sent elsewhere pronto.
        So long for now.
                    My love to you,
                        Dotty.

August 23, 1943, Diary

Start of the 4th week of basic. To R.R.I. this week for second work out.

Letter from Art to Dotty
Camp Roberts
Tues. Night Aug. 24, [1943]

My Dearest,

Tonight we have a whole half hour for ourselves between preparation for rifle inspection, inspection, a training film, etc. However your morale building letter of last Thursday came last night, and I do love to hear. Perhaps you do too, so I write. That isn't the only reason; darling, for I walk, and talk with you many times a day tho I can't always get it on paper.

We continue our work on the P.R.I. Range. Almost all of the work is done by the "coach and pupil method which I believe I have described. It has many advantages, and we learn a great deal from helping each other. I am working on preliminary rifle instruction with a swell guy from Birmingham. Unlike many of the boys, he is a hard worker and we are really getting a great deal from our work. I think the results will show up next week when we fire, for they tell us that a rifleman is made before he fires a shot.

Oh, I almost forgot to tell you about a little outing I had last night. Ten fellows were picked out from each company in our battalion to go to Paso Robles (15 miles south) for a little swim. We got out of an hour of repetitious instruction, leaving about seven. We swam for a half an hour and then saw a little of town. There wasn't much to see, but it was civilization. We ate a bite, shopped a bit, and returned to meet our bus at nine. I mailed a card from there which I hope you receive. The picture is one of a very old mission only three miles from Camp. If I get any chance, I intend to see this. There are hundreds of interesting sights in and around here and I do not have time to do any of them justice.

I just found out yesterday that the site of this camp was once an estate belonging to Randolph Hearst. However, I can't see what he might see in this section for an estate, although certain seasons are probably very nice.

Found a very good book on 'The Wisdom of the Chinese. It contains excerpts from the various philosophical writings. I can read two or three paragraphs and put it down without losing the thread of thought.

It is almost time now for inspections and I must finish this. We have inspection every night this week, and training films three nights. The C.O. (Company Commander) is doing everything possible to make crack shots out of his boys.

Goodnight and sweetest dreams, my sweet. I look forward to every letter you write with happy anticipation. I constantly pray for the continued increase and blessing of

<blockquote>
Our Love,
Bushy
</blockquote>

P.S. I hope you can translate this scribble.

P.S. II. The news is breaking quick and fast during these days. History will have many pages for these important events. Peace will come!

Letter from Dotty to Art
Wed. August 25 [1943]

My Very Dearest,

One letter got here in very good time, the other—not so good. I received the one postmarked the 21st on the 24th; the one postmarked the 23rd arrived here on the 25th. I wonder how long it would take if it were not airmail?

Thanks so <u>much</u> for the pictures—I am delighted with them. I carry them around in my purse, and run to take a fresh peek every little while. You've no idea how it refreshes me just to gaze into those wonderful eyes, and that nice big mouth full of teeth with an irresistible impulse to grin right back at you. You look more better all the time, Darling. I may keep the pictures, mayn't I? And <u>who</u> is the <u>tall</u>, handsome brute striding beside you in one of the pictures? He makes you look no taller than me! Mary Ruth is about to die off because I can't tell her who he is, why he is, what's his name, where did he come from, is he nice, is hitched or attached? or! Please enlighten, for both our sakes. [Photo, "Ken Cooper & Art 8.8.43, Camp Roberts."]

Ken Cooper & Art 8.8.43, Camp Roberts

I read your letters through so many times that Mother accuses me of memorizing them. I do, almost! Hmmm—March ain't so bad, brother. I can think of a pretty nice wedding that happened in March. Just looking forward to any <u>certain</u> time makes it seem a lot closer. If only we can start now doing part of the planning, then when the day really does come we'll be better able to carry out the plans effectively and quickly if need be. It gives me such a thrill to talk about making plans!! Shall we try to make it in March? That is quite agreeable to me. Then if I can see you before that time and receive that little trinket, I'll have a little time in which to be "engaged." Hah.

Darling, I love you, whether you get a commission or not, so don't do a great deal of worrying on that score. (Pardon the wavy lines—Mary Ruth ran me into the bathroom to finish this so she could turn out the lights and perchance get some sleep—you know how much "desk space" there is in here!) Guess what—Carl wound up in the engineering branch, too. What do you think of that? He will have a tougher time than you, because he hasn't had nearly as much math. I hear tell that in A.S.T.P. the study is quite intense, but the discipline, etc. are not nearly as bad as in basic. As for adjusting to married life, do you <u>really</u> think that would be <u>hard</u>?

Now for the financial part. I figure that by March we together will have saved a tidy little sum. Quite a bit of what I save will be spent on the wedding (how much or how little depending on how elaborate our plans are.) I hope to save enough so that I will not have to work for at least a month or two after we are married. After that, I am afraid I'll have to work, regardless of your scruples about the matter—at least a part time job until the war is over, unless your rank rises sharply enough so that your pay plus my allotment will cover expenses. I'm really not very expensive, and do not expect much "comfort" until we have our own home. Flo plans to work full time.

Last night all of us and Flo went to Tyson house to hear an outdoor concert of recorded music. Tyson House is connected with the university—it is a sort of religious and recreational center; it is a lovely old mansion-like place, with gobs of beautiful sloping lawn, part of which forms an amphitheater. A loud speaker affair sends the recorded music out for quite a distance on the evening air. The concerts (there is a series of four) are sponsored by the Knoxville Symphony Orchestra. You were very close to me as I as reclined on the lawn, looked at the stars through the branches of the beautiful and varied old trees, listened to the good music, and—thought of you.

It is getting very late, and I must lie myself off to bed in the very near future. Speaking of futures, ours is wonderful because of

Our Love,

Dotty.

Letter from Dotty to Art

Friday Night [August 27, 1943]

My Dearest,

No, the paper is not mine, nor the pen with which I am writing, nor the desk at which I am sitting, nor the room in which I am spending the night. But I am me, and that which I am writing—it comes from me. Mary Alice was sick today and also alone because her husband is working on his brother's farm; I came to pay her a short visit after work, and here I remained—ensconced for the night. She is in the habit of retiring early, so I'd better make this short. Shucks.

Now where were we? Guess I had better wait until I hear from you before I get too involved in all this planning business. I have a whole raft of questions to ask you as soon as we start the "planning project."

It seems as if I have gone somewhere or done something special four or five nights out of seven for the past three or four weeks. It certainly makes the weeks fly and also makes them interesting, and yet, even though I want the time to pass as rapidly as possible, I can't help feeling a sense of regret that time must always pass so swiftly. Last night Record Breakers turned out to be something quite unusual. It was, first of all, a come-as-you-are party (I described my attire in a previous letter, nicht wahr?) We had quite a variety of fashions—shorts, halters, bare feet, negligees, street clothes, etc.—I didn't look so bad, after all. Mary had a number of cute, silly games planned—we all laughed a lot. Then came the refreshments, and if you know Mary like I know Mary you know that the refreshments were wonderful. Lemonade, mixed candies (mostly gumdrops) and a luscious Devil's food cake iced with chocolate fudge. Mmmm. Yes, our mouths were watering too, but Florence had cut but one or two pieces when the whistle sounded for a surprise blackout. [These were common during the war.] Imagine our surprises (and consternation) to be caught in the midst of such an intriguing process! Flo quick cut the cake and we all grabbed for a piece before we turned out the lights. Thus we had a good time sitting in the dark munching refreshments and singing, singing the good old campfire numbers (minus the campfire!) Secondly the party was a shower for Flo—cute little 10¢ gadgets mostly. Ho, hum. Why should we play any records?

Oh, oh. Most <u>awful</u> thing. Like a situation you might read about in a book. Hold on, and don't split <u>both</u> sides—Mary Alice gave me permission to tell you. She and Foster live in a rooming house, and have just the <u>one</u> room, single beds, semi-private bath. She didn't expect him home till late tomorrow, otherwise she would never have invited me to spend the night with her. Well, to proceed with the story Mary Alice was already in bed and I am sitting here (in nothing but my slip) writing to you. Comes a knock on the door, and Mary Alice opens it (a crack) to reveal—you guessed it—Foster, wanting to know why he can't come in! Oh, woe, oh embarrassing situation! So the poor boy had to go sleep with one of his relatives. I sat in petrified silence until Mary Alice had explained the situation and shut the door on him. Then we both just laughed and laughed. It was tragic but oh, so <u>funny</u>! What would you have done in my shoes? Yes, Dear, I love you, too. And that love flies out across the country to kiss you goodnight.

> Your
> > Dotty.

Letter from Art's parents to Art
Friday Aug 27 [1943]

Dear Son:

We are always glad to hear about your work and all that is happening to you, but this getting up at 5:30 and keeping on the job until midnight doesn't sound so restful. I can only repeat "It can't last forever."

The Engineering doesn't sound as if you are going to get just what you wanted, but in this war game one must take what is given, and again I repeat "Better Engineering with training than being a private with no training. No doubt but what the training will be a very thorough job. Melba Reid has been in service nearly 18 mo. and has never done anything but train. Rolland is still in training and Mr. Case says that he has given up trying to find out what he is training for. Seems that it's a continuation of his live-low.

Your Dad had quite a nice trip to Nashville yesterday. A long day from 5 am to 10 last night, and the weather was hot, dry and dusty—but getting his glasses adjusted was worth the trip. Excepting the visit by two big (size) Army officers from the Cookville Area, I had a regular routine day.

I agree with you that one can't tell what the morrow will bring. Just listen to what we are in for: Beginning Sept. 1 we must put this

[Stamp stamped here on the letter that has questions and spaces for the answers.] on the back of all our 3800 cover sheets and fill in the requested information. Then we begin a record (3 copies) from my big book, giving the order no., Serial No., Name, race classification plus the information found on stamp as above. That means handling the book and coversheet at same time and what a sweet job its going to be. What about getting a 30 day furlough for the month of Sept.?

Sgt. [Sergeant Alvin C. York] sold the Café this week to Charlie Rains. Took Charlie's property and so much cash and Charlie plans to use the building as a store building. We lose our neighbors " The Rankins" next week. Iva & Allie are moving to Pleasant Hill to work in the hospital. They are getting good jobs and the children will go to school. Nerene enters high school.

Barbra Lyons is home from Summer School. She will graduate next year and hopes to teach. A lot of the school this year will be taught by high school grads.

Haven't heard about Chesterlyn lately but am sure she will go back to U.T. Seems that her engagement is off in spite of the fact that she had agreed to a Catholic wedding. He (the lucky fellow) was to have come in June, telephone that he couldn't get away until July and didn't come at all.

We will soon have chickens big enough to fry if you come on that furlough. We have our wood in and cellar full but no time to cook. Will send you some more cookies soon as I can get either nuts or raisins to use in them. Either would keep them fresh.

We are getting the Blue Books together and will send you any we think you can use. Try to get them off in day or so.

Awfully dry and hot here now. No rain for about two weeks and growing things are getting thirsty.

Will send this along and try to write soon again.
Love and all good wishes from us both.
Mother

P.S. Your weekly letter came Thursday PM. and the letter from Mary came Saturday a.m. This is the longest time for any of your Sunday letters to come. We usually get them Thursday a.m. or Wednesday p.m. The folder "Camp Roberts" is quite interesting. Thanks for it.

[The following note from Art's father was written in the margins of the letter.]

Dear Boy: Just a line. Mother took the afternoon off. Very warm. Sgt [Sergeant Alvin C. York] home in bed with Rheumatism. The letter from Mary was very nice. So glad you could write her. We must try to write her too. By the way, whenever I go to Nashville I always try to pick up a book or two. One of the best, I believe was "The Conquest of Fear" by Basil King. It is very good, I do want you to have and read it sometime. I bought it for 69¢ at the Methodist Book Store. I will list in my letter to you, the book I recently picked up. <u>God Bless You</u>, dear son, from <u>Dad</u>

I am making wonderful improvement in trouble of Kidneys. I am very very much better in this regard. Much love.
Hope you got my letter with NY Times clippings? Goodbye
        Dad

Letter from Dotty to Art
[August 29, 1943]
Sunday

My Darling—
    It is very late, and I (it seems to be a usual thing) am seated upon the bathroom floor. And why am I so tardy in beginning my epistle to you, you ask? It is because of <u>The Robe</u>. You must read it as soon as you possibly can—it is a very compelling book. It shows how people who had only a remote contact with Jesus yet felt that they were impelled to find out more about the man. So vividly and realistically does Lloyd C. Douglass draw the scenes and the characters and life in the time of Jesus that you feel as if you were actually living then.

[The following has now been typed instead of handwritten.]

    You can easily tell that some time has elapsed between the above and this because of the change of ink. It is now today—the day (one of them) on which I hope to get a letter from you. As soon as I finish this I will call home and find out.
    There doesn't seem to be much news. I saw Louise Marshall the other day and she said that she had seen Mrs. Colbert. She tells me that

Mrs. Colbert is expecting a baby. I hope the severe shock she has experienced from Prof's death will not have a serious effect on it.

Mary Ruth leaves for good old MC tomorrow. Would that I were going with her. Let's go—shall we? (They put question marks in the wrong place on this typewriter)

Dean was home yesterday! He was just here on a weekend pass, but just a little bit of him was thoroughly enjoyable. I can think of a certain soldier that I would much rather see and hear and talk to.

Shucks it is time to go back to work. Work has been somewhat of an ordeal this past week with the temperature ranging around 101° nearly [all] day. You know our humid heat!

Bye now. Must run—but fast.

> Our love is forever,
> Dotty.

Letter from Art to Dotty
Camp Roberts, Calif.
Aug. 29, 1943
Sunday Afternoon

My Dearest Heart,

John Charles Thomas just finished singing "Through The Years," but it wasn't Mr. Thomas that I heard. I heard your soft voice whispering those words as you sang that song many weeks ago. I heard you promise our love through the years as I held you close and kissed your eyes to sleep. Darlin, it is in moments like these that you seem so near and yet so far. Ted, Ken, and I just returned from church where we heard "The Holy City." The soloist did a very fine job and I could hear Hargrave on his trumpet playing the same number back in 219 Carnegie [on the campus of Maryville College]. My soul thirsteth for the highest expression of human emotion for music.

Your description of the coming of Fall in East Tennessee did things to me. I know and appreciate more than ever before just how wonderful the season is there now. I also enjoyed your description of the trip to the Park with the Intermediates. Someday we will have our own to take on all the rides. Yes, we will too! You spoke of David being home but tell me something about Dean. What branch of the Service did he get?

You asked about what kind of engineering I will get. I have absolutely no idea what it will be. That will be determined at the Star Unit where tests will be given. As far as the place where I will [be] sent, I only hope now for the East. If it were U.T., I could only faint for the nonce. I could then wait to be brought back to life by the cooling hand of my little nurse in the fair city of Knoxville.

By the way, tell me all the details of this wonderful trip you are planning. Your last letter contained the first mention of the trip in several weeks. You must be planning to leave just a week from today. I am very happy that you are going North. How long do you expect to be away? How soon will Sammariet be heading for their training? What is Jenks doing now? Get accustomed to travelling, darling, for we may do a great deal. I intend to bring you West for one place, New York for another. Don't forget that you are planning to visit me if I can't get a leave around Xmas. I know by experience that you will not have a great deal of time for any writing while visiting, but I hope you can send full details of everything you see, feel, and think. If at all possible, see something of Washington. It is a wonderful city—the most beautiful I have ever seen. Perhaps you can also see Philadelphia. Remember me to our brother & sis and also Jenks. I started to write her, but got only half through.

At very odd moments I have been reading bits from The Wisdom of the Chinese, "Confucius" etc. I am amazed at how closely these ideas coincide with the concepts set down by Christ. Compare this, for example. In regard to the meaning of true goodness, Confucius says, "The subdual of self, and reversion to the natural laws governing conduct—this is true goodness. If a man can for the space of one day subdue his selfishness and revert to natural laws, the whole world will call him good. True goodness springs from a man's own heart." Many passages such as this one remind me of the words of Christ. We must read more of this Eastern philosophy and religion.

In the last few days I have discovered the presence of a Jewish and Catholic boy living across the room from me. We have already had interesting discussions, and I know that more are to come. Sheldon Beren, the Jewish boy, is a Harvard product, with all of the cultural background that goes with Harvard. Daniel Downey, the Catholic, attended Notre Dame where he majored in philosophy. I hope to attend service with both of them before long. I am happy to find a number of men hear [here] who have religious convictions. A high percentage of our barrack attends Church each week.

Your good letter of the 25th arrived just a few moments ago. Didn't you recognize Ken Cooper in the one picture? The tall brute? He was here when the letter arrived, and we enjoyed your questions. I enclose more pictures. The extra one is for Mother.

I am as happy as you to think that by Spring we may be able to go ahead with our plans. However, let us be very careful not to be optimistic. The possibilities are good, but everything depends upon the

A.S.T.P. situation as I find it after I get to school. There has been some indication that it is not for Post-War work for which we are preparing. I wish we could find out something just a little definite on this thing. You spoke of the ceremony: I favor a very simple one if it is to be during wartime. Particularly should it be simple if I am still a lowly private or even a Pfc. Next week I get another pay check, but after deductions, it will be only thirty-five bucks. With Christmas coming, a ring to purchase, and travelling expenses to consider, I perhaps will have difficulty saving as much as three hundred dollars by March. However, I intend to save everything possible. Keep your fingers crossed.

Find out all you can about Carl's luck in the Star Unit. We can certainly profit by the experience of that couple for our immediate paths may be similar. As soon as he is settled I hope to write to both of them. I also will write Mother while you're away and Mary Ruth will hear from me also. You haven't mentioned Daddy of late. How is he getting along?

I enclose a brief editorial from The New York Times which is a masterpiece of description. Little gems such as this appear periodically in The Times which is without doubt, the best newspaper in the country. I wonder if you drop this in the mail after you get done with it and mail it to Dr. Hunter with my compliments. I think he might enjoy it.

By the way, we spend all next week on the range with the rifle. We arise every morning at four o'clock, begin marching before six, and return to the company area by seven each evening. Upon our return we must clean our rifle of all the carbon formed while firing. That means little sleep for Bushy during the next few days. There will be no chance to write until next week, but be sure and let me know where my letters can reach you. At Samarriet's, I suppose.

The hour is late, I arise early in the morning. I hasten to dream land to walk and talk with the most wonderful dream who is more than a dream, for she is a living reality. I think of you constantly, dreaming of you nightly. Our love will grow and grow "Through the Years."

Ever thine own,
Bushy

August 30, 1943, Diary

Up at four and began march to K.D. (Known distance) range by six.

Letter from Art to Dotty
Sept. 1, 1943 (Wed. Noon)

My Own,

Here on the firing range, the few shady spots that are to be found attract men at the noon hour as beautiful flowers attract the honey bees. This is our third and perhaps our hottest day on the firing range and we are beginning to feel the affect of continuous loss of sleep and intense heat. All around fellowmen are sleeping peacefully as we want to go on with preliminary fire. By the middle of the afternoon this will be done, and firing for record will begin. I think the men as a whole are having more fun right now than at any time since we entered the service, even though this is perhaps our hardest week. Every man longs to make good in this phase of our training. We "bolo" (Army slang for making a mistake), we do poorly, and complain, but all of us get a great kick out of rifle fire.

Thursday Morn
(Very Early)

For the second time this week the first platoon was unlucky enough to get pit detail in the morning. Then we left company a half an hour ahead of the others and arrived here on the range long before sunup. I am amazed at the efficiency with which the army works in many things. The schedule on the firing range is just one example. A thousand men are out here this week firing on one hundred and twenty-five targets. Each company (there are four) has its number of targets and two platoons fire at a time from each distance. You see, we fire from 200 yds., 300 yds., and 500 yds. From the last distance we fire from the prone position. For the others we fire prone, kneeling, sitting, and standing. Also in these we fire rapid fire as well as slow fire. For the latter we fire at will but in the position we must go from standing into the prone or sitting position, load, and shoot nine shots in 51 sec. That is plenty of time but shooting at a steady cadence for maximum effectiveness offers the principle difficulty.

Two platoons from our company are on the firing line all the time. One platoon works in the pits and one platoon scores the shooting and taken care of all jobs. This pit detail is a rather interesting job. The targets are in a long line about four feet apart and behind a ten foot embankment. They are on pulleys in such a manner that they can be pulled up quickly into the firing position. Two men work each target, and as it is fired on, we pull it down, put a small spotter in it to show the man where he hit, and run it back up where we disk it. This is just another way of showing the man a littler more clearly where his bullet struck.

Most of the time we have to be on our toes every minute, but there are lulls when we have a chance to relax a little. At night this week, we have absolutely no time to call our own. We usually get in by seven thirty, get through supper about eight, then we must spend every minute on our rifles. A great deal of carbon collects in the barrel when we shoot, and this must be washed out with soap and water. If we are lucky we get a chance to take a shower and to bed by ten.

Sorry to have to write this with pencil, but it would be foolish to take pen on the range.

Camp Roberts, Calif.
Sept. 1, 1943 [Art's dates]

My Dearest,

We fall out in a very few minutes, but I hope to get just a little written. This is our third day on the firing range and things are going well. We are getting up each morning at foursometimes 3:45and begin our march about 5:30. As we leave the company area, the stars are bright in the sky above us. As we move across the parade ground the hills around the camp show up as dark outlines against the sky and in the East the light of the new day begins to appear. We march for about an hour (the range is three miles from camp) and the dawn continues to transform night to day. Shortly after our arrival, the sun peeps over the edge of the hill land and the new day has actually begun.

9-3-43
Friday Morning – 5:20

I must try to get this odd bits together and in the mail this morning. As I write the first news of the long awaited invasion of the fortress of Europe is being reported. Twenty-five years from now darling, this will be an important date in our history—an invasion force coming just four years to a day after war began. The picture is changing rapidly and will continue to look brighter until victory and peace come.

I finished firing for record yesterday afternoon. Sorry to have to say that I made a poor showing in comparison with my buddies. I shot only 156 out of a possible 210 but that is well above the qualifying mark. The M1 rifle is a sweet weapon and I feel that I know how to handle it.

By this time you will be getting ready to leave on your well deserved vacation. I had hoped to get this to you before you left but there was just no time to finish writing (as if I could ever finish!). I plan to sleep most of the week-end, but I will write at length Sunday.

Give my loving regards to Samarriet Inc. I hope to write mother and Mary Ruth while you're away. Please tell me all about your wonderful trip. Give regards and best wishes to Jenks.

Thine Own,
Bushy

Letter from Dotty to Art
Thurs. Night
Sept. 2, 1943

Mine Own,

I somehow knew that you were listening when John Charles Thomas sang our song, "Through the Years." How about having that sung at our wedding, perhaps by Harriet (if she can be there?)

My soul was very much athirst for music the other night. I sat down at the piano and played for a while, but rather than assuaging my thirst for music it offended my ears and angered me. Thus when Flo called and asked if I were going to the outdoor concert of recorded music at Tyson house, I agreed immediately and went, rather than staying home and doing a number of odd tasks as I had planned. It was worth it. The music, the stars, the coolness of the evening all did wonders for my pent up spirits. I could almost believe that I was at Maryville that night—such "old faithful" disc clubbers were in attendance as Arling Kressler, Gabriel Williamson, Flo, and myself— and one of the numbers was a song by our friend Kipnis. Gabriel is headed for Richmond and seminary; Krees is still here with the T.V.A., having been removed from draftable material because of arthritis in his hand. When I mentioned my proposed trip he said that he might take a week off and go North at the same time (as me). His home is in Allentown, Pa., you know. If that works out I may have company on the trip up. (Aren't you even a little jealous?)

I spoke of the cool weather a little too soon—we had almost a week of cool weather, but it got hot again and has been exceedingly hot ever since; in fact, we have enjoyed (?) some the highest temperatures of the summer!

By the way, you may say <u>Corporal</u> David W. Barber, Jr now. Dean was here Sunday (didn't I say something about it in Sunday's letter?). He has just been transferred from heavy artillery or equipment or some branch of the infantry to the Air Corps. He says he wants to be a pilot.

You had better not ask to be sent any particular place for A.S.T.P., but just hold your breath and pray for the East. I heard of one boy who asked to be sent to U.T. and ended up in <u>Maine</u>! Carl hasn't been sent anywhere, yet. He is still at the STAR unit.

I hope I don't leave a great deal unsaid in my letters. Daddy accused me tonight of being very close-mouthed. If you share his opinion, let me know immediately, and I will become a chatterer or bust. I never was a very great one to prattle much.

Now for my trip! I hope to find time to write you all about the scenes, sights, sounds, reactions, thoughts, and people. I'm afraid I won't get to see much of Washington since I'll only be passing through both times. I leave here Sunday morning on the early Tennessean, and arrive Baltimore about nine or ten that night. Sam is to meet me there and take me to the abode of Samarriet. Will leave said abode sometime Wednesday and go to Philly, there to be met by Jenks and paraded around who knows where. Since I haven't yet found out about my reservation for the trip back, I don't know whether I'll get back home Saturday night or Sunday. At any rate, it will be a full week, and 'tis only a week. Wish it were more. Among other things and people I shall try to see in Phila. is Arlene. I got a letter (airmail!) from her today telling me how to get in touch with her. Remember my telling you, some time back, about getting a letter from her and one from Bob in the same mail? She said that she got my letter and one from Bob enclosing one from you on the same day. Looks as if we had this telepathy business just about sewed up between us four, eh. What? If you try to write me at all while I am gone, address is to Jenks' house (211 South Ave., Glendolden, Pa.) since I will be there the latter part of the week. I'm afraid if you send it to Harriets that it will get there after I'm gone. Do you care to hear my wardrobe, or is it only girls who are interested in such things? On the train I shall wear my green (uniform-like) suit, big green hat that you like so well, new black shoes, new black gloves; a couple of white blouses will make a change for the green suit; and my new black dress which you have never seen. There you are, whether you wanted to hear about it or not.

Confucius and Chinese wisdom is interesting. Now you can understand why I received immense enjoyment from concocting that chart on "Comparisons of Scriptures of World's Ten Great Religions for Brother Dollenmayer. He, by the way, is now a Chaplain in the army, Prof. Vine will not be back, and the enrollment is down to about half its usual number. School just won't be quite the same this year. It is unfortunate that Mary Ruth had to strike it at such a bad time. She seems happy about it, though. We got a letter from her today—she isn't homesick, her stomach hasn't become upset from the excitement, she likes her roommate, and she has made the acquaintance of "Superman." Horrors. I hope she doesn't make it too deep a friendship. (Now—slap me on the other cheek, too, and give me a nice saucer of milk. Meeeow)

Well, of all things! So the boy in the picture is Ken Cooper. Well, blow me down with a feather. Now that you mention it, I believe he does look a little bit like Ken! You all must have had a good laugh on me that time. Thanks for the other pictures, darling, also the Camp Roberts Dispatches. Very interesting. Mothers pleased with her picture, Daddy likes them, too.

Now for questions about wedding!

1. Church or home wedding? Place?
2. Formal (long dress) or informal?
3. Relatives <u>and</u> guest, or just relatives? (I have quite a few)

Think on these things. Our love will indeed grow "Through the Years."

   Your

    Dotty.

Letter from Art to Dotty
Camp Roberts, Calif.
Sept. 5, 1943

My Dearest,

September 5th, and so the weeks go by. Time, like an eternally moving stream, carries us into the dawning of the morrow with a relentless for useless to resist. We cannot hold the passing moment and that is all the more reason for enjoying it to the full. We cannot hasten tomorrow but we can know that dreams come true in the dawning of each new day.

Today as you were leaving I heard you speak very distinctly to me. I was writing a note to my aunt when all at once I stopped in the middle of a sentence to listen to your voice. Darling, my prayers and thoughts are with you every moment of your wonderful trip. I too wish that I could be making the trip with you, but, of course, that is out of the question. You must have felt a tingle of loneliness surge through as the train pulled away from the station and you found yourself alone on the train. It was in part an echo of this that I heard this afternoon.

You will enjoy this trip, nevertheless, to the full. Travel can be one of the most broadening experiences than we have. As we travel, seeing and meeting up with new faces, new environments, and new ways of living, we realize in a new way the existence of our fellowmen. Instead of Washington being a place you've heard about and have only vague ideas about, it becomes a human city with life and beauty and movement. Instead of Maryland farmland being a jigsaw picture with many pieces missing, it becomes rich fields, colorful farmhouses, and neighborly people. One of the finest educations to be had come from seeing a new section of our varied and ever changing American countryside. I am overjoyed that you could make this trip.

Again, fate decrees otherwise in plans that Ted and I have made. We had settled on next Sat. as the time to go to Los Angeles, and a ride seemed certain. Yesterday I learned to my dismay that my platoon has guard duty next week end. The following week-end Ted will have it, as there goes our trip. I do hope we can make one trip together before we leave.

I can tell you more about guard duty in my letter next Sunday, but home is a general idea. As a platoon we will dress in our best uniforms, don leggings, gas masks, etc. and march to the guard house. We will be assigned certain posts and then divided into three reliefs. Each man will walk his post for two hours, be relieved for four hours, and walk again for two hours. This continues for a full twenty-four hour period. We must remain in the guard-house at all times if we are not walking post. There is nothing extremely difficult about guard duty, but it is considered a milestone in army training.

As I described in my mid-week letter, we spent a rugged week on the firing range. Friday we completed the last of the record firing and had some shooting with the carbine. This is a small gun, way lighter in weight, and designed to replace the pistol as a defensive weapon for officers. It is also used by men in the heavy weapon's outfits. I am not sure what we take up next week, but at least some of the time will be spent on the machine gun.

By the way, before I forget it, I want you to get a season ticket for the U.T. Concert Service and present it to Dad from me. Get it with yours so that you two can enjoy the thrills that I must miss. Because of existing conditions, I think we'll have to make it about the same price range as we had last year—about six and a half I believe. Let me know the amount and I will send it along on or before next payday. After all, I'm taking you away from him, and the two of you should enjoy every minute you can together—particularly such minutes as you can have at the concert.

Again and again I am reminded of the fact that man is basically good. The fellowmen in my barrack are rougher, of course, then the group at Maryville, but they too have ideals, religious conceptions, and cultural loves. The corporal in our outfit is a college graduate having been elected to Phi Beta Kappa. He did honor work and was offered a teaching fellowship at Harvard. Today I met with half a dozen fellowmen to discuss problems of peace and causes of war. It is hoped that we can get together each Sunday for such discussions. Another evidence of the higher type that I find around me can be seen from the songs that we sing while marching. There is an almost total absence of the dirty type of thing that usually goes with marching. We sing "I've Been Working on the Railroad," the Air Corp Song, and several times we have taken up marching hymns. It gives me little thrill to swing along to the moving cadence of "Onward Christian Soldiers."

By the way, we have taken more pictures and I will send them to you as they are developed. Where are ones that you told me about taking? I would love to see them. Yesterday Ted and I took shots of each other in full field equipment—steel helmet, full pack, etc.

I enclose a couple of poems that Dad sent to me. Both are very fine, and I think you will agree. I continue to enjoy my reading in Chinese Philosophy. I long for the day when we can share our reading.

This we had to clean our rifle for inspection, but I managed to attend church services. Our Sun. schedule is rather messed up since we began eating only two meals—breakfast at nine and dinner at three. It breaks in the church hours in the morning and breaks into the middle of the afternoon. I think that we will soon vote a change.

Tonight Ted, Ken and I joined for a few minutes in a group sing at the Service Club. It was swell, but not as half so wonderful as that beautiful moon that you perhaps watch from your Pullman window as you northward.

The hour slips by and I need a dream or two. You come to me in the beauty of your true, lovely self, as I dream of the future that is ours. I kiss you and whisper
     Our love,
     Bushy

Camp Roberts, Calif.
Sept. 7, 1943

Dearest Heart,

Your wonderful letter arrived last night and I felt as though I had a week's vacation. It always does a great deal for me to get your letters. Last week when I was coming in from long hard days your letters refreshed me greatly. I only wish I could write to you as often.

I have a very short time, but I will try to take up a few pertinent points that you mentioned.

Wed Noon

We have just returned from the field to hear the great news that Italy surrendered at 9:30 (Bonfire War Time) this morning. Coupled with great news from the Russian front, it seems that events are moving even more quickly than we had thought. We have been able to get no detail. But it has certainly given the morale here a big boost. I wonder if Germany will not attempt to defend only an inner circle of defense. We'll say more about this later.

Back to your questions: of course, we hardly know how the final plans will be determined by events, but I now favor a church wedding. There is something sacred about the altar that we could not find elsewhere. I think that we should make it a simple affair, yet make it outstanding in its simplicity. I favor a formal as to the long dress, and, if we make it a church affair, let's have guests. Because of the general situation of travel, my relatives will probably be few in number, but I have a few friends in Maryville (Dr. Hunter, Dr. Orr, etc.) that I would like to invite.

Thursday 9th

Please, darling, let's don't try to do too much planning just yet. After deductions I receive only $35.75 per month. It will take some time to amass enough to get married at that rate, even if I am able to save as much as $25 per paycheck.

Yesterday we hiked about fourteen miles in our daily round. This included our eight mile hike last night. We started out about eight, hiked out to a grove, pitched tents, and returned—all by twelve. Up this morning at 5:30 for another day. Will try to describe the joy of marching with the light of a California moon in weekend letter. Am on special detail Sat. and Sun. Six o'clock Sun. go on Guard Duty until Mon. morning. Hope to have time to do a little writing.

Look forward to description of your wonderful trip. Must send this out. Enclose pictures. Am sending a little package next week—I hope.— Not size 5—yet!

> Goodnight, my Love,
> Bushy

Letter from friend John H. to Art

39 Stafford St.
Worcester, 3, Mass.
Sept. 7, 43

Dear Bushing;

Now, what do you think of my loyalty and consideration in continuing to write while you are occupied with army duties? I owe Bob Lord and Bev Davis letters as well, besides several seminaries, my mother and George Howard. It is obvious that I am involved in something again, is it not? Well, to tell you the truth, I am, very much so: I have joined the army.

I haven't had peace of mind for so damned long that I finally went home, weived my deferrment, and had myself put in class 1-A. I go for my final physical around the sixteenth of this month. If I pass—and I hope that I do—I shall be in the armed services within a short time. It did my heart good to hera you say what must have been churning in your mind for years and certainly has been an accepted fast in mine for as long as I have known you: namely, that you have dedicated your life to the Christian ministry. If ever there was a man more evidently qualified for the clergy than you I have yet to see him. I don't see the light in the same manner as you—which is not a criticism of you but perhaps evidence of my own unenlightenemnt—but I recognize a complete sincerity, a deep love of right, God and man, an overwhelming desire to spread the light of what you see as truth and best, and an all pervading sincerity and empathy with your fellow man in you which is so infrequently found as to mark you as specially inspired and selected. It is typical of you that you would not hasten the issue just a bit in regard to your complete assurity of your place in life and thence be exempted from army duty. Many and MOST of the newly self determined ministers have done just that—Dexter Rice included, I am very sure, but not You. For that I am proud and appreciative of you and your friendship.

My folks are to move to Cincinnati this month. Daddy has been there all summer in government employ. He was at Washington for a good while. He is a co-ordinator of shipping and ship building. A darned good job. Mother, Brother perhaps Sister and he are taking a house in the Westwood section. A very nice district, I understand. I shall not go with them, of course, I haven't the faintest idea when I shall see my folks again. I shall not go to Cincinnati, of course, after my physical, I wondered at your statement that on your furlough you plan to take a ring home do Dotty; do you mean a wedding ring? I hope so. It would be fine were I able to attend your wedding, but the knowledge of your being joined with so beautiful a girl is more than satisfactory. I shall write to Dotty some day again. I hope she has continued to advance in her job. It speaks very well for her that she has gone as far as she has already!

Bob Lord has made a corporal so soon. He has also qualified for the A.S.T.P. that seems so desireable. I am glad. You are in that, are you not? I hope to make it myself, but shan't be disappointed if I reach only yard bird rating. [John is referencing perhaps becoming a soldier whose job is to do only menial work at the military base.] I'll be a durned good yard bird, let me tell you. You seem to be well, able to take it, Bushing. I admire your guts and your spirit. Keep it up, and yet further up. I must write to other less interesting parties now; so God Bless You, dear Friend.

> Aufwiedersehen,
> John

Letter from Art to Dotty
Guard House, C. Roberts
Sept 12, 1943

My Dearest,

Here I sit on my bed in the guard house but not under detention. We formed for guard about three-thirty this afternoon and marched from our company area to the guard-house. The guard is divided into three reliefs for each post. The first relief has just returned and I go on at eight o clock. I work then from eight until ten, am relieved, and go on guard again from now until four. I look forward to both of these for the moon is almost full tonight and I will have plenty of time to dream of our dreams.

I had hoped to write of many things yesterday, but, rather than having a free afternoon, I had K.P all day. Your wonderful letter describing the first place of your trip arrived, and I was so happy that you are enjoying it so much. I mailed two letters to Samarriet's but had no chance to mail one to Jenk's address. Forgive me, darling, but the army leaves no time in its schedule for personal desires.

Last Wednesday night we had an hour of lecture after supper and then fell immediately for another of the now familiar night problems. We hiked out about four miles by the light of a half moon. A cool nightly breeze drifted past as we marched, night shadows intrigued us from the hills, and stars offer a choral background for the melody the moon seemed to sing. In the moon-shade of a beautiful grove we pitched pup tents. The purpose of the problem was to do all of this with the minimum of noise. We were supposed to say nothing during the entire problem.

On Thursday and Friday we began a new phase of our training when we worked on the tactics of the rifle squad. I hardly have time to bore you with detail of this but it is a culmination of all of our training thus far. Next week we fire the machine gun (we didn't do this as I thought we would). Monday, after guard tonight, we go on another night problem.

I want to write at length about our planning, but the guardhouse with all the yelling and talking on every mile is not place to concentrate on such an important thing as our love.

I go on duty in a very few minutes. Hope to be able to write more early tomorrow morning. May be able to write again Tuesday or Wed. Sent paper out with ASTP write-up and small box. Hope both arrive O.K. Tonight I dream of our love.
    Bushy

Mon. Morn 6 o'clock
Just now getting off guard.
Enjoyed every minute of it.

Letter from Arthur Bushing Sr. to Art Jr.
Jamestown, Tenn.
Sept. 13, 1943
5.00 P.M.

Dear precious son:

Your good letter with enclosures of pictures depicting rather realistically what it means to be a soldier in Uncle Sam's Army came this A. M., having been mailed Sept. 10th 11.00 A.M. Fast travel.

So glad always to hear that you are well and getting along nicely. By the way, you will forgive my having opened by mistake the letter from "John" here enclosed, which came with a bunch mail for this A.M.

Well, the news is a-plenty this time, although I may have to report it in brief. Mother is completing some 3200 cover sheet notations, on the 16th to list all registrants per listing requirements as shown on copy already mailed. We will have to engage Florence to help on this big job, and she has agreed to come Thursday A.M. We have two weeks to complete that job.

Here is some sad news. Jim York was killed on his job at Clinton, Tennessee last Thursday. He was riding on the front of a switch train (he was working as fireman). As the train was going around a curve he must have lost his balance. He fell head foremost and the train did not stop before running over his mangled body. Funeral was yesterday (Sunday) first, short service at home and then on to Wolf River. Mother and I attended the first service. Large crowd; beautiful flowers. Very sad occasion. [Jim York, or James Preston York, was Sgt. Alvin C. York's brother.]

The paper (Local) is improving and had a nice edition last week with most space taken about the Bond Drive. It shows that a community should have an outlet for its notices and items of news interest to the people.

Mother is through with her season's canning. We bought apples which seem very scarce, and the cans are full for our winter needs.

We will get off a nice present for Fred—as are hoping in good time. Mother is a very good salesman. She found a buyer for the Looper house and as it was at a price higher than I would have thought possible to get at this time, I agreed to sell; for with painting a house and repairs always coming up of one kind or another, I thought Mother and I should be relieved of the worry with so much undone even at home. We got $2000.00 for the place, and sold it to Mrs. Ralph Lyon. She had insurance money and was able to make a good substantial down payment. If she gets some $500.00 from the Government due Ralph shortly, she wants to apply that on her notes and that would leave only a small balance for her to pay, in a year or so, if she needs the time. She needed a home for herself and the girls, and she can keep teachers (Board them) and make a nice comfortable place for herself and the girls. Of course, we will put most of the money in Bonds.

Here is a Money Order $20.00. Do trust you have a fine trip to Los Angeles. It will be wonderful for you to see these Coast cities. Had a nice card from Dorothy from Philadelphia. She will be returning soon, I assume, and I will want to get a line to her. By the way, I deposited the $25.00 to your account and Dad will just make this $20.00 a little present so that you can have a good time and not miss good eats and good hotel accommodations. We trust that and pray for you a whole lot dear boy, may the Peace soon come to a war torn world and a new world Open up for further civilized advances. God bless you dear precious son mother sends love. By the way, I sent the books without finding red covered little Algebra book. Will continue to look for some mother will look around for socks its Sent about 2/3 of little Blue Books. More later

Letter from Art to Dotty
[September 14, 1943]

Dearest Heart,

Lights are almost out, and this seems to be my only chance to dash off a note. There is so much to say; so little time. Darling, I love you and long for you constantly. Walking guard last Sunday night I walked and dreamed of our future. Last night as I went through a long night problem thinking of our years ahead. Tonight I watched the full moon slip off the eastern horizon to fill the earth with a beauty and a hope of higher things.

Tonight is our first free night in weeks. Thursday night we will probably be out most of the night on another problem. Ted and I plan to leave Sat noon for L.A. unless something unexpected comes up. I will try to write again before Sat. Thought that Ted had mailed your package. However, he couldn't get it off and I don't know when I will get a chance to mail it.

I enclosed a couple of poems that I want you to read and keep. Dad sent "The Lover's Prayer."

I will probably be taking A.S.T.P. test in a few days. Am going to ask for U.T. or Vandy. Keep fingers crossed, my dearest.

Goodnight, darling, I must get some sleep—for a change. I live and dream of the day when our lives become one.

   Thine Own,
   Bushy

No letter since first one from Me. Hope to hear tomorrow. I love to hear from you.

Sept. 13, 1943
Monday Night

My Dearest,

No, I'm home now, but I swiped some of the hotel stationery to write you on. There is so much to tell that I may have to send this in installments, not only because it may be too much for one envelope, but also because I may not have time to finish it tonight.

I received your two wonderful letters and the pictures tonight. One of the letters arrived of Harriet's after I had left and she had no way of getting it to me except to forward it on here. Thus I didn't get it till today. Your letters inspire me no end, darling.

Now where were we? Oh, yes—after taking leave of Samarriet and little "Bliz" I boarded the train and spent an uneventful ride (on my suitcase) to the big city. After getting off the train I ascended to the upper regions of the station by means of escalator (my first ride on one) and there was Jenks! The nearly feminized Jenks is just the same, yet different. If you get what I mean. Jenks decided that we should have a hotel room as our headquarters, since it would consume too much time, energy, and money to go back and forth from her room in Glenolden. Hence the Robert Morris Hotel, twelfth floor, was my "home" during my stay in Philadelphia, and a nice one it was too.

The first night included John, supper at a Chinese restaurant, and a visit to the planetarium and observatory.
Tues. night.

John (John Lewis—never to be confused with John L. Lewis!) is quite a guy. He had infantile paralysis at the age of 15 or 16, so his spine goes > instead of |. But it does not handicap him in the least! He goes anywhere he wants, does anything he pleases. Jenks says he is strong as an ox, is first man on any tennis team he joins, rides horseback a lot, etc., etc., etc. He has an extremely active mind of a high caliber—it makes you feel mentally alert to talk to him on any subject, and he can talk on most any subject! He has perfect pitch, and an almost perfect sense of time; every now and then he would ask me the correct time and then tell me before I could tell him, always where there were no clocks or watches in sight. He is exactly the kind of person that would appeal to Jenks, perhaps the only kind. At any rate, Jenks is a changed woman, and I do mean woman! I think you would like John (I know he would like you).

The first night in Phila. we met John and went to a Chinese restaurant in Chinatown for supper. All the waiters were Chinese, they wrote down the order in Chinese, and the food was very definitely Chinese, also very definitely good. Delicious would be a more apt term. John and I exchanged match tricks, so I decided to I decided to [written twice] swipe some of them as souviners (?sp.) I enclose one for you. [There was actually still a match inside the envelope when we typed this letter.] For the evenings entertainment we went to the Planetarium. There we watched the artificial stars move across the artificial sky to show their bearing on the seasons. We even saw how the stars would look from Australia; do you realize that there are stars in the heaven that we never see from this side of the earth that are seen by people on the other side, and vise versa? After the intriguing lecture on the stars we went to the observatory atop the building, and looked at the moon through the large telescope there. John acted interested and spoke a few friendly words to the man in charge, and soon that man was showing us stars all over the place. I was amazed that any man could know the stars so well that he could train the huge telescope on almost any star he chose with hardly a glance at the locality of that star.

The next move was to Whitman's for ice cream. While we were there who should walk in but Betty Querns, one of your former tablemates. She sent her regards to you. So endeth the first night.

Thursday's program included a luncheon with a cousin of Jenks', a shopping tour, and supper & a show with a couple of girls from Sharpe and Dohme. I felt as if I were already acquainted with Nelda (Jenks' cousin)—she used to write letters to Jenks at Maryville that were masterpieces of cosmic literature. She writes poetry, too. She is married to a newspaper man who works for the Associated Press, who also writes poetry, and whose name is Ed Creagh. This Ed talked in a very quiet, matter of fact tone, but said surprising things, cute remarks, or sly digs that you were apt to miss if you didn't listen closely, because <u>what</u> he said was somewhat obscured by <u>how</u> it was said (purposely so). Nelda an Ed have a fairly small but extremely well-chosen record collection, from which we heard several gems before & after lunch. Darling, I longed to have you there beside me meeting and enjoying these people as I did. Here is a sample of Ed's poetry:

Horse De Combat

My steed did breeze
O'er bush and shrub
With utter ease.
Aye, there's the rub---
And rub and rub
And rub and rub.
Arnica, please!

by Ed Creagh

On my shopping tour I became acquainted with the <u>big</u> department stores. Fun. I could easily get lost in one. In one store window I saw a white satin wedding dress that looked as if it had been <u>created</u> for me! The show was Deanne Durbin in "Hers to Hold." Frankly, I was disappointed in it. She didn't sing much, and the plot was weak.

What happened on Friday and Saturday? See your next installment of "The First Trip North" as told by

Your loving fiancé,
Dotty.

Letter from Dotty to Art
[September 15, 1943]
Wed. Nite
Installment II

My Dearest,

Came Friday, the day with a lot of plans up its sleeve, and such an itinerary! In the morning we took the electric train out to Glenolden, the place containing Jenks' abode. She has a very nice room with a Mrs. Lake, who is a hospitable and pleasant soul. But before her comes the tour through the new labs and offices of Sharp and Dohme. Jenks ceremoniously escorts me through the whole place, introducing me to all her pals, colleagues, and fellow mischief-mixers. They seemed a nice sort for the most part. She has a very pleasant place in which to work.

Now we can go back to Mrs. Lake. She fed us a lunch that surely must have originated in a southern kitchen (hot biscuits, 'neverything).

Jenks' house in Glenolden is not far from the Tinley's house in Norwood, so we must needs go over and pay a visit to the Tinley's. And guess who was home there—Spike Tinley, home from the Marines for a short visit! In case you have forgotten, Mrs. Tinley is Harriet's mother-in-law. Spike and Sam are step-brothers. Spike is looking well, still as bashful as ever.

From the Tinley's we board the electric train again and swish back into Phila. I don my new black dress and shoes, and we are ready to meet all the girls included in the "The Reunion." After we had met all the trains we found that we had acquired Arlene (!), Phyllis Heaton, Marion Northrup, Charlotte Colby, and Beth Pascoe. What fun we did have talking over old times and new, catching up loose threads of acquaintanceship. Beth was on her vacation, Charlotte is going into WAVES, Phyllis is almost a graduate nurse, Marion is beginning med school, and you know about Arlene. Arlen, by the way, has had her hair cut quite short—it makes her look quite different, and quite pretty; most becoming, in fact. We went to a <u>most</u> interesting place for supper —it may have been a dive, but it was extremely interesting; it was the Frenchified part of a French restaurant, supposedly having the atmosphere of a French village. It was a basement room (rooms?), with all brick archways and dim cubbyholes, some decorated with somewhat crude drawings and French words painted over the bricks, in addition to some interesting pictures (some of them riske') and paintings hung on the walls. Tables were lighted by tall candles stuck in old wine bottles. Entertainment there was, also: three Hawaiian musicians played American current hits, sung in French by a friendly little French fellow. The whole thing somehow reminded me of a Barnwarmin' scene.

It was so refreshing to see my friends again, especially Arlene. Bob was to be home this past week-end, and she was (needless to say) quite thrilled. She was the last to leave, and we saw her off at 11:00 P.M. After that, Jenks and I suddenly decided that the evening was quite young, so we went to a show, and didn't hit the hay till 2:00 A.M.! More fun!

Thanks for the "more" pictures. I get a great deal from them—if you only knew how much time I spend gazing at them. The close-up of you in your visor—cap, etc. is <u>excellent</u>. (You take a wonderful picture, Darling). You didn't have to look so realistically vicious in the one where you were pointing that wicked-looking bayonet. [Photo dated September 4, 1943.]

I am afraid I must leave again, although I still have much to tell. It is taking me almost as long to tell of my trip as it did to experience it. Through it all runs the constant stream of

My Love,
Dotty

September 4, 1943 [photo mentioned in Sept. 15, 1943 letter]

Letter from Art to Dotty
Camp Roberts Calif.
Sept. 16, 1943

My Dearest Heart,

Thursday night and we actually have a little extra time to ourselves. I will write as much as I possibly can tonight. Your card from Philly came yesterday along with a letter from little "Sis" and a wonderful package. Darling, it was very thoughtful of you to be so loving as to send me the sweets. The candy we get here is only second rate, and even in civilian life it is seldom that one can find candy to compare with Gimbles. The one thing better would be candy that your own little hands could make and I know that you are too busy (I really didn't mean that as a hint).

I look forward very much to further letters concerning your well-deserved vacation. To date I have received the first and the card. I really think that I am not getting all my mail and haven't been for three or four days. I have only one letter from home in almost two weeks. Glad that Jenks is writing. I will answer at first opportunity. Have been trying for several days to write Mary Ruth and will answer her letter shortly.

Tonight I was overjoyed to receive four math books from home and a whole stack of Little Blue Books. In case you haven't seen the edition, it is designed to be read while travelling and the books can be carried in a shirt pocket. Almost all of the classics are to be found in this series, and I will be able to do a great deal of reading during my ten minute breaks in the field.

Yesterday we had preliminary firing on the light machine gun and today we fired for record. It was lots of fun and everyone did will. Pardon me, darling, may I brag a bit? All right, I will anyway. With the all important aid of a good instructor and a good gun I fired one of the top scores in the company. I only wish I could have done better on the rifle.

Sat. is the day that Ted and I plan, for the fourth time, to go on pass together. If nothing changes our plans we will leave here about eleven thirty Sat. morning for Los Angeles. We hope to get a good sleep Saturday night for we will probably return early Monday morning— getting little sleep. (If these sentences sound screwy, just remember I write in a room with twenty-five men—all talking, yelling, relaxing. 'Tis difficult!)

Next week I take over duties as squad leader of my squad of fourteen men. There is not a great deal to it, but the experience is good. The job rotates from week to week, and it just happens that my time is coming up. Part of our time next week we are on the combat range where we fire live ammunition. Should be lots of fun.

Will try to write a card or letter from L.A. Will also write at earliest possible moment next week. By the way, I thought Ted mailed your package last Sat. Not out yet, but I will mail it soon as possible. I continue to hope and plan for our future. Wonderful days and years, will be ours. As the moon peeps over the eastern horizon I whisper to you

              Our Love,
              Bushy

Letter from Dotty to Art
[September 16, 1943]
Thursday Nite

My Dearest Own,

It's—ah—Friday, now. Last night after work, I saw "Stage Door Canteen." It affected me strangely—when I got home I still wanted to cry, or something (oh, yes, I shed a few tears—after all, I could as easily put myself in her place), but couldn't quite get it out. I was all stirred up, but couldn't seem to get rid of the stirred-upness nor settle down to anything, such as a letter. After struggling with myself for almost an hour I finally gave up and went to bed. Ah, me. Forgive me, darling, for getting all worked up over the absence of your presence.

Hmmmm. We were still on our trip, weren't we. Came the time to turn my steps and thoughts homeward, and I was reluctant to do so. I was unable to et a reservation for the trip home, so I decided to take the night train and trust to luck that a seat would be available.

The seat situation was fine until I got to Washington—there the fun began. I boarded a bulging train and my heart sank. The coach in which I finally halted was as crowded as any of the others, but somehow it seemed promising. I started out sitting on my suitcase, which was with a number of other bags in a peculiar corner. I can explain my position best by drawing a picture of the seats in that coach. [Dotty drew a diagram of where she sat on the bus.] Finally, among the baggage I found a camp stool (canvas seat with out arms or back), and there I sit for several hours. The soldiers (there were several,) fed me, talked to me, and saw that I eventually got a real seat. This "real seat" turned out to be beside a very interesting soldier, although he slept most of the time. He is an "accultist" by religion (they go in for astrology, believe in a certain evaluation of the soul). We swapped views awhile. By the way, how do you reconcile your views of life after death with the 2nd coming as prophecied in Revelations?

At 2:00 A.M. I finished the book I had borrowed from Jenks. It was Hartzell Spence's (of One Foot in Heaven fame) Get Thee Behind Me—, the story of a preacher's son, who feels the hand of the parsonage on his shoulder all thru life, who is never quite the same as other fellows. A preacher's son is set apart, inhibited, and often lonely. A preacher is too busy with the affairs of others to be a good father to his own son. Bushy, darling, you must read this book some time. Remember—it is highly probable that our son will be a preacher's son!

The rest of the night was uneventful. I got little sleep, because

1) The couch was well lighted—all night.
2) Available space & the fact that I sat beside a man did not permit curling up into a comfortable sleeping position.
3) I had no manly shoulder on which to rest my head, no arms to snuggle into—any old soldier won't do, you see.

So, at 6:30 Sunday morning I arrived back home. After breakfast with my family (even Mary Ruth was home) and a bath I went to bed and slept till dinner, after which I returned to bed and slept the rest of the afternoon.

Oh, woe, oh, alas! Mr. Hamilton is leaving us! He has accepted a call to a church in Chattanooga; he will be here only a few more Sundays. Isn't that tragic? Tragic for us, fortunate for Chattanooga. As one's mind refuses to believe in the death of a friend, so does my mind balk at contemplating this news. I just don't like to think about it! Who will marry us? With Mr. Hamilton gone, and Samarriet probably unable to make the trip in March, who will do the honors? (Provided there are any to do!) Pete, perhaps?

Tis the funniest thing about my watch. For some time it had been running a little fast, and I kept setting it back, rather than parting with it long enough to have it regulated. At the beginning of my trip I set it at the correct time. Since that moment (all during the trip and ever since) the watch has not wavered from the correct time!

Mary Ruth has a boy friend! By now they have had three dates, so I guess they are on their way to going steady. You know Maryville! The fellow is John Kirstein—remember him? He told Mary Ruth that he used to mail your post cards for you. P.S. He also read them. She thinks he is quite nice. It is really quite an achievement to get a man (sucker) at Maryville now—the manpower shortage is acute if cadets are excluded. And they seem to be.

Dearest, if you can save enough money for a ring and a train ticket, the rest comes out of my pocket. Besides I shall get a job and work shortly (about two months) after we are married. And remember, I'm saving <u>for us</u>, too. "What is mine I'll always share— —." <u>We can do it</u>, Bud!

Well! Carl pulled the cream of the crop out of the hat, or something. He is to receive his Specialized Training at Princeton! How's he doing? Flo plans to leave immediately, if not sooner. They certainly have had it lucky, nicht wahr?

To return for the last say about my trip: every time I boarded a train I felt a surge of loneliness, a deep longing for you. Every time I met a new personality or established new friendships, I wanted you to meet them also. I rest me in the thought that some day, perhaps soon, that very thing will take place, for we shall be together always. I am comforted when I feel that you hear me when I call to you across time and space. "Love is a Song that never ends"

        Dotty.

September 17, 1943, Diary

The purpose of the modern stage (i.e. the theatre) is purely for entertainment with all the glory of the art gone. Since such is the case, no art appears; but merely a shallow story centuries old, which provides a release from reality for the masses who attend.

Letter from Dotty to Art
[September 20, 1943]

My Own,

Imagine my surprise this afternoon when I ran into Olson Pemberton on the street after work. He stood and talked for about twenty minutes about everybody we knew. The occasion for his being in Knoxville is the fact that he is on his way home to see Sam, who expects to be shipped out or across very shortly. He said that John "Squawky" H. is trying to get into Princeton. There is going to be quite a gang there, for one thing or another. He said that seeing Cordelia occasioned a long letter to Ted, and that seeing me would do the same for you. I hope he means that.

The weather here has been chill and rainy, in the traditional September manner. I trust that the heat has also broken out where you (bless you) are. If it hasn't, you let me know, and I'll send you one of our coolest raindrops. We have had a fire in the front room fireplace for three days. Every time I came within the glow of its warmth I think of our many happy trypts [?] before such fires. Oh, happy days, come thou soon again!

As for the poetry—Darling, the "Lover's Prayer" is a beautiful thing. Your Dad knows how to pick 'em! So do you. Joyce Kilmer's poem reminds me of one Jenks wrote. An odd style.

Remember the tall pine tree in the very back part of our back yard? It is now no more, for Dad "cut down the old pine tree," Saturday night. It was very perverse, and fell just exactly in the opposite direction from that in which Daddy was striving to make it fall. It fell across Johnson's yard, but did not damage except to break a small telephone wire. Felling a tree is exciting.

It is also exciting to attend a square dance. The hiking club held a banquet and square dance Saturday night. Mary, and Florence and I went to the dance, which was held at the Y.M. On the way we saw Arling Kressler just standing on the street corner watching the people go by, so we persuaded him to go along. He lives at the Y.M, you know. He had never been square dancing before, but he joined in and did fine. In fact, if it had not been for him, I might not have been asked to dance at all. Men are not so plentiful, you know, and I do not attract moths to my flame like Mary does. Question: how did I ever attract you? Answer: You ain't no moth! It was lots of fun, but golly, I missed you!! I was in quite a whirl when it was over.

Yesterday—it rained. I sang a short solo in the anthem at church. "God shall wipe away all tears," etc. Yesterday was Uncle Tom's birthday, so Aunt Mary and Uncle Tom came down here for dinner. Mother used every pan in the house, getting dinner, so I washed dishes far into the afternoon. (It's always my turn, now!) Then Aunt Carol called and asked me to come up to her house to help entertain an air cadet who had invited himself out, because she and Florence had to leave before the cadet did. Would I, please. Yes, I would, I guessed, although I had planned to entertain you (by a letter). He wanted to play the violin, so I accompanied him for a while after Flo left. He was a nice fellow, and would as soon play hymns as anything else. He quit on the Moonlight Sonata. He seemed very appreciative of my patience with his playing, and complimented my playing highly (which shows that he didn't know too much about it.)

May I brag a little too? I have been bragging to nearly everyone about how I have gained weight in the past three weeks. Now hold on ———I haven't gained that much! Just 2 1/2 pounds. I now weight 105 1/2. Isn't that wonderful? Yes, it is, too.

I wonder what the cabin is like in March? Do you think you can compete successfully with a March wind? I can just see that cosy (?) front room with a roaring fire in the huge fireplace, the curtains drawn across the French doors onto the porch, and most vividly of all me in your arms. Sigh. What do you think?

By the way, do you hear from Dick Boyd? He seemed unhappy at the close of school, sort of at loose ends. How are things with him now?

By another way, how are your folks? I haven't heard from them in some time. I sent them a card from Philadelphia. I think of them often and wish I could see them. Tsk, tsk.

Congratulations on your high firing score. I am counting on you to make a top score on that A.S.T.P. test you are taking soon. I still think it would be too good to be true for you to be sent to U.T. for your Sp. Tr., and yet it is highly possible! I have all my fingers crossed, and I'm ampidextrous [ambidextrous] along that line! (Do I mean double-jointed?)

Harriet and Sam should be in Hartford by now. They are really pulling up roots, now. But they was planting a bigger tree.

I do hope you and Ted make it to Los Angeles this weekend! You've tried so hard. You should be rewarded for the persistence if nothing else.

Yes, and I adore getting letters from you too, my darling, for you are the one I

        Love,

         Dotty.

P.S. Aren't mail peculiar? I received two letters from you today, one postmarked the 15th, and one the 17th. Ho, hum. I sleepy. Goo night.

Letter from Art to Dotty

Station Hospital - Roberts
Sept. 22, 1943
Wednesday Evening

My Dearest Own,

My surroundings at the present seem entirely apart from anything remotely connected with the Camp Roberts that I have formerly known. For more than two weeks I have been troubled with a constant headache. The dispensary seemed unable to alleviate my trouble and finally today I was sent here for observation.

At the moment I am stretched out full length on the ground in front of the Red Cross Building just across the street from my ward. The grass is soft and green beneath me and my senses tingle with a feeling of luxury at being able to relax complete in such surroundings as the sun sinks lower and lower into the Western Sea. Yellow snapdragon borders the grass and a lovely rose is directly to my front. Birds, starlings, I believe, are sailing overhead a cooling breeze carries away with it memories of the intense heat of the afternoon. As much as I regret to miss training, I think that I am going to enjoy to the full these few days of rest.

So far, the doctor has been unable to decide just what ails me. It may be a recurrence of my old sinus infection or it may result from intense heat and eye strain. We know that it is nothing very serious and you must promise not to worry about me at all. I am hoping that the trouble can be cleared up in a couple of days at the most. By that time I will have had a chance to catch up with a bit of sleep and a lot of writing. After all, it has been some time since I have been able to tell you I love you in ten lengthy pages. To begin with, I love you, darling. That doesn't go on for a mere ten pages but ad infinitum.

Part of the training that I am missing is not too important, but some of it, I fear, will be. Tomorrow the company goes out five miles from Camp to a combat range. Here, battle conditions are simulated, real ammunition is used, and tactical problems are carried through. Tomorrow night the company will pitch tents out there, spend the night, and continue the work the following day. It will be difficult to make up this type of work.

This is a good place to begin a description of my week-end in L.A. —what a week-end! After four attempts, Ted and I were at last able to get a pass at the same time. We left about twelve-thirty. We had hardly gotten away from our company was when a car came along and asked if we were going to LA. We had expected to pay $10 or $12 for a round trip but this was free. It turned out to be a mother, father, and soldier son. The parents, from Oklahoma, had brought a car out to the boy and were leaving it with him. He was taking them to Los Angeles to catch the train.

We stopped for an hour in Pas Robles where Ted and I had a chance to buy a few essentials. We soon continued south via the inland route, passing near Bakersfield, the big oil field out here. We rode for miles with barren plains, more barren hills, and oil derricks lined row on row. On one stretch of the highway we could see the rode for sixteen miles, and there were many spots where we could see for eight and ten miles. As we neared L.A. we passed through a beautiful range of mountains, but they had little to compare with our Smokies.

Mrs. Tootell lives in Pasadena, a suburb of L.A. As we neared our destination we passed large groves of olive trees, orange trees, and grape vineyards. We also past the Rose Bowl where our favorite Vols made U.T. history. By eight o'clock, two hungry lads were making the most of home-cooked food and enjoying many of the comforts that can only be found in a home.

After family histories had been brought up to date, we decided to see a bit of Pasadena at night. Ted's cousin, a nurse, wanted to show us the high spots, so out we walked after ten o'clock. A moon just past the full began to show itself thru the palms and the sleepy city seemed to nod its head.

V.V., Ted's cousin, took us to the little theatre there where semi-pros were soon to open the fall season. In the true Spanish style, the front was a lovely garden surrounded by a balcony on three sides. We slipped in an open door and peeped through a crack to view the stage.

A play was being rehearsed, so we slipped up the shadowed stairway to view the action from the balcony.

Later we wandered to the City Hall, a massive structure done entirely in the Spanish style. Here we found an inner garden filled with trees, flowers, and strangely enough, empty benches. Spiral staircases led up from the four corners to two or three levels. From one spacious balcony opening we looked out on a large fountain in the very center of the garden. Tall towers touched the starlit sky to the right and to the left; across the way palm trees scattered the moon's rays. We halted there and for several minutes contemplated the quiet beauty of silence. The experience can best be described by comparing it in a small way to the College Woods in the light of a moon. You were very close to be that night, and I whispered a prayer for our love. As the night passed into the wee hours, we returned home, love excursion had been highly successful.

I think I will make this a chapter ending. I just realized that I fail to mail a note to you that I dashed off before I came to the hospital. You probably haven't heard from me in several days.

The last part of this has been written on Thursday morning. Soon after breakfast I had my head x-rayed for possible sinus infection. As yet, no report is forth coming. I am getting drops in my nose which may or may not relieve me. Hope to mail another letter this afternoon. Please, darling, do not worry about me. My difficulty is not of a serious nature, and I will soon be in there pitching again.

Our love goes on and on as our spirits grow closer to the God of Love.

> Thine own,
> Bushy

P.S. Write to my old address unless I mention otherwise.

Letters from Dotty to Art
Sept. 22, 1943

Darlingest,

What's all this I hear about your maybe having a furlow before Christmas? How come you tell your other girls before you tell me? Furthermore, why does Muriel get a card from you when I don't get anything? Take it easy, darling, I'm just kidding. After all, I've almost been counting on that xmas leave as a sure thing, and besides, I'm glad you find time to send a live to Muriel now and then. By the way, I saw Muriel this afternoon for 15 whole minutes. I as usual got off at 4:45, and she was leaving on the 5:00 bus, because she wanted to get back for the wedding. Janice Grayheal and Lynn Crawford got married in M.C. Chapel tonight. Would like to have been there.

Ever since I got back from my vacation has been a sort of slack season at the office, so in a a way my vacation has been extended. I have enough to do to keep me busy all day, but not enough to rush me. And besides, I have another new girl (harrrumph), which makes two assistants. Right now, however, I don't have enough to do to keep them both busy all the time. Anyway, s'nice!

We have so much good reading on hand now. It angers (?) me because I don't have time to read it all. We have have Clarence Day's <u>Life with Father and Mother</u>, <u>The Song of Bernadette</u>, and <u>For Whom the Bell Tolls</u>, which I feel I must read, to say nothing of a few other not so good books and several magazines that I'd like to read. Do you think I'll ever have time enough to do all the things I want to do? I guess not. Sad case, sad case. At least I'll never be bored for long.

Florence is with us yet. Carl has not yet arrived at Princeton, he's training starts October 6., so if he finally gets there any time soon he and Flo may have a little time together before he buckles down. Dean is home, again. This time he has several days. Nice, huh?

The concerts are "out of this world" this year! Six wonderful concerts instead of four, one every month from November through April. I am enclosing some literature on them—thought you would enjoy seeing it. Daddy doesn't know what is going to happen yet—that is to be a surprise for his birthday next week. It was sweet and generous of you to want to get Daddy's ticket, but <u>please</u> let me take care of it— you need to save all the many possible, remember? Either let me pay all of it or let me go halves with you. The seats are more expensive this year, so the best I could do was a $6.60 seat for all of us. Mother is buying her own, and we will all three sit together. Our seats are way up in the balcony, but in one of the center sections. [Dotty draws a diagram of the stage and the location in the audience where they will be sitting.] Not bad, I'd say. If we can see.

And remember, if it isn't all its half, and no "butts". Oh, Darling, I'll miss you so—being with you was a large part of the joy of concerts. Oh, I'll enjoy them intensely, but it can't be quite the same. Hey—the Ballet Theatre is March 27—I wonder. Could be, darling!

I think of you constantly. It's an all-consuming thing, this

     Love,

      Dotty.

Friday,
and the hour
is Midnite!

My Dearest,

Since it is so late I can only write a little, but I had to talk to you a while. I was hoping that this would be a red-letter day, or at least a letter day, and I got part of my wish. The wonderful little package made it a red-letter day, but letter was there none. Oh, Darling, its beautiful! I go around sticking my chest (?) out and proudly displaying my pin that is unlike any pin anyone else is wearing. So there. Oh—Gee—I love it. Just wait till I wear all my medals and pins someday. Ouch.

Tonight we gave a farewell party for Mrs. Hamilton and Latane. It was at Aunt Carols', and was given by the young people, said young people being a bunch of girls, now! I had the pleasure of buying and presenting Mrs. H. And Latane with a gift (apiece).

I demand to know why (this should have been in the last letter) the name of Pvt. Arthur S. Bushing was not listed among the college class presidents, etc. in the article on the 81st Inf.Fr.Bw. that appeared in the "Camp Roberts Dispatch"? I was quite annoyed at the omission! See that it doesn't happen again. Just the same, your tops on my list of class presidents, Bud, on account of we got

Love,
Dotty

Mann, Thomas, <u>The Beloved Returns</u>, p. 163

"I must say I find it amazing how quickly and easily men change their views, when the course of events and the misfortune of a man they had believed in gives them better instruction!"

Perhaps prophetic of the German people of 1943-44.

* Letters from Art to Dotty

Station Hospital
Thursday Night - 9/23 [1943]

My Own,

These days of rest and relaxation may do much for me for it is giving more time to think than I have had in many long months. Creative thought and philosophical thinking can only thrive when the mind is free from the mad rush of living in a materially-minded world.

You know, of course, the attitude that I have taken toward marriage during a war. I have felt it unfair to tie you down, so to speak;

and in case, I didn't come back to leave you a widow with diminishing odds for a second marriage. Too, I thought of the possibility of you being left with the added burden of a child to rear. These things led me to feel the marriage wasn't for us until after the war.

When Specialized Training loomed on the horizon, both of us saw the prospect of me taking part in reconstruction rather than destruction. We saw our reasons for hesitation fading and our hopes leaped high with the thought that lengthy delay might not be necessary.

My ideas are changing gradually and I think that I can see them beginning to gel. In the first place, I think it was wrong for me to take the responsibility of making your decision for you. You are certainly able to see the consequences of marrying a dope like me, and it should be entirely up to you. The chances are excellent that I will not see action on the front lines; and, if I don't, I would very likely return. In case something did occur, you would have my insurance to provide partial security.

There is another feeling that has been surging within me for the past few days. You know how I have always felt about contributing to others whether it be from the desk in a classroom, from my pen, or from the pulpit. I also want to give the world children—strong children mentally, physically, and spiritually. My dearest, our children will contribute to the world around them. If I were to go to a fighting front tomorrow, I would be happy only if I knew that in your care I had left a son or daughter to take up where I had to leave off.

Station Hospital
Friday Morning. Sept. 24

My Dearest Heart,

Last night my morale went up ten degrees when I found a little library here at the hospital. It isn't large, and the variety is not great, but it has good books—enough to keep one busy for many days. As I mentioned before, I have been trying to review a little math and physics for the tests that I must take in the next few days. This time at the hospital will offer the one excellent chance to do this. Last night I spent an hour on algebra and this morning I spent some time on physics. It's a wonderful feeling to be able to get down to work on something constructive. How I long to be settled in school and really working.

There is little change in my condition this morning. The only treatment that I have been given has been nose drops three times each

Pe, California, 1943 [Art is in top row, 7th from left.]

day, but so far these seem to help but little. I do hope that I can be fixed up by Monday at the latest.

I am finding the men in my ward a rather interesting lot. While my outfit is made up of a bunch of eighteen and nineteen-year olds, these men have had two and three years of service, some of it overseas. Their stories show the less romantic side of Army life. Our men are fighting for more than the proverbial "love and glory." War is not a pretty thing.

I sometime wonder if men must always fight against each other rather than work together. If only the enormous forces that are being utilized for destruction could be gathered together and put to work for the good of mankind, the world would change overnight. It isn't as simple as that, however, and many years will pass before we learn the simple truth of plain Christian living. If we believe in progress, we must believe that the day will dawn. "How long, O Lord, how long?"

```
        HOPE    9-25-43


There are shafts of light

        A sunset fair

                A smile or two

                        A lilting song

Amid grey, long clouds.



        FANCY FLEEING       9-25-43


By cobwebbed paths I trace my course

        Back

                Back

Hoping to lose myself

                on a path that is lost

Hoping to find myself

                on a trail since gone.

O Past,

        Call me not

                Remain sealed and pure

                        Pain not this less sweet hour.
```

Poems by Art Bushing, 9-25-43

THE COMING OF NIGHT IN THE VALLEY   9-26-43

Cool winds of autumn blow across
The lawn, and clouds are being tossed
To odd shaped castles in the West.

The colors never seem to rest
But toss and turn on th' far hill crest,
And the night is drawing nigh;

The birds cry home as in the sky
They turn about and westward fly
To warming nest and love.

TO A LONE TREE   9-30-43

                                    it
Alone he stands on the high hill crest
Alone against the wind
                    the sun
                            the rain

I too rough the elements
I too dig deep into the earth
            to find solid rock
                    to find my source of strength

I too stand alone against the wind
                            the sun
                                    the rain.

A lone tree on a distant hill, the rough elements that
surround one in Army life—these things seemed to fit
together in the above manner. One feels strong because
the tree is strong.

Poems by Art Bushing, 9.26.43 & 9.30.43

203

As I remember, I left off yesterday with my L.A. trip with our return home Sat. night. We arose the following morning at a late hour. By the time we had finished a healthy breakfast we had to get ready for church. On our way we stopped at The Green Hotel—one of the largest in town. With a business-like air we walked directly into the lobby as though we belonged there. Though I love simplicity, I admire the splendor that one sees in such a building.

After absorbing the sights here, we hastened on to church. No chapel on any post in the world can offer the worshipful atmosphere that a church affords. The sermon was called "The Ministery of Silence," ["The Ministry of Silence" delivered by Mr. Petrie] and the minister described perfectly moments such as we have known in the college woods, in the mountains, and in the silence of the quiet church alter. Everything went to make the service wonderful and inspiring. I have a program back in the barracks which I will try to send to you.

Another highlight of our trip came in the afternoon when we visited a Chinese Garden with an ajoining [adjoining] Art Gallery. Like an enchanted garden from story-book land, in this hidden spot were strange birds and flowers. Chinese oddities filled corners and crannies. In the gallery were on display a number of very fine paintings.

Upon our return to Mrs. Tootell's, we found another missionary who had known the Kidder's in China. We had only a short time left, but she insisted on taking us to see more old friends. It was good that we did for we saw many things of interest in addition to seeing the very close friends of Ted's. We passed by the famed Santa Anita Race Tracks where an Army Unit is now encamped. We passed by the foot of the mountain in full view of Mt. Wilson Observatory; and, on our return we came by Calif. Institute of Technology. Our time was short and we had little chance to view much of the campus, but it had the appearance of constant care and planning. The buildings, as one might expect, were designed along Spanish lines; and the total impression was one of culture and refinement.

From Pasadena we had an hour's ride by streetcar over to Hollywood where we were to meet our friend. The ride was interesting but uneventful. We passed the famed "Brown Derby" and a couple of other well-known spots, but had no time to see the "Canteen" and other places of interest.

Chinese Garden, Pasadena, on September 18, 1943

The one dominant impression that I received in Hollywood was the false god of material hold sway, and the mad rush seen on every hand was an unavailing effort to please him.

After a long night's ride, we arrived in Camp during the wee small hours to hasten to sleep. The trip was certainly worth a great deal to both of us. New faces, new customs, new ideas can always be found with new sections of the country. From your own travels I know you can verify that.

By the way, I read with intense interest your vivid description of Maryland and Penna. Your letters always inspire me and help me to carry on.

This letter seems to be a series of disconnected notes, but every line I write is bound to every other line by the strong hand of love which makes our hearts one.

To continue the thought of the note of Thurs. night, I anxiously await the moment when our plans can be made definite. If I can get back to work within a few days, my training will be over in five short

Pasadena Presbyterian Church, September 19, 1943

weeks. When I know that Specialized Training is certain, the whole outlook will be changed. With patience, let us wait yet a little while, my sweet.

In the last two days I have written to Mary Ruth and Mother. I must try to write a number of back letters in the ensuing days.

By the way, it is too bad that Rev. Hamilton is leaving. How about Dr. Orr and Dr. Gates. Both did much for us at Maryville. If Pete is around, it would be swell to have him do the job. I'm really not hard to please on that score. I am racking my brain for a best man. John (H.)

always had an eye for the job, but he has decided to enlist. Perhaps Hargrave could get a furlough. Might get Pete for that.

In reference to John's enlistment, I feel in part responsible. I told him that I thought he should. The self-discipline that he will be forced to take on may proving the making of him as a well-rounded individual. He needs to find himself.

You haven't mentioned my request that you buy a season ticket for Dad to the U.T. Concert. I will send the money next pay day.

In order to make the afternoon mail I close this chapter. Will write more tomorrow, darling. Meanwhile I dream of
Our Love,
Bushy

* Station Hospital - September 25, '43
Saturday Afternoon

My Dearest Heart,

I almost hesitate to write in moments like these when my morale is at low tide and I have a sordid outlook. There is much to be happy about. Today, for the first time since I came to the hospital, I received mail—four letters and a package! Oh joy! For the first time in many months I am beginning to get caught up with my correspondence and I also have time for reading. The food is excellent—the sunsets enthralling.

However, my headache continues unabated and the doctor is doing absolutely nothing for me. "Take aspirin," "Take aspirin," he says, as if that would cure me. I can stand the pain; I've been doing that for more than two weeks now; but I do wish I could think that a cure was in sight. Perhaps they are phoning Wash. to see if they can go ahead with treatment.

I'm sorry, darling. I did not intend to get out of hand; but I am exasperated sometimes at the sluggishness of the Army. I realize that in any organization so large, everything takes much longer; but some of it is unnecessary.

Today I helped wash dishes and clean up the ward kitchen—more the activity than anything else. When God designed me, He never intended that I should spend my life vacationing in a hospital. I know that the rest is good for me but I am already beginning to fret. Remember, dearest, when I grow old you must never let me stop work even if I am only writing or digging in my rose bed. I think I would be a nervous wreck if I remained inactive for any length of time. After all, life is activity; death is merely stagnation.

A letter from John last week indicated his pleasure at my decision for the ministery. I did not mean by any measure, that I have made a clear decision. I have offered myself without reservation to full time Christian Service if God wants me there. I am still awaiting a definite call.

This afternoon I wandered down to the library to revive nostalgic memories of former days. With more than a little pleasure I caressed the small collection with a loving eye. You alone, my sweet, take precedence above my love for books. In case you are not destined to be the mother of a gang of P.K.'s, you must accustomed yourself to life with an incurable bookworm. However, I can assure you that we will never need ration-points. Bill Shakespeare will always be food for thought!

Your vivid description of the cabin in March sets my heart aflame, for I too have been day-dream of the seclusion of that spot. Darling, I miss you more with each passing day. Yet a little while and this too shall pass away. Patience, though the hardest to acquire, is perhaps one of the most noble of the virtues.

I am happy that you are able to go to square dances, etc. Please mix with others whenever possible. I know how much it meant to that air-cadet to have you entertain him and I want you to do that sort of thing every time the occasion arises!

One thing you failed to mention in regard to that 2 1/2 lbs. Where, my dear, did it go? Wt. is swell, like clothing, if worn in the right places. I too have my fingers crossed.

I still hope to catch the afternoon mail with this, so for now

All my love,
Bushy

P.S. Heard from Muriel. Hope to write her soon. Hey, maybe Hal could be around for Best Man. Yes? No?

Station Hospital - Roberts
Sept. 26, '43 - The Babbet [?]

My Dearest,

My fifth day in Ward 19 has come and gone. As I talk more and more with the men here, I find revealing things that interest me greatly.

While waiting for church this morning I struck up a conversation with a Phillipino (sp?) lad who is here in my ward. Although he has been in this country for ten years, I had difficulty understanding all that he had to say. Nevertheless we were soon talking about religion and the various sects. In belting phrases he explained his simple but firm faith in God. We talked until time to go to the service, and then went along together. Remember Kipling's words? — "There is neither East nor West..." etc.

I think I mentioned the fact that these men are older and more mature than the fellows in my company. Many of them have returned only recently from active duty in the combat zones. I am glad to see that the morale is good. These men have not become stagnant as a result of their long months in the service. They are thinking about our policy after the war, about the problems on the home front, about religion. This morning I heard a group debate for two hours on the matter of socialized medicine.

I must mention something of the work of the Red Cross here. Just across the street from my ward is the R.C. Building where patients are entertained. Shows are held every Tues and Friday night, and special musical programs, game nights, etc., are planned all the time. Church services, both Catholic and Protestant, are held every Sunday morning. It was a real thrill this morning to hear one of the patients, perhaps one just returned from Guadalcanal, request "God Bless America." It isn't a lot of bunk to say that these men know what they are fighting for. As another example of what the Red Cross is doing, there are fifty girls here tonight who have come from Bakersfield, (125 mi S.E.) to entertain the patients. Poor girls, they have already danced three times today, and tonight they dance here. One of them who ate at my table tonight is an English teacher—small world!

For the first time in months I am beginning to write a few bits of verse again. I enclose these that I jotted down yesterday and today. Perhaps you could copy them on the typewriter and save them. They are barely worth saving, but for sentimental reasons—! Thanks, darling.

Had a nice letter from Jimmy Smith yesterday. Also letter from Muriel which I answered today. I don't have Jack's address, but want to write him.

Tomorrow I intend to insist on some action being taken in regard to my case. I have rested around here doing nothing long enough.

Night shadows lengthen and I must prepare for bed. (I hope I don't spoil you as I write every day.) Both day and night I dream of

Our Love,
Bushy

Station Hospital - Camp Roberts
Sept. 27, 1943

My Own,

This morning the ward doctor checked with me as to my progress which was nil. The x-ray revealed clear sinus so that eliminates another possibility. We made out forms for me to go to the Ear, Nose & Throat clinic, but I will probably not be called until tomorrow sometime. Meanwhile, it seems almost certain that I will be shifted to another company when I do return to active duty. Tough, but it can't be helped.

I was interested in a brief discussion which I had with the doctor sandwiched between questions as to my headache. I had heard little about it, but there seems to be a bill in Congress now intending to introduce socialized medicine in this country. I know little of the details, but the plan seems to involve medical aid for all persons under this Social Security Plan. Many of the doctors with whom I have discussed the subject are thoroughly against it. The officer this morning told me that he would either leave the country or give up medicine. Something of an exaggeration, of course, but nevertheless indicative of the feeling of medical men toward the movement.

It is going to be interesting to watch the whole socializing stage through which the United States is passing. The New Deal has given strong impetus to it, and where it will stop is a matter for the wave of future alone to decide. I read recently an article which spoke of the post-war period as one of stabilizing. I rather doubt this. We are still a young nation; and, for the first time in our short history, we are flexing our muscles to find them fully developed in maturity. I speak of physical maturity; with nations, as with men, physical maturation procedes mental maturity. There must still be a period in which we "settle" to take definite form and to assume clearly defined ideas. Post-war development on the home front will make their place in history. Darling, it is no small blessing to be living in such kaleidoscopic times.

This afternoon I basked in forgotten pleasure as I played Brahm, Shubert, Wagner, etc. to my heart's content. The Red Cross has a very good machine and a serviceable library of music. I can see where I will spend many pleasant hours with these records. Music is one of my most serious losses.

Tonight I continue my dream-like existence in the library where I have just begun Thomas Mann's <u>The Beloved Returns</u>, a study of the later life and love of the Master Goethe. Mann is one of the truly great modern writers, and we must read more of his work. As I go more deeply into this book. I will attempt to discuss its merit.

With these new found pleasures to enjoy I am becoming a bit more reconciled to my fate here—particularly since I have no choice in the matter. Nevertheless, I long to get back to work.

"Tis late! For now
   Goodnight, my Love,
    Bushy
P.S. Filipino is spelled "Filipino" and not otherwise. (See letter of 26th)

Letter from Art to Dotty

Station Hosp. — Roberts
Sept. 28, 1943 (Tues. Night)

My Dearest Heart,

Again my morale soared to a new high today when I received four big letters. One from Hargrave, one from Ted, and two—yes two (of 22nd and 24th) wonderful letters from the sweetest, most adorable, most lovable girl in the entire twenty-five hundred miles that separates us.

You really will be worried when you hear that I wrote an entire letter to Muriel as soon as I received her letter. "Two-faced" they used to call me—when I appeared at the masquerade with a small mouth. I will also confess again that I wrote your dear sister and also our mother. Tsk! Tsk! You had better better watch me, dear. As to the furlough, I think I said "I hoped to have a furlough by xmas." I continue to hope—needless to say. It will either be several weeks early or many weeks late, I fear.

I am glad that your work is light for a change. It certainly sounds as if you are getting up in the T.V.A. when you have two assistants. It seems as though you are growing accustomed to bossing. Easy, easy, easy! I do hope you can find time for some good reading. The books sound swell and I know you will enjoy them. <u>No, darling, you will never have time to do all the things you want to do. Life doesn't work that way. Life is a series of choices; those who choose wisely the things that will take up their time are the ones who reach heights of greatness.</u>

It was with a feeling of intense longing that I looked over the concert schedule for the winter season. My one consolation will be that there will be many, many concerts in the years to come which we can enjoy to the fullness together. I am so happy that the three of you will be able to go together. You are so insistent upon the point of Dad's ticket that I suppose I must give in part way. I must insist upon paying at least half, however. I will forward the money as soon as I get the monthly pay check.

Lights out

I just returned from the show "We've Never Been Licked", with the setting at Texas A&M. [a WWII propaganda film released by Universal Pictures] Was there with one of the Aggie boys who took part in the picture. Enjoyed it very much. Now I am doing one of your tricks as I write in the bathroom.

I suppose there isn't too much of news to relate. Bill writes for advice regarding a prospective engagement to a girl from home—Philly, that is. Poor guy, he has his troubles. First one & then 'tother. It's a pity he couldn't have found The one early in his career, as I did. Another proof of how very, very lucky I am, darling. I am advising him to take his time. Neither Rome nor love were ever built in a day. Ft. Robt. Calvesbert is stationed at Pensacola. Meteorology, remember?

I thought often of the choice I made on that memorable day of Mar. 9th when I chose between three months at Maryville and meteorology. It was a choice deciding our future, and I have no regrets. I hope I never, take time to regret any choice I make, for it is a mere waste of time to worry about it then.

> *"...I shall be telling this with a sigh*
> *somewhere ages & ages hence*
> *Two roads diverged in a a woods and I,*
> *I took the one less travelled by*
> *and that has made all the difference..."*

212

Remember Frost?

I must sign off for tonight, my love,

Thine own,

Bushy

P.S. I. Always anxious to hear of Carl's welfare. Send me his address when you get it. Also Arlene's. I have written a letter to Bob & her, but address back in barracks & I can't get it.

II. Nothing at all on my trouble today. Headache persists unabated.

Letter from Art to Dotty

Station Hospital, Roberts
Sept. 29, 1943

Dearest Heart,

If ever cloud has a silver lining, I suppose it is also true that every silver lining must also have its cloud. Almost three weeks ago I wrote Dad and Mother concerning our plans to get married after I get settled in school. Today I received an answer. I enclosed both Dad's letter, which I feel bears with it the feelings of Mother, and an excerpt from my answer which I wrote almost immediately.

Darling, I am more than a little torn up about the whole situation. On the one hand, I feel bound in filial duty to Mother and Dad and their wishes; and yet, on the other hand, I am torn by a deep and consuming love of you, my dearest.

More deeply than I realize, Mother was hurt last Xmas when she learned of our engagement. I think you understand something of her reason: my age, the war, the desire to see me "firmly established. And yet, with all of this, it is with a rebellious spirit that I try to comply with their wishes.

As I told Mother in my letter, I regret deeply that I did not discuss our engagement with them prior to making it definite. Not that it would have made the slightest difference in my plans, but it would have given them the satisfaction of not being "left out" on an important and far-reaching decision of mine. Mother and Dad have done much for me, and I can't help feeling a sense of responsibility to their wishes even though they conflict with mine—with ours.

In the hurly-burly of the moment—my mind has been in a tumult all day—the picture seems about this: Until I can effect a change in the attitude that Mother and Dad are taking, our plans will be delayed. I sincerely believe that I can bring them around to our point of view by the time we could go ahead anyway.

Darling, please go over these things carefully, point by point, in your mind. Weigh each value involved and give me your frank thoughts on the matter. It is not as I wanted it, nor is it a happy situation. I suppose no situation is ideal. But above all, I want you to be assured that there is nothing whatsoever personal in the feelings that Mother and Dad expressed. Both of them have a very high opinion of you, and feel that I could not have made a better choice: They honestly feel that it would not be to my advantage to get married until I am settled down "in the business or professional world". With all my heart, I disagree!

Unless they bring up the subject, I think it unwise for you to make any mention of the subject by letter. I will keep you up to the minute on the chain of developments.

Just a thought in passing: I think it would have made a world of difference if they could have seen us growing closer to each other. Due to my own ignorant neglect, they failed to see our engagement coming on. As yet, they have not recovered from the start it gave them.

I was finally called this morning to the ear, nose, & throat clinic. The doctor found nothing! "Come back Friday and we'll look some more," he said. When I returned to my ward, the doctor sent me over for another x-ray for sinus. The one last week didn't show the part he wanted to check. You know, I may get out any week now! My headache is no better—in fact it has been worse during the last twenty-four hours. The pain is bordering on monotony.

With the hope and pray that "all things work together for them that love the Lord" * I say goodnight, my darling. Our years will be happier for the difficulties we encounter on the way.

Eternally thine,

Bushy

* The quotation is not quite correct.

[The following letter was written by Art to his parents. Then Art recopied the letter by hand so Dotty could have a copy of that letter, and know what Art had written to them. Note the quotes.]

Dear Mother and Dad,

"......................

"I owe far too much to both of you to take such an important step without your consent. I had not forgotten that I promised Mother I would wait until after the war to go ahead with plans; and yet, as I see it, the circumstances have been greatly altered.

"In the first place, there seems no probability that I will see combat duty, and this eliminates the problem you once suggested of leaving a widow. In the second place, it seems that I may be tied up with the Army for several years. You speak of getting settled down in 'the business or professional world' and yet it seems to me that if I have a firm connection with Uncle Sam I could hardly expect more security. If it is to be for a number of years, I hardly think you could expect me to wait to settle down. It would neither be fair to myself nor to Dotty.

"In the discussion so far, I have intentionally failed to take up the suggestion of getting married after I get started in school. I asked for your advice on this and you gave it to me. Perhaps you are right. I can't quite see it in the same light but, as I said before, I could not be so ungrateful as to go against your direct wishes.

"It was with some surprise that I read what you had to say regarding my honors work. When Dr. Shine gave me a "B", he explained the difficulty of grading work which was still in an unfinished stage. He gave me every reason to believe that he was completely satisfied with the work that I was doing when it was cut short.

"Let me say again that I have no intention of going ahead with my plans while you feel as you do. For almost a year the memory of hurting you deeply has preyed upon my mind. I hope that you can someday forgive me for my hasty action. Not that I regret having asked Dotty to marry me; I feel perfectly justified in that. But I do regret more than words can say that I failed to first discuss the matter with you. I can only hope that you will someday see my point of view......."

[The following was on a separate piece of paper inside this envelope.]

Mann, Thos., The Beloved Returns, 1940
p. 133: "I have always noticed," Adele went on, "that society, especially our German society, actually takes pleasure in bowing down. It likes to spoil its favourites and superiors, and force on them an exaggerated pose

*of authority, until both sides suffer and nobody gets
any pleasure from it."*

Coming from a German, I am inclined to think that this
generalization is a correct picture of the German people. If so it
accounts for much of their history both past and present.

Letters from Dotty to Art
Sept. 27, 1943
Monday Night

Darling,

How are you? I hope? No, I haven't worried too much, but oh how
I wish I might have been there to soothe that aching brow! I hope that
your stay in the hospital alleviated your headache as well as giving you
a much-deserved rest. I hope to get a letter tomorrow saying that you
are better, nay, that you are feeling fine.

I'm so glad you and Ted got to take your long awaited trip to L.A.
You described the moonlit scene so vividly that I was indeed
transported to your side. How did you like Mrs. Tootell? Isn't she
interesting to talk to?

Yesterday I travelled to Maryville for the first time since those
memorable days in May. I thoroughly enjoyed every minute of it, even
though each minute was fraught with very poignant memories. I had to
leave Mr. Hamilton's last sermon a little early in order to catch a bus in
time to get me there in time for "Y". Frances Lane rode over with me.
Did you know that she didn't go back to school this year? She was given
a training course this summer at gov't expense (I think) and is now
working at Clinton for Tennessee Eastman on the project that nobody
knows anything about. She said that her decision to stay out and work
this year was an extremely hard one to make. You can see why.

Mary Ruth is in fine spirits and seems to be getting a great deal out
of school. There seems to be an awfully nice gang of girls on her floor,
very congenial, etc. She would love to hear from you. So would I!

Y.W. was inspiring as of yore, with much of Muriel—it was the
Sunday on which the "Y" president introduces each member of her
cabinet, who in turn says a few words.

Muriel and I had a long talk. She is trying to get a church job in
Peoria, Ill. I wonder why. Hmmmm—not so terribly far from Chicago,
is it? I loved seeing her again and talking things (!) over with her. She—
ah—wrote a little note which I am enclosing. I wrote a similar one to
Hal.

I talked to your ex-Joe-roommate. He is as blond and bedimpled as ever. Also talked to Dr. Hunter. He at least is still once of the stable Maryville elements. Also met "Mary Ruth's John. He is very nice; goes with other girls on purpose, so as not to get Mary Ruth involved during freshman year. Thoughtful, huh?

Pardon the spellings in the last sentence or two—I was sleepy but now I am awake (for how long?)

When the choir marched in, when it sang by itself, when the multitude of voices filled the chapel with hymn, when Dr. Gates produced a quiet, inspiring message, when the stars moved along with us, as the bus travelled—when all these things occurred, you were with me Darling. You will always be with me, because eternal is our

Love,
Dotty

September 26

Dearest Bushy,

Dotty is looking over my shoulder! She has been over all afternoon. Gee, its' great to see her—and that beautiful watch!

She's been telling me all about your work and showed me all your snaps. I was talking some today for Hal.

Thanks for your card. I'll love a letter! She's writing a note like this to Hal now—before she goes home.

I'm hoping like everything for that furlough. (Want to see you.)
Love Muriel

Sept. 29, 1943

Darlingcal,

"Everybody's doin' it, doin' it, doin' it. Everybody's doin'—what, why getting married! Witness the enclosed clippings. Isn't that silly? Now I wonder why they go to all that bother, all that fuss and feathers? Do you know, huh? I do. ("Because God made you") By the way; do you think we'll like it at the cabin that time of year? Sure, I'm game! I can just see it—all the doors to the outer cabin shut tight, against the cold and dampness, the curtains pulled over the French doors, a roaring fire in the big fireplace, and a great, great love to keep us warm and make the room shine with its glow. Shall we?

"Heaven Can Wait" has come to town, so I plan to see it some night soon. Yesterday was Dad's birthday. He was extremely pleased with the concert ticket (and his new pants and his new tie). I wanted to go to the show "My Friend Flicka" [starring Roddy McDowall] with Mother and Dad, but found I had to go to first meeting of Nurse Aid class. After waiting 45 minutes at the appointed time and place without a single kindred soul arriving, I decided that something was screwy, so went to show after all!

And now, I give you
Eternal Love,
Dotty.

P.S. As Muriel says, "I'd <u>love</u> a letter.
P.P.S Florence leaves tomorrow for Princeton!

Letter from Art's Parents to Art
Sept. 30, 43

Dear Son:

We had hoped to have a letter today telling us how you are and still have a chance of getting it tonight. Do hope you are so much improved as to be out of hospital. As comfortable as it may be there we are sorry that you are having to miss some of the training, especially if its going to make a difference in your going on with rest of group.

So many of our boys are being sent home that we sometimes wonder how they plan to keep an Army. I haven't had time to check up on the number out so far, but we certainly have an average of one per day. James Howard Gualls is out, and our neighbors are hoping that Fay will be sent home. He went in as limited Service.

Melba Reid was in to see us short time ago and. The poor fellow has failed out on his Specialized Training again. He is terribly disappointed for after all these months of training and with a commission within his group, and this the second Commission he's lost by failing on final exams is surely enough to discourage a fellow. He is in N.C. at present. Glen is in New Jersey and gets over to N.Y. quite often it seems. Fay is in Mass. Ward Story is in training (school) in Texas. Haven't heard about Eston lately.

Things here are going on about as usual. We have just completed a long hard job and only got it finished at time given by getting Florence to do about 35 hrs. of typing. The Army certainly expects one to keep busy.

We are having lovely weather with real cool nights, and I'd give a whole lot to have a few days off to do some outside work—no such luck.

36 months with no vacation is beginning to get tiresome, but the work must go on.

The town is very quiet with all the young people gone it seems. The Froggie girls and Looper girls are in Ward Belmont, John Sloan and Bill Johnson are in a Boy's school at Sweet Water Tenn, and Maud Catherine went back to Murfreesboro. Bill Ruth Wright went back to Maryville, but Doris is teaching. Teachers seem hard to find here for they are using teachers who have no training whatsoever. Renzo Beaty's wife and her mother (Albert Taylor's wife) are both teaching.

I haven't heard that you got the socks which I sent and included a "G." key harp. Didn't know if that was what you wanted, but the best I could get. They now have some heavy ones I could send. I later sent two pair of brown (kaki) dress socks—all the kind I could get in your size. If you need more of those I can send them. We haven't heard that you got the $20.00 money order your Dad sent, but I'm sure it reached you. So glad you had the trip to Los Angeles. Your Dad got a nice letter today from the pastor of the church you attended. Hope you can get other similar trips. I hope to get one trip to the City sometime this fall, but don't know.

There is no end to the work here, and with the calling of Fathers the work will be greatly increased by appeals etc. We hadn't gotten our Inventory Report in the mail until we get instructions about a "recap" of the entire 98 pages, which means another hard week's work—Orders are Orders, so we "carry on."

Do hope to hear that you are well again and that you are getting on with getting ready for your Exams. Let us hear about the Xray etc. Hope the trouble is nothing serious about your eyes.

We are hoping and praying for your continued success and protection.

Love from us both
Mother

[The following is a note from Art's father written in the margins of his mother's letter.]

Dear son: Mother some better. Now I have a sore throat, with little anxiety mixed in praying that word from you will be encouraging. Please don't worry about us here. We know you will be led along the right road, if for any reasons your Army plans don't come out as you thought due to your present incapacity which as you wrote might mean some new rearranging X God bless you. Dad

P.S. Will continue to write frequently if only short line until we hear news from you.

Letter from Art to Dotty

Station Hospital – Camp Roberts
Sept. 30, 1943

My Darling,

Almost every evening now I come to the little library on the grounds to read, write, and recall something of the joy I once found in the library at Maryville. Surrounded by shelves containing a representation of the knowledge of the ages one feels a sense of power, a sense of pride, a sense of exultation. Night after night I come in and merely walk up and down between the stacks, caressing familiar books with a loving gaze.

I suppose everyone learns to love the tools with which they work. The aviator learns to love the power of his motors; the farmer takes justifiable pride in the excellent condition of his livestock; the housewife never stops changing and improving the home that is her life. It is this feeling I have that I "belong" when I enter sanctuary of a library.

Each evening I try to take a roundabout way to reach my destination in order to exercise my pent-up muscles and to see the scenery at hand. You perhaps have noted the location of the hospital from the little map which I sent you. Directly to the west of the installation there is a sharp drop in the terrain and a more or less flat plain extends on for a couple of miles. Upon this plain are located the rifle range, the bayonet range, and the grenade course. My memory picture of these places is one of hot, dry sand, a burning sun, and a parched tongue. Tonight, the panoramic view from the edge of the hospital area seemed a world apart. In fact one hardly noted this open area at all.

On the northern side, close at hand, runs a long ridge of bare, California hills. Far to the west, perhaps ten miles away a range of low-lying hills runs north and south. It was behind this range that I saw the sun slip slyly as if seeking a moment's rest from a hard day. There was not a cloud in the sky, but a golden glow lingered in brilliance for many minutes. As the glow settled and slipped too behind the hills, blue shadows emptied themselves on the distant horizon and overflowed onto the plain below.

Night was at hand; the day had passed into the dark abyss of yesterday. The whole experience captured me completely and carried me back, back. We were together, my Love, as we watched the Day bow to his successor Night. I held your hand and we looked into each other's eyes. We understood. We had witnessed another of God's miracles and we smiled knowingly. I recalled Arnold's powerful "Dover Beach."

Little is new in my situation here. Today I received the remains of my month's pay. It's always "remains" when deductions are taken. I have a total of $35.75 each month to take care of running expenses and savings. You're getting a poor buy when you get me, dear. The corporal who brought my pay told me that I would be definitely transferred when I return. Ken's outfit, I think.

I enclose a letter I wrote to Bob and Arlene several days ago. Since I don't know when I will be able to get back to the barracks to get their address, I will let you forward it to them. Send it to Arlene and she can send it on to Bob. Read it if you like and add anything that you wish.

I also enclose money order ($3.50) for the concert ticket. I wrote Dad today as a birthday greeting.

All my love,
Bushy

Letters from Art to Dotty

Station Hospital – Camp Roberts, Calif.

Oct. 1, 1943

Dearest Heart,

Even in days like these when I am doing but little—reading a bit, writing, seeing the doctor, or a show perhaps – I sometimes sit up with a start. Why, here it is October already. Looking out of the window today I saw leaves beginning to turn. The bright green of former days is fading now. A dull green is still present, but the predominant colors, the ones that strike the eye, are the multi-shades of brown and yellow that make the time of year so beautiful. (How much it would mean to see these colors in the Cumberlands and the Smokies now!)

Yes, as unexpected as it seems, Fall has arrived. The noon day heat still brings beads of sweat to the brow, but this is only for a short time. Early mornings and late afternoons are cooler than before. Again too, the path that the sun takes is noticeably shorter now, and the darkness comes at an earlier hour. As I walk home from the library, I pull my robe more closely around me. The wind whips down the street and whistles in the eaves.

It is the time when one thinks of gathering pumpkins in the field and gathering in the last vegetables from the garden. The time when one gets out the old rake and rakes away the leaves from the iris bed in the afternoon when the day's work is done. I used to cut a little extra stove wood after supper for the joy of the exercise and also because it came in handy when the snow covered the ground. Yes, Fall is here, and when the wind whips down the street and whistles in the eaves, one thinks of a crackling fire, flames shooting high, the lights

[Letter stops here.]

My Darling,

Over again to the E.E.N.J clinic this morning. One side of my sinuses opened and "irrigated" (I believe they call it.) This afternoon I felt worse but tonight much better. Another x-ray today. Think it may prove to be sinus after all. Doctor told me to return next Wed., so I'll probably be here at least another week. Since I know I will be transferred anyway, it doesn't make too much difference now. I intend to enjoy to the full my stay.

Lights going out in a few moments. Nurse, a pretty thing, insists that I must say "Goodnight." Tsk. Tsk! I will say "Goodnight" to her but to you

Ever Thine Own.
Bushy

Letters from Dotty to Art
Friday Night
Oct. 1, 1943

My Darling,

I might have known that it was the mail system that was screwy, not you. In my last letter I hinted that I would love to hear from you, because after I received the first letter you wrote from the hospital I didn't hear again for five ½ long days, and naturally I wondered what went on. So, yesterday I got two of your letters, (postmarked three days apart!), and today I got two more; and furthermore, they were all mixed up—both of the letters I got today were written <u>before</u> one of the ones I got <u>yesterday</u>. So, forgive me for implying that you hadn't written—you wrote plenty, it just got mixed up in the mail. And such nice letters they were, too. Ah-h-h-h—, I'm a lucky gal! And the poetry

222

—I especially like the one with the meter and the odd rhyming scheme (or perhaps I don't know much about such).

"Heaven Can Wait" was such an interesting tale, and I liked it (enjoyed it is the word) a great deal. I hope a certain heaven I know of doesn't have to wait several hundred years. And, Darling, if becoming a preacher makes you anything like cousin Albert , I'll divorce you! (P.S. – I ain't worried.)

How I would love to get my hands on your head. I'm egotistical enough to believe I could help it. I'll come if you but say the word. Queer that they can't locate the cause—you don't suppose it couldn't something psychological, do you (you'd probably be the last to see it, if it were) or a nerve out of kilter, or something? If they don't let you go back to work soon, or you'll be in worse shape, if I know you. I do hope they will let you stay with your company. Gee, whiz!

Speaking of shapes, mine ain't so bad. The three (!) pounds seems to be pretty generally distributed, and I exercise every night. I'm not trying to get fat—I just know that I ought to gain a few pounds for the sake of my general health.

After studying the matter over, I have come to the conclusion that I put a vivid description of the cabin in two letters. Please excuse.

You could work up a good debate on the subject of socialized medicine. It seems to me that there are strong points on both sides.

I am enclosing a poem that Daddy got somewhere. He didn't write it. It is right cute, but lays it on a bit thick, I think.

Florence left this morning on the early train. The lucky thing. Last night we (Aunt Carol's family, Addison, Dot Barton, and some people you don't know) had a picnic out at Uncle Charlie's place on the bluffs over the river (just off the new highway to Maryville). That is one place we must go, you and I.

Muriel was planning to come over Sunday, but found that she had to be there Mon. morning for Mu Gamma [Alpha Mu Gamma] breakfast in woods, so her visit is postponed.

Fred Proffitt died yesterday. He had a series of heart attacks. Very sad, nicht wahr?

'Tis extremely late. I must needs retire to dream of
      Our love,
        Dotty.

Sunday
Oct. 3, 1943

My Own,

Yesterday I received the letter bearing the shocking news of you parents' reaction to our cherished plans. It has been the center of all my thoughts and prayers ever since. I shall try to present my frank opinion about the situation. I am always afraid that I will say the wrong things when I am stirred up like this. For once in my life I feel like being unreasonable instead of sensible; I find myself disagreeing at every turn with the points presented in your father's letter.

First of all, darling, I sympathize with your position. By agreeing with me you disappoint your parents, and by taking their advice you make it difficult for me. I started to say you would "hurt" me, but the only way you could do that would be to tell me you didn't love me. In any case, which ever way you turn, you make one or the other of us unhappy. None of which does your headache very much good.

If only we can make them see the picture clearly. I think they would agree with us if they did. Thanks for the assurance that there is nothing personal in the feelings they express. I find myself having to grab that assurance tightly when I read some of the things in that letter of your Dad's ("recurrence of that disappointment ...precipitated as Xmas," and the comment about your honor's work, for instance). Bushy, dearest, you are your parents most prized possession, and it is their greatest desire to see you rise to the very top of some ladder, and they resent anything or body that threatens that rise. Apparently I represent such a threat, else how could they feel as they do about your honors work and ASTP? My surprise at the reaction is as great as yours. Why, you surely saw more of some of your classmates than you did of me during the time you were working on your honors work! And besides, I had nothing whatsoever to do with the fact that it was cut short, and that seems to me the only reason your grade was not higher.

It is life with you that appeals to me, not the material things you have to offer at present, not 50 dollar allotments and insurance policies. I want the security of The Wonderful Life, the security that comes from being one with you in spirit and body, the security that comes from being able to help, soothe, or comfort you when you need me most. As for your taking your place in the business or professional world, I <u>know</u> you have the ability to do such when the time comes. The great problem is that we don't know when that time will be, and in waiting for it to come and our blossom of youth, our love and passion, our ability to adjust to each other cannot but be dimmed. We very definitely want children, and the time for me to have them is not 8 or ten years, but <u>now</u>!

Our marriage will not be hasty, your decision to marry me was not hasty in the least, and our decision to put marriage off till after the war was made when the picture was vastly different from the way it looks now. Can we not make your parents see this? We must. If you come home anytime soon, we must all get together and talk this out, and this time I want to be there. As the situation is now, we are all made somewhat unhappy by it. There must be a better solution. God will show us the right way if we can open our spiritual eyes far enough to see it.

Mother and Dad went to Maryville this afternoon, so I am alone and lonely. But, boy, can I concentrate on this letter!

Our first Sunday without Hamilton found a slim attendance, and this was world-wide communion. My spirit touched yours as I partook of the bread and wine.

I was offered the superintendency of the Junior Department of the Church this morning. Since I am planning to take the Nurse Aide course, which will require Sunday morning work at the hospital, I declined. I will also have to give up my primary class, and that too will be hard. My new class of kids (I just got them this morning—Promotion day) is eager to learn—quite a contrast to the class I just passed on, which had to have <u>any</u> sort of knowledge crammed forcibly down its throat.

All bad things, as well as all good things must come to an end, so surely your headache is diminishing by now. If it isn't do I have your permission to come out and blow it away?

Madge Evans moves in with me Thursday of this week. I am going to enjoy her company, I think.

I await your next letter eagerly. I await all of them eagerly. I must go to C.E. now. Meanwhile and always,

I Love you,
Dotty.

P.S. I love your Mom & Pop, too.

P.S. I've gained another pound, making my total weight 107 lbs. I asked Mother tonight if she could tell I had gained, and she said "no." So there.

Station Hospital – Camp Roberts, Calif.
Oct. 2, 1943 (Sat. Night)

My Darling,

It seems a bit strange that in all of the writing I have done since I came to the hospital I have consistently failed to go into any detail as to the system under which the hospital works and in general my physical surroundings here. More important things have been before my mind up to now, but tonight I think I will go into a little description.

In the camp are there are a number of dispensaries—one for every regiment, I believe—where the men are sent when they go on "sick call." (This merely involves reporting to the first sergeant before seven o'clock and indicating the desire to see a doctor). At the dispensary the ailment is treated and the patient usually returns immediately to his company for duty. If the case is serious, or the treatment beyond the scope of the doctor's equipment, the patient is sent to the hospital.

Once here, as I have found, the poor patient is stuck! Sometimes treatment is given in one of the clinics in the hospital and then returned at once. However, the suckers I referred to above are the ones who are admitted to a ward for observation.

These wards—there are thirty that I know of—will hold thirty-six patients. Each ward has its doctor, a day nurse, a night nurse, and three ward men. The latter do most of the work with the nurses being on hand at infrequent intervals and the doctor being around only in the morning.

We wear our pajamas and robe when we go to meals or anywhere else in the hospital area, and actually we wander about pretty much at will. I have mentioned the library and the Red Cross Building before. There is also a "PX" (Post-Exchange) where we can get magazines, candy, soft drinks, milk-shakes, etc.

Perhaps I have mentioned the fact that in the winter, we will have rain without ceasing here. (One month last year there was rain twenty-eight out of thirty days). This rainy season too has been provided for. Connecting every ward, every office, every single building, is a ramp. The areas where patients must walk are enclosed, I really believe that one could walk for ours [hours] in the hospital area, and never be exposed to the weather.

When men are to receive medical discharges, they are taken from the sick wards and placed in another part of the area. Here they work on odd jobs ("details" is the Army term) until the release is made final. I was amazed to find how many are discharged here. In the last thirty-day period, eight hundred men are supposed to have left. Of course, many of these are wounded men who have returned from the combat zone.

Taken as a whole, the hospital seems entirely apart from the Camp Roberts I knew for thirteen weeks. The tempo is down to a slow cadence, where one has time to think. This is literally true, for one doesn't have time for creative thought while in training. Yes, this vacation is proving very much worth while.

I continue to think a great deal about Dad's letter which you probably have by now. I anxiously await your reaction to the whole thing. Meanwhile I try to shape our plans in accordance with changing events. I maintain a profound belief in faith and prayer. I believe in His plan for us. May it hasten the day of fulfillment of
> Our Love,
> Bushy

* Letter from Art to Dotty

Station Hosp. – Camp Roberts
Oct. 4, 1943

Darling,

Monday afternoon and I have a bit more time for writing. Last night there was only time for a hasty sketch.

My general situation seems just about the same, with no particular improvement. Today the ward doctor gave me the report from the E.E.N.J. Clinic. "No indication of sinus trouble." He is sending me to another doctor, but it will probably be tomorrow or the next day before I see him. I return to the E.E.N.J. Clinic Wednesday. Since I am waiting to be called, I can't go down to the company today and probably not tomorrow.

The news concerning Specialized Training may alter our plans just a bit. Particularly in regard to the Xmas furlough which we had counted on. What I am hoping is that you can get another leave sometime after I get in school, and make another trip. I still keep my fingers crossed that my school will be within reasonable travelling distance. I should also be able to see you at the end of my first three months. Oh joy!

I mentioned in my letter last night, Dad's last letter softened up the viewpoint expressed previously: "... You are thinking of your future plans, of course, but trusting God as you are willing to do, I am sure, why not rest calmly upon

His leading and I am sure, parents' or no parents' fond wishes, you will be led into the path He has marked out for you to our satisfaction and your ultimate greater happiness. That is all we can be expected to hope for—for you have your own life to live which we must fully realize is up to you in the last analysis; and we do not want to kill off by any unreasonableness on our part our opportunity to share in that wonderfully fine living you are hopeful of being able to provide for those you love. So just rest in the Lord; keep your outside enthusiasms in check, because your Uncle Sam wants you to keep before you what is the important matter before you and the world—the winning of this terrible war..."

You see, deep down Dad understands our situation. We shall see what the future brings. After a term in school it will be far easier to plan. Almost "Everybody's doin' it, doin' it, doin' it" but most of them have a bar or some similar security for tomorrow.

Your letter of the 29th indicates that you were not hearing from me regularly. This should be changed by now, for I have written every day. This is the first time that I have enclosed letters for two days in one envelope.

I enclose a few pictures taken in Pasadena. The view looking N.E. in City Hall is almost the point I described which was flooded by moonlight.

Hope to catch the afternoon mail.

I linger in

      Our Love,
      Bushy

Letter from Art to Dotty

Station Hospital - Camp Roberts, Calif.
Oct. 5, 1943 (Tues. Night)

My Dearest Heart,

At last I can announce a partial solution to my difficulty. At last I have been told what is wrong by the psychiatrist. I spent more than an hour with him this afternoon. Darling, we have long since decided that utter frankness is the only practical way for two people to maintain a relationship of love and faith in each other. Therefore, I will attempt to outline the complete diagnosis as the doctor gave it to me this afternoon.

From my recent letters you have been able to gather that all attempts to find the source of my headaches from a physiological standpoint have failed. It was left then for the psychiatrist to discover a psychological concerning my personal history, my reaction to the Army, etc., he suggested that my trouble probably comes as a result of conflict of emotions and desires. He built up a case revolving around my feelings toward combat, the uncertainty of Army life, engineering in A.S.T.P. rather than some other branch, etc. I suggested our problem of getting married as against the viewpoint that Mother and Dad are taking, and also the desire I have always had for the ministry. He pointed out that a combination of all of these conflicts—some conscious, some unconscious—were the cause of my constant headaches.

I am inclined to agree that this is the possible answer. You know how I build up an emotional strain. Perhaps I should turn loose my feelings about the Army rather than kidding myself that it is a bed of roses and all O.K. Perhaps I have had too much control, if you see what I mean. The emotional tension of Army discipline should have a release. I thought that I had such a release but perhaps I was wrong. Further proof of this is seen in the fact that, although I have enjoyed two full weeks of physical rest, I am more nervous and restless than when I came into the hospital. I find it very difficult now to sit down and concentrate on physics or math as I try to review.

The doctor gave me this advice: "Do away with indecision." (In the Army? That's a laugh!) "Choose your career; decide a definite courses on your marital question." On his report he made three recommendations:
1) No oversea's duty in combat;
2) Return to active duty;
3) Return in four weeks for a check-up.

Knowing me, you can imagine how I feel about first of these. I don't expect combat duty with the A.S.T.P. program in view, but it does hurt to be told "unfit for oversea's duty." However, there is no help for that.

I believe that I can reconcile most of the problems and uncertainty that surround Army life. At least I have some idea of what I must do. Some of the other conflicts will require time. My first problem will be to completely accept the fact that I am of a nervous disposition. I must attempt to avoid the gradual building up of nervous tension. It was in this respect that you helped me so much at school. With you each night I was able to completely relax and forget the strain of work. Don't you see, darling, I can't live without you. With my soul, mind, and body I need you. But, that too is one of the conflicts that I must resolve— perhaps the paramount one. (It just occurred to me the irony of my dream to write a detailed study of frustration. Now, I'm the victim of many frustrations.)

I hope to get back to duty tomorrow. I will have plenty to do, and it may be that I will not be able to write again until the week-end. It will be difficult to get back to writing at such infrequent intervals again. Ted says they have even less time now than before. Will write at earliest possible moment. Meanwhile,

"....pray for my soul,
More things are wrought by prayer than this world dreams of."

Thine eternally,
Bushy

* Letter from Art to Dotty

Station Hospital – Camp Roberts
Oct. 6, 1943 – Wed. morning

Dearest,

I will only have time to mention a few things, but perhaps I can finish this letter tonight. As I mentioned in my letter last night, I am getting out today. I leave here at one o'clock.

I intended to mention that I would leave to your discretion just how much you say about my difficulty to Muriel and the others who know I have been here. The whole situation is so indefinite that I think "nervous disorder" should cover it. I would prefer that we say nothing about the first recommendation. I have not mentioned it to Mother and Dad, and think that I will not for a while. After all, it was only a recommendation and represents nothing final.

Thurs. Night – Barrack

Just a moment to dash off a few notes. Your wonderful reaction to Dad's letter was typical of understanding, lovely you. Letter from Dad tonight indicates changing attitude on Mother's part. He himself would concede to any practical plan that we might work out. He asks me to say nothing about the matter but to give Mother time to adjust to the idea. She is coming around to our way of looking at things.

"... You have a life to live and plan for, you both are praying about the matter; God will surely guide you into this great adventure for your happiness and His glory. Now Mother is slowly but surely coming to see that she must not be selfish about this matter nor in anyway thwart this natural longing for companionship... Be a little patient. Mother will finally write her feelings about your plans, and I feel sure will finally concur in what you wish to plan and do! It will take a little time. Your succeeding in getting specialized training will help a lot. God bless you. I love you dearly as I shall love Dorothy as a very precious daughter in law..." Dad Oct. 4.

Don't you see, my darling, things will work out for us. Our prayers, our hopes, our dreams will come true.

Here is some big news also. I will be leaving this company in a few days. Saw the C.O. tonight. I will also take my A.S.T.P. exams tomorrow. Very glad to get them now rather than later. Think I can get electrical engineering which I intend to apply for. Ted has wonderful news. He will get three months refresher in Chinese and then will probably get shipped abroad. Perhaps bars by that time. My training will likely last twelve to eighteen months but will know definitely within a few days.

Fri. Afternoon

Just returned from taking examinations for A.S.T.P. Plenty stiff but I think I made a fair showing for the most part. Will know in a few days. Let's keep our fingers crossed. Since I spent all day taking tests I wasn't with company again.

Ted, Ken, and I plan to go on pass tomorrow. It doesn't make much difference where. Will probably be our last chance. Don't know how soon I will be sent to 80th battalion. I think they lack seven more weeks which will give me just about twenty-one weeks of basic. I should be a good soldier by the time I am through.

I really think my headaches are improving. I try to forget about them and I am also trying to resolve my "conflicts." If the problem is a psychological one, I know that I can conquer it.

Last night we were out on another night problem. This time we ran a night compass course, hiking about seven and a half miles. Some fun! Oh yes, and yesterday we fired the mortar. (I thought I had heard that the infantry was motorized!)

Many of the men were not accepted for A.S.J.P because they lacked the proper courses. Some were rejected because of the fact they were pre-med or med students. Some of them will be able to return to school

Land Ahoy! "Carmel by the Sea" 10.10.43

Garden Spot on St. Near Beach "Carmel by the Sea" 10/10/43

when they are accepted which isn't bad at all. Others will remain in the infantry I guess. (Pardon the rough scribble but I am writing in a very peculiar position—sitting and writing on my foot locker at the same time.)

I will try to get this off now and write again at the earliest possible. When my transfer comes, I may have a wee bit of time.

For now, all my love
         Thine own,
           Bushy

P.S. Appreciated letters from "Ma" (Barber) and Mary Ruth. Will answer soon.

Letters from Dotty to Art
[October 9, 1943]

[In this envelope of two letters from Dotty, was also enclosed a typed letter from Art's Dad, which is also included.]

with reference
Dear boy: I tried to reply to your letter of Sept. 12
to your plans and seeking our advice in connection with same. Not reading it as carefully as we should have, our reaction was at first that you might not be seeking our advice as much as our concurrence in what you and Dorothy have pretty definitely decided upon. In that case, there wouldn't be much that we would care to say nor would your letter suggest anything much different than recurrence of the disppointment which you precipitated at Xmas, I will assume that you have not yet made definite promises nor committed yourself about getting married before the war ends. This is the promise you made your mother because as she sees it you cannot do any better work (ASTP) than you did in your honors work at Maryville which of course you fell down on because of too much attention to outside matters which must have diverted your energy—as pleasant as love making is. We have only your best interest and ultimate happiness at heart, and we feel at the moment that you should aspire to finish up your specialized training in the Army without any crack-pot idea that a $50.00 allotment and a $10,000 Life insurance policy should appeal to a girl starting out in life with you. You should have and she should insist that you get a good job; find your place in the business or professional world and

Ken Cooper & Art Bushing on the rocks in Carmel, CA,
with the Pacific Ocean in the background, October 10, 1943.

demonstrate thereby that you have your feet on the ground, and
are practical about matters of this kind as you are sentimental.
Well, dear boy, it will be interesting to hear again from you as to
why you now consider changing the comforting promise you
made your mother that you would put off this question of
marriage until after the war and now feel that your marriage is
imperative just as soon as you can gauge what your course is
going to amount to in specialized training for Army service.
Mother sends loving wishes and will try to write you over week-
end. God bless and keep you in my prayer. Whether the above is
going to be of any help in your final decision is of course up to
you, but be assured that whatever you decide Dad will always
pray for your largest possible success. Mother will worry but I
know enough about life and Emerson's Compensation that the
price is paid for all our unreasonable insistences. Write soon
again.   DAD

Your letter of Sept. 20 just to hand. Have just read it hurriedly. So glad you had such a wonderful time, and then the news of your good shooting. Sgt. York is in the office and he said when I mentioned it that he knew you got that ability from your mother. Good bye and best wishes.

* Letters from Art's parents to Art
Sunday Afternoon
Oct 10, 43

Dear Son:

Your letter of Wednesday the 6th came last night. We are more than glad to hear that you are back in camp, but somewhat nonpleased by your statements concerning the findings of the Dr. We thought you were getting on so well, and were happy in the thought that you were getting an opportunity to take the special training when so many million others are less fortunate. We thought we could count on you above all others to not let anything prevent you from making the most of the opportunity.

I feel that your first duty is to your country, and that you should make every effort to be the best soldier you know how to be.

Now as to the question of your getting married; if you feel that you can't do your duty as the soldier, without taking on the extra duty of a wife and home by all means get married. We have only had one hope in mind and that was for your success and happiness. If you feel that you will be content with the kind of life you will have as a married man in Uncle Sam's Army there is no reason for us to object. We had hoped for something better for you, but you have a perfect right to live your own life in the way you want to live it.

It's too of course that the Gov't will put up $50 per mo. for a wife, but $22 of it comes out of your paycheck. However that may not seem a problem to you, and you may never have any problems; but whether you do or don't, you have my permission to carry out any plan you may have, any time you like.

One thing we are counting on you to do is to make the best soldier you are capable of making. You are only one of ten million who has had to make changes in plans, and not one of them would have had this thing happen, if he could have prevented it. Now that we are in it, it's everyones duty to carry on as best he can.

Thanks for the pictures. We think you look rather thin, although you say that you weigh 160. We are real anxious to hear what will happen about the two wks training you lost, if you will have to make it up, if you will go on with your old company, or how you will get your exams if the others have taken their's already. You were to have been through basic by Nov. and as fast as time flies that time will soon be here. I presume you will tell us all these things as they come up.

Your Dad has spent most of the day, except the church hour, in the office. In fact he is have to spend a lot of time, Sundays, in office if we keep the work up.

I took part of yesterday afternoon off but didn't do a big lot of work. Have had a cold for several days, but it's getting better. I have most of the outside jobs done, and we will no doubt have a lot of work weather yet.

We got a big load of 8 to 10 ft. lengths of 1 to 2 in poplar strips for kindling. Yesterday afternoon one of the Patton boys cut them up for us, and we now have all our wood, coal and kindling for the winter.

Monday

Talk about a hectic day, we surely had one today. 66 boys to get off with busses <u>two hours late</u> and one queer duck (a fellow transferred to us from Oregon) ambled off had to be hunted up and rushed over to Crossville via car. Oh well it's all in the days work, but we certainly haven't done any work which gets anything really finished. Edd York [George Edward Buxton York] got home at 2 a.m. this morning and had to leave on the 10 a.m. bus to go back. A phone bill is $62 this mo. Fine business:

Lots of love from
Mother

[Below, a note written by Art's dad in red at the top of Art's mother's letter.]

Dear boy—hope you received my letter mailed this a.m. Believing you should now find your problems easier of solutions with assurances from mother and that we feel you can overcome what seemed difficult—we'll wait word that you are much better now.   Dad

**Letter excerpt from Art Sr. to Art Jr.
posted in its entirety below,
October 10, 1943**

[Hand written in the left margin:] Mother completed nice long letter to you. Will mail this pm. She gives her full consent to you carrying out any plans you want to now make about Dorothy. [Hand written in the top margin:] P.S. From now on you will hear often from us. Mother getting over one of those frightful colds but much better. 66 boys leave in the morning and 85 married men to get blood test Thursday. Boy, oh boy how we have to work but we love it!

*** October 10th Letter
[typed as well for your convenience]**

Dear son: Your letter from Station Hospital dated October 6 with pictures taken in Pasadena came last evening. We were delighted and disturbed, dear boy, for while Sinus is a painful ailment, as we understand it, your several problems of which we have been pretty much in the dark (these matters which you have had to discuss with your officer in the Hospital seem from here, pretty serious. It appears to us that if this condition in your mind continues, you cannot go on with anything like the service your Uncle Sam is entitled to. Why a conflict in your mind about fighting or killing anyone should have entered your mind as to seriously impede your training, at this time, seems tragic. No one in this War—fighting for our very freedom, delights in killing just for the sport of killing. This is Defense; an all-out struggle to keep from the women and children of the United Nations, the horrible brutality of Dictators that now threaten to cut off the heads of their own morale-shaken people, and dear boy, remember there are other good christian young men who don't like the business any better than you do, but are going to do their bit toward ending this terrible shambles. Jews are being killed and have been killed by the thousands simply because they were Jews. Don't you see, dear boy, that placed as you are—one of 8,000,000 men as you aptly put it, by conscription to be sure, to serve your Country, that you must not fail America. Everything is being done to teach you how, not only defend the Country, but to defend yourself on somewhat equal terms with the enemy as that occasion arises—if it arises. The Army is not a Sunday School affair, to be sure; its tough alright; there will be tough spots in every real fighting situation; it calls for virile men conscious that there never was any similar situation in the world's history when sacrifices great and <u>small</u>—but had to be faced and all personal consideration of one's comfort and plans held in abeyance until Victory was won. Being in, you will not, surely you will not let us down or your Country down by entertaining your own ideas, so to speak, of expecting to win a war <u>without fighting</u> for that victory. You are at the forks of the road, as your officer indicated, and must cure yourself of <u>even thinking further of having a problem on your hands to solve along these lines</u>. Now here is our solution for another problem upon which you have been anxious to get our advice but which, if a <u>problem</u> to you, should never gotten into that stage. Can any one ever love you more than your Mother and Dad. No, there may be another love equally precious and endearing, the love of husband toward wife etc., but precious son, we do love you, and think of the happiness to which you are entitled in the new relationship you are anxious to establish as soon as possible. In the light of your present conflicts, more especially in connection with your plans, you have my blessing and I know Mother is ready from the depth of her heart to forget and forgive any disappointment she and we may have had, about your planning for marriage just at the earliest possible and resonable moment. I especially feel that crediting you now with having thought it all through (which we at one time felt you might not have done) I am convinced that you will <u>make good</u>, and that with a prayer in your heart, you will fight to make this happiness you seek in establishing a home—altogether possible. So sonnie boy, God bless you. I want you to write me at once on receipt of this, that you will have no further worries about the step you feel you and Dorothy would like to take. It should make you want to fight for specialized training which your Government offers you, and surely <u>having problems that worry you and unfit you</u> for <u>being even a good rookie</u>, is not the manly way to face life's duties and obligations in even the present situation. I love you dear boy, and I am not a bit disappointed in the dear girl you want to make your wife, but now to have allowed worries to have gotten you down as a man and a soldier—well, you will <u>buck up</u> and <u>snatch at the happiness</u>, and be your own dear and real self. From now on you must feel free to write me for any advice you may think I can helpfully give you. I pray for you always. If and when you write me that you are your own dear self again, I want to get word to Dorothy of my delight in truly concurring in your plans, and express to her acceptance by me of that precious place she will occupy as a daughter. I know you will have

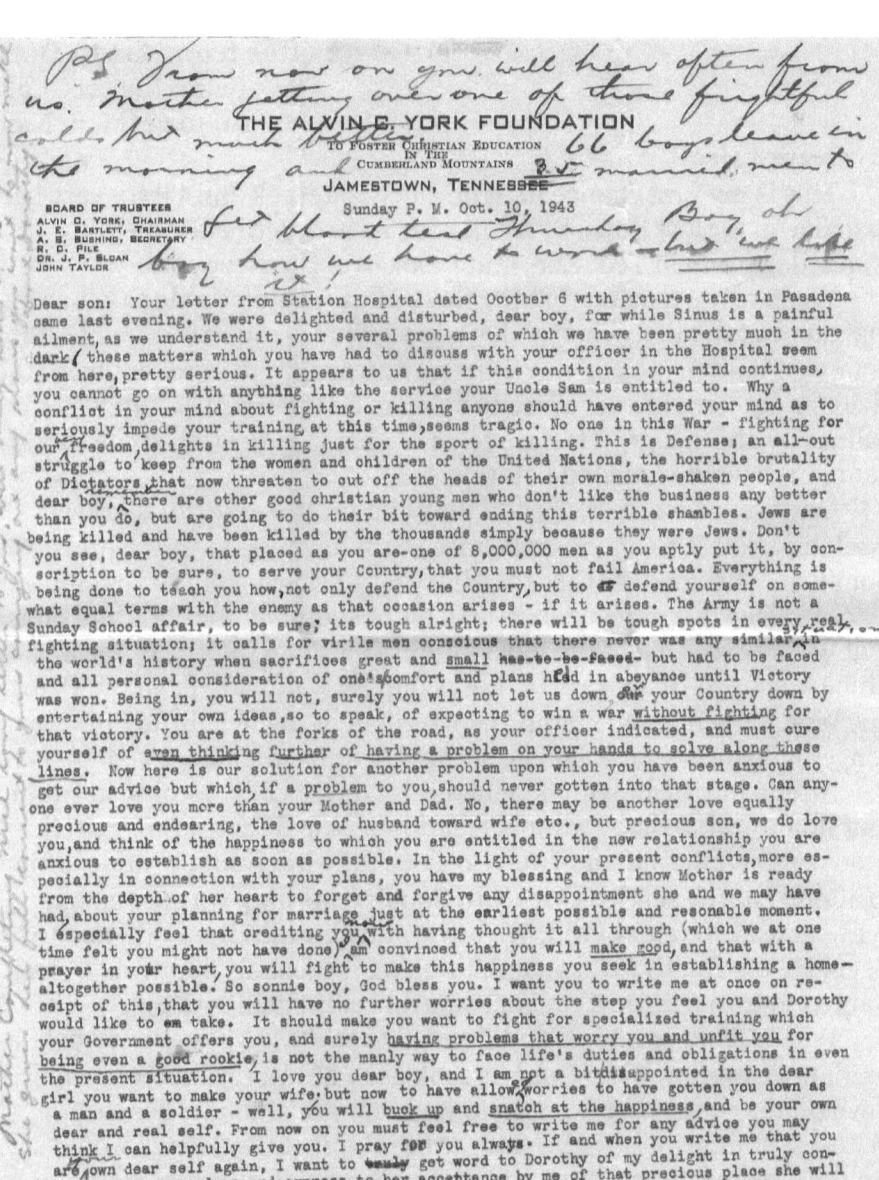

Sunday P. M. Oct. 10, 1943

Dear son: Your letter from Station Hospital dated Ocotber 6 with pictures taken in Pasadena
came last evening. We were delighted and disturbed, dear boy, for while Sinus is a painful
ailment, as we understand it, your several problems of which we have been pretty much in the
dark, these matters which you have had to discuss with your officer in the Hospital seem
from here, pretty serious. It appears to us that if this condition in your mind continues,
you cannot go on with anything like the service your Uncle Sam is entitled to. Why a
conflict in your mind about fighting or killing anyone should have entered your mind as to
seriously impede your training, at this time, seems tragic. No one in this War - fighting for
our freedom, delights in killing just for the sport of killing. This is Defense; an all-out
struggle to keep from the women and children of the United Nations, the horrible brutality
of Dictators, that now threaten to cut off the heads of their own morale-shaken people, and
dear boy, there are other good christian young men who don't like the business any better
than you do, but are going to do their bit toward ending this terrible shambles. Jews are
being killed and have been killed by the thousands simply because they were Jews. Don't
you see, dear boy, that placed as you are-one of 8,000,000 men as you aptly put it, by conscription to be sure, to serve your Country, that you must not fail America. Everything is
being done to teach you how, not only defend the Country, but to defend yourself on somewhat equal terms with the enemy as that occasion arises - if it arises. The Army is not a
Sunday School affair, to be sure; its tough alright; there will be tough spots in every real
fighting situation; it calls for virile men conscious that there never was any similar in
the world's history when sacrifices great and small has to be faced and had to be faced
and all personal consideration of one's comfort and plans held in abeyance until Victory
was won. Being in, you will not, surely you will not let us down or your Country down by
entertaining your own ideas, so to speak, of expecting to win a war without fighting for
that victory. You are at the forks of the road, as your officer indicated, and must cure
yourself of even thinking further of having a problem on your hands to solve along these
lines. Now here is our solution for another problem upon which you have been anxious to
get our advice but which, if a problem to you, should never gotten into that stage. Can anyone ever love you more than your Mother and Dad. No, there may be another love equally
precious and endearing, the love of husband toward wife etc., but precious son, we do love
you, and think of the happiness to which you are entitled in the new relationship you are
anxious to establish as soon as possible. In the light of your present conflicts, more especially in connection with your plans, you have my blessing and I know Mother is ready
from the depth of her heart to forget and forgive any disappointment she and we may have
had, about your planning for marriage just at the earliest possible and resonable moment.
I especially feel that crediting you with having thought it all through (which we at one
time felt you might not have done) am convinced that you will make good, and that with a
prayer in your heart, you will fight to make this happiness you seek in establishing a home-
altogether possible. So sonnie boy, God bless you. I want you to write me at once on receipt of this, that you will have no further worries about the step you feel you and Dorothy
would like to em take. It should make you want to fight for specialized training which
your Government offers you, and surely having problems that worry you and unfit you for
being even a good rookie, is not the manly way to face life's duties and obligations in even
the present situation. I love you dear boy, and I am not a bit disappointed in the dear
girl you want to make your wife; but now to have allow worries to have gotten you down as
a man and a soldier - well, you will buck up and snatch at the happiness, and be your own
dear and real self. From now on you must feel free to write me for any advice you may
think I can helpfully give you. I pray for you always. If and when you write me that you
are own dear self again, I want to truly get word to Dorothy of my delight in truly concurring in your plans, and express to her acceptance by me of that precious place she will
occupy as a daughter. I know you will have decided, after receipt of this letter, to buck
up and be truly a christian soldier and man. Win the battle and write me. DAD

Actual letter from Art Bushing Sr. to Art Bushing Jr.,
October 10, 1943

decided, after receipt of this letter, to buck up and be truly a christian
soldier and man. Win the battle and write me.   DAD

Camp Roberts, Calif.
Oct. 10, 1943 (Mon. Night

My Dearest Heart,

This is my first chance to write since last week and I'll try very hard to make up for lost time. To begin with I will describe the hastily planned trip which Ted, Ken, and I took over the week-end.

We hardly expected that the three of us would be able to get away together but the jinx seems to have been broken. Shortly after the noon hour we found ourselves travelling northward. With excellent luck (the civilians out here are very nice to soldiers on the road), we arrived in Salinas by about 4:30. This is a town of about 30,000, en route to Santa Cruz where I visited before.

Our first concern what's to find room for the uniform fills every available spot. We soon found a nice room for three in the "Hotel Cominos." [Located on U.S. 101 Highway.] Assuring ourselves of a place to sleep, we proceeded to do a bit of shopping for odds and ends that we needed. One of the most interesting spots we found was a Chinese shop with all sorts of things imported directly from the Orient. Mr. Wong, the man in charge, displayed all of the delightful congeniality of his race, and he seemed overjoyed to meet Ted.

After a bite of supper (Ken had eaten practically nothing in twenty-four hours), we went to a double feature movie. We threw our tired heads on the pillow about twelve o'clock fully intending to arise in time to attend church services. At 10:10 Sunday morning we opened our eyes—at least Ted and I did. We arose and showered, leaving Ken to sleep. He too finally awoke; and, thinking it was only about six o'clock, wanted to turn over and dream some more. We pull him out.

We ate a big breakfast and decided to make our way to Carmel—a small town on the coast. Our bus took us to Monterey, another small town on the ocean and from there we hitch-hiked four miles to picturesque "Carmel-by-the-Sea" as the Dept. of Commerce would say. On the coast we found trees and undergrowth far different from the scattered scrubbs [shrubs] which we have around camp. "Quaint" is the only term by which I can describe the town we found. It is small—few more then five to six thousand I would guess. Artists, poets, writers—a queer lot has assembled here where the "best" beach in N. Calif is to be found. Our time was extremely short, but we spent much of it walking along the beach and watching the surf break on the rocks found on one side of the bay. I took off my shoes and got my feet in the blue Pacific waters. Later revisited the local art gallery. We started back about four and by nine-thirty we were again in. A swell time!

It means so much to be able to spend a week-end away from here with a someone of similar interests. I will also thank my lucky stars that I have been able to be with Ted, Ken, and the others of the M. C. gang here in training.

Glad to report that my headaches seem to be improving. For two or three days I hardly knew I had them. I am still in the 81st, and the situation seems generally messed up. Another fellow who missed eight days of training (I missed twelve) was transferred to the 80th Battalion (where Ken is). Sat he was transferred back here. We may get to stay. I can barely hope for it, but still...!

Your letters of the 5th and 7th received today. Have still be [been] unable to read parts of the former. I know how wonderful it is to get mail–particularly yours and I could hardly object to your writing the poor lonely guy. Interesting letter his. How many of my daily letters even arrived? Must hasten to a close. Will be happy to hear from Dad.

I look at the full moon tonight and whisper are eternal

> Love,
> Bushy

P.S. Look for a package sometime in the next few days

Letters from Dotty to Art
Sunday
Oct. 10, 1943

My Dearest,

I had a sneaking suspicion that your headache had a psychological basis. Remember?—I mentioned it in one of my letters last week as a possible source of your difficulty. Oh, ah. There I go, being an I-told-you-so person. What I really mean is that I understand you pretty well, Darling, and shall try to use that understanding for your greatest possible well-being. For some time I have realized that you were somewhat nervous, and that one of my greatest (and most enjoyable!) tasks as your wife will be to calm, soothe, and relax you when necessary. Ummmmmm. Lead me to it!

But please don't worry so much about things. There doesn't have to be such a problem about us—just remember that I stand ready, waiting to receive you at such time as you can come to me, or I to you. As for your parents, who seem to feel that marriage might impede your rise in Army life, their attitude will surely change if they realize that it is a lack of marriage rather than marriage that may hold you back! So let's not worry about it, huh? Just pray.

Please feel free to turn you loose on me your feelings about army life. Your real deep down feelings. Tell-all. Use cuss words if you want to (if you know any). I can take it—I am aware of the fact that the army is no bed of roses, etc. But whatever you do, don't hold your feelings inside if they are strong feelings. It isn't good for you, anymore than it is to bottle up anger without giving any emotional or physical outlet. So open up, Bud!

Since you didn't expect any overseas combat duty anyway, why waste any time worrying about that?

Now that you have viewed a possible source for your headache and have resolved to resolve the conflicts, has the ache receded? Or will it take a visit for me to complete the job? If you have gone back to work (I'm so glad you can, now) you should complete your training sometime next month and then be sent somewhere, so a visit might be arranged soon, my darling, because a month will _fly_ by at the rate the weeks have been passing lately. Oh, I can hardly wait to see you. Already I am jumping up and down with excitement. Even a month and a half or two months isn't awfully far away. I just _know_ God wants us to get together soon.

Mary and Aunt Carol and I had a powerful prayer session Saturday, and you in particular were much prayed for. I pray for you almost constantly, but it does me a great deal of good to hear other people doing it also.

Yesterday morning, after I got your letter written and into the mailbox, I sat out and soaked up the sun as I combed and combed my hair. A little later Mary, Uncle West and I went out and dug up the last of the potatoes that remained in the ground. My first potato—digging— more fun! We sat down to a dinner of chicken and dumplings, baked sweet potatoes from the patch, gravy made with Aunt Jemima pancake flour, tomatoes, field peas, and jello with pineapple plus chocolate cup- cakes (made by Mary) for dessert. Oh, boy, did I stuff! Aunt Carol has a new and better kitchen stove in the cabin, by the way. During the rest of the afternoon I slept a little, gazed at my beloved view for a while, and suddenly and all too soon it was time to start thinking about going home. On the way home I rode in the back seat, accompanied by four other fine hens. One silly chicken stood up for the last ten miles despite the fact that its legs were firmly tied together.

Imagine my surprise (and delight) when I walked in last night to see Mary Ruth in our midst. We got caught up on our talking. Next week she is bringing a gang (and I do mean mob) over for a skating party, etc. Oh, college days, where art thou? Whither didst thou fly so fast? Ah, gone but not forgotten!

It is now tonight. All day I spend writing you a letter. Tsk, tsk. Christian Endeavor tonight was a joint supper meeting, and Mary led, and I sang a solo ("Prayer is the Soul's Sincere Desire") which was punk on account of my cold and on account if I can't sing anyway. But I love to try. And on the way home we saw a star shoots clear across the sky, with a green tail tacked on behind. So we made a wish. Guess what mine was! That's right.

Enclosed please find one photograph of a girl (the shortest one) that loves you like nobody's business. That other girl is her sister. Cute ain't she? (The tall one)

> Good Night
> My Love,
>> Dotty.

P.S. Mother says, quote, "Let go and Let God."

Tues. Oct. 12, 1943

Dearest,

I borrowed this paper from the beauty parlor lady so that I could use these few moments of waiting to write you. I'm going to have my hair done (by some lady besides me for the first time in months), then Mary Alice and I are going to eat supper in town, then go to the Masonic Temple to roll bandages for Red Cross for a couple of hours. By the time I get home there won't be much time left before bedtime. My Nurse Aid class starts next week, and that will meet two or three nights per week, from six to nine. I hope your letters won't suffer therefrom. The work may prove hard and tiresome after working all day, but I am looking forward to it with eagerness. You know me and hospitals.

There is a letter from you at home waiting on me—wish it were before me now—I would probably have more of value to say.

Yesterday on the bus going to work in the morning I crowded on the front as usual. The bus driver is a dry wit, or thinks so anyway. A man standing behind him was talking to him about people getting squeezed in the door, to which the bus driver replied, "Yeah, I'm right jealous of that door—it gets to do all this squeezing!"

We bought a new mattress for my bed in honor of Madge. Going to bed is now a wonderful event, whereas before it was just one of those things. Will write more later.

> Your Very Own,
> Dotty

―――――――

October 12, 1943, Diary

To San Miguel Mission this morning for a ten or twelve mile hike. Built in 1797, the mission was one of twenty-one built along the coast by missionaries from the old world. It was a great work that the padre did as they brought culture and eduction to the Indians. The original walls, six feet thick, still stand, and the entire mission has been renovated since 1928. After a half an hour or more here, we went to the USO for punch and doughnuts. Eight of the first squad, including myself, sent to "J" Range with A Company. Listened to lectures this afternoon. Tonight hiked fourteen miles over some of the roughest country I've seen. More than one fell out.

October 13, 1943, Diary

Spent entire day on famous "J" Range with A Company again. The training is good—we crawled under live machine gun fire and had other good conditioning courses. The squad tactics course was by far the toughest of the lot.

October 14, 1943, Diary

Up and on march by six-thirty for French Village. Was among the first to go through. Sixteen went.

―――――――

Letter from Dotty to Art
Thurs. Oct. 14! [1943]
Record Breakers.

Hi, Hansome!

With the Voice of Nelson Eddie singing "Evening Star" from Tannhauser the room (oddly enough) is quiet, and I can concentrate on this letter.

Yes, your daily letters got here okay, and was it a thrill to get them! Oh dear, I'm spoiled now, and it seems terrible not to get them so often, but I know you are terribly busy trying to get caught up, so don't you dare try it.

Now they are playing ballet music from "Faust," and here I sit, with rapture on my face, in my soul, and very much in my feet, and can't do anything about it. Ah, woe.

How wonderful that you three could get another weekend off. I think you've had more than I have. But my goings in between weekends have more than made up for the few times you have been places.

Which reminds me. The Maryville concert series this year includes the Fachman string Symphony (again!), Aileen Ferrill (she sounds like Harriet a great deal) and a young piano prodigy. I shall try to get a ticket and go, by all means. If I can stand it without you, darling. Frances Lane is here tonight, with a boy friend in whom she seems very interested. They are holding hands and looking into each others eyes up a storm. Makes me lonesome, Bud.

What, another package? It will be most welcome, naturally, but why aren't you saving your precious money? Yes, dear, I love you too. With all my heart, soul, body, etc., etc., etc., And etc.

I should have written you last night. I was an extremely silly mood, and giggled at the least excuse, sometimes with no provocation whatsoever. You would have gotten a crazy letter.

Say, I always did like electrical engineers! Remember, when I was working in the payroll office, how I went around bragging about "my" electrical engineers all the time. Just wait till you get to be one. Boy, won't I brag then!

Do you like Toll-house cookies? Well good. Maybe you'll get some. Soon. It is time to leave, now, so I'll sign off. Big weekend ahead (for Mary Ruth).

All my Love,
Dotty xxxx

Letters from Art to Dotty
Friday Morning 10-15 [1943]

Dearest,

When I returned to the company area last night, I found my transfer already at hand. As soon as I was able to wash up, eat, and turn in my equipment, I came over to Co C 80th. These men are four weeks behind the 81st, so that means an extra four weeks. I should be a well trained soldier by the time I finish twenty-three weeks here. So far it seems O.K. here. The men seem to be in the 18 & 19 year old age group and their training has not been as stiff as ours in the 81st. They were very unhappy this morning when they got up at 5 o'clock. I have been arising at 4:15 & 4:30 most of time.

We take up dry machine gun fire today—this I have done twice already. Should have a little more time here for a few weeks. Will right long letter over the week-end.

Very find letter from Daddy Barber yesterday. I must hasten this to a close. Details will come as quickly as I can get them on paper.

Eternally thine,
Bushy

Oct. 14, 1943 (Thurs.)

Dearest,

The letter on the reverse side should have been mailed when I went to the hospital. Just a brief note to tell you the wonderful news. In a matter of a few seconds last night I made the choice that decided our future. Went before the A.S.T.P. Star Board last night. I had given up all idea of getting the language branch, and planned to ask for electrical engineering. The Lt. who interviewed me was extremely nice; and, after several complementary remarks (something one almost never hears in the Army), he asked me if I were interested in language and area study. With cautious discretion I told him definitely yes. The choice was made; our whole future was decided in that moment of choice. In a flash I caught something at the importance of the situation, and yet actually there was little choice to make. I was never cut out to be on engineering although I do think I could have made a success in that field. Dr. Hunter last Spring advised me to stay in school rather than take meteorology. Later he said that he wanted "to save me for the humanities." I hope that this will be a second time that I have "saved myself for the humanities."

Letter from Art to Dotty

Oct. 17, 1943 The Sabbath
Camp Roberts, Calif.

My Dearest,

I find some difficulty in getting accustomed to writing so infrequently, but there seems to be no help for it. There just isn't any free time in which to write. As I told you in a hurried letter written

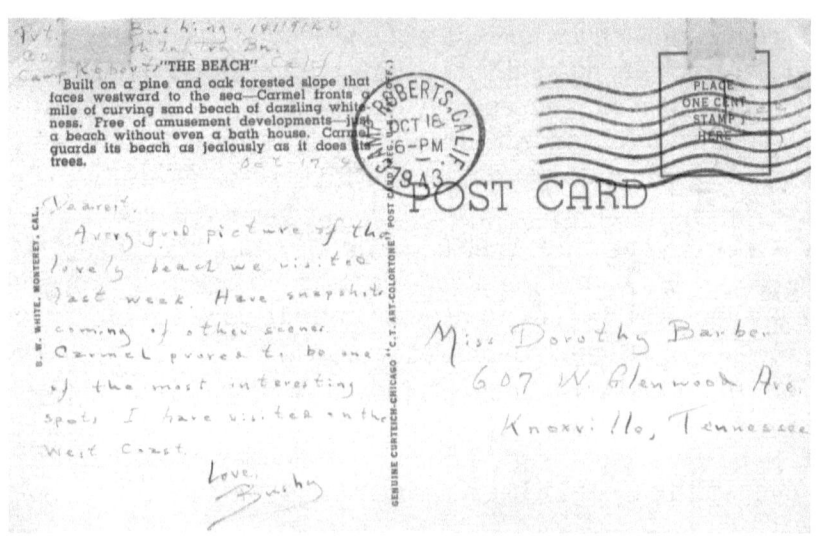

Art to Dotty, October 17, 1943

Thurs. and Fri., I have been transferred to the 80th Bn, Co C. This came rather unexpectedly, for I thought it would be arranged for me to remain with my old outfit. However, this is the Army!

I will try to take up the news in the degree of importance and hope to get through all of it. My paramount thing is the fact that I have been accepted for language and area study. I have not allowed myself to dream that it might be possible, but "all things work for good for those who love God." (not verbatum) Language is really a minor part of the training for I only learn to converse in some foreign tongue. The main study will consist of the customs, habits, and history a particular group of people. At the end of the nine months of training, I will probably go ahead as a junior officer in a military government. One of the important factors to us is that the transition from this work back to English will be far easier than the transition from engineering back to English. I should be well fitted for diplomatic service, the teaching of a foreign language, or for several other types of educational work. You know me well enough to know that I can put my heart into this type of work in a way that I could never do in engineering.

Our own plans will of course be influenced by these rapidly changing events. The maximum training that I get will probably be twelve months—the minimum nine. We must await developments after I get in school but my hopes are rising.

I seem to move from one point of uncertainty to another. At the moment there is the possibility that I may be able to go on bivouac with my old company next week and make up training the following week. That would mean I could leave with my buddies Oct. 31. Here is the situation: I have had no chance to talk with the C.O. in the 80th; but, if I can get his permission and go through a tangle of red tape, I may make it. The boys get up at twelve tonight and start marching at two. I can not see my C.O. until tomorrow morning. However, if I can get out to the bivouac area by Tues. in time for training, I can get credit. It will certainly be a race against time.

Now that I know what I am to study in A.S.T.P., I would be willing to stay here for twelve weeks of training, if necessary, but it would certainly be a waste of time. If I do have to stay around here for the remainder of this cycle I will get through Nov. 27.

Ken Cooper and Art, Front door of 1st Platoon C. C 80th Bn.
10.17.43

248

There have been several changes to be noted in comparing the 80th & the 81st, one for me they haven't been for the better. The men in my platoon seem to be largely high school boys—eighteen and nineteen years old. I have never heard a filthier lot in my life. I constantly say, "Forgive them, Father, for they know not what they do," but it is still disgusting. I do find an unusual set of officers and non-coms, however.

The company was taking up the light machine gun when I came over. Since I have already fired it, the sergeant sent me over to the ammunition tent to load belts Friday afternoon. I also did this Sat. instead of standing inspection.

I don't recall how much I told you about our schedule last week, but I will describe some of it at the risk of repeating. It must have been last Tuesday that we marched to San Miguel (about six miles away) to visit the Mission there and also the U.S.O. The march was, of course, for purposes of conditioning, but we spent more than an hour in the Mission. Established in 1797, it is one of twenty-one such missions built between San Diego and Frisco when the territory was just being explored by the white man. Twenty padres work here, and the old buildings have been kept in a very usable state of preservation. The walls of the old chapel are six feet thick, and wood carvings from Spain of the patron saints stand against the walls. My respect and admiration for the work of the Catholic Church has increased many times from such contacts as this one. At the U.S.O. we had a donut and drinks and then returned to camp. In the afternoon I went to the "J" orange, and Tuesday night we hiked fourteen miles over some of the roughest country I have ever seen. Some of the hills we crossed we [were] as steep as the "Chimnies." [Chimney Tops is a mountain in the Great Smoky Mountains National Park.] The following day I spent the entire time on the "J" range where we crawled under machine gun fire in addition to several other interesting experiences. It was Wed. night that was accepted for language study. On Thursday we took up another highly important phase of basic when we went through Village Fighting. A full size French Village has been built about two miles from Camp, and combat conditions are reproduced as accurately as possible. In going through this, we fixed live ammunition and had bullets whistling all around. Rather exciting as you can imagine.

Sun. Night

This afternoon I saw a list of the colleges where language is being given in the A.S.T.P. Such schools as Yale, Harvard, and Princeton are included, but there are also for schools on the West Coast. I don't mean to be a pessimist, but U. of Cal. opens Nov. 2, and my old company graduates on the 31st of Oct. I firmly believe that God is guiding my fate, and I trust him about everything thing else in the world.

I must trying to write a note to Dr. Hunter tonight, but perhaps I will not have time. At any rate, I must say Goodnight.
Eternally thine own,
Bushy

P.S. I want to study the point you made concerning the second coming of Christ and eternal life. Will comment at earliest possible moment.

Thought for the Day—
God placed within the heart of many the spark of the divine, but some times man almost smothers this spark with base actions on the animal level.

(The presence of Ken and Ted and other such friends makes my surroundings bearable. Without them my faith and belief in mankind would be seriously strained.)

Letter from Art to Dotty
Camp Roberts, Machine Gun Range
Oct 18, '43 (Monday Night

My Dearest,
Dusk is fast fading but perhaps I will have time to dash down a few notes before Cerberus rides across the land.

Tonight I get another lucky break. I am helping guard amunition and equipment on the machine gun range until midnight. I say lucky because the rest of the company is out marching over the hills until the same hour. I will probably be in a warm tent all night.

Fall made a convincing entrance this morning and throughout the day. Dark and ominous clouds rolled up last night, and this morning we had two or three hours of drizzling rain. The first, by the way, which I have seen since I came to Roberts in June. After the rain clouds passed on, a cold, fall wind blew throughout the day. Fall is here!

As I thought my plan to complete training with my own company was too perfect to be accepted by the Army. (Details tomorrow, I can no longer see even the line that I write.)
Tuesday Morning.

I spoke to my new C.O. yesterday morning and he promised to do what he could to see if I could take my bivouac training with my old outfit. Last night he told me that classification office said "no". The

BIGGEST COLLEGE ON EARTH

On 200 campuses, the Army is training engineers, chemists, doctors

Soldiers, picked for merit, study there — and are paid for it!

THE largest university on the face of the earth has taken shape in America to meet the challenge of total war.

Extending from coast to coast, it already is established on more than 200 campuses, with more to be added. Its name: the Army Specialized Training Program. Its purpose: to provide vitally-needed trained specialists and technicians for the Army. Under it, hundreds of thousands of Uncle Sam's brainiest soldiers, many of whom would never have been able to go to college in civilian life, are being sent to the best universities in the country.

Any soldier, no matter what his age, who has the necessary education and has scored a minimum of 115 in the Army Classification Test, is eligible for this training and may be sent to such institutions as Harvard, Yale or Stanford to study engineering, languages, or whatever the Army feels him best suited to learn.

Moreover, the soldier gets his regular Army pay and his tuition, food, clothes, books and room.

Now, why are the armed forces doing this? General Marshall, Chief of Staff, says: "The Army was compelled to assure itself that there would be no interruption in the flow of professionally and technically trained men." The Army needs engineers, doctors, chemists, linguists, mathematicians, physicists . . . and is willing to train them.

Granted the need exists, now does A.S.T.P. work? It's quite simple.

A Chance for All

FROM the day of his induction every soldier has an opportunity to be considered for this program. If he is under 22, has scored 115 or more in the Army Classification Test and has a high-school education or its equivalent, he is definitely a prospect. Soldiers over 22 need that same 115 minimum and at least one year of college. They also must have a substantial background in one or more foreign languages, or their col-

lege work must have included a year of mathematics and physics. Those who have had more than three years of college must have majored in engineering or they must know at least one foreign language.

Full details can be obtained by writing to the headquarters of your Service Command.

Picking His Course

IF A man's record indicates that he's potentially eligible, he's called before an A.S.T.P. Field Selection Board sometime during his basic military training. If he gets by this, off he goes to a Specialized Training and Reassignment(STAR)Unit. Here another board decides on whether the soldier is suited for collegiate training, and if he is, the board assigns him to a field, depending on the

A typical classroom of S.T.A.R.'s

Army's needs and his own aptitudes.

Suppose, however, that you're a young fellow in high school not old enough for the draft. You'd like to go to college, but you'd like to serve your country too. If you've reached your seventeenth birthday you can take the Army's pre-induction exam which is designed to indicate your qualifications. These tests are given at nearly all high schools and colleges. The next one, a test of general education, will occur November 9. Those who receive an acceptable score in those tests are eligible to be candidates for military scholarships under the Army Specialized Training Reserve Program. These scholarships entitle the 17-year-olds to become A.S.T.P. reservists, receiving free tuition, housing

and board at a college, picked by the government.

They are called to active duty at the end of the term in which they reach their eighteenth birthday. They are then assigned to basic military training, after which they are sent back to college if they are still qualified.

Men between 18 and 22 who still have not been called into the Army can assure themselves of getting special consideration for A.S.T.P. training after their induction. To do this they must qualify in the same test given to 17-year-olds.

Right now there are probably 150,000 soldiers, men from all sorts of families, picked solely on their merits, attending university classes throughout the country. They are on active duty and the life they lead is strictly military.

Some of these men are taking courses which will last from three months to almost two years. The Army says you can train an engineering specialist in that time. Prospective doctors adhere to the standard curriculum, which takes somewhat longer. At the end of each 12 weeks, the university reports to the Army on the progress of each student. Those who haven't passed the exams go back to other duty.

May Get Bars

AFTER a soldier has completed his A.S.T.P. training, he is assigned to a troop unit in his specialized field. If he has the necessary qualities of leadership, he may be recommended as a technical non-com, or for an Officer Candidate School.

The A.S.T.P. has proved to be a solution for several critical problems. The Army, suffering from a lack of technicians, has built itself a replenishing source of supply. Colleges that were threatened by depleted enrollments are able to carry on. Educators are certain the program has given a new purposefulness to higher learning. And the soldiers themselves . . . Well, listen to Private Bill Collins of China Grove, N. C.

"The Army's sending me to Harvard," says Bill. "Can you imagine me going to Harvard as a civilian? I used to work at a filling station for fifteen bucks a week."

— LLOYD SHEARER

TW—10-17-43

"Biggest College on Earth," published Oct. 17, 1943

consolation that I take at the moment is that my buddies may be sent to U. Of Cal. which begins Nov. 2. Perhaps I will get a school in the East now. While on guard this morning I just realized that I will have a total of twelve extra weeks here—six at the beginning, two weeks in the hospital and four weeks tacked on at the end.

By some happy chance, the corporal in my platoon seems to have taken a liking to me, and has been able to get me out of a great deal of repetition work. While the rest of the company fixed machine guns in the rain yesterday, I spent the day loading amunition in a tent. As I mentioned in the note I wrote last night, the company was out on a night problem until twelve. Since I have had the work which they took up, I was slated to clean machine guns all night—that is until the others returned. My good corporal friend said that he needed me to help sort equipment on the machine gun range, so we returned there immediately after supper. Our work was done by seven o'clock and I slept most of the night. I only had to stand guard for about two hours between three-thirty and five-fifteen. Today we have the morning off. Most of the men have gone for the A.S.T.P. exams, and I suppose this is the reason. In the afternoon we hike to San Miguel Mission where I was last week.

I have still had no letters since I was transferred last Thursday. I know that I have mail in camp, but I suppose that it will take some time to get everything cleared up. By the way, any time that you write to anyone who might write give them the change of address. Hope to write Mary Ruth soon.

For now,
>
> All my Love,
> Bushy

October 18, 1943, Diary

Arose early to go out to ammunition dump. Brought ammunition back to machine gun range. The 81st rolled out about midnight last night and pulled out for bivouac. The first rain to fall since I arrived began this morning about seven and drizzled on until about ten. I fear that training conditions will not be improved now. Lucky for me, I was detailed to load ammunition in the tent all day. Asked the C.O. if I could make up bivouac [a temporary military camp] with 81st and so finish in two weeks. He checked with Classification but the answer was "no." Four extra weeks here! The company out on a night problem tonight. My good friend Cpl. Van Pevenage put me on guard duty at ammunition tent. Slept most of the night.

Letter from Art Bushing Sr. to Art Jr.
Oct. 19, 1943

My dear sonnnie boy: It is a glorious morning here with Mother and I feeling in fine trim for the day's work. We are beginning our 4th year with Selective Service. Work is near-up to the minute, but for how long we can't say. 40 boys entered service of the group which left last Monday morning. Induction station divided the group putting hall in the Navy and the other half in the Army. 26 were rejected.

We received your wonderfully fine letter of the 14 and 15 mailed the 16th, with the news for which we were waiting so anxiously. All's well that ends well," and we hope everything is going to be fine for you in your new division. We are delighted with your prospects as outlined in your letter for your specialized course. It all seems wonderful, and your choice, we feel, is a good one especially if you finally try teaching later on.

Now dear boy, I am rushing out this letter to you for two reasons more especially: Do forgive me for misjudging you in regard to what I very mistakingly thought had assumed a problem for you and which I rather bluntly cautioned you about—all quite unecessary as your fine letter makes clear. We are proud of you. In a world such as we find it, manhood and manliness; courage to face great obstacles are always confronting us and when we are thus challenged, we come to grip with realities and if fight we must—fight we will. God grant that I may not have caused you any suffering for having so misjudged you. I know deep in my heart, dear boy, that you will give a good account of yourself in any and every field of endeavor, and yours is going to be a successful life largely because of good training, lack of which I have largely failed.

On October 15, I mailed you a P. O. Money Order for $10.00 and of course,

Getting some 40 married men examined Thursday, having had that many last week. We are going a little too fast in this, as we have no idea that our calls will or should exceed say 50 or 60 men each month. Many men are getting disturbed, of course, as we approach their number. Joe Ligon is wondering if he will have to go. Supt, Linder also wondering and so down the line.

We await your further word about your outlook and know always that Dad and Mother are backing you and will always looking to your greatest happiness and success. More another time. Love from Mother. These clippings, as I hope, will be welcomed to you for the pleaure they may give for the passing moment—or we know how busy you must be.
　　　　　Dad

Letters from Dotty to Art
Tuesday night. 10-19-43

Dearest,

　　I got your little letter with the big news in it tonight. I can hardly wait for the letter containing details. There are so many things I don't understand. What all does this language and area study stuff involve? Will you be sent across? What will it mean for us and our plans? When did the four weeks start and when will they end (more important)? Isn't it odd that you got languages when you thought you were headed for engineering and Carl got engineering when he thought he was headed for languages? Are you happy now that it is definitely decided? What were some of the compliments the sergeant gave you? I am so glad for you, Darling - - so glad that you are going to be placed in something that you can throw yourself into with real enthusiasm. The fact that you will be in language, etc., eliminates the possibility that you might be sent to UT, worse luck. H-m-m-m m-m--- it seems as if it ought to be a school <u>somewhere</u> in the East! I hope.

　　Mary Alice is much better and has improved rapidly ever since she got here almost. She says she feels fine except for the soreness in her throat. I got to be a nurse aide a day before my time. Which reminds me--I am going to enjoy my nurse aide work <u>thoroughly</u>--I can just tell. Last night I attended the first meeting of the class. We didn't do anything but make beds, and be lectured to a little bit, but just that much caught my interest, and I came out feeling all pepped up whereas I had gone in feeling extremely tired. Now how do you account for that?

　　One of the boys in the office is leaving this week, a fellow who is Miss Lee's right hand man, and every one likes him a lot. So-o-o, the office is having a dinner in his honor tomorrow night at the S&W cafeteria, and I was requested to do a reading on a spur of the moment program that is being planned. That means that I will have to cut this a little short and go learn Solomon Sickletop over again. Remember? Also remember that the greatest thing in my life is

Our Love,
Dotty

My Dearest,

There are so many things I wanted to ask you, I'm afraid I'm going to forget some of them. I may have to go up stairs and get your letter yet! Naturally I am waiting breathlessly to find out whether or not you are going to get through Oct. 31 or Nov. 27. Don't worry about what school you are going to be sent to I can come to California, you know. Ha. I had to go get the letter after all. Too bad the 80th Bn. doesn't measure up to the 81st. One consolation is that you won't be in it very long at the most. Pardon these piecemeal unrelated sentences, but I am just saying things as I think of them. By the way, that verse you quote so frequently reads thus: "All things work together for good to them that love God, to them who are the called according to his purpose." Now you can quote verbatim, Darling. It is a beautiful promise and oh, how true.

You say that you will probably go abroad as a junior officer in a military government. Does that mean that I can't go too, I hope not? My hopes rise and fall so fast--it would be very interesting to chart a graph of said hopes. Which reminds me. Thanks so much for the Chinese works of art. They are so delicately intricate. They will go into my hope chest and some day they will hang on your study wall or some ither sich appropriate place.

We all had a good time at the party last night. I really work with a very nice gang and couldn't ask for a more congenial bunch. After we had eaten, the girl who acted as master of ceremonies began looking pointedly at me, and then introduced me as the little girl who, when she found there was to be a program, just wanted to do everything. I managed to get through Solomon Sickletop without anyone knowing that I had the paper in front of me, although in reality I looked at it two or three times. Sidney is going to the navy, (he thinks), so we presented him with a little doll size washing set; it seems he had heard that they have to do all their own wash in the navy. Then Barbara Lennon and I sang a duet, after which we all sang some of the old songs. Barbara is my assistant, and she has a very nice soprano voice, which she is taking lessons for.

After the party I went to nurse aid class, there I took pulses, temperatures, respirations, and made some more beds. I'll be able to do it scientifically, Bud! Then by the time I finally got home and read your numerous letters and opened the package, it was too late to do anything but go to bed. It is getting to be that time again tonight, but I want to talk a little while longer, Can I, huh? I took Mary Alice to the doctor tonight, and he thought her throat looked good, so tomorrow she is leaving to stay with her mother-in law in Lenoir City a few days before she goes back to work.

The "bill" for authorization for cleaning out my files finally came through this afternoon and we started right to work on it. I'll be plenty busy from now on getting that done. It took us three hours to get one drawer done, and we have several hundred drawers, so you can see that it will take time. The drawers look beautiful when we finish with them. We are sending a whole lot of old and useless correspondence and applications that we no longer can use away to be stored. Oh, joy!

Goodnight, Darling. I think of you constantly and dream of
Our Love,
Dotty

Letter from Art to Dotty

October 21, 1943 (Thurs.)

My Dearest,

Last night I received the first mail since I came to the 80th—two wonderful letter from you. (dated 11th & 12th). I really felt the need of the boost they gave. However, I was just a bit disturbed by the schedule you are trying to keep up. I know how much you enjoy taking part in everything constructive, but I hope you will not attempt too much. I want to comment on your letters at length, but it will have to be over the weekend I guess. This I am dashing off during ten minute breaks in the field. Tonight we have another night problem, and Friday night, as usual, I will be busy until light out.

As is always true, I am enjoying my surroundings more as time goes on. Most of the fellows are still kids trying to act "grown up," and often I get disgusted with some of them. However I find a few of the more serous type. A fellow by the name of Friedman, who bunks next to me, is a Harvard lad; and represents the better type.

Even if things were bad enough to feel like "cussing" as you suggested, I would refrain after hearing some of these fellows. No, I haven't reached that stage, darling. However, I must admit that I am not overjoyed at all this extra training I am receiving. Some of it is more than a little boring since I am doing certain phases of the work for the third time.

(A couple of interims)
Friday Noon

(Continuing the same of line of thought:) Up until this point I can honestly say that I have enjoyed the work. I have been kidding neither you nor myself when I have told you that I like it. That is one reason I might question the suggestion made by the doctor. From all that I can observe of my own feelings, I have never held any pent-up emotions within me. Nevertheless, I am having to philosophize a great deal to rationalize this last delay.

Friday Night.

Bit by bit, break by break, I am getting this letter written, my Sweet. Your letter written Tues. night just received—quick service. I think I answered most of the questions that you raised in previous letters. Perhaps I can discuss them at length tomorrow & Sunday.

In the brief moment that I have in which to finish this, I want to tell you, Darling, just how much your understanding letter concerning my headaches meant to me. Due to my failure to explain very clearly the doctor's diagnosis, Dad and Mother failed to grasp the exact situation. With your customary loving understanding, you reached a new and supreme high in revealing the <u>oneness</u> that Love affords. Darling, I constantly pray that I may be worthy of your love, that I may be worthy of being your husband "through the years." A constant tower of strength will our Love ever be.

Goodnight My Own,
Bushy

P.S. Today the first day that we haven't had rain since it began on Monday. California weather! Much colder now.

October 23, 1943, Diary

No inspection this morning, but spent entire morning in drill, physical training, etc... 81st returned this morning about nine-thirty from hectic week of bivouac. Much rain and extreme cold they report. However, the marching seemed to be the worst thing. When they returned, Lt. Schneiweiss pulled a rifle inspection and gigged enough to clean up supply room and go on K.P. Dirty trick! Ted had K.P. Washed fatigues and wrote letters this afternoon. PX has Hershey's chocolate bars. Mass attack on the counter. First time that we have had real pre-war quality candy. Six big letters forwarded from 81st. Hal, T. Pratt, Muriel, Dotty. Wrote letters with Ted and Ken tonight.

---

* Letter from Art to Dotty
Camp Roberts, Calif.
Oct 23, 1943 (Sat. Night

Dearest,

Today I was happy to get some of my mail that has been held up over in my old battalion—six letters in fact. Hal, Muriel, Ted Pratt, home and two of your descriptive epistles. It made me feel like a new man.

Hal understands that we are planning to be married this winter. Darling; I can't help feeling that it is a wee bit early to make things too definite for us, and particularly too early to say much. I know, I have been guilty of the very same thing of being so thrilled with the possibility of an early culmination of our plans that I have mentioned our hopes to more than one friend. But just as this incident demonstrates, one little word is like the proverbial snowball. What's say, let's surprise 'em? Wait until we make a definite date?

That leads to another point, and a far more important one for us. You ask in one of your recent letters just how this new chain of events (area study) will affect our planning. It is still hard to say just yet, and remember that this must of necessity continue to be tentative. However, as I said before, I want to be at the earliest possible, the earliest practical moment. Since I may be abroad in twelve months, I certainly want to hasten that blessed day in every way possible. From the vantage point of many uncertain details, it seems to me that the end of my second twelve-week term would be a practical point to stop long enough to acquire a life partner. By that time I should have my studies well in hand, and my bank account should be a bit nearer the point where the safety margin can be seen. Recent letters show a changing feeling on the part of Mother and Dad. Roughly, that will be the latter part of May or the first of June. At the moment, the end of the first term doesn't seem to be too practical.

Another point that I have intended to take up in previous discussions is the one of the place of the ceremony. Since Rev. Hamilton has left, I wonder if you have ever considered Voorhees Chapel [on the campus of Maryville College]. Maryville holds many memories for us, and that would be a fitting climax to our meeting, our many hours together, our engagement. This is merely food for thought. Let me know what you think about it.

Sunday

I am happy that you are enjoying your Nurse's Aide so much; and yet, as I said before, I hope it will not be over strenuous. There is a limit you know as to how much a person can do. Please do give me all the details you have time to write. I'm really not in that bad a shape, Darling. I am interested in everything that you do.

Wish I could have heard good old "Solomon Sickletop" again at your party, but the thing that I miss far more is your beautiful voice. Among many other things, I long for the day when you will be with me to sing as our hearts desire. I know it has meant much for you to find a congenial group to work with in the T.V.A. You have maintained remarkable interest in the work there. Even though you enjoy I hope that it will not be for long. Your abilities as a housewife far exceed any other aptitudes which you may have.

By the way, I want to clear up a point that confused Dad and Mother in regard to my sickness. The conflicts which the Doctor suggested, were merely suggestions. He said that such things as I mentioned might well be the source of my trouble, but there was no out & out statement to that affect. He also suggested that the conflicts, if there were such, might be unconscious rather than conscious. I have never had nightmares of shooting a Jap, nor have I actually worried a great deal about any of the problems which he suggested. I have thought a great deal, of course, about them; but I never thought I was "going nuts" because of them. Dad seemed to feel, before I explained, that I was failing to put my country first. I would have no fear of facing death tomorrow if it were for the good of the war. After going through basic here, there is no physical effect that I fear. (Men returning from conflict, tell me that basic in Roberts is far worse than battle conditions as they experienced them.)

I am sending Mother one of the best groups of Camp Roberts' pictures that I have seen. I have been on almost every range and in almost every situation shown. Hope she likes them. In this letter I enclose a couple of poems which Dad suggested you might enjoy. "The Immortal" has compact phrasing which I like.

Hope to write again in next few days. Take up mortar tomorrow for fourth time. Bivouac out on this Combat Range Wed. Ted leaving next week.

Goodnight my Dearest Heart,
Bushy

The Immortal

THE wine of immortality
Is his alone to quaff
Whose pen corrodes with salt of
  tears
Yet · shapes songs-words that laugh.

O bitter burnt his bread may be,
But he shall savor crumb and crust
Who breathes the atmosphere of stars
While plodding through the finite dust.

Jessie M. Dowlin in "Green Mountain Verse: An Anthology of Contemporary Vermont Poetry." (Farrar & Rinehart).

Poem enclosed in letter of Oct. 23, '43, from Art to Dotty

Letter from Dotty to Art
Sunday
Oct. 24, 1943

My Dearest,

Here it is Sunday again. They roll around rapidly. It seemed so good to go to church again. I have missed two Sundays, one with a cold, one with Mary Alice. This Sunday the service was very uplifting to me. Al Cole, our favorite tenor, was home today on leave (he is the navy), and he sang "Panis Angelicus." It is one of my favorite selections, and he did it well. Its beauty went straight through me so that the tears came to my eyes. With me, worship is closely allied with intense appreciation of music, or beauty of any kind. Is it so with you, Darling? Our pulpit was supplied this morning with a woman, a Chinese missionary who was lucky enough to be sent home from Hong Kong. Her story was extremely interesting.

Your poor cookies will be dry as a bone by the time they reach you, I'm afraid. You mentioned in your letter of the 19th that you were not getting your mail, and my package was probably in with the mail you didn't get.

Muriel is coming over this afternoon, and I must go to the bus in a little while to meet her. What a session we are going to have! You will come in for a large part of it, but don't worry—I won't spill too much.

Mary Alice's mother-in-law came after her Friday and took her home (Martel, Tenn.) with her for the remainder of her "sick leave."

They are playing Tchaikovsky's "4th" on the symphony this afternoon. I hope you are hearing it.

Can it be that the hand of God is working toward the furtherance of our plans? The more your situation develops the more it looks as if something of the sort were true.
I am almost glad you are unable to finish with your mates if it means that you may be sent East to school. Oh, selfishness, thy name is Dot!

What are you hearing from your family nowadays? I still have heard nothing from them, but perhaps I should break down and write to them anyway.

I want you to have this poem I found on the back of "Seek" a sort of "Today" that Mother takes. Written by Nancy Carpenter it is called

IN MY HEART

Lord Christ, I'm blind!
I cannot see
How Thou wilt work this out
For good to me.
But, Lord, by faith—
Though not my own—
I take Thee at Thy word.
Trust Christ alone.
He never fails!
He satisfies
As God and Lord and Friend!

And joy supplies,
Though dark the day,
And weary—I
Can't understand just how,
Nor why;
Yet by Thy healing hand I know
That darkness will depart,
And I shall see as well as hear
Thy handwork in my heart!

Must go now, and get Muriel.
        I Love You,
           Dotty.

Letter from Dotty to Art
Tues. Night
[October 26, 1943]

Darling,

How are you? You haven't mentioned your feelings for some time, and I've been wondering how your headaches turned out.

I don't suppose your California weather has at all paralleled ours. We have had cool weather for some time, and the past few days have been downright cold, with a raw wind and a cold drizzle containing a few flakes of snow (invisible to most people but me). Imagine such weather in October. Feels like Thanksgiving!

Last night I had a good in Nurse Aid class. I had worked hard (harder than usual) all day, and as a result was as grubby and dirty as they come. How fortunate that we were to practice giving baths last night. Bed baths. So, I put my partner to bed, pretended that she was a patient, and proceeded to give her a bath. Then we were required to remake the bed, with said patient still in it. After giggling through it we switched places, and my partner did the same to me. Oh, joy!

Tonight is Mom and Pop's wedding anniversary. Mom said to tell you "Hello," and she hopes you will be as happy after 28 years of married life as she is! That goes <u>double</u>, Bud.

I am sitting here going to sleep on myself, so I'd better cut this short. (Nothing has ever happens to me, anyhow. Except I love you, I love you,

        I love you
           Dotty.

Letter from Art to Dotty

Camp Roberts, Calif.
October 26, 1943 (Tues.)

My Dearest,

Yesterday I received a wonderful box of delicious cookies. I have no fears as to the quality of food I will be eating in future years. It makes even Army chow a little more bearable when I know that before too very long I'll have a cook all my own. Not that I intend to marry you for your cooking ability alone, Darling; but that will be a definite point in my favor.

Yesterday I heard lectures and had practical work on the mortar—part of this for the fourth time. I did enjoy a Retreat Parade that we took part in last evening. This is the second I have taken part in. They are full dress, of course, with band playing and flags waving. Very enjoyable and always good for the morale. There's something about a parade! Last night we marched out for a patrol problem lasting until midnight. Everything was carried out well and we returned without mishap. The amazing and unexpected happened again: we had the morning off today. Only a clothing inspection interrupted an entire morning of relaxation. I tried to catch up with a sadly neglected diary. I guess my letters will have to bear record of the past four months, My Sweet.

Tues. Night

A slight change in our schedule announced tonight. We were scheduled to bivouac tomorrow night on the Combat Range—about seven miles out. We were to return Thurs. night. Just a few minutes ago we were told that we are to be out until late Fri night or early Sat. morning. Rough schedule I would say. Rumors are flying think & fast as to the bearing this may have on our completion of basic, but I disregard all of them. I have heard too many "latrinagrams" (as we call them) before. I think I will leave here on or about Nov. 27—no sooner. It is interesting how fertile an Army Camp is for rumors. Like wildfire they spread and morale seems to feed upon new ones. No matter how many times they prove wrong, men are willing to grab at any new one that comes along.

Get up at four in the morning, and have much to do tonight. Hope to write while on bivouac. Enclose pictures taken at Carmel. Ted will be leaving with his camera in a few days so these may be the last for awhile. All my love, Bushy.

Thurs. Oct. 28 [1943]

Dearest,

I find that this one little piece of paper is <u>all</u> the stationery I own at the moment, so maybe if I write small I can crowd this letter onto it.

Forgive me for talking out of turn. I'll try to keep my big mouth more shut hereafter. The plans, even if tentative, are so wonderful that I want the whole world to know, and especially my close friends. But things do get around! Yes, let's do surprise them.

I shore wuz proud to get a letter from you today, 'cause today makes the 6th day since I last received a letter. And today came <u>two</u>! Joy!

Did you write your Mother & Dad as full and complete an account of the Dr.'s Diagnosis and what led up to it as you did me? I meant to tell you to if you hadn't, because I don't see how they could misunderstand if you wrote them what you wrote me. I still haven't heard from them—do you think I should write?

Why does it not seem practical (aside from the back account) to go ahead at the end of the first three months? I am willing to wait as along as is absolutely necessary, but I hate to see any time that we might possibly be together not taken advantage of. Nine months together seems much better than six months, but naturally I <u>would</u> feel that way. Anyway, tain't as long as has been, Bud!

Our church is still without a preacher, and without even the prospects of one as far as I know. Yes, I have considered the chapel, and although it holds many <u>dear</u> memories, I still prefer our church. The chapel doesn't seem quite as warm nor as close nor as holy as the church. I am not using the words I want, but perhaps you can catch a little of what I am trying to say.

Please don't worry about my schedule being to complicated. My interest is so great that I don't think of getting tired, therefore I'm not. If I looked upon it with regret or begrudged the time in any way, it would make me extremely tired.

Can't stay awake any longer.

       All my love,
        Dotty.

P.S. Must tell you about my almost "date" tonight at record breakers.

Ken Cooper & Ted Kidder, U.S. Light Tank M-3.
Weight about 15 tons, 37 mm gun & three machine guns

* October 24, 1943, Diary

Heard Chaplain Adams this morning with Ted. K. And Ken C. As usual, very good sermon. Also attended Catholic Mass with Dan Downey (phil. major from Notre Dame) and Jim Campbell. Enjoyed the service, but felt the need of explanation in several places. Noticed that there seems to be a certain consciousness of being Catholic. There was frequent mention of "we as Catholics." Must go again sometime. This afternoon Ted, Ken, and I went to the Service Club after mail call to write letters until eight o'clock. Our fellowship has made a tremendous difference in my Army life. Few there are in the Army who share the ideals of Maryville students. Sent Math books home tonight since I no longer need them.

October 25, 1943, Diary

For the fourth time I took up the mortar today. Must admit that I'm a bit bored with all the duplication in my training. However, the weeks will pass. Tonight we took part in the Retreat Parade. With the band playing and everyone on his toes, these parades add much to our morale. To make the day a full one, we had a night problem tonight near P.3. Reconnaissance Patrol by squad. I went with the second squad and acted as second in command. The problem was carried out better than usual. In bed by midnight. Box of delicious cookies from my little cook.

———

Letter from Art's parents to Art
Monday Oct. 25 [1943]

Dear Son:

With us to "fall is definitely here." Yesterday we had rain most of the day and we knew that cold weather was coming. There are practically no green leaves left, and the red, yellow and gold ones are falling fast.

On Oct. 15 we had enough snow to put a white blanket over everything but it soon melted of course. On Sat night of same week we had a freeze which killed dahlias and chrysanthemums, and anything else in bloom. Last week week was the week to remember as a probable last week of fair weather. I was able to get home early one afternoon and get some lily bulbs transplanted. Later on I hope to reset some shrubs.

I found time yesterday to make some cookies and got off a box of some 35 to 40 you this morning. Hope you get them in good condition, and he sure to give that nice Corporal some—that is if Corporals eat cookies, and you dare offer them to him. We are so glad to hear that your headaches are improved and that you are going ahead with your training, even though much of it is a repetition of what you have had. If it should turn out that, as a result of the delay, you get and Eastern College it might work out for the best anyway.

You will have been away a long time if you get no furlough until the end of your first three months training. I had hoped that my baby chickens would be just right for frying while you aren't here, but if you stay too long they will be too big. I had a hen set under the wood shed,

266

and come off with nine chicks during the hottest part of the summer. They have grown very nicely, though.

Bros. Parker is our preacher again, but the Nicholas family left Jamestown and as yet the Baptist have no preacher.

The Looper girls we're home over the week end but I didn't see them. There is absolutely nothing in way of news to tell you. I don't see many people except are registrants.

We carry on from day to day, but never know what morrow's mail will bring. Over a week ago we got six new Storing Cabinets, but haven't had time to put them together. They are knocked down Cardboard. At the same time we got about 5000 envelopes #1, 2, & 3. So it looks as though we are to go on keeping busy.

On Oct. 15 your Dad sent a money order for $1000. We haven't heard that you received it, but I'm sure you will acknowledge it in due time.

Today's paper tells of the smart guy over at Murfreesboro who got 4 yrs Federal prison term for attacking the Exam physician for Selective Service. So wire still for Judge Davies since he's the same fellow who was the judge in the Fentress C. Case.

Will send this along and try to write again soon. Your Dad will right tomorrow or next day. Lots of love from us both and all good wishes for your continued success. Mother

[Art's father wrote in the margins of his mother's letter, written below.]

Dear boy, I have just a big letter in and heart for you. Have some very good clippings from NY Times —especially from "Sat. Review of Literature." Everything will work out fine for you regarding your plans. I am going to help you in every way. So be of good cheer I am praying for you daily. Dad

---

October 26, 1943, Diary

Slept until seven this morning. Half day off because of last night. Whata life! Never thought that the Army would come to this. Spent most of morning writing diary. Am too far behind. Brief clothing inspection. Out to 80A this afternoon for map reading. Ken C. sending applications for med sch. Ted came over tonight and the three of us wrote letters. About seven o'clock the company was told that we are to have two nights of bivouac instead of one.

October 27, 1943, Diary

Up at five and began march to Field Fortification Area at seven-thirty. Heavy rain last night foretold no good for us. As soon as we arrived we began digging fox holes in ground baked for months in the heat of a California sun. By two o'clock some still unfinished, but light tanks ran over us. Hardly exciting.

Letter excerpts from Art to Dotty
October 29, 1943

"I have tasted everything that basic training has to offer... We marched to the field fortification area, about seven miles from camp. No sooner had we arrived than we began to dig fox holes in ground which had baked in the Calif. sun for many months. We dug until noon and we still had feet to go (Dimensions 2' x 3 1/2' x 5'). As soon as we had eaten we returned to dig. Finally about two o'clock, although some were not finished, we ducked down in the bottom and had a light tank roll over us. During the remainder of the afternoon we took up anti-tank mines and barriers until sun-down. At supper we were issued our "C" Rations for the following day. And then came mail-call. Tired, dusty faces lit up with expectation; letters from friends, from sweethearts, from home. I want to write at length sometime on the place of mail-call in Army life. It plays an all important part. As darkness settled down, we marched a half-mile farther on to our bivouac area. Here we pitched tents and prepared for bed.

"Thursday (yesterday) we had our "C" Rations for there meals. Rations for one day are contained in six cans—meat and beans, vegetable bash, meat and vegetable stew, and three cans of bread unit. The latter cans contain fine cookies of concentrated bread, three pieces of hard candy, and powder for drink (coffee, chocolate, and lemonade). Everything can be eaten cold; but, of course, all of them are far better when heated. A few complain (a few always do) but I found the rations better than some meals we have in the mess hall.

"Late afternoon and we are getting a bit of rest. Soon after supper we will start out on a cross country march, returning very indirectly to

Dear son: Mother and I enjoyed, as we always do, receiving word from you. We must not forget you even by seeming neglect on account of much work here. As a matter of fact, we think of you the more when we put off writing you at least once a week each. Note in your last that you want us to send out the French book you mention, which we will try to do at once. I want to make it a habit to cut out, at the time it occurs to me, short articles which I hope you may interesting. So glad you mentioned what we might send you for Xmas. I will attend to this the next time I am in Nashville. Wish you would suggest in more detail the kind you would like, and know would serviceable for your needs. Just name the kind make you would prefer, and we will start from there.

Yes, the time will pass swiftly now for completion of your basic and in this connection I am going to find the time to write you frequently. We are again caught up on the work and today was really a picnic for we worked leisurely along and accomplished a good deal toward next week's work. By the way, we note you will be sending back the books no longer needed. We'll be looking for them. It has cleared up today and the weather is somewhat warmer. Very quiet about town. Chesterlyne and Jessie Ray were home from school but have returned to Nashville— as I suppose mother wrote you. John Sloan and Bill Johnson are reported coming home from their Military School near Chattanooga for the week-end. The Academy is located at Sweetwater, Tenn.

Lester stopped the other morning before mother left home to report the arrival of another little baby girl. Mother has a little present for her, when Lester returns with some shelled corn which we ordered from him.

I do hope your lot will be cast East for your specialized training so that you may be able to run in to see us or Mother and I or one of us, run in to see you. I understand that you will not have a furlough before the end of your first three months in School. In my next I want to list some of the books I have recently read, and my planned reading for the winter months ahead. Mother just completed a very good story which she enjoyed as I did also, an old book - the author Robert Chambers. It was entitled, "The Fighting Chance." A society novel so to speak-but excellent writing. His day has passed, but Robert Chambers wrote some fine novels.

Well, dear boy, I hope what my letter lacks will be made up in the articles I enclose. We understand you are getting the Atlantic Monthly. If not I would be inclined to do some clipping from this magazine every month to send you.

God bless and keep you, dear boy. I hope the experiences you are passing thru will be a source of satisfaction to you in the years to come. If the world is turned upside down, as we all know it is, you will know how much of sacrifice it cost and how sweet will be the ways of peace when men cease fighting.

Mother sends love and we both will write you soon again.

Dad

End I have that confidential letter
almost completed which I told you
sometime ago I would write you. I will
mail it tomorrow - so look for it. It
is front news since I wrote to tell you how
many Bonds mother now has and putting

269

Letter from Art's dad to Art, October 29, 1943

Camp Roberts looking NE
(Note: East Garrison in background 10.31.43)

Camp Roberts looking Southeast

Camp Roberts looking East

Camp. This will end a rather hectic three days and nights. I haven't washed for three days, except for my hands, and I shaved face in the field a few moments ago for the first time since Monday night. You can imagine how filthy I feel..."

Letter excerpts from Dotty to Art
October 31, 1943

"There is a fellow working in my office who is very interested in music, and buys records (good ones) with all his spare cash. His home is elsewhere, and he is not at all familiar with this part of town, so when I asked him to Record Breakers he hadn't the groggiest notion how to get to Uncle West's house, and the more I tried to explain the more confused he seemed to get, so I invited him home with me for supper as the simplest way to get him here safely. He came to work all dressed up in his Sunday best that day. Was my face red! However, all turned out alright; he was an interesting guest, for he is an intelligent follow, an interesting conversationalist, and actually knows more about music than almost anyone in the club. <u>But</u>—he can find his own way around from now on!"

November 2, 1943

[Regarding attending Gounod's Opera "Faust" the night before, in the Alumni Memorial Auditorium.] "Oddly enough Steve, the boy I described in my last letter, has a seat next to mine. He had a libretto, and also knows French fairly well, so when he chuckled I knew that something lively was happening, so I would ask him what they were singing and he would tell me. Now don't go getting jealous, darling. I was thinking of you, but hard, and he was thinking of his girl and of what a good time he had ushering at the concerts last year."

November 1, 1943, Diary

Sixteen hours of K.P. today. Company on night operation until twelve or later. The thing that is so disgusting about the Army is that one can work the fingers to the bone and still get a kick and a curse. It doesn't prompt initiative. "This too shall pass away."

November 2, 1943, Diary

Morning off because of night operations. G.I's barrack and visited with 1st platoon, 81st. Most of them leaving today—at least orders announced. Find tonight orders cancelled. Wonderful letter from Dad: "...God bless and keep you, dear boy. I hope the experiences you are passing thru will be a source of satisfaction to you in the years to come. If the world is turned upside down, as we all know it is, you will know how much of a sacrifice it cost and how sweet will be the ways of peace when men cease fighting..." He sends swell articles from Sat Rev of Lit and NY Times. It is truly inspiring and challenging to have such wonderful parents.

Letter excerpts from Art to Dotty
November 2, 1943

"For the sake of our future and for the future of the children we plan for, we can't afford to allow anything to interfere with my complete success in the training. Dearest, as I wrote the last lines I knew that they conveyed the wrong ideas. You could never "interfere" with my success, but rather you will ever be the guiding light that enables me to attain a respectable career and security for us. However, the set-up at college may not prove entirely conducive to a marital status and yet again it may. A few more weeks will tell. Tonight I looked over my financial standing. The most that I have been able to save while here has been $25.00 per month in addition to the $6.25 for bonds. When I get in school, of course, expenses will shoot up. A little band, size 5, remains to be bought [wedding ring for Dotty], and the most that I can hope to have by Mar. 1, will be $150. Not much to get married on, Rose Bud!

"Will be glad to hear about your 'almost' date. I have always believed in "share-the-wealth." The guy must have had a keen eye for beauty. For, Darling, your beauty shines as a beacon light reflecting a ray of
   Our Love,
   Bushy."

Even in Time of War, Think of Art

By Elizabeth K. Phelps Stokes

IN time of war, think of art
    As world harvest through the ages
Of passion fruit whose vital heart
    Outlives fighting men and sages,
Even in time of war, think of art
    As ecstasies of lonely hands
Near to heritage, yet far apart
    From the boundaries of lands,
Ecstasies that lift by their power
    Man from his plough and cart
And fill a wildly longing hour
    With as deep and lusty a roar
And sharp and exquisite a dart
    As from the boiling blood of war,
Even in time of war, think of art.

The Saturday Review

Poem enclosed in letter dated 11.2.43

Letter excerpts from Art's parents to Art
November 4, 1943

"Sgt. & Mrs. York were at Camp Campbell Tuesday of this week. After discussions, and conferences, checking up on previous operation and xrays the discussion is that Edd [George Edward Buxton York] is not to be operated on. And according to rules should not be kept in the Service. He wants to stay and Sgt. says he wants him to stay, but I don't know what they will do about it. My opinion is that he'll be coming home to stay one of these days...." [from Mother]

"I don't want you to run short of needed funds, so I will, not later than Saturday P.M., send you a money order for a ten spot. This will enable you to get along if your check doesn't arrive in time and if it doesn't come at all, just write for such expense money you may need. This or these little items of money for your expenses are Dad's little present to you to enable you to increase or show your savings while in the Army of some fair sum. And in this connection, besides the $500.00 I mentioned as a little present to you and Dorothy, I want that your own savings while in the Army should approach a like sum, and what that lacks I want to make an additional little gift to you so that you and

273

Dorothy start out with at least $1000. This will have to be our little secret for the time being, but not necessarily a secret from Dorothy. I hope you understood my confidential letter. Things are improving as far as Mother's attitude is concerned...." [from Dad]

Letter excerpt from Dotty to Art
November 4, 1943

"By the way, how is the liquor situation around Camp Roberts? It may amaze you to know that the amount of money spent for legal alcoholic beverages in this country is three <u>billion</u> more than the national debt for the same period of time. Some of the boys overseas write home that beer and cigarettes seem to be the only things that aren't rationed, and that beer is the only thing cold that can be gotten to drink. Isn't [that] deplorable?... You must have had a long, hard week of it out on bivouac. It's a good thing I wasn't there—I would hate to have been kissed by all those whiskers. (Huh—you know good and well that I would love to be kissed, whiskers or no!)"

November 4, 1943, Diary

To hospital this morning, but told to return tomorrow. Going for final check-up on my old trouble. Mortar fire (H.E.'s) today. Tonight Ted and I over to see Joe Louis at Sports Arena.

November 5, 1943, Diary

To hospital this morning for a final check-up on my nervous disorder. Doctor thinks my condition tops and says I should have no more difficulty. He explained more fully the various symptoms that may develop from sub-conscious conflicts. By recognizing the results that may develop, I should be able to curtail worry and anxiety.

"Last night we [Ted & Art] went to the Sports Arena for an exhibition given by Joe Louis in person. Never have I seen more perfect physical form than he has. Joe works with an ease & a pose that is indicative of an artist. It was a delight to see his rhythmic movement, his lightning speed, and his impassive face. It think he barely blinked the entire bout (three rounds).

Louis has been touring the camps all over the country since August and will continue through Jan. He has with him his old sparring partner and two or three other boxers who perform. It must be some routine for Army life."

Letter from Art to Dotty

Nov. 6 '43
Sat Morning 8:20

Darling,

As I write machine gun bullets crackle over my head and an artillery barrage is being poured into the hills ahead of me. A few minutes ago the entire battalion moved out from the line of departure in open squad columns (5 yds between men & 10 yds between files). A thousand of us moved across a vast field while the machine guns & artillery opened up. Now we have taken the prone position, still dispersed, and watch the tracers. Now P-39's, four of them ..... far in the rear and come in from our rear at tremendous speed, flying very low. As they get to a point over head, the guns open up and fire just to our front. Three more follow the first group. They circle again, coming in over a long range of hills. Dropping very low, they get before the horizon and become almost invisible. All at once, they shoot into sight, travelling at tremendous speed, and now only fifty feet above our heads.

The P-39, better known as the Bell-Air Cobra [Bell P-39 Airacobra], is one of the fastest planes we have. [The letter abruptly stops.]

Letter excerpts dated November 7: "Your description of "Faust" made me long to have been there with you, Dearest, but there will be many times to come. Glad that you were able to enjoy it with the "boy you described in your last letter." What's his name? By the way, I showed

Ted the program for "Faust," and he saw the date for Sigmund Romberg. He may ask you to get a ticket for his girl (Cordellia Dillenger (sp?)). I told him you would be glad to do anything you could."

"Ted is still here, and the inseparable three saw a beautiful show last night. "Lassie Come Home," based on the book by Eric Knight. It is the story of a faithful dog done in technicolor, with the setting in Yorkshire, England. I hope you can see it when it comes to town. The background music was exceptional, I thought. This morning we had a good sermon and joined together in Communion. It seemed very fitting that our last service together should end with the hymn, "Bless Be the Tie That Binds." Ted and I spent almost all of our spare moments together—shows, passes, Service Club, Church. He's a grand guy as were all of the Maryville [College] gang. I shall miss him...."

"I look at the growing moon and whisper words of love to the one I love most in all the world. I long to hold you close and smother your sweet lips with kisses, Darling, for
> I'm in love with you.
> Bushy"

Letter excerpt from Dotty to Art

Dated November 7: "Is it possible that in just 20 more days you will be through with your training? At long last? And may I dare hope that I can see you in the interim between basic and school? That's just three weeks from now! Oh, I hope, I hope!"

November 8, 1943,
Letter excerpts from Art to Dotty
[from Camp Roberts to Knoxville, TN]

Dated November 20 "Sat. Evening": "Here I am keeping our Sat. Night date. Are you there? I have a sneaking suspicion that you are as—lights dim, stars, a soft glow from the fireplace. Well, I can dream, can't I?

"I survived the 22 mile hike in good style. A bit sleepy of course but not too far gone to miss my date.

"In regard to your immobile 106-107, you know that I think you make a delightful lap full just as you are. Gain more if you wish (and can), but be sure it is added at the proper points. Tch! Tch!

"Out of the ten Roberts men who went down for language, only two made it. Gordon Stone spoke French fluently and made very high on his long, aptitude. He is now an engineer to be. Ted was told that language is closed except for experts. Our immediate future looks a bit shaky, Darling, and I must admit my displeasure at the prospects.... As has always proved the only way, I place our future in the hands of one higher than human comprehension. The whole thing will work out to our best advantage.

It seems that one day I write news that puts us in high spirits—the next day, we are down again. That's Army for you. Please, Darling, don't worry about the latest developments; but be prepared for whatever comes. Even engineering on the West Coast would be better than combat unit in the Pacific. We have much to he thankful for. I can still claim the love of the most adorable, lovable, the most beautiful girl in the wide world. We have each other!

November 8, 1943, Diary

On "J" Range today. Assigned to ammunition tent and worked there all day. My cohorts on the loaders were sergeants and corporals. Tonight I guarded the tent with one of the staff sergeants. Wrote a long letter to Dotty by moonlight, and to bed by eight.

November 9, 1943, Diary

Up about seven and into company for breakfast and clean-up. When I returned to "J" Range worked on ammunition detail remainder of morning. Easy afternoon including completed physical. Tonight crawled under machine gun fire on "J" Range. Not bad at all. Beautiful moon.

Letter excerpts from Art's father to Art

Dated November 10: "Sgt. [Sergeant Alvin C. York] showed Mother another Warner Bros. Check $6,000. Making a total of $153,000.00 to date. By the way, Fay Qualls is expecting to get a furlough in two weeks. He has been stationed in Mass. Sgt. Says that Ed. York is now on the border line of being retained in the Army as a 1-A (L) (limited service) or may even be discharged. He had an operation sometime ago and the Army wanted to again operate in the same section, and for some reason for the necessity of the thing, but leaving it up to Ed., he declined to go through with it thinking that it might leave him in a worse condition ultimately.

"Very interesting about seeing Joe Lewis. He must be a fine specimen of physical manhood. Here is a phrase I have always liked—The manly art of self-defense; known as boxing. You can punish a man to be sure, but you need not kill him and in the sport world you don't.

"I gather from the last letter that you may be a bit lonesome, dear boy. Well, know that we too are awfully lonesome without you, but it is to be remembered always that our happiness and joy will be that much more when we are priviledged to all meet again and overflow with the peace that will assuredly be ours at your homecoming. So keep up a good stiff upper lip; the days are clicking off; your new assignment let us hope will bring to these parts and we will certainly want to send you a ticket no matter what the cost—to run in from no matter where you are to be stationed. God bless and keep you, dear boy. I will write again this week end without fail. Mother sends love and we await such news as you are able to send us and find time to write.

Enclosed - Money Order
Dad

November 11, 1943, Diary

Up early and to French Village (three miles out). Coincidentally I went through it just four weeks ago today with the 81st. First time I went through in an assault position and today flank machine gun. We went through in two-man teams with an officer with each team. Live ammunition and plenty of chance for casualties. Lunch and supper in field and night problem—squad approach march and assault. Good problem. Lt. selected me as an advanced scout for our platoon.

November 12, 1943, Diary

Morning off, but I spent most of the time going to finance office for delayed pay for Oct. Inspection this afternoon when Lt. wondered when I had shared. This morning it was.

November 14, 1943, Diary [Sunday]

Most of the language and area men called to Classification this morning where they were transferred from this branch to engineering. Reason "men must now be twenty-two or have two years of college." To Church with Ted and Ken. Most of the afternoon in preparation for bivouac. Wrote letters for a short time tonight in slot "Rec" Hall with Ted. Not much sleep between nine and twelve.

Letter excerpts from Art to Dotty
November 11, 1943

"It was also just four weeks ago tonight that I was transferred to my new outfit. The experiences of the past weeks have proven disgustingly broaden; I have lived with a type of fellow I never knew existed. The filth of mind and the low level of human that surround me is deeply disgusting. It is revolting to my whole nature.

Friday

"Perhaps it is good that I was interrupted yesterday—I would probably have ranted at some length on the subject of my discussion. Briefly now, it has been an addition to my realm of experience, but it has added little to my view of the ideals of man.

"Beer is sold on the post but it contains a very low percentage of alcohol, and I doubt that anyone ever got drunk on it. Drinking is deplorable, but the filth that fills the minds of some men is even worse. The beastial lusts and desires seem to cover up all signs of decency and manhood.

"...The main idea of bivouac is to see how much the individual can take. We eat at odd hours, sleep little, and simulate actual battle zone conditions, at all times. This means that we have guards for the entire

November 14, 1943 - Camp Roberts "we three..."

battalion, and guards for the company at all times. Sleeping will be a major problem because of the cold. We are not allowed to have fires at any time. We will get mail—I hope you have time to write at frequent intervals—but it must be carried on our person or destroyed. No newspapers are allowed and nothing to identify us can be left lying around. I look forward to bivouac with a great deal of anticipation. It will be something to look back on and recount to you and the children as we sit about an open fire."

———

November 15, 1943, Diary

Arose 1:00 A.M. Left barrack 2:30 Tactical march until 6:30 West and then South. Easy march, J old moon. Time for thought. Assigned to area upon arrival & began at once to dig in. Breakfast (C Platoon) about 9:00. Continued to dig thru noon & camouflaged. General rode thru about 3:30. Dinner about 4:00. Slept for an hr. Supper. Night problem until 11:00.

November 16, 1943, Diary

Slept until 7:45. Morning off until 10:00 Ph, Ed. & Duty fighting. Compass course in squadron of four. Lost. Returned near starting point. Began again. Lost. Returned by 6:30. Supper and bed.

November 17, 1943, Diary

Up at 5:30. Phy. Ed for a few minutes and fell out about 8:00.

...on a defense platoon problem. I was outpost. 5 hr afternoon we were on the attack & climbed some of the roughest hills I have seen in Calif. (Chimney) [Art could be referring to the Chimney hike in the Great Smoky Mountains National Park. It is very steep, like stairs.] Lecture on Russia, boring. Compass tonight when we did nothing a le Ft. back by 10:30

November 18, 1943, Diary

Attack by squad this morning & defense this afternoon. Guard tonight.

November 19, 1943, Diary

Combat reaction course this morning followed by a 5 mile compass problem. The former proved to be one of the best that we have had. It consisted of a series of problems requiring one to find cover when fired upon and then return the fire. Live ammunition was fired at us; one poor fellow had four or five inches of his bayonet clipped off. Five mile hike afforded scenic view of Camp. Only a few of us went through the complete course.

November 20, 1943, Diary

Tried to sleep last night without blankets and only raincoat over me. Little success. Never more miserable, cold, awaking every half hour. A hot meal did wonders at midnight. March began about 2 o'clock. The old moon was past the half, but it came up to provide a beautiful setting for our start. Just as we began to move, a fog bank rolled in from the ocean. In murky darkness we climbed, we marched. Twenty two miles in about seven and a half hours. Met by Gen. Lawrence and band. A grand feeling to be returning and only slightly tired.

November 21, 1943, Diary

To church this morning. On task force and had to go in formation. Slept eleven hours last night and felt good today. Letter from Ted today who was sent last Tues. to Compton Jr. College near L.A. Out of ten lang. students going down, only two remained in lang program. Ted had three choices: took 3 mo. Chinese refresher.

Letter from Art to Dotty
[November 23, 1943]

Friday morning

"Dearest,

We are waiting at the head of a deep gultch [gulch], waiting to go on the Combat Reaction Course. This I think is the last Range I negotiate in basic. Oh Happy Day! On it, we are fired at with live bullets, the lead hitting within inches of us. A wrong move here means —well nothing good at any rate. When we finish this we go on another compass course (only five miles long), and the day's work is almost finished.

Sunday Again

"The Combat Reaction Course proved interesting to say the least, and I came through without a scratch. Non-coms were placed at various stations along the gultch. We were fired upon, and the problem was to hit cover and return the fire at targets which appeared. It was fun and excellent experience.

"The compass course was not difficult and proved highly interesting. We climbed from about six hundred feet above sea level to fourteen hundred feet. At the top of the mountain we had a marvelous view of the country side. Stretching ten miles directly East we saw Camp Roberts, surrounded by rolling hills; and far beyond a high range of mountains. The entire hike was worth the few moments we had looking at several hundred square miles of territory...."

Bivouac Area P-17 (about 10 mi from Camp)
Nov. 16, 1943 (Tues.)

Dearest Heart,

Here it is, the second day of bivouac and not half bad. So sadly, no pen; but pencil will suffice.

I arose at one o'clock Mon. morning, and the zero hour (two-thirty) we left the battalion area. On our backs we carried full field equipment, i.e., a pack containing blanket, shelter half, ten pole and pins, extra under clothing, rain coat, toilet articles, mess equipment; gas mask, rifle, over shoes, etc, etc. The moon was just past the full, and the air was just cold enough to make hiking pleasant. We marched at a steady cadence, arriving here about six-thirty. We are south-west of Camp and into the mountain range, over which lies the Pacific.

Although a bit sleepy when we started, my brain cleared rapidly and I spent the time in productive thought. We marched without talking and so there was nothing to interfere with the thought process. In a rough way, I outlined the religious development of the Christian. As I have time in the next few days I will fill this out, smooth it up.

AS soon as we arrived in our area, we were assigned to our position —at least five yards between each slit trench, tent and trenches in the shadows—and began to dig. We were supposed to be through by the time the General came at 2:30 for inspection. Being through involved digging our trenches, camouflaging them from air and ground observation, pitching our tent and camouflaging it in a similar manner. THe General rode through in a jeep about 3:30, but hardly got out. In the late afternoon we had about an hour off and I curled up in a gultch for a bit of shut-eye. Mon. night we went out into the hills for a problem and returned ready for a sound sleep. Though the ground was hard, it was not cold and I slept very soundly.

Still Bivouac
Thur Night - Twilight

Tuesday morning we arose at the amazing hour of 7:45. (The 81st had only twenty hours scheduled for the entire five nights), and didn't get that much. From eight until ten we were off. Physical training and dirty fighting made up the rest of the morning. The first regular training came in the afternoon when we ran a compass course through the mountains in squads of four. We are right in the mountains here, mountains that are very much like the Chilhowees and the foothills of the Smokies. The first time around we found ourselves back near the start. Our time was almost up, but we started out again. At last we arrived at our area in time for supper. "What d'ya do in the Infantry?" We do, and how!

Sunday now.

Wed. we had one of our toughest days as we climbed up and down one hills as steep as the Chimneys, attack, defending, etc., etc., ad almost infinitum it seemed. This continued through Thursday, but meantime we were getting plenty of sleep. Every night during the week we were able to get at least eight hours, and sometimes it was as much as nine or ten. Thursday night I stood guard for an hour and a half and still slept eight hours and a half.

Only on Fri. night were conditions such that sleep was next to impossible. We struck tents early in evening and rolled squad rolls (one blanket, overcoat, extra pr. shoes, clothing, etc.), and also made up our full field packs. I curled up in my rain coat and tried to sleep. For half an hour at a time it was O.K. But every thirty minutes I had to get up and walk around to get my blood thawed out. The experience was hardly a pleasant one. At twelve we arose and enjoyed a hot meal including hot coffee. We stood around (waiting as per usual) until about two o'clock when the return march began. The moon came up before we ate, but by marching time a heavy ocean fog rolled in. In this murky dampness "Forwarded March" was given.

Mon. Night   11/22/43

"....Twenty-two miles we marched, arriving in our battalion area by ten. Oh happy hour! I whistled for joy on the return, knowing that basic—the tough part—is history. So ended bivouac.... Remember that anything I write concerning troop movements or my change of address is strictly military information and should not be repeated. I think that I may be shipped to a school here on the coast for further testing. I can only hope that I will survive in lang & area study. From here—East? Well, perhaps. Will write more about these things in next couple of days. For tonight, goodnight, My Dear. Eternal is Our Love, Bushy."

November 23, 1943, Tuesday, Diary

Poison Oak spreading all over my legs today. Unable to exercise at all. Merely took part in tests and lectures.

November 24, 1943, Wednesday, Diary

Infection worse. To dispensary this morning where doctor wanted to send me to hospital. I suggested a rest in the barrack, and was confined for forty-eight hours.

Letter excerpts from Art to Dotty
November 24, 1943

"Tomorrow is Thanksgiving and we have much to be thankful for. We are at war it is true, but I am thankful that I have a country to fight for; and especially since it is such a wonderful country as these United States. Climate, soil, scenery, people, schools, churches—all the finest to be found. Variety in everything, and new things, new ideas constantly coming to the fore. Yes, I am thankful to be able to play a small part in the war we are fighting for America. I am thankful also for the background that I have had which has prepared me for the road ahead. Home, Church, and School. The Church habit was of course, developed at home. Those hours of meditation, in absorbing the teachings of the minister have done much to mold my character. School, (I am thinking of Maryville) [Maryville College] took me as a boy and made of me some resemblance of a man. The friends that I made (students & faculty alike), the institution which I received, the religion atmosphere of the campus, and, most of all, my association with the sweetest little co-ed in the country—these things developed and matured me. Still looking back, the thing for which I have most reason to be thankful is Home—Mother and Dad. Not only did they give me whatever capacity I possess, but they directed my thoughts, they molded my nature to the point that I was ripe to absorb much that Maryville and Life itself have to offer. Along with the gift of a sound body and an average brain, I have found the source of eternal strength and the reassuring presence of God's love. I am thankful for these factors in my background. But there is a third thing for which I am grateful at this Thanksgiving season. I have a country and a background, but more important still I have a future to live for. That future (whether you know it or not) is built around you, My Dearest, and the home that will be ours. For the love that we have found and will continue to find in ever-increasing abundance, for you understanding, for the strength that your faith affords, for our hope and dreams I am thankful. May God forgive us for failing to live up to the best that is within us; and may He bless us and keep us strong that we may live the life of true Christians. These are my thoughts and my prayers as we enter this Thanksgiving Season."

Letter excerpts from Art to Dotty
November 26, 1943

"Congratulate me, or something, Darling, tomorrow I get my diploma showing that I have completed thirteen weeks of basic training as a rifleman, Infantry. It is a day that I have looked forward to for a long time. Tomorrow morning we march in full dress review before General Lawrence and all the "brass" (officers of high rank).

"One would think that six weeks of pre-basic thirteen weeks of basic, and four weeks of post-basic would be enough for one soldier. Not so for Bushing. Yesterday a full schedule for next week was posted. However, shipping orders for some of the men are already here and rumors fly thick and fast that we will be out by Dec. 1. By the time you read this I may be on my way some where. I certainly hope so.

"...Today we had a full field inspection with all of our equipment displayed. You would be amazed at the exactness which is required for these inspections. Every article—there must be thirty-five or forty—must be in one place, facing one way, etc. ad infinitum.

"...Tonight, we had a company party in the mess hall. It was begun with supper & the hilarity followed. The beer and noise were so disgusting that I made a speedy get-away. The beast that is within man too often hides the divine which is of God. I long to return again to civilization and to taste culture again.

"...I must tell you of a vivid dream I had last night. Yes, we were at the alter, my sweet, you and I. Pete, Corbett, and the whole Maryville gang must have been there. Reality was once a dream, and that which we dream today will be the reality of the morrow. I live and pray for the eternal growth of Our love, Bushy
P.S. Don't forget that anything I mention in regard to troop movements should not be repeated."

November 26, 1943, Friday, Diary

Still unable to drill but fell out for full-field inspection. Entire battalion out behind guard house and plenty of brass looking us over. Everything is set up in minute detail. Interesting to see sharing brushes, tooth powder, etc., being tossed from line to line. Had to miss retreat parade tonight.

November 27, Sunday, Diary

The day that I have looked forward to for many long weeks, the day that has been pushed back again and again. This morning we (the battalion) passed in review before Gen. Lawrence and the rest of the brass. After this, we went to Theater No. 2. where we listened to cut and dried speeches. Here too we received our diplomas. 'Tis a grand feeling to know that I have "successfully completed thirteen weeks of basic military training" after twenty-three weeks of work.

Letter excerpt from Art to Dotty
November 28, 1943

"You no longer need refer to your service man as a trainee. AS of yesterday morning, I am now a soldier in Uncle Sam's Army having "successfully completed thirteen weeks of basic military training." Yes, Darling, I graduated—but I almost didn't. I almost had K.P.—and that would have been ironic.

"...With all the pomp and ceremony that the Army can muster, the 80th Battalion marched in review on the "largest parade ground in the country" yesterday while General Lawrence inspected. After the parade, we marched to one of the theatres for speeches. Here too we received our diplomas."

---

* December 1, 1943, Diary

The Army discipline, its strict regimentation has tended to give me a sense of inferiority. If the doctor was correct in his analysis of my condition at the hospital, ie, that nervous mental conflicts caused my headaches, then I think that perhaps a sense of inferiority has been another symptom. Here one is never told that a job was well done—if so it is extremely rare. There is no particular opportunity in basic for ability in general to be recognized.

December 2, 1943, Diary

Sgt. Bauman left last night on three day pass: and, in leaving, he told me goodbye. I thanked him for the many breaks he has given me, and, in turn he paid me a number of complements. One of which was that he had wanted to make me a squad leader. He was very wise not to since I was a new man. Nevertheless it was nice of him to consider me.

Letter excerpts from Art to Dotty
December 2, 1943

"From a company of almost two hundred and fifty men, twenty two of us (not on orders) were left, and today it narrowed down to about eighteen. However, instead of training today all of us gold-bricked through a G.I. Party in the barrack. In other words, we scrubbed the barrack with brushes in a half-hearted fashion. Our corporal told us that we had to work all day, so take our time. We did! I think that the basic engineers will leave tomorrow and that will leave about seven men in my platoon.

"....Of course I'm jealous when you tell me how handsome are the men you fed and rub. I'm jealous when I know that someone else is playing the violin with you, talking with you, or even seeing you. However, I don't want you to stop because of that. Why wouldn't I be jealous of the most precious thing in the world to me. Oh, by the way, My Sweet, I have a feeling I've fallen for you. I guess I'll have to admit I love you, Bushy"

December 4, 1943, Diary

Table waiter this morning and most of morning spent in kitchen. Basic engineers pulled out about ten o'clock. Authentic rumor has it that they are going to Puget Sound University. Tonight Ken and I spent a wonderful evening with Sibelius and Grieg at the chapel. Company has only about twenty-five or thirty men left.

Letter excerpts from Art to Dotty
December 4, 1943

"I intended to ask you if you by chance read an article in Dec. Reader's Digest on Birth Control. Written by a Catholic , it presents their convictions against it. I am sure you have read many such articles, but I would be interested in your reaction to this one. Without knowing all that I would like to know about it, I am included to agree with the Catholics.

"...I think that our previous discussion of this point has been rather vague. It is something, my sweet, upon which we should reach a mutual decision or at least understanding. Read the article if you haven't and let me know what you think.

"...Dad's letter included more news concerning Sgt. Another royalties check arrived recently to boost his picture profits to $160,000. That's on the g.t. [?], of course. As Dad says "what a chunk Uncle Sam gets of this!

"...In case you hadn't suspected, I expect to get a very important gift for the sweetest bundle of charm this side of the Atlantic. However, I can't get it here in Roberts. Fact is, I can't get it until I reach a place where I can get the best. Soo, it looks as though I will have to send it by mail if you are to have the gift by the 25th. It may be that there will be a delay to even at that. Point is, would you want me to hold it just in case we could get together within a few weeks? I don't like the idea of sending a ring by mail. Doggone it, I want to be there to place on that kissable little hand."

December 5, 1943, Diary

I awoke this morning to hear a steady downpour patter on the rocks outside the barracks. Ken unluckily had K.P. so I went to church with a fellow named Bendi. Very nice communion service. Rainy and dismal all day.

December 8, 1943, Diary

In charge of detail to oil rifle slings. An all day, inside job. We have to be kept busy. Ken and I saw "Happy Hand" starring Don Ameche tonight. Good picture of the effect of war on an average Am. family and particular the reaction of the father to the death of his son. The job well done. First Sgt. Hoagland told me that I leave Friday with eleven other language men for Santa Rosa Jr. College, Santa Rosa, Calif. S.T.A.R. Unit there.

Letter from Art to Dotty
December 8, 1943
Wednesday Night

My Dearest,

At long last I can report news: Darling, I'm leaving Camp Roberts. As much attached as I have become to the place, I feel like shouting. Friday morning at ten-thirty I pull out. It's still a military secret of sorts: but, by the time this reaches you, I will have arrived at my destination. No, it isn't East, or at least not yet. As I suspected, we are to go to a S.T.A.R. Unit for further testing and classification. It isn't entirely official, but it is almost certain that we will go to Santa Rosa Junior College, Santa Rosa, Calif.

The best I can make out his that this is about eighty or ninety miles north of Frisco. Here I am sure we will get "fluency" tests. Unless my degree and other pertinent points in my background make a strong impression, my chances to remain in language may be seriously hampered. In such case I intent volunteer for Japanese.

Only one man from our company got into the Japanese study— somewhat separate from the other languages. It seems that three years of college are required plus a score above 130 on A.S.E. Test. I should be able to make both of these. As I understand it, this is the only branch in which men are vitally needed. My interview etc. will clarify a great deal.

I don't know how much time I will have to write tomorrow night. I want to study French as much as possible and write a note home. I may not be able to write until Sat. for we will probably not reach Santa Rosa until late Fri. afternoon. Mail will be forwarded from here until I can get you my new address.

'Twas a wonderful prayer that Daddy wrote. I was glad to get it. Your letter came tonight. Please, please, my Sweet, do not try to kill yourself with work. I am really worried about your health with such a heavy schedule. For the sake of our future & the future of the little ones to come, don't overwork.

Pray for our success in the coming days.

Thine own,
Bushy

December 9, 1943, Diary

Physical ("short-arm") this morning. Few small details just to keep us occupied. Got in a couple of hours of much needed sleep. Ken on K.P. again but finished by 7:30. We went down to the chapel and heard Nutcracker Suite and other selections. Afterward went up to the altar for a few moments of prayer.

Letter from Art to Dotty
Santa Rosa J.C.
Sat. Morning Dec. 11, '43

My Dearest,

Well, here I am, dreaming it seems. To my front is a small orchard; to my rear is a college campus. Forty of us arrived about eight-thirty last night and we still can't realize that all this is true. They call us "Mister" civilian "G.I." our barrack, the best cooks from the hotels and bakeries prepare our food. There is almost nothing of the former regimentation and our inspections are mainly to see if we have our clothes button and shoes shined. Really, Darling, this seems like an almost perfect set-up so far. Frisco is only fifty-seven miles away, and connections are good by bus and by thumb.

As yet (this is Sat. afternoon) our situation is a little confused. The S.T.A.R. Unit at Roberts was supposed to have performed the function of this place and there is just a very faint possibility that further testing will not be necessary. However, since I took no language tests whatsoever, I expect to be subjected to embarrassment. I understand that every possible break is given, but even so my sadly neglected speaking knowledge of French will not stand up. So far I can't find out very much about Japanese, whether or not there is still an offering. In a few days, I should find out.

My Dearest Heart,

The last three days have been so filled with varied activity that I have not had time to write even to give you my new address. Here I am at the Hospitality House a little tired from sightseeing in glad to get the chance to sit down and talk with you.

To start where I last left off, Friday morning found the language and areas study men ready to ship. Since the preceding night had been our last time together, Ken and I had gone down to the chapel to listen to the Nutcracker Suite and a couple of other favorites. After that we had gone up to the altar for a final prayer together. Friday morning we left the 80th Battalion about 10:30. However, Art train didn't leave until 12:30 so we stood on the platform at the Camp Roberts Station. One of the last things I saw as I left the parade ground was a Tennessee car from Nashville.

We had a nice trip to San Francisco, arriving about 5:30. After a good meal in the train station, we boarded a bus and pulled out for our new home. I think I described the beauty of a sunset in the Golden Gate. I saw that site on my way to Roberts last June. Friday night I saw the beauty of the full moon over the Golden Gate Bay as we crossed the Golden Gate Bridge. A great shaft of light poured down on the rippling water. It seemed as though the lights from Heaven were shining down. We crossed the bridge and continued on our northward way.
Sunday night

As per usual this seems to be another disjointed letter. My letter was interrupted by an unfortunate incident, and now I'm back at school.

I must get these various bits together and send them to you, Darling. After all, I haven't written now for four or five days. My trip to Frisco was intended to be a shopping tour, but I when I arrived last night most of the stores were closed. I hardly had a chance to get started. Perhaps I can go back again next week.

After I got in town I found a place to sleep and then took a sight seeing tour. Enjoyed the Stagedoor Canteen, a couple of USO's and the Hospitality House. At the last I ran into several Australian boys who arrived in America Friday. It was highly interesting to talk to them and get their first-hand impression of America. Also I ran into a boy from Ohio in A.S.T. there in San Francisco. Like me he neither smokes nor drinks. That is really an amazing discovery in the Army.

This morning I arose about nine and found the location of the nearest Presbyterian Church. It proved to be the Finest, the oldest on the coast. An excellent sermon which I must tell you about. A good Scotsman he was, and good sound thinker.

I must write Mother and Dad tonight, I haven't yet been able to write them either. I promise to write again as quickly as possible.

For tonight, goodbye and sweetest dreams.

> All my love,
> Bushy

Co B ASTAR Unit 3964
Santa Rosa J.C.
Santa Rosa, Calif.

Letter from Art to Dotty
Santa Rosa, J.C.
Tues. Dec. 14, '43

My Dearest Own,

I'm still dreaming, but don't bother the wake me. Last night we were asked whether we wanted coffee or fruit juice for supper. Today we were <u>asked</u> to clean up an area, and the sergeant almost apologized when he asked us. Friday night there will be a big dance in the gym & we are allowed to go for dates and take them home. Bed check at one o'clock. I can't decide whether I want to blonde or a redhead. Which do you think, Darling? (Well, at least I can dream of my younger days, can't I?) Now you should be a bit jealous unless you know me better. The food is better than the best civilian restaurants. I just can't believe it! We have class A passes, that is we can go into town every night that we are free & any week-end. After six weeks, we can get three day passes.

Well enough description for now. When classes begin our time will be full I imagine. As yet we are just waiting around, playing football all afternoon both yesterday and today. The classification section here awaits word from the Ninth Service Command as to our status. The complication is that we were through the S.T.A.R. Unit at Roberts. There seems to be another technicality concerning the new requirement for fluency, whether or not it is retroactive.

Suspense and uncertainty are the keynotes right now. For the sake of sanity I am expecting the worst while hoping for the best. From encouraging words that we have had, there seems to be some ground to believe that I can remain in language though not fluent. However, the

Ninth Service Command may put its foot down. It seems that in regular A.S.T. Schools, the new language taken up will be taught in the language in which we are supposed to be fluent. That is, I may be studying Chinese in French. If such is true, it would be almost futile for me, and I may as well switch to engineering now. Everything is so confused that I refuse to worry or think very much about the whole situation. It is a grand feeling to leave the future in the hands of a Higher Power.

In case I stay in language, the chances are that I will remain here for from two to three months. I came back from Frisco with a fellow who has been here thirteen weeks and still doesn't know when he is leaving. However, in that case, I think I would have a better chance for a S. Eastern school. If I go into engineering, I should ship by the middle of Jan. In any case, I will have to dream of a White Christmas. Our plans for an early meeting seem to have come to naught, Dear.

I went to town tonight in the hope that I would do some Christmas shopping, but the stores were closed. I will have to send letters of apology I fear. Did get a present for Mary Ruth in Frisco. However, have had no opportunity to get it mailed as yet. Could you pick up a book of poetry by Masefield on Yeats for Daddy. Inscribe it please and present it to him from me. I see no chance of buying anything until after Christmas. I bought a lot of cards at Roberts, and I still haven't sent very many. In case I can get in town Sat before stores close I will get Mother a present.

As usual, I am writing at a late hour. Have had no mail from Roberts but it should be up by tomorrow. I miss your letters a great deal, Darling. But even more I miss you. The school here brings me very close to Maryville, to what it represents, and to the things we love. Goodnight, my Own, and dream of
Our Love,
Bushy

P.S. In case a small recording comes, save it until Christmas Day. Remember!

PS. II. Luther Burbank [an American botanist] lived here in Santa Rosa. Hope to go through his gardens Sat. or Sun.

Letter from Art to Dotty

Santa Rosa J.C.

Dec. 17, 1943

My Dearest Heart,

For more than a week I had been without a letter from you; for more than a week I have thirsted for word from you. As usual my patience was rewarded by your wonderful letter of the 8th. If you were doing nothing else, you would be making your contribution to the war-effort by keeping this "G.I." with a high morale. All I ever need is one long letter (of course, two are never turned down!).

The details of your training at St. Mary's was news, for I have not had the chance to read about it in the papers. I rarely get to see a newspaper except to view the headlines. Glad to know that you will graduate from "basic" in two weeks. I faintly remember something about basic myself. I think you mentioned before that you are to take 150 hrs. so that means you have about 70 more to go. I am glad you were getting it, but will also be glad when it is over.

Glad we agree on the Reader's Digest article. Such points should not be left until our wedding night to discuss. As you say, we never know until we try, but I hope we can have some degree of certainty.

As time goes on here I am getting a clearer idea of just how things may work out for us. I think the chances for staying in language are very good, in fact I think we can almost assume then I am in. We still await word from 9th Service Command to get final word on fluency testing, but my work has been so intensive in the last few days that I believe I could pass even that. Six and eight hours of French per day is a big help.

If (there is still an "If") I do remain in the program, the chances are too good that I will remain here for at least a couple of months and maybe three. I couldn't wish for a more wonderful setup—except to wish for the one indispensable in my life, you my Own. From here I will probably go to a school out here on the coast. The situation may change, but that seems to be the only thing to expect. At least if something better comes up, we will be happy, whereas if we expected my courses to be taken at Chapel Hill or Vandy, we would be terribly disappointed with U.C.L.A.

With the picture thus just a bit clarified, I am trying to do a bit of planning in regard to our immediate future. It still seems the wisest to wait until the end of my first regular term and A.S.T. By that time I will be settled in regard to the work and our financial status should be much improved. As you can easily see this may necessitate your coming out here.

Now I'm getting around to the point I made concerning a bit of certainty in regard to children. The story I get here doesn't include much possibility for a wife abroad in this business. In fact it would seem that I may go along with a regular unit for the purpose of interviewing prisoners, interpreting, etc, and it may work into a job lasting sometime after hostility ceases. There is always the chance that I may be away for many long months. If such were to happen, it probably wouldn't be wise for you to be in the states with a couple of little Bushing's on hand.

Well, I'm really taking the point too far. There is a great deal of conjecture in all of that. What I do want you to think very seriously about is the fact that we may be separated for a very long time once I get into my work. We must prepare ourselves psychologically for that possibility. You have every right to want to put the marriage off until after the war, as we once thought would be necessary. As for me, "give me my love or give me death." I don't care to wait; and I know you share the same feeling. Our home may be delayed, but Our Love can be halted by nothing. God-given, it will live on eternally.

'Tis Friday night and I will write a long letter Sunday. Must go from the sublime to the concrete with a few details. The big news for me at the moment is the fact that none other than Kenneth C. rolled into Santa Rosa, J.C. last night. Yep, for the third time the kind hand of fate has thrown us together—two who look at a star and see the same thing. He will probably leave with a couple of three weeks, but we can enjoy a great deal together here at Santa Rosa.

In regard to Xmas presents, I was able to get one for Mary Ruth, but still haven't been able to get it in the mail. No place here on the campus. Will mail it for sure tomorrow. If you can do this one thing for me, Darling, get an album for Mother and Daddy. I leave the the selection to your excellent judgment. Something they both liked. Will send money order for $5 in letter. Will send more later if needed. I can't possible get a chance to buy anything for them; and, even if I could, I wouldn't want to send records 3000 miles.

I face the same dilemma as you in regard to Dad. He would love to have a nice picture of you if you have one. I hardly know of a book that he doesn't love, unless it would be such a book as poems by Yeats or Masefield. In case you bought that for Daddy, you could send it to Dad since the records will take its place. If it is a picture you sent, put it in a folder for him. He could probably use such a thing as a wallet or a travelling kit. I'm sure he doesn't have the latter. Say, I think I'll get him a travelling kit. You will probably already have something when you get this, so I'll go ahead and get that tomorrow.

Big dance tonight in gym from 8 - 12. I didn't like my red-head so I came home. However, between waltzes I managed to book the enclosed Calif. mistletoe. It served its purpose here, so I pass it on. There is plenty of it on the campus. (Don't believe everything I say. I've spent the entire evening with Ken in the writing room, writing this letter. To heck with the dance and the Jr. College kids!)

Darling, needless to say, my mind will be filled with thoughts of you and home during the coming week. May your eyes open on a very Merry Christmas Day and may the Spirit of Christ enter into our hearts as never before.

Through the eternal years will prevail
　　　　Our Love,
　　　　Bushy

Letter from Art to Dotty

MERRY CHRISTMAS!

Santa Rosa, Calif.
Dec. 21, 1943

My Dearest Heart,

I find myself in a lonely mood tonight, thinking of you. I had hoped that along expected letter would be forthcoming in the evening, but no letter did I receive. In fact, my Dear, I have received only one message from you since I left Roberts, seemingly months ago. I know that you are extremely busy, and I know that the mails are loaded far beyond their capacity. The latter reason is more likely, but that doesn't prevent me from longing to hear from you.

Speaking of letters, I had a long one from Phil, Phyllis Eggy Evaul which I will enclose if I have room (hope I haven't!). It amazed me to find that they are only about thirty miles from Santa Rosa. Ken and I must go down at the earliest possible moment. It will be wonderful to see Phil again and recounts old times. It will be worse than a convention of old hens. In addition to many other bits of news, Phil mentions that "Peggy (Carter) Northup is living in San Francisco while her husband is in submarine duty." Unless I'm mistaken, she's a Maryville flame that flicked before my Awora dawned on me. Perhaps I should look her up to say 'hello'. Yes? No?

Ken and I had hoped to go down to see Phil Friday since our vacation begins Thursday afternoon. Almost everyone is getting a three day pass, but 15% of the post must remain. I was one of the unlucky ones to be "selected" to stay. I don't mind too much, but I did want to feel free for those few days. In addition to seeing Phil, we wanted to spend a day in the Petrified Forest. However, we can do these things later.

We have accepted an invitation to Christmas dinner together with a family in town, and I will be able to get out for that. About twenty-five families have invited men stationed here, and so we decided to take opportunity. It will be wonderful to be in a home on Christmas even if it is a strange one.

Last week-end we took our past but stayed in Santa Rosa. Sat. night we did a bit of shopping, returning early to bed. Sunday morning we attended church at the local Presbyterian. I mailed a very fine program earlier in the week. The music was especially good. Sunday afternoon we had a real treat in store. The local county orchestra and chorus presented a concert in the high school auditorium next door to the College. The chorus gave the "Messiah" as you will note in the program. You can well imagine the thrill that we received! The soprano and contraltos were excellent in their performance. I did the bass the injustice of comparing him with Dean Stiles, and I fear I couldn't enjoy him too much. The orchestra was far better than I expected. The day was certainly well-spent and I think it is typical of the cultural opportunities that I will have while here.

Our situation has changed none at all since I wrote you last. We continued to study French six hours a day in class, and I am spending every possible moment that I can find it night. I am learning but fast! However, I still have great difficulty in conversing. With practice, it should come. We have had no official contact with the S.T.A.R. Unit since we began work on our own. I suppose that they know that we are still here. Any day I expect a statement in regard to our status, but I certainly am willing to wait. Every day that passes increases my chances of remaining in the language program.

Darling, I must again and make an explanation and an apology concerning the Christmas present for Mother and Daddy. I had fully intended to send the money in this letter, but Ken and I find our pools very low, since we do not expect to get paid at the end of the month. We must "be prepared" for unexpected expenses, and I still must buy Dad's gift. I know you will understand, and I think you can safely trust your future "le fiancé".

By the time you receive this, I think your Christmas present will be well in hand. I hope the present and the record arrive on time. You know, I so wanted to be there, "ma bonne amie." I had never planned that the mailman would convey one of the most precious gifts that I could give you. However, perhaps the little record will bring my voice to you, bring me a bit closer. I hope you can hear it alone, at least the first time.

Darling, the ring which you will have on when you read this will symbolize the bond that makes us one. It is to remind you that our hearts look to each other for strength through the years of eternity. It is to remind the world that I have placed my claim upon you as my partner—the one who will share my joy, my sorrow, who will bring forth my children, who will give meaning and purpose to all my efforts.

As you put it on your finger, or rather as <u>I</u> placed it on your finger (I will be with you, my Dear!), let us pray again to our Father who is the author of our divine love. May we give thanks for the blessing of his holy guidance in our lives, for bringing us together, and for revealing his plan for our lives together. May we renew again are promise, our dedication to His service, whether it be full-time or only part-time. May we seek His purpose for our lives and His Love as the cornerstone for that home which will be ours. For the joy of living in Christ's Way, for the eternal flame of Our Love, we pray.

May your joy be full at this glad season, and may our hearts reach a new understanding of the true meaning of Christmas. God bless

     Our Love,
     Bushy

Letter excerpts from Art to Dotty
December 23, 1943

"Thursday night; the night before the night before Christmas.... Here I am, Darlingical. And here's a kiss just because that cute librarian and the two others in the entire room are not looking. Another—great big one this time —— —. Ah-h! Gee, it's nice here. No noise, almost no one else, a little Christmas tree all lit up on the desk—uh oh! Watch it! someone else is coming in the door. I better not hold you so tightly someone might think—oh let them. They can see that ring, can't they? We belong to each other, don't we? I know though, we'd both feel better if I took my arms down—at least, until we're alone again. By the way, Dear, I love you, you know —————. All night long I could go on daydreaming....

"Two wonderful letters arrived from Roberts yesterday and today your first letter came direct. Three days isn't bad at all for a letter in the Christmas rush. I suspect the mail realized how happy it would make this "G.I." Tanks for the article, program, and news. I enjoyed all, especially that "you" that is in all your letters, my Dear.

"I too feel that "it sort of hurts," Darling, that the prospects to see each other grows dim. I fear that my hopes were a bit higher than I had allowed you to guess. The one thing that keeps my chin up is the dream of the long days beyond these war-torn years when we will know again some degree of normality. When we can live as to [two] people, deeply in love, should be able to live. Until we can share our total selves in the bonds of married love, our faith and hope and love will continue to strengthen our lonely hearts. Thine Own, Bushy"

Letter excerpts from Art to Dotty
December 24, 1943

"My Dearest Heart, 'Tis Christmas Eve: the radio brings carols of rich voices praising the name of Him whose birthday we stop to commemorate; the room is quiet, the night outside, still; 'tis Christmas Eve in California—'tis Christmas Eve all over the world tonight. My evening has been spent writing to Mother and Dad, writing to you, and dreaming of home, of my Sweetest Dream.

"In the early part of the evening I almost did a very bad thing—I almost allowed myself to feel sorrow for "me." I was on the verge of being a homesick and lonely little boy on this, my first Christmas away from home.

"A nation wide, in fact, a world-wide program began, giving little glimpses of Xmas Eve with the fighting men around the globe. I begin to think how lucky I am to be here in the recreation room of a college campus, far from the burst of bombs and the splatter of bullets. By the hand of a kind and purposeful God, I am here tonight rather than "over there." I can worship on this Christmas Eve, knowing full well that tomorrow I will not go out to see and kill the enemy.

"I have been selected for a higher purpose in this World Struggle and it is for me to prove myself worthy of the opportunity. I'm a very lucky "G.I." even though three thousand miles separates me from the ones I love on this Christmas Eve.

"I pray, not for special consideration in this time of crisis, but for strength to make the maximum contribution to the rebirth of a new and better world in which Christ will be brought closer to the hearts of men. And so, on this Christmas Eve, I miss home and you, but I'm thankful to be here."

Letter excerpts from Art to Dotty
December 25, 1943

"My Darling, I so wanted to call you today. I so wanted to hear your voice and to hear you say "I love you." This morning, before I had to leave for my Christmas dinner I called long distance to find approximately how long it would take to get the call through. I found in all likelihood that it would be long past my appointment time. I intend to try again tomorrow and I do hope that I can make it....

"Ken and I found ourselves in a lovely house for our Christmas meal. The couple was middle-aged, with the son in the Service in Alaska and a daughter working in San Francisco. The daughter was home and a couple of men with whom our host works. After a wonderful meal, it was suggested by the men that the ladies take us for a tour of the scenic valley.

"After several attempts we found gas and continued on our way. Through "The Valley of the Moon" we drove to Sonoma, I town just twenty-miles away. This poetic name attached to the lovely little valley was given it by Jack London who built a home on one side of the rolling hills. Although not quite the same, it reminded me of our little valley in the mts. At Sonoma we saw another mission (Mission San Francisco Del Solano) in the chain extending from Southern Calif. north. The one at San Miguel (near Roberts) was in the same chain. This was the most northerly of the missions and the last to be established—1823 was the date. Just across the street we saw the spot where the "Bear Flag" was hoisted for the first time when California declared herself independent and free from Mexico. Almost immediately the Stars and Stripes replaced the Bear Flag, and Calif. became a part of the United States. On the same corner was an old hotel or inn frequented by Kit Carson, Tremont and others. On the forth corner of this crowded cross street was the old adobe barracks for Gen. Valleau—a military leader for the state in its early days. We drove then passed his home and on by the location of Jack London's home.

"We return to the home for a bit of cake and coffee. By nine we excused ourselves and attempted to express our appreciation for the wonderful time. It was much nicer than if we had taken a three day pass into Frisco, and certainly less expensive. I fear I can never be at my social best with young ladies on such occasions, however, I am constantly thinking of a certain wonderful girl. Almost unconsciously I compare them with you, My Dearest, and the [they] fall so low on the scale that I must force myself to act the part of a gentleman. You were with me every moment, Darling, during Christmas Day. I pray that the next 25th of December we will be together to share the joy of the season."

Letter excerpts from Art to Dotty
December 26, 1943

"My Own, As Ken just told me, I'm depressed tonight. At eleven o'clock this morning I put in a call to you. At that time I was told that there would be a five or six hour delay. I was perfectly willing to wait, so I parked myself here in the Day Room immediately after the noon meal. I tried to study French; I tried to write letters. I kept listening for the phone and ended up by doing almost nothing. I checked at 5:00, 6:30, 7:15, 8:00. Finally at 8:00 P.M. the operator told me that there would be another delay from two to three hours. I have to be in by 10 o'clock, and that would be midnight at 607 West Glenwood [Dotty's home], so I had to cancel the call after waiting nine hours.

"I am depressed, Darling, for I so waited to talk with you. I wanted to hear you say the ring arrived, that you were proud of it, that you love me. I wanted to hear your voice.

"I do hope it arrived without your knowledge, but you didn't play the record until Xmas Day, and that my Special Delivery didn't arrive so early as to spoil the surprise.

"By the way, while I think of it here's a bit of important data to save. I give it to you because I may lose it. When I get the wedding band, I should have this number—Dia. Sol. 40-6254.—to refer to. Put it down in a place where we can locate it easily.

"The thing for me to do tonight is to go to bed and try to sleep off my depression. Not a thousand years of sleep would keep my lonely heart as I dream of you, My Dear; but the time calls for a stiff upper lip and resolution. With patience I await the consummation of Our Love, Bushy"

Letter excerpts from Art to Dotty
December 29, 1943

"...I must mention one other thing very briefly before I say goodnight. You seem to feel for some reason that you can't wear the ring because for some reason I wasn't there to put it on. I was there, My Darling, very definitely. I do hope the record arrived O.K., and if it didn't, perhaps my special delivery spoke for me. If I am blind on some bit of social custom, enlighten me; but I fully intended for you to wear the ring. I can hardly wait to hear how you like, if you do. Remember, Darling, the size of the stone hardly represents my love. Stones just don't grow that big!"

Letter excerpts from Art to Dotty
December 31, 1943

"...Your Xmas package arrived tonight, and I was delighted with its content. The scarf will make a wonderful dress addition to my "G.I." wardrobe, and the sweater will be no less nifty. As for the pen, well you just and wait and see all the letters that will be coming now....

"I still anxiously await a letter telling me that you have a new bit of jewelry. Have had but one letter this week. Still counting on getting it tomorrow....

"Life would lose its grand adventurousness if we could look beyond the veiled curtain of time, and yet how anxiously we await the coming of each new morrow, and how much we long to know what is in store. The Year which already moves across the expanse of these United States holds much for every individual the world over, but for a relatively few does it hold as much as it does for two lovers whose lives will be joined in the bonds of marriage before its end. God has been very kind to us, and I believe that His plans enfold us in a new union with Him—Mrs. Arthur S. Bushing! I'll be the proudest & the happiest guy alive....

"One year from tonight I may be thousands of miles away doing my bit in some theatre of war. My success in this work will have an important effect on my post-war work for I may continue with the government long after the Peace is made.

"On this New Year's Eve, let us pray together to the ever-mercyful Father who has granted us Love, the most wonderful of his blessings. May we pray for forgiveness for straying from Christ's example, and for strength to become more like Him. May the New Year bring a new vision of World Brotherhood and may the foundation for that Brotherhood be laid. Give us strong leaders, Christ-led, who will rise up to meet the challenge. For ourselves, let us pray that it may be His divine will that we, who love each other beyond the expression of human words, find in 1944, divine union of our lives, our minds, are all. This be our prayer on New Year's Eve Amen, Bushy."

1944

"Enlisted Man's Temporary Passes"
and "Registration Certificate"

January 1, 1944, Diary

Santa Rosa

Ken and I spent New Year's Eve in the Day Room writing letters and wondering a bit what the ensuing months have in store for us, for the world. Today was a little different from our other school days here, and a heavy Calif. dew began after lunch. Ken and I hitch-hiked to Oakland, having very good luck, and took bus from there to Centerville. On way past four Kayser Ship yards, famous for Liberty Ships. Inquiring at the only place open, we found the location of Phil Evaul's house from the men in the local tavern (Phil's influence spreading!) Marched each other to keep warm while we waited for Phil. Later talked till one

---

Letter from "Daddy Bushing" to Dotty
Jamestown, Tenn

Jan 28, 1946
Dear Dorothy:

I hasten to inform you that came early Sunday am, my first copy (January) of Fortune Magazine. We are delighted with it and I could hardly lay it down for more religious duties – Mother likes it because it deals with real people - with facts rather than fiction. Editionally, it surpasses most of everything with which I might attempt to compare it. Thanks a lot. We'll save copies for you & hubby. Very cold here yesterday, but today not so bad.

Hope you and the folks are getting along nicely. Work going along as usual. It looks as if the work will close out sometime in May at which time we will again take up Agriculture – maybe. Monday, you know, is one of our busiest days, and this has seen some 30 or 40 people, mostly discharged GI's milling around in here.

Loving wishes from us both.
Daddy Bushing

Letter excerpts from Art to Dotty
Santa Rosa Jr College
Jan. 1, 1944

Happy New Year, Darling,

Outside the clouds hang low and the damp air penetrates the outer garments as soon as one steps outside. Mist is falling and one is glad to remain in the warmth of the heater. The French class takes time out to celebrate the New Year—some reading, others writing. I have slipped out to an empty room to think and write.

Just within my view stands a giant oak, one of a number of such trees composing a beautiful grove in the central part of the small campus. These trees seem to lounge in their repose; their gnarled and moss-green limbs languidly searching the empty nothingness of sky around them. A beautiful cathedral effect would be given by the light of a full moon as the arms rainbow the air, but on such a day as this a weird, haunting effect lingers in the mind, even after a casual glance. Almost unconsciously one is reminded of the Moor-setting from "Wuthering Heights" or a dream fantasy as Poe [Edgar Allan Poe] might describe.

The heavy, gray blanket of cloud seems to close in tighter, the mist continues to fall, 'tis a dreary day that greets the New Year, and a time for a backward look.

The past twelve months have been full it seems. My twenty-first year has in reality been a year of transition. Just a year ago I was still a struggling senior at dear old Maryville. It was in the early part of February that I applied for Advanced Meteorology, the suggestion having been made by Dr. McClelland. March 9th, it was that I was knocked off my feet by orders to report for active duty to Chapel Hill for Pre-meteorology. That would mean giving up my last three months at Maryville, even though I would receive my degree. I said good-bye to many of my friends; there was no recourse I presumed when the Army called. We telephoned Atlanta to see if I could get a twenty-four hour delay—I had almost no time to pack. The Atlanta office told us that I could refuse the appointment. The choice was mine to make. Since Meteorology was merely a war-expedient; and, for a number of other reasons, I stayed. Dr. Hunter wanted me to do that, for, as he said later, he wanted "to save me for the humanities." I hope he was correct.

Soon after, the choice came again to me to give up my honors work, my first scholastic love, my other studies, and accept a position on the teaching staff at Maryville. At the time it seemed to be a choice between teaching and entering the Army. I sincerely wanted to be in the Service, and yet I was told that the College needed my service. I accepted the opportunity. I still wonder how I went into the classroom eighteen hours a week to attempt to teach physics to men with far more hours in physics than I. The six weeks of teaching was a memorable experience.

The event of my graduation was hardly the thrill I had always looked forward to, for it was actually an anti-climax. I had really completed my work two months earlier. At the time of graduation I was a full-time instructor. Remember how we graded papers until five o'clock on my last afternoon before graduation? I could never have finished if you had not been there. Graduation Day dawned; Mother came; my happiness was made complete. Without her work and planning my four years at Maryville would have hardly been possible. Along with graduation, are memories of our few days and nights together—with Roblene, Dick, Jack—alone with the moon in the College Wood. [Art is referring to the night he proposed to Dotty in the woods of Maryville College's campus.]

A welcomed two weeks of rest at home and then, on June 1st, I reported to Fort Oglethorpe via Knoxville. I found little that is the Army there, but my stay was short. With old college friends (seven in all) I spent six days crossing our gigantic country to arrive at the now famous (at least to us) Camp of Roberts. Six months of strenuous, outdoor work. I still must insist that the moments which I did not enjoy were few and far between, and the experiences I gained were immeasurable in value. I think the outstand gain was the proof of the very practical value of the standards and ideals which I established at Maryville. Christ's is the only practical way. It was there too that I discovered that I must avoid certain pitfalls in regard to my nervous system. (I still question sometimes the diagnosis given me by the Doctor.)

From Roberts to Santa Rosa for a real rest. But 1943 did not bring the final answer to my future in Specialized Training. That decision is still to be made.

Yes, 1943 was the year of transition for me. In it, I change from a college boy to some semblance of an Army man. While the last few weeks at Maryville added fuel to the flame of my ego, the months at Roberts tended to make me less certain of my own abilities. The Army does that I fear particularly in a branch where regimentation is so strictly adhered to. In Specialized Training I will again have a chance to demonstrate any intellectual ability that I may possess. So the old year is dead, long live the New! I expressed our prayer last night. I can only say now: May God bless and keep us during the next twelve months as He has in the past. May we be creatures of His Divine Will. Yes, it is to be "the year" in our lives....

"Telepathy at work again. The prayer that I wrote in my letter last night (New Year's Eve) was almost identical in thought to your words which came today. '...For their hearts and minds shall become as one....'

"In regard to the Nurse Aide: Just how do you expect to finish it? By my math, it will take 50 weeks to complete 150 hours. I hope you don't expect to be in Knoxville for the next eleven and a half months....

[Sunday morning, Jan. 2]

"Since the day I finished basic I have been growing—that which I always threatened—yes, a moustache. Wanted to surprise you with picture but thought I'd better give you a chance to refuse the picture first. I do like it, Darling."

January 2, 1944, Diary

Phil gave a great sermon today in his little church in Irvington. Good crowd, very nice people. Peggy lovely wife and Phyllis a sweet baby. Had a grand time talking over Maryville and "doings" of friends. Phil 'n family have an apartment here and come down from seminary every week-end.

Letter from Art to Dotty
Santa Rosa Jr College
Dec. 4, 1944 [Art meant Jan. 4, 1944]

My Dearest,

At long last, after the fourth attempt, were at last able to talk to each other. I was beginning to wonder if the jinx had us. Even last night I expected a delay of several hours, and the call went right through. It was wonderful to hear your voice again, Darling; and it did my moral no end of good. Second only to the effect of your voice was the exhilarating effect of the wonderful letter which you wrote on Christmas Day. Only one writing from the depths of the soul could have written in such a warm and vibrant way. As I read and re-read the letter, you seem to be here with me; you seem to be whispering in your soft voice those heart-felt words of love.

I am, of course, extremely happy to know that you like the ring. If I had had the opportunity I would have probably spent days picking it out. As it was, I rushed into Frisco, rushed to the first store in town, bought the most fitting ring I could find within our budget. After I got there, I did spend time in deliberation, but it didn't take too long when I saw the one. I saw who it was made for. Until I can give you a ring which will have an even deeper meaning, this one will bind our hearts. By the way, in case you are still wondering, I love you, Sweetheart!

Oh yes, I promise to tell you about my trip last week-end. Jan. 1st, dawned on a cloudy, dismal day (we have hardly seen the sun since Christmas Day). Ken and I left the campus about four o'clock in a steady downpour. Luck was good, and we were soon in a car going all the way to Oakland. (As you know, Oakland is just across the Bay from San Francisco.) Among the more interesting things which we saw were the famous Kyser [Kaiser] Shipyards—four in all—at Richmond. It was there too that we saw the famous "L's" brought from New York City to transport the shipyard workers. The "L's" were the elevated trains that were only recently torn down to be replaced by an improved subway system.

The rain was pouring by the time we reached Oakland, but our kind host took us directly to the bus station. We had time for a snack and boarded a bus for Centerville. We tried three or four times during the week to call Phil and make our plans. However, we had no luck and finally sent a telegram Fri. night telling him when to expect us. By nine o'clock we were flounding [floundering] around the streets of Centerville trying to find where the local Presbyterian Pastor lived. Everything was closed except the local tavern—so, in we go to ask where the minister lives. We found out! Fine place to inquire. Phil 'n family were still at a dinner six miles away & he had left word for us to call him up when we arrived. Operator was abed, so we waited in front of his house. The rain had fortunately ceased, but it began to get cold. Ken and I began to march each other around: "By the left flank, march! by the right flank, march! to the rear, march! etc., etc., etc."

About ten o'clock Phil returned and we met Peggy & Phyllis. I sort of fell for the baby to begin with. Couldn't help thinking how proud I would be if only——! Patience, Bushy. Not only do they have a nice cottage at the seminary, but they have a little apartment at Centerville for the week-end & for summer. Peggy knows you and asked all about your welfare. We talked until long past midnight—in fact, it was after one o'clock. Certainly grand to be able to talk over old Maryville days.

Sunday morning we drove out three miles to his church. I was amazed at the crowd; the place was almost filled, and the sermon was very fine. Phil has changed very little since I knew him last, but his depth of thought has, of course, matured. He took his text from the first Chapter of Deuteronomy, verse twenty-one: "Behold the Lord thy God hath set the land before thee: go up and possess it, as the Lord God of thy fathers hath said unto thee; fear not, neither be discouraged." You can imagine the sort of New Year's message that Phil could make of that.

We returned home, talked some more, ate a good meal, talked some more. By the time we were warmed up again, it was time to leave. We came back by bus, making good connections via San Francisco. Oh yes, in the harbor we saw an aircraft carrier in addition to a number of cruisers. The rain continued almost all of the week-end, and it hasn't stopped yet.

Another interesting tit-bit was the food situation in the Bay area. Civilians were unable to bring meat of any kind last week-end. Meanwhile, we eat like kings up here at Santa Rosa—the Army, that is.

The only trouble with writing you, Darling, is that when I start talking, I can't seem to stop. I should write Phil, and half a dozen other letters tonight. Should also study French. Better do the latter.

Am still have [having] a great deal of difficulty with French conversation. Hope that doesn't indicate innate trouble with language. Hear that language are often restricted for first three months of training. That's another reason for us to wait until end of first term.

I have been reading a bit more about birth control. Suggest you do the same. The only time that we can be together will be on week-ends. If we depend entirely on the "safe-period" our complete enjoyment might be limited seriously. I was surprised that the Presbyterian Church has given full approval to Birth Control. We should examine every side of the question. I intend to read as much as possible, and perhaps discuss the thing with Phil or someone else who could advise. "Go thou and do likewise."

I must wait until later to continue our talk. Your Xmas letter was wonderful, your voice ditto, your presents ditto, and you, you, My Sweet are the object of

All My Love, Bushy

P.S. I. Please send Samarriet's address.
II. Still no fluency test.

"One thing I want to tell you before other things arise concerns the class in military science yesterday afternoon. We usually have lectures or training films which vary in interest. Yesterday it was varied in that we had two guest speakers. A short film was shown dealing with the race problems and prejudices that exist in America today. The entire picture was very realistic, and no blows were spared. Following the showing of the picture, a Congregational Minister and a Jewish Rabbi were introduced. They are two of a party of three sent out, along with many others, to work against prejudice and hate. The Catholic Priest was unable to come. The talks centered around the brotherhood of man, and the common aim of all religions to seek but One God.

"These men are being sent out by a Christian-Jewish movement which is nationwide. The plan is certainly needed for more than ever before I realize that we as a people do not live up to our ideals. I thought of the Brotherhood at Maryville with Bob, Dick, Jack, and the others; and how we were unconsciously driving after the same goal. I thought of the very fine relationships I had at Roberts with Dan Downey, the Catholic boy from Notre Dame, and Sheldon Beren, the Jewish boy from Harvard. We too were finding common ground on which to discuss the problems of religion, of philosophy, of life, from our various vantage points. The racial and religious problems are very real in our country, but I think that we are working on solutions in a realistic manner. Much remains to be done....

"By the way it just occurred to me that you might like to know my daily schedule. At eight-fifteen (C.S.T.), when you are just getting down to a hard days work, it is six-fifteen here and we are just rolling out. We dress and fall out for reveille at six-thirty. Between six-thirty-five and seven-five we make our bunks, sweep, and clean the barrack. Then to breakfast and back to fall out at eight o'clock for the first class. We have no supervision for this, but the seventeen French men from Roberts carry on our own study. We spend the first hour and a half reading and translating a French newspaper which we get. Later we take up a short dictation exercise and usually a bit of vocabulary. We spend from one to two hours conversing in French on a subject that happens to come up. Although still weak in this place of my work, I think that I am gradually picking it up. I think our plan to work ahead without supervision has worked out amazingly well. There are, of course, a few

313

who take the time for reading or writing letters, but most of us go right ahead with the work.

"Our noon hour is from twelve to one, after which we fall out for military science. I think I mentioned this class before. From two to three I take ph. ed.; three to four study; and from four to five my one class with a regular instructor. Here again we emphasize reading and speaking. At ten of five we return to our barrack and fall out immediately for the Retreat. To me this is always and [an] impressive ceremony, even thought it is sometimes sloppy as carried out here. From Retreat we go to supper, after which the language students are free. I usually come to the Library or write in the Day Room. From about nine-thirty to ten-thirty, I shave, shine shoes, read my Bible, and prepare for bed. Lights out at ten-thirty. And so endeth a typical day at Santa Rosa...."

January 7, 1944, Diary

For the first time since we have ben in Santa Rosa, rumors began to fly today concerning shipments. Texas and Oklahoma we hear. The places may be incorrect but something is cooking (to use current vernacular). Wish I had my interview out of the way.

Ken and I to town tonight. Did a bit of shopping. Enjoyed the relaxation. Ken expecting to leave any day.

January 8, 1944, Diary
Stanford University

More rumors concerning shipments, as we studied this morning. When I returned from lunch found that I was on orders and had to be ready by two-thirty. Like a bolt out of the blue it came. It seems that only those of others who have more than 135 A.G.C.T. [Army General Classification Test] are leaving. One group going to U. Of Minn. to study Norwegian, while we go to Stanford to study Dutch. By chartered bus to S.T. Arrived in Stanford about 8:30. And so begins a new chapter in my dynamic living. I had given up hope of going East, and Stanford is a very fine school.

Letter from Art to Dotty

On the Road to Stanford
Jan 8, Sat. night

Dearest Heart,

The unexpected happened again and I'm on my way to Stanford U. Rumors began to fly yesterday as to shipments—the first rumors since we came. Texas, Okla, Minn, etc—this morning new rumors sprang up. I thought some thing was happening, but I hardly knew what.

Less than two hours before we left, we were told that we were on orders. I was taken completely by surprise. Five of the French students, six or eight German,—in all about twenty of us are heading for Stanford. Rumor has it that we are to study Dutch. The amazing thing is that I have still never had a fluency. Ken, who expected to ship a week ago, remains.

Hope you can read this. I am writing on the moving bus. Just coming down to The Golden Gate, and again I have the privilege of seeing the sunset in the Bay. A beautiful sight, Darling, I wish you were here!

Hope to get this in the mail in Frisco. Will try to write details tomorrow. At least for the present I can be reached at

ASN 14119120
AST Unit 3905
Stanford University
Palo Alto; Calif.

Will be very close to Phil on week-ends, and only about ten miles from San Horea where the Pratts live.

Still believing in the Divine Plan for our lives. I send

All my Love,
Bushy

January 9, 1944, Diary

The Lord truly loveth his own. I could hardly believe my eyes this morning when into Encina Day Room walked Ted Kidder just arriving from his S.T.A.R. Unit. Not for than a week here I been away from either Ken or Ted. I'm very, very lucky. Ted Pratt's family live only a few miles away in San Jose; Phil Evaul comes to Centerville every week-end; Oliver Van Cise is stationed in Frisco. Chapel here very nice. Very lovely for a wedding.

Ted Kidder

Letter from Art to Dotty
Co F ASTU #3905
Stanford University
Palo Alta, Calif.
Dec. 9, 1944 [Jan. 9] Sunday Afternoon

My Darling,

    The Lord truly loveth his own: Here I am in language and area study, at Stanford University, one of the best schools in the country (even if it is a long, long way from Tenn.); with friends near at hand, San Jose less than twenty miles south, and Centerville less than ten east, ———and one other big thing: Guess.... No, Ken didn't come down, but—yup, that's right, Ted Kidder walked in the door this morning. I have never seen such luck since the day I first set eyes on you. Well, not many times anyway. We arrived here about eight-thirty last night, and Ted rolled in very early this morning. Wonders seem to never cease.

Last night we spent in one of the big engineering halls, but this morning we moved over to our regular assignment. Three of us are in each room—I'm with the nice fellow from Brooklyn and another from Chicago. Ted, of course, will not be in our dorm but will have a room in a frat house. We are divided according to language and also classification. He has a 9-L rating, which means that he will get only three months' work here. We are 4-L, which means that we will probably get six to nine months of training. The dorm which we have is considerably nicer than Carnegie; and, since we will not be in the rooms much anyway, it will not seem crowded. ["Carnegie" is the dorm where Art stayed on the campus of Maryville College.] Anything would be better than to be living in a one room barrack with seventy or eighty fellows. That is an exaggeration, of course, but we did have about fifty in the barrack at Santa Rosa.

From the scattered bits that we have been able to gather, it seems that we "caught the last boat from Lisbon." Men are being kicked out right and left in the S.T.A.R. Units. As I told you illegible note I wrote on the bus yesterday, I still can't figure out how I got shipped without the fluency test. I'm just lucky, Darling. (Pardon the change of stationary, but my barracks bags haven't arrived as yet, and I have to use anything I can find!)

At noon yesterday I had no idea that I would ship for weeks. With about a two hour notice, I packed and was ready to leave by two-thirty. We finally said good-bye to Ken and Santa Rosa about three-thirty. Twenty of us were coming to Stanford—in the French and German groups it was the men with a A.G.C.T. [Army General Classification Test] Great about 135. More than once I have had cause to give thanks for the grades I made at Oglethorpe.

Sunday Night

Tomorrow we will get our schedule and get in full swing on Tues. We are supposed to be here to study Dutch, but that too may change. I would be very happy to get Dutch but the area that we study with it will be the Dutch East Indies; not Holland. Anything I get will be good. We were told this morning that Stanford will give a full credit for our work —credit that will go a long way toward a Masters, My Dear. It seems that we are to get three hours of language per day and three hours of area study. We study from seven to nine-thirty in the evenings. Strangely enough we are told that the guys who flunk out here, do so in the area study rather than the language. It seems that a "B" average is required and we have two or three test per week.

Of course, the most important thing that we are interested in is the possibilities for married couples. Now don't get excited, Darling: I only came last night. However, I'm hopeful. It seems that if a "B" average is maintained I can get out every week-end, and maybe one night during the week—if I'm married. The most important thing is for me to make a good record during the coming weeks. Ted is here for Best Man, Phil, Peggy, Helen Pratt-Tapp, Dr. Pratt. We saw the Stanford Memorial Chapel is comparable to some of the cathedrals in New York. A marvelous structure. Your letter came on finances. I agree for the most part. We can discuss it more at length later on. As the calendar looks now, the first term will end about April 8.—Easter. I wonder how Ap. 9 would fit into the monthly period. No conflict, I hope!

Darling, I feel as though I have a very delicate and costly piece of glass were balanced lightly in my hand. Any moment a break a breath of air may dash it to the ground. I am lucky beyond words to be here in language. It could turn out to be well nigh perfect set-up for us. Let us retain our wild hopes; let us pray that my situation works out here. If it does, our plans to be married will be greatly aided. The point I am trying to make is that the situation looks good, but we can't be sure until I see how work goes here during the first month or so.

I had hoped to write Mother this week-end to wish her a recovery a week ago. Give her my loving and wishes. I do hope the flu didn't keep her inactive too long. Received M.R.'s letter, and hope to write her sometime. Don't expect to have much time from now on, however.

Haven't written home and must do so tonight. We'll write at earliest possible moment when I find out my definite schedule. Don't worry if the letter is delayed. Ask Sis to give the Echo my new address. It should be permanent for awhile.

With a thankful heart for all our blessings, with the growing hope that our most wished-for hopes may be fulfilled, I pray for

> Our Love,
> Bushy

..................14119120
Co F. ASTU 3905
Stanford University, Calif.

Stanford U.
Jan 12, 1944
Wed Night

My Dearest Own,

As the days go by and I get a real start in my work here, I feel that I can hardly call my time my own. I can see from the start that we are making that we will be going at a furious rate in a very short time.

This week we are merely getting an introduction to our work in area study, but our Dutch is going ahead at full speed. Right now we are learning vocabulary at the rate of 60 words per day. As I expected before, the area study is to prove the most important phase of our work.

I have two teachers in Dutch and then will change each six weeks. This, of course, to familiarize us with the different accents. One of my teachers came from Holland four years ago, and has a fair command of our tongue. The second, however, a delightful personality, about thirty-five I judge, has been in this country only six months. She was a volunteer worker in concentration camps in France, and was secretary to the Dutch Embassy in Lisbon. She is familiar with ten languages, but speaks only five. With only two lessons behind us, we will be giving sentences in Dutch tomorrow. Some speed, nicht wahr?

Phy. Ed. Program twice each week: I went swimming in outdoor pool today. Better come West, young lady! The real Calif. weather that I always dreamed of here now.

Ted and I hope to get together with Ken & Van Cise Sat. in Frisco. He's (Ted is) being reclassified, but nothing serious.

Light giving out and so little time to tell you of the dreams and plans for
Our Love,
Bushy
Encl. Money Order.

January 14, 1944, Diary

Ted and I had written Ken and Van Cite to meet us in San Francisco Saturday, but letter from Ken says he's shipping. Lucky bum's going East, but I don't know where.

January, 15, 1944, Diary

Ted and I hitch-hiked into Frisco this afternoon after 3:30. Met Van as planned at Pepsi-Cola Building. Swell to see the guy again. He's tied up with a Red-Head in the City it seems. Out to Granati to get a watch—my xmas present from Mother and Dad. Very hard to get a good watch, but I luckily found a nice Gruen. We saw "Thousands Cheer," [a 1943 MGM musical comedy, directed by George Sidney, intended to boost servicemen's moral] and Van slept. Spent night in dormitory Saint Vincent De Paul's.

January 16, 1944, Diary

Arose too late for Church. To Golden Gate Park where we spent a couple of hours in the Young Museum. Later to the Aquarium and Chinese (former Japanese) Tea Garden. [The title "Japanese Tea Garden" was reinstated in 1952.] Had to push ourselves all day, but enjoyed very much what we saw. The museum in particular had much of interest.

Letter from Art to Dotty
Stanford University
Jan 14, 1944

My Own,

I'm up to my neck already in work and I love it! Yet already (as my Dutch teacher would say) we have learned about two hundred words in Dutch, we are already conjugating simple verbs, and today we took thirty-five Dutch sentences in a dictation test. The amazing thing is that we are learning the stuff.

Even more interesting and certainly far more important is our area study. This week we are merely taking up the geographical location of the vast clusters of islands in the S. Pacific in from the Fijis to Japan, and general background material including population, relative sizes, etc, etc. But even now the material is being pushed at us an amazing speed.

It is only as time goes on that I can grasp the vast scope of what this work entails. I'm even now losing myself in it. By the time nine months have gone by we will have a thorough knowledge of the peoples, (including customs, hist., etc, etc, the geography (this includes weather, terrain, resources) and the problems of an area which, if placed in our hemisphere would stretch from Bolivia in S. Am. to the mouth of the St. Lawrence in Canada. We will be acquainted not only with the East Indies, but also Japan, China, the Philippines,etc.

Sat. Morning

I could continue at some length but, I must give you a bit of the news. Ted and I hoped to get together with Ken and Van Cise, who is also near Frisco. Letter from Ken last night says that he is leaving for the East. Didn't have time to tell us details. Still hope to see Van tonight. Next week we may try to go down to visit Ted Pratt's family, only twelve miles south at San Jose.

Darling, as each day goes by, I need you, I long for you more and more. I hope and pray and work that I can send for you at the end of this term!

That is another subject on which I could spend hours, but I must hasten on. Learned yesterday that Dutch is second on the priority listing. As I think I told you we are the second group in the country to get this particular assignment. There are only a few more than a hundred of us here, half in the second term—the rest just beginning. The general impression seems to be that by the time we are finished here, large scale operations will be in progress in the Pacific and our value to the Army will be greatly enhanced.

Sat. Afternoon

As you can see, this letter is being written bit by bit. I am now waiting for inspection prior to getting my pass.

By the way, Dear, the type of thing I was writing in the foregoing paragraph must be taken as confidential. I will probably be telling you such things from time to time knowing that you are interested and knowing also that you will keep such things. It is, of course, all right to say what I am studying, i.e., Dutch and area, but details as to numbers etc. really make no difference to others.

As I said before the plan and scope of the program continues to unfold and I am greatly amazed at the infinite possibilities not only during the war period but also in the post-war period. We will be trained for many varied types of work—to do anything from assisting in the planning of a campaign to organizing native assistance to aid our troops. We will have the background for a thorough understanding of the problems following in the wake of invasion. After the war there should be innumerable possibilities in the industrial, commercial, diplomatic, and educational fields.

I could go on and on, but that isn't the most important thing at the moment.

Sunday Morning

Van did come last night, and it was great to see him. He's going strong with a little girl out here. How fickle men are! Will right later concerning "the most important thing at the moment."

Hope to go through Golden Gate Park and Palace of Fine Arts today. I love you, Darling!

Sunday night

This letter is going into the mail tonight if I have to seal it without signing my name and send it along. I carried it with me all day trying to get it in the mail.

Ted and I did go to the Golden Gate Park and a wonderful time we had.

Since I began this <u>three</u> wonderful letters arrived from Santa Rosa from you. You know, Darlingcal, I hadn't heard from you in more than a week! Have so much to write about that I must wait until later. Must write Mother & Dad and also study—a lot.

Only the days and years can prove the eternity of
    Our Love
    Bushy

Letter from Art to Dotty
Stanford University
Jan. [21]
Friday Night

My Dearest Heart,

I have failed miserably in my attempts this week to write you, in fact, much to my regret, I haven't been able to write even a tiny note. Reason: well, yesterday we had our first our test in Dutch and today our first area test. Even the little time I have for study does not seem to be enough to adequately prepare the tremendous amount of material that we are attempting to assimilate.

Your wonderful letters have been literally pouring in, and I love to get them. I only hope that I will have time tonight to answer a few of the questions and discuss some of the all-important questions at hand. I promise that when and if I get my working schedule organized I will

322

do better at this business of writing the one who inspires me to do all that I can possibly do to achieve success.

Now for a few of the questions: About coming to Knoxville for the wedding. Darling, for more than one reason that seems out of the question. The principal reason is the fact that our furlough, when it comes, is not good beyond Denver. Even if I could get a special leave (which is doubtful), it would hardly be possible. Van Cise just returned from his home, taking seven and a half days of travelling time. It is very unlikely that one could get a plane—I would have to have a priority rating which could be taken away at any point along the way. Riding free by plane would have to be on an Army bomber, and one is seldom lucky enough to catch the ride.

Well, the secondary reasons are of no consequence. As much as I regret it, it looks as though it will have to be in Calif., Bud! But even so we have a Maryville congregation on hand. Ted as best man, Phil to assist the preacher (perhaps Mr. Pratt), Peggy, Helen, Van Cise—we could hardly expect many more of our schoolmates if we were in the 4th Church.

Well, like you, I speak as though every small detail were settled. The prospects are certainly encouraging, Darlingcal. Dad and Mother agree if I can clear the details. There are many of the latter. I hope that I can as clearly as possible delineate the major difficulty as I see it. I think that we can consider the financial problem as one which we can cope with adequately. We may have to scrape and pinch, but both of us know how to do that.

After only two weeks of adjustment to this radical and rather swift change of life (from bivouac to a library of 2,000,000 volumes), I find myself up to my neck in intensive study. I have no idea that I might go under, don't misunderstand. But men are being removed without discrimination, not so much at this particular moment, but just wait until the end of the term. The Dutch test I took yesterday came back today with far too many errors. I fear the same for the area test. Of course, this is only the beginning, and I will get the feel of what they want. But nevertheless, the competition, the requirements of my teachers is going to require my full attention.

It is hard, terribly hard to see what I mean, Darling. Perhaps, I hardly know myself. To do the job that I must do requires putting everything else in the back of mind. That is hard for one who has spent months thinking almost constantly of the one he loves with his whole being. But for the sake of that love which we cherish, I must quickly learn to concentrate with every bit of mental energy that I have.

I firmly intend to make a good record, my Dear. I have to! You see, I am confused. There is a problem which I recognized, and the solution is the thing that worries me. I fear that I am going to neglect you, my Dear.

Almost two hours have slipped by and I have said little, covered only a few points. Much more to say later. I made a miscalculation; the date would be Ap. 2nd rather than the 8th. Don't know how I could have made the error. Now is the bond, I hope!

Ted and I hope to visit the Pratt's tomorrow & Sun. I am trying to begin definite plans, my Darling, for the great step which will further unite

> Our Love,
> Thine own Bushy

Note address—No Palo Alto
necessary!
Thanks for suggestion. Will certainly watch my grammar and spelling.

January 22, 1944, Diary

Ted and I hitchhiked to San Jose this afternoon. After slight difficulty we found the Pratt's home. Grand to see Helen again and to meet Ted's mother. Rev. Pratt in Nevada. Shortly after we arrived, Van Cise rolled in. We looked at annuals and talked Maryville until a late hour. Roland Tapp is in Italy in Air Corp.

January 23, 1944, Diary

Up late and had good breakfast. To Church with Helen. Rode around a bit before a swell dinner. Van, Ted, and I did K.P. and then took pictures in aprons. Phil Evaul 'n family came over from Centerville, and we had a grand time talking over Maryville.

My Dearest Heart,

Outside a steady drizzle (Maryville variety) is coming down, and it sounds good from the inside. Ted and I just returned from a very wonderful week-end. I was delayed a bit yesterday afternoon but we were able to leave by five o'clock. By six we were in San Jose, and shortly after we found the Pratt home. Greetings were exchanged and very soon were eating a swell home-cooked meal. Before we had gotten a good start, in walked Van Cise, and our little party was complete. Mr. Pratt is in Nevada just now, but we had a grand time rehashing all the Maryville news.

Helen is looking well, and gets lots of mail from "hubby" Roland in Italy. I hope I can write as interesting letters to you, My Dear. She is doing some Church work, and seems as happy as one could expect. I hope you can find full time work when I go across; I would be very unhappy to know that you were not busy enough to keep occupied.

We slept very late this morning and arose to stuff ourselves with waffles. Heard a good sermon in return for another good meal. Earlier in the morning we had gotten in touch with Phil 'n family & about two-thirty they arrived (just after we had finished K.P. with aprons—pictures later). You can imagine what a grand time we had for the next few hours. [photo on next page]

By the way, I am assured that Rev. Pratt will make arrangements to be here just in case we can use him about April 2nd. I had to tell them about our tentative plans and they are almost as thrilled as we are. Helen promises to write you soon. (The address is 101 Glenn Eyrie Ave., San Jose.

I'm going to find out tomorrow the name of the professor in the Far Eastern Area dept. who is a Maryville man. From him I hope to get a couple of leads on the housing situation in town. About how much can we figure on for rent?

That brings up another point. I think, Darling, that I will have to rely on you for some of the budgeting since my expenses will be almost nil. There will, of course, be fifty per month from Uncle Sam, but I suppose it may take a couple of months for that to start. I feel certain that you can secure an excellent job later on. My first look will be for a clerical job here on the campus. If that doesn't turn out satisfactorily, I will inquire in the local church. However, I think that's all that can be

"San Jose, CA, 3.5.44 Art, Van, Ted—hiding behind aprons."

done in a leisurely fashion since we don't want you to begin for some time.

In regard to my last letter, this budget business is along the same lines. There will be more than one thing in which I will be unable to take full responsibility because of my work. I think your suggestion about the safe period and the use of artificial methods is good, and possibly the only satisfactory one for us. The details here again I will have to leave to you for the most part. I intend to get a lot of dope from Phil, but probably will have no time to read further on the matter.

I must write a long letter home tonight, telling further about our plans; I must study, and also sleep a little. However, I promise that this week I will write more than last. Forgive the unavoidable neglect, My Own. All by a life-time of expression can I tell you of my devotion. This is mutual:

> Our Love,
> Bushy

Forgot to mention that I am acting cadet sergeant of my platoon—an empty end meaningless honor. Begin a couple of weeks ago and only lasts a month.

My Dearest Own,

I have just fifteen minutes to dash off a letter telling you that which will take a lifetime to tell. I love you! Your Record Breakers edition arrived last night. Glad to get a new pictures of you, even though I see you clearly in my every thought. Your beauty, my Darling, shines before me like a guiding star in the chaotic darkness of the blinded world. (That site which Christ brought is slowly but surely being found, but how slowly!)

I enclose pictures which may give you some small idea of my mustache. I classify it as "B" (for braggin') It is much fuller than when the Roberts pictures were taken.

I'm investigating rooming situation. None too good, but I'll find something. Rumors are none too good for a A.S.T.P. but I think I'm safe. How would this labor draft effect us? Don't know yet.

Working every minute, and making progress. I love you with all my heart, my Dear. Good night and sweet dreams of
        Our Love,
         Bushy
P.S. Will outline some work for you in regard to geog [geography] of S. Pacific. Extra picture for "Mom"!

Dearest Heart,

Should have at least one letter from you tonight since I have had only one this week. However, I will be able to finish this up tonight—I hope.

I will try to discuss first things first, and get onto the lesser things later. Reports persist concerning abandoning A.S.T.P. It is certainly being cut considerably, and very few are being accepted. I was very lucky. I repeat, to be able to stay in the program, my Dear. Well, anyway, there is always the chance that parts of it will be deleted.

Engineering, first I think. From all I can gather, Dutch would be one of the last to fall by the wayside. I think I mentioned that Dutch was considered second on the priority listing when we came to Stanford.

Unless, something drastic occurs, some indication that the Dutch will fold, I favor going ahead with plans on April 1. Darling, if I had been undecided for so long, it hasn't been because of my heart but rather in spite of it. I have tried very hard to keep perspective and see from the long range viewpoint. As you will learn, the Army is uncertain to point of exasperation.

Our time together will pass all too swiftly, and the separation then will be far harder than anything we have known before. The war in the Pacific will last for longer than we in America have been able to realize.

Fri Night

Hilton Wisk has just returned from the Pacific where he took part in seventy-two bombing raids. (I just missed seeing him the week-end Ken and I visited Phil.) Hilton thinks it will take at least three years out there. After studying the Far East for only a short time, I fear that I must agree with him. I think that it will take at least that long to root the Japs out. Many factors enter in that I will discuss later, but I merely wanted to point out a big factor for your consideration. Our separation will certainly be an extended one. There is always the chance that I may return a physical wreck from wounds, or from malaria. There is always the possibility that———. Well, I think you are aware of all of this. I once was against getting married during the war because of these possibilities. I have change my point of view. More than ever before I believe in the Divine Guide who watches over each one of us. I believe that His plan is for our lives to become one now and through eternity. If His plan is for my return to love and to serve you, to love and serve others, I will return with the capacity for doing.

If you are willing to face the future with me, realizing at least in part what may be involved, I favor getting married—but soon! With me here as I do my work of learning almost everything about the Far East, you will far better understand what I am doing while away; and our later years will be far more complete. And, by the way, I warn you now that I plan to have jobs for you relating to my work.

I must spend a couple of pages telling you about Jack Feldman some time. He's Ted's roommate; short, fat, about thirty years old, Dutch ancestry, Staff Sgt., non-G.I., jovial, ever trying to do something for some one. He seems to have innumerable connections with everyone. Told me tonight that he thinks—in fact, he is sure that we can find an apartment, furnished, for lesson $30 per month. Sounds plenty good, and I think that is about right for our budget. Hope we can keep within that.

What type of work are you interested in most? I think a job on the campus would be just about ideal, there will probably be good positions of varying type in town. Would you prefer a wedding in this Stanford Chapel, or in Presbyterian Church San Jose, or the Pratt home? The latter would, of course, require diplomacy on my part to work around. I understand that the school encourages weddings in the beautiful Chapel.

Your Sunday letter came tonight—six days, six very long days, but, honey, you couldn't help it. You wrote. I was certainly sorry to hear about your frustrated trip to the cabin. By the way, I want you to come out via the Union Pacific Route as I did. We'll try to return the Southern trip. I want you to see the mts out here. Also happy to hear about "Ossie" L. He sounds great.

That leads me to another point—one of the minor ones I promised. Ted, Jack, and I have tickets to the Ballet in Frisco tomorrow night. And what tickets they are! Fourth row, orchestra. That's another one of Jack's connections! We'll try to give you a complete description Sunday. All the time I look on, I will be thinking of my own little ballerina. Can hardly wait for your personal appearance and complete performance of your own ballet, Darling! In case you wonder, I love you immeasurably.

Congrats on graduation etc. Proud of you, Bud. Just hope you can keep up the training here. By the way, can you get a leave of absence from T.V.A.—twelve months or something! When I go across, you will probably want to return there, nicht wahr [is not it] ?

I just thought of something else. I had better sent from my pajamas if I plan to sleep in elite company. G.I. shorts or not the most fashionable night-wear. As for your hair, Darling, I love to smooth it down messy or not. I assure you that you will not have to go to Reno for the matter of the curler. (By the way, Reno isn't far away, just in case you realize that you have made a bad bargain. I'll do the best to pull the wool over your eyes!)

Hope to write long letter again Sunday night. Did better on that area test than I expected, but must do better.

I spend my dreams concerning Our Love, Bushy

P.S. Princess Juliana coming to see the Dutch students next week. [She became *Queen* of the Netherlands in 1948.]

"....The best argument for Christianity is not an argument—it is a Christian. Oh, darling, you have such a wonderful opportunity for presenting Christianity to the men in your outfit who now are indifferent to things of the spirit and lead such low lives. You have the power within you of being a strong spiritual force and of bringing that force to hear upon the lives of those around you. God bless our love and grant that it may bring some light into this world of darkness. Eternally yours, Dotty"

January 29, 1944, Diary

In pouring rain Ted, Jack, and I hitch-hiked into San Fran this afternoon. Picked up tickets at Opera House, and after supper went to Russian Ballet. Saw "Billy The Kid," "Helen of Troy," and "Dim Lustre." Had second row orchestra and enjoyed it very much. Had difficulty getting bed but finally found something in Cartwright Hotel dorm.

January 30, 1944, Diary

Up about 9:30—breakfast in Canteen USO. To First Presby. Church on Van Ness and Sacramento. Dr. Creighton very good and Jack who is Catholic enjoyed it very much. Out to Lincoln Park in rain. Spent a couple of hours in Palace of Legion of Honor [now called the "Legion of Honor" museum in San Francisco]. Very fine paintings there. Grand view of Golden Gate Bridge and the ocean.

Letters from Art to Dotty
Stanford University
Jan 31, 1944
Mon. Noon

My Dearest Heart,

I had hoped to write along letter last night, but— Well, anyway, I have a few moments now in which to tell you about my week-end. Jack Feldman was able to get excellent seats for the ballet in fact, the best in the house. We were in the second row, center section and also important was the fact that we had 90¢ reduction in price. The seats cost only $1.87.

As I expected, the performance was very fine, but I must admit that the one we saw last year at U.T. [University of Tennessee in Knoxville] was better. "Billy The Kidd," "Dim Lustre," and "Helen of Troy" were presented. It was with intense longing that I thought of you as the movement and rhythm developed. The San Francisco Orchestra was playing, and it in itself was worth going a long way to hear. As wonderful as were the ballerinas, I still prefer my own little dancer. Can hardly wait, Bud!

It was pouring down rain on Saturday night, but Sunday dawned clear. We attended First Presbyterian Church again, and later went out to Lincoln Park, and the Palace of the Legion of Honor. Wonderful pictures there—originals, Turner, Rembrandt etc.

Describe later

See ff pages to hear of my plans for
> Our Love,
> Bushy

> Stanford University
> Jan. 31, 1944
> Monday night [typed]

My Dearest,

Since I get much more on a page this way, since I write much faster this way, since I love to use a machine, since a typewriter is at hand, since I want to write a great deal, and for a couple of other reasons which I can't think of just at present, I will use a machine. I began a letter at noon concerning my week-end, and this too I will try to finish tonight. However, your wonderful letter of the 25th came tonight, and there are enough questions in it to keep me busy for some pages.

Ted and Jack are really wonderful to help me plan, for as you may well guess I have very little time to attend to important details. Jack promises to take care of flowers, organist, and he asked tonight if he might inquire concerning arrangements for the Chapel. Wish I had time to spend a couple of pages describing it, for it is worthy of all of that. In addition, as I mentioned before, he plans to look into the rooming situation. By the way, he isn't going to get married for me! I too am looking out for these things, but he has innumerable connections, and they will certainly come in handy for us.

Here is the general set-up as I am trying to plan it. I would hope that you could be out here at least a week early. That is so we could have the last week-end of the term to plan the last minute details. Hope Helen has written you, for it would be wonderful if you could spend the week with her. If I can make arrangements for the room by that time, you would be able to work on it a bit. The rooming situation is going to be tough, but I am going to work at once, and should be able to report progress soon. I thought before that I would have a big final on the last Saturday, and so I figured it would be better to have the ceremony on Sunday. However, it seems: that the big tests are over before the last week. If this is the case I would prefer to walk down the aisle, or rather watch you come down the aisle Saturday afternoon. Perhaps we can plan a reception or something with all the gang (there will be quite a bunch you know), and then spend the night in our apartment here in town—if we have it by that time. I had hoped to plan for the honeymoon to Yosemite, but it is a long way (two hundred miles), and Carmel-by-the-sea may prove more suitable. Those arrangements too I will have to begin to inquire about. If we do get married on Saturday, I think that we should wait until Sunday to travel. Saturday night is a very bad time to be running up and down the coast. You see, my furlough will not begin until 3:30 on Sat. afternoon, Ap. 1, so that means that the ceremony must be sometime after that—perhaps 5:00.

By the way, just what would be the situation if April 1st didn't work out just right? Oh me, oh my, Darling! That would be bad in deed. Frustration at that point would be unfortunate to say the least. However, I don't suppose there is much that can be done.

I favor the long dress by the way, and I think that the color is very nice. I always did like red, no matter what color it is! (Do you suppose it is just a bit—well, you know? Maybe not.) If you like it, Sweetheart, I adore it. So there! Phil can't perform the ceremony until he is ordained in May. Perhaps we can have another one then. How about having him give the bride away? Can't think of a better person at the moment. Be nice to have Helen, Peggy, and Johnny Astles' wife involved some where. I think you should rapidly build up a correspondence with Helen. 'Twould be wonderful to have Mother ("Mom") come out. Fraid I can't defray many expenses. In fact, my Dear, I think I will have to let you pay your own way. Ain't I hoorrible! If we can afford it, I would like a double ring ceremony. However, the wedding ring is more expensive than I thought. Checked up on it a couple of weeks ago. I can't hope for much better than $150 after I get the ring. Wedding expenses, honeymoon, and expenses for setting up household must be defrayed. I sometimes wonder how I have the nerve to ask anyone to marry me, when I'm practically in the poor house. We may have to figure a bit close for awhile. (Hope you can find an alarm clock to get me up. If and when on week nights I can get away, I must be back here by 6:30) Would love to have you quote Ruth to me. That is the sort of thing that we need to work out on the preceding week-end.

My first area test was nothing to be proud of, but it was by no means the lowest in the class. However, the one on Saturday showed a great improvement. Last week's Dutch test also showed improvement. I am getting the hang of what is expected and I am going to aim for the top now.

"Sixty-Eighth Series of February Meetings Begin with Dr. Anderson..."
Maryville College, Feb. 2, 1944

I hardly have time to say much more, but I will mention that we did get the opportunity to entertain Princess Julianna today. [Newspaper clipping below.] The advanced Dutch boys talked at some length in Dutch in a prepared program in her honor. Very simply dressed she was, and very unassuming. I only see one star in my heaven, and she moves westward. "Western Star"—remember?

As the days and weeks swiftly pass, I renew my determination to make a record of which we both can justly be proud. I am striving for my country first, but I am also striving for

Our Love,

Bushy

P.S. Mother and Dad are working their heads off in the office. I intend to write than, but I fear that it would almost [be] impossible for either of them to come.

When will the engagement be announced? Think we better hold wedding banns for awhile. Always keep the fact in mind that ASTP is still subject to the will of an unpredictable power.

February 5, 1944, Diary

Ted, Jack and I to S.F. this afternoon. Out to Granati to leave my watch. The crystal was not put on correctly and it was cracked. Back into town to see "Desert Song" from air view. Very fine musical and the technicolor beautiful. The acting a little Melo dramatic at times. Dennis Morgan & Irene Manning. Bed in St. Vincent De Paul's Dorm.

February 6, 1944, Diary

Up late and breakfast downstairs in very nice Canteen. Out to Prside and strolled around Place of Fine Arts. Out to G Gate Bridge and walked across. Fog rolled and we couldn't see much. Back to town and down to dock. Saw a number of cargo ships loading. Back to Stanford in time to hear organ recital.

Letter excerpts from Art to Dotty
Stanford University
Feb. 6, 44 (Sunday Night

"....Some of the men who will be leaving at the end of this term have apartments, and we will perhaps be able to find one of them suitable.

"Don't be too hopeful, but I am going to try very hard to get an apartment here on the campus. We shall see what we shall see!

"As the days go by, I find that more and more I am able to concentrate with better results on my work, even though an all consuming thing is Our Love.

"I want to spend considerable time telling you of a recent letter from Mother, but I haven't the time tonight. She is not fully reconciled to our plans, for which I am deeply sorrow. However, I am doing that which I think is best for us and for our future. Will discuss this at length next letter.

"From the very depths of my being comes the source of my Love for you. Ever thine own, Bushy

"P. S. Better check again my address, Darling! What about announcements? How about mom?"

PRINCESS JULIANA visited Stanford for about five hours Monday. In the photograph she is seen greeting Paul H. Davis, secretary of the University. (The picture was taken by Bill Hyer.)

Princess Juliana visits Stanford, published Feb. 3, 1944

Juliana Visits Stanford

By BETTYE MONELL and ESTHER BELEW

With the parting remark, "I would like to spend months visiting Stanford as one can't possibly see all of it in a few hours," Princess Juliana of the Netherlands ended her tour of the campus yesterday.

The Princess, who came to the Coast for an informal and unofficial visit last Friday, arrived here at 10:30 yesterday morning and was welcomed at an informal reception by the Dutch teaching staff in the Hoover War Library. After signing the register and viewing a special Dutch exhibit in the library, the Princess was honored with a carillon concert.

Her Highness visited the Memorial Church and then had lunch at the Union. Following the luncheon she visited Lagunita where she was presented with a yellow orchid corsage, a gift of the women's organizations on campus.

She left the campus at 2:30 p.m. after attending an ASTU Dutch class. However, the departure was delayed a few minutes while Princess Juliana met and spoke to "Pete," clerk of the Union who was born in Holland.

"The whole campus is simply wonderful," said the Princess when asked of her impressions of Stanford. "I would like to send my daughters to Lagunita. We have no dormitories in Dutch universities. In fact, the universities really have no campus, they are just buildings," she continued. "But there are as many bicycles here as you would find in any Dutch school," she concluded.

Princess Juliana wore a dusty pink dress with brown accessories and a full-length ermine coat. She is traveling with her secretary, Dr. William van Tets, and Mrs. Tets.

Feeling that the Princess would be served Dutch dishes elsewhere, it was decided to serve a typical American meal at the Union, according to Anthony E. Sokol, associate professor of Germanic languages and one of the arrangers of the tour.

Accompanying Princess Juliana on her tour of the campus were John P. Mitchell, acting president of the University; Paul H. Davis, general secretary; Harold H. Fisher, director of the Hoover War Library; and Dr. Sokol.

"Juliana Visits Stanford," by Bettye Monell and Esther Belew. Published in The Stanford Daily on February 3, 1944.

"On Monday I talked with the Chapel Secretary to make arrangements for the wedding. April 1, 5 o'clock! No charge for Chapel, $10 for organist, $3 for janitor, and $3 to the Sec. for making arrangements. Not bad, nicht wahr? Will have to get license in San Jose which will be rather handy. Ted says that Mary got Dave's and hers. If I can't get out, perhaps you can do same. You can bring the blood test and it has to be taken within a month of the wedding.

"Very happy to know that April 1st will be suitable for you. I will prepare myself with the necessary precaution, however. In regard to the wedding ring, the one that goes with the engagement job is surprisingly expensive. Also very beautiful, I might add....

"P.S. Can you bring your camera?"

February 12, 1944, Diary

Early passes for the three of us, and a station wagon ride to Beach. Strolled around and took pictures. Bought Redwood Burle for Mother. Saw nice collection of ship models. Ate swell meal in Clift House. Met a couple of natives from East Indies in Dutch Air Corp. Tried my halting Dutch. Was thrilled by the sight of the sun sinking into the depths of the Pacific Island, thirty miles out visible. Intended to get wedding ring tonight but no time. Rushed back to Curran Theatre to see Noel Coward's "Blithe Spirit" (grand comedy but Buick could have done us well) with Clifton Webb. Stayed in Civic Center.

February 13, 1944, Diary

Ted, Jack Feldman and spent night in a dormitory at the Civic Center (Frisco). Up in time to attend First Presbyterian Church. Heard Dr. Henry Sloane Coffin Moderator of the General Assembly. Very excellent sermon.

February 14, 1944, Diary

My old trouble is returning, and I see that I must guard against it carefully. My Saturday's Dutch test came back today with far too many careless errors. Not so much carelessness, but I think the trouble lies in the fact I allow myself to become tense and nervous during a test. I am making my work here a life and death matter when it really isn't at all. I see even more clearly than before something of the problem that I have to face, not only now but later. Even yet I have not adjusted (as I so proudly thought I had) to the life of an army soldier. I still have a long road to travel before I can claim conquest of self.

February 15, 1944, Diary

Am learning a great deal from my contact with my roommates. Mina Dallas is a Greek boy from Chicago. He has had the influence of work at Liberal Chicago U., and is rather mature in some of his thought. An interesting and productive clash between his pessimism and my idealism. Very studious, he should be a leader in the classwork. Marvin Flowerman from Brooklyn is a Jewish boy of no mean ability and offers a far more complex figure. More concerning him later. Our room only one rated "Excellent" today in company inspection.

February 18, 1944, Diary

Associated Press released the news tonight that 110,000 men now in the Army Specialized Training will be reassigned by April 1st. 35,000 are to remain, but whether this will include any language has not been told. If any languages remain it seems only logical that Dutch would be held. However, the Army is never logical. The discussion has been brewing for some time, and it seemed to be a constant pressure against it. An intermediate conclusion is that the move is a political one. Of course, it makes impossible carrying out of plans for the wedding. I fear that poor Dotty will be rather upset, as of course I am. But such is the uncertainty of Army life.

Had a long talk with T Sgt. Jack Feldman (Ted's roommate) who is a psychologist of no mean ability. He is attempting to help me with my old nervous difficulty which developed at Roberts. He analyzed my care in much the same way as the doctor before. Think he may be able to help.

Took overseas physical today.

Art & Sgt. Jack Feldman 2.44 [February 1944]

February 19, 1944, Diary

Little of news to add to the little we know concerning our future. The officers known nothing. A large scale attack is in progress on the Jap bastion of truk. O.W.I. (Officer of War Information) has released no details as yet. If nothing more, it indicates the vast striking power that we are amassing in the Pacific. Ted and I had excellent luck crossing the Bay to Centerville. Up until one looking at slides of Maryville with Phil and Peggy. We were just a bit homesick to see the beautiful scenes which mean most to us. Letter from Mother today, but nothing from Dad in a month. Am worried.

My Dearest Heart,

For a week now I have gone with only a Valentine to console my lonely heart: I do miss your letters, my Darling. However, I know that you must be extremely busy during these days and I readily forgive.

You too are probably hearing the same radio reports in Knoxville that we are hearing in Palo Alto. Drastic changes seem to be taking place in the Army's planning in regard to A.S.T. of course, rumors have been rampant for weeks in regard to it, but the news that will be clarified probably by the time you read this is the first definite thing that we have had.

As yet we don't know what effect the whole thing has on Dutch 4-L students at Stanford. The reports tonight have been that 110,000 men will be called out; 35,000 to be left. As I mentioned, when we came we were told that we were seconds on the priority list for language study. This is subject to change at any time, but surely if any language men at all are left in training, Dutch are likely to be among the lucky ones.

The full impact of this, even though I always have known it to be a possibility, has not quite dawned upon me. To be practical, I must admit that the dreams that we have so carefully cherished are at once placed in peril. A temporary delay in further planning must be made until the situation clears.

Darling, it is hard for me to think that the day we have long awaited may be postponed again. I know that it must be especially so with you. I wish that I could be there now, on the couch, the lights low: to stroke your hair, to cover your face with warm kisses, to try to express in my inadequate way the love that I hold for you. I wish that I could tell you that He is planning our lives and not we ourselves. That women for thousands of years have had to forego for a time the joy of a home and a husband while he went away to fight for his ideals. That man throughout the ages have left hearth, home, their Love, to obey a higher duty, the duty to their homeland. As the poet said, "I could not love thee, Dear, so much, loved I not honor more." My duty, my honor, my obedience to the will, or even the whim, of the Army of <u>our</u> country comes before every thing else.

I know that you know these things. I know that no matter how it hurts, and it hurts deeply, that if circumstances forces us to delay beyond April 1st, you will be able to bite your lip and ask Him for

Strength to wait with patience. We waited long to find our Love; we have waited long to fulfill our plans for union; if necessary, we can wait still longer.

I am speaking as though all hope was gone; it isn't. There still remains the possibility that I will remain here, and that we will be able to go ahead with plans. However, there is also the other chance, and we must not willfully blind ourselves to it.

If the language men are to be reassigned, I may be out and away long before April 1st. If it so happens, I will probably be sent to some camp, probably Camp Roberts, for reclassification. We can't know what the future may bring, but we can always trust and hope in His plan for us.

I will discuss this more at length later. Ted and I [are] going over to Centerville to visit Phil 'n family. Will try to write from there. I enclose a note from a S. F. paper concerning Dibble Hospital. Menlo Park is about a mile and a half from Stanford. [Article below]

Finishing this up in class break Sat morning. Hope to hear from you today.

> All my love,
> Bushy

"Army Needs Hospital Workers" found in letter
postmarked Feb. 18, 1944

February 20, 1944, Diary

To Sunday School and Church with Phil. Peggy remained thu is met Phyliss. [?] Ted spoke to the S. Sch. Class and played for both services. Phil is mature in his thought and gives an excellent sermon. We spent a pleasant hour after dinner and did not leave until five. Great success reported from initial raid on Truk. Many Jap ships and planes destroyed. We were given a notice today concerning A.S.T.P. "Certain language groups" will remain. This may include Dutch.

---

* Letter from Art to Dotty
[February 20, 1944]
Sunday night
Stanford

My Dearest,

Events may be occurring during the next few days that will profoundly effect our future. I fear that my letter was a little crude Friday night, and I sincerely hope that it did not break the situation too harshly.

I returned tonight from Phil's just in time for a formation where we were given a form letter concerning the A.S.T.P. Its contents you know with possibly one exception: "Certain language groups" will be retained. Whether this means Dutch we can't know as yet. It may! As I said before, I think we have a good chance. It will probably depend entirely upon the present strategy of the High Command. That we don't know.

So, my Sweetest Heart, there still lies hope in the human breast. We may still be able to climax our hopes and plans within a short time.

I don't want either of us to build up a false hope without realizing the possibility of disappointment. Nevertheless, it seems wise at this particular moment to continue our plans. That will be easier than to call them off entirely. When I say "continue" I intend to imply that we should continue at reduced speed, so to speak. Continue knowing that at any moment the worst may happen. Before the time for you leave comes, the situation will be clarified. I will write at the earliest possible moment if anything new takes place.

By the way, I had a talk with Phil today concerning this and that. He does not favor the use of a shield (or rubber) by the male, but says that a diaphram worn by the female is far more satisfactory. That, with jelly, is almost foolproof. A shield involves putting it on and taking it off just before and just after intercourse. The diaphram can be worn throughout the night without any discomfort whatsoever. He says that you should see a doctor, preferably a woman, to be measured. Although a bit more expensive, it will last for some time. Perhaps you should investigate this method. Phil and Peg have found it very satisfactory.

Two letters arrive tonight, the first in more than a week. One of the 11th and one of 13th. I fear you misunderstood something that I said long ago. I had no intention for you to withhold our plans now that they are more or less definite. By all means, tell everyone.

I favor the announcements, and will send "Mom" a list just as soon as possible. Will try to do that tomorrow. Sorry for the delay.

'Sinteresting to hear about your "misguided friend." Poor boy! I feel sorry for him, but rather proud of your choice. Why yes, my Dear, I think I might consider your proposal. Come out and see me sometime, Bud. I'll give you the answer!

I must to bed to pray and dream of
　　　　　Our Love,
　　　　　Bushy

P.S. Phil has some wonderful slides of the campus [Maryville College]. I grew more and more homesick as I view them.

I enclose excerpt from Mother's last letter. I think that it says more than I could to explain Mother's feelings.

February 23, 1944, Diary

Senator Barkley has broken his association with the FDR because of the veto of the tax bill. Barkley says he will resign as Democratic Senate Leader. This is merely one of many rifts coming into the open in the Party. There has already developed a strong anti-New Deal Southern Bloc. Many political leaders think that a Republican victory is certain next November. Willikie is making a strong bid for the Rep. nomination, but the Gallup Poll still shows Dewey in the lead.

At the risk of making a poor showing on my Dutch test tomorrow, I attended the concert given by Marian Anderson tonight in the Memorial Auditorium. Although the performance was in keeping with fame that she has established, I felt that the response given Miss

Anderson was a bit cold. At least it was not in keeping with the warm reception given an Artist on the Maryville Stage.

Letter excerpts from Helen L. Tapp to Dotty
February 24th 1944

"Dear Dot,

"I have two exciting letters from you to answer. I'm down in Pasadena right now so your letter was forwarded to me....

"I will be thrilled to death to act as your matron of honor. The dress you speak of sounds darling, and I do hope that I will be able to wear it....

"I betcha I'm almost as excited as you are. Are you sure you want me to be your matron of honor. I've never done it before. I'll be scared to death. But then you've never been a bride before, have you? We'll be in the same boat.

"Sunday was Roland's and my first wedding anniversary. He had written my aunt down here to have some roses for me. I was tickled to pieces. And there was a gardenia corsage to wear to church. He also sent a cable. I was glad for it, because I haven't been hearing from him quite so regularly. He has been transferred to North Africa—Algiers, I think—to the ferry transport service. Had some trouble with his ears while dive bombing in Italy. Sounds providential to me—he was making out of Italy just when the worst that battle began. And he's not in combat at all now. Wouldn't it be lovely if he could come back in time to attend the wedding. Would he be invited? But he doesn't think he'll be home before the end of the European war.

"Mom and I are thinking up all sorts of plans. Don't get worried—I don't mean big parties, etc. Tell me, about how many will you expect to be there? I mean what would you be having very many outside of the wedding party?

"What about this new stuff concerning the govt. interrupting some of the ASTP boys in their training? It was to affect some Stanford boys. Art said he would have at least six more months after you got here. Such a delightful six months!

"You are probably wondering why you haven't heard from me. So I better hurry and get this in the mail. And I'll write you again as soon as I get back to San Jose and find out a few things. Wouldn't it be swell if we had found a house in Palo Alto by then?

"All for now. I think this is going to be more fun. Were you maid of honor for Florence? Gee, I hope I'll know what to do at the right times. I can't remember one thing about my own wedding. We were married in Dad's church in Ohio, I know. And only the immediate family was present. And my voice shook when I was repeating the vows. That's all I remember. I asked the organist to play "The Old Refrain" and "I Love You Truly" because I like them so much, and then I didn't hear whether she played them or not. Some stuff.

"I really am stopping now.

With love——and best wishes—Helen"

Letter from Art to Dotty
Stanford University
Feb. 25, 1944
Fri Morning

My Darling,

I have not intentionally neglect to write again this week, but I have found myself rushed as per usual. At the expense of my Dutch, I attended a concert Wednesday night [February 23, 1944] to hear the grand performance of Marian Anderson. Thursday I had my weekly Dutch test, and tomorrow I have an area quiz. No rest for the wicked and A.S.T!

As I say the concert was rather wonderful. All that I have ever heard concerning this Anderson's voice must be true. She has equal facility over in her high and low ranges, and her tones are beautiful. Most of the time she appeared like a shy schoolgirl, looking down as she sang; but her personality did add much to the enjoyment of the program. The auditorium was packed as you might guess—tickets were sold out two weeks ago. However, the response was not so warm as an artist receives at Maryville. It was with a sense of deep longing that I heard her while you are away. Not only at such moments but every day and every hour I miss you, My Sweet....

My grade in area for the eighth week (ending next Sat.—week from tomorrow) should be a high B. I made that grade on the second hour test and quiz grades have been high. The Dutch exam yesterday suffered because of the concert, but conversation is the main thing, and that is improving.

Darling, the uncertainty of my situation here makes planning extremely difficult. As yet I have received no word from you to know your reaction to the confused state, and I am anxious to hear it. One thing that worries me is to know just how long you can wait to hear that

I am to remain and still get here by April 1st for the marriage. To be very frank, I hardly know what to think of my chances of staying here. As far as we know, absolutely nothing has been heard here by the officials. It seems likely that a large shipment is expected soon for our dining hall (there are two) is closing this week. I think that we may stick around for a few weeks even if we do leave eventually.

By the way, say absolutely nothing about this, but Ted and Jack may be in line for a good set up in D.C. Jack has good friends with influence. In fact he has given me some dope that may prove extremely valuable in the event that Dutch closes. I have my fingers crossed.

I received an <u>Echo</u> the other day in which your name was permanently spread on the front page. Proud of you, Bud! Wish I could have heard the talk.

Full House Hears Singer

By CYCLONE COVEY

Featuring songs of Schubert—four on the program and two as encores—Marian Anderson sang Wednesday night to a sold-out house in Memorial Hall. As much for her characteristic reserve as the phenomenon which is her singing, Miss Anderson is always a relief from the effusive majority. of. her. profession,. who freeze unfelt smiles upon their faces and abound in pretended graciousness.

Well the outstanding number of our comely and sedate contralto was "Poor Me," one of the spiritual group, low-pitched, sustained, and absolutely finished in its execution. And though her forte is flowing melody, she included about an equal number of fast selections, such as a couple of the Schubert Lieder and the "Se Florindo a fedele" of A. Scarlatti, which were fairly rippled off.

Most enjoyed by the audience were probably the partly talked spiritual, "Ain't No Hidin' Place Down There," a novelty ballad, "Cuckoo," and the inevitable closing "Ave Maria"—all three encores.

Up to the concluding group of spirituals, incidentally, the program was arranged chronologically, including selections from the 17th to the 20th centuries. The lament "When I Am Laid in Earth" which closes Purcell's "Dido and Aeneas." opened the recital, and was the only number not up to par, or her recording (Victor 17257) which is the standard phonographic impression of that music.

Miss Anderson sang also two compositions of Haydn, "La vie" and "My Mother Bids Me Bind My Hair"; Massenet's aria, "Pleurez mes yeux" from "Le Cid"; and a group of contemporary works including Vaughn Williams' "Silent Noon."

Marian Anderson Concert in Memorial Hall
on Feb. 23, 1944 (Mentioned in letter dated Feb. 25, 1944.)

Lewis Mumford, head of the English Dept. here and an outstanding man in American literary circles, is giving the sermon in the Chapel Sunday. I would give a great deal to hear him, but we plan to visit the Pratt's in San Jose this week-end

In a world filled with chaos and uncertainty, there remains one hope on which to build our lives—that hope is Faith. With Faith I pray for

        Our Love,
        Bushy

Art Bushing & Jack Feldman, Stanford Quad, Feb. 1944

February 25, 1944, Diary

Jack Feldman and Ted visited Headquarters today. Buy methods on his own, Jack gleaned important information concerning a STP. Nothing official has been released as yet, but it seems that the whole thing may fold at any moment. H.Q. merely awaits a telegram from Washington. We will probably go east to the staging area perhaps in Penna. My specialized serial number is 405.

Letter from Dottie tonight. She refuses to accept the inevitable conclusion concerning our plans. Poor girl, I wish I could be with her to comfort her. It certainly isn't easy to readjust my thinking to the idea that again our plans are friend nought.

February 26, 1944, Diary

Entire post paraded today in Stanford Bowl (supposed to be the largest college bowl in country—holding 90,000). In honor of Sgt. who died saving a buddy. Silver Star and Purple Heart awarded his father. Marching none too good, morale low. After 3:30 Jack, Ted and I made a fast trip to the city in the jeep—45 min. to Market St. Looked at Dotty's wedding ring and wanted very much to get it. However, our plans may be delayed for very long time. Saw "Ali Baba and the Forty Thieves." Hitchhiked back to Stanford.

February 27, 1944, Diary

Arose in time to attend Chapel Services on the campus. Lewis Mumford was to speak but he is sick. Dr. Trueblood gave the sermon. The Chapel is a beautiful structure, and it would have been so wonderful to have been able to be married in it!

* February 28, 1944, Diary

Letter from Dotty tonight. She is going full speed ahead with plans for a wedding on April 1st. Has tickets for trip, and her other plans are nearing completion. It will be a real blow when she finds out the bad news. Went over to see Jack and Ted tonight—first lesson on how to become a Classification Expert. Closed shop it seems, and yet not too much involved. I feel far better as to the possibilities for my, for our future. In case I could get stationed with a good position. Hmm!

My D earest Hear t,

To begin wi th, this ma chine skip s with mark ed re gulari ty, but I can do li ttle or not h ing about it. Blame it on the mach ine, and no t the drink .

I was overj oyed tonigh t to get t he Valentin e with the pict ure, but at the same t ime I was a lmost heart broken to get your letter of last We dnesday. A t that time you were go ing ahea d at full s peed with p lans for Ap ril lst. D arling, it is hard enough for me to real ize that ou r plans mus t again be dela yed, but it cuts deepl y when I kn ow how hurt you will b e. I kn ow you will be brave, but that do esn't keep the shock ing from hurting. Only with a firm reslo ve to turn to Him for a st rengthening of our Fai th can we f ace this cr isis and th e many more that will come w ith calm ou tlook. Try to m aintai n the firm belief that He is planning ou r lives, an d He knows the way that is ours to fo llow. We d o belief th at, My Dear .

I have some news that may help so me to take our minds f rom the immediate. I t hink I m enti oned th at Jack has offered to help me i n every way possible t o get a goo d position when we lea ve here . Because of my cleri cal experie nce, he ass ures me tha t I can get a rating as a cler k, with a c ouple of st ripes attac hed. Bett er than tha t, he is wo rking with both Ted an d myself to make us what is known as " Classificat i on Special ists". He is a te chnical ser geant, and r eceived his rating in t he field of clas sification and adminis trative wor k. The wor k invloves beco ming famili ar with cer tain forms, and thei r various use s. He s ays that we can learn the work th oroughly in fi ve or si x hour s of study. More than that, he i s working t hrough cert ain frie nds higher in the serv ice t o find places fo r us We kn ow that t here is a grave shor tage of suc h technicia ns in the n ew expa nding progr am that the Army is un d ergoing at the present time . I have w ritten aski ng Sergeant asking tha t he help u s in any way that he can.

Speed is ve ry importan t in the en tire situat ion, for at the pres ent moment, we have mo re chance o f getting i nto some thi ng like that than we may have for a long time to co me At the mome nt, we are in Detached Service, w hich means t hat we are not assi gned. L ittle red tape would be i nvloved in pulling us right out, and into a good job. If t his la tter opport unity only mate rializes, t here would be excellen t chance fo r advanceme nt, and probably a sergeant's rating very shortly. We are wor king for an opening in the East , and that seems a def inite possi bility

D arling, I d on't want t o build our ho pes up a gain for so me- thin g that may not wo rk out, but this to me look s brighter than anyt hing so far . It is no military s ecret that technicians a re need ed; and, hav ing a great faith in J ack, I think we can be come equi ped for the work under his able d irecti on. (You sh ould see som e of the le tters of re commendatio ns from Cha plains, off icers,

Letter from Art to Dotty, February 28, 1944, pg. 1

and one from Mayor LaGuardia. What a guy! Makes me think of John in some ways.

Today nine men were taken out of the advanced group of Dutch students, and yesterday an order came through for two of my group. If other things had not indicated it, that is enough to prove that we are no longer consider as essential to the Army program. Another thing it proves is that men with certain technical training are needed and will be taken out at any time for special assignments. If we can only get out hats in the ring in time, there seems to be excellent possibility for a break. Even if we have to go to a classification center from here, I think that Ted and I may have a chance for the same thing. Jack of course has nothing to think worry about with his rating.

The meaning of all this is that with a rating and a chance for advancement I could conceivably land a permanent job in this country. If and when, My Dearest, the plans that you have worked on so feverishly may not be in vain. As you well know by now, nothing in the Army is certain. The thing that we least expect usually seems to happen. Don't count too much on this latest development, but still it offers food for speculation. This isn't intended to be exactly a secret, and yet I think for the present we should confine it to the family.

Nothing would please me more at the present time than a picture of the sweetest girl in all the world, My Love, since I must put aside my dreams of you as my wife in the coming weeks Do you suppose that perhaps....? If and when you do, please put it in a nice folder for me, Darling. It might prove difficult for me to find a suitable folder for it here or where I will be when I receive it.

The sands run quickly the hour of pleasure, and I must to bed. Darling, in this time of heartache and sorry know that my thought and prayer are with you constantly. I long to hold you close to me and telling you that our plans will be fulfilled. If I can't be with you in body, feel my spirit entwined with thine as we look with chin up to the future of

OUR LOVE,

Brahm

P.S. By regular mail I am sending pictures of Stanford, and a paper to "Mom".

Letter from Art to Dotty, February 28, 1944, pg. 2

March 1, 1944, Diary

Frat houses with Chinese etc. closing out. Ted and Jack moved over to brander this afternoon. Over to Quad to talk Dutch with Merrouim Hymons for an hour tonight. After study period went up to Ted's room to go over a few points with Jack concerning Classification. Am learning a great deal. If I have a little time should be able to insure good position later. Jack is writing to friends which he has to do what he can for me, and letter from Sgt. [Alvin C. York] should help.

---

* Letter from Art to Dotty
Stanford University
March 1, 1944
Wednesday Night

My Dearest,

I am sure that by this time you have my letter of last Sunday in which I crudely broke the news that our plans must of necessity be postponed. I feel very close to you, my Darling, as we share this misfortune. My heart cries out to be with you to lend comfort and solace.

For the present that cannot be, just as our plans cannot be carried out. So, we are not in the final analysis the "captains of our fate." Through no volition of our own can we foresee or determine the events that may befall us. However, it is in our power, with the aid of His guiding hand, to control to a great extent the way in which we react to any given situation. That is to say, we are capable of finding a vast reservoir of strength, by which we can adapt ourselves to life in its broad complexity.

And so, I know that the bond of love binding our souls to each other will be strengthened during these days of anxiety and pain, and that we will be able to look upward and outward with courage and determination. We shall look ever upward into the face of Our Father to find the strength that alone can sustain us and we shall look ever outward into the veil of the future to foresee the happiness and joy that will make our lives together a veritable heaven.

We may not find material riches for our search will lead us in other pathes. We shall seek the joy of living, of working, of serving. We shall seek to prove that Christ was more modern than the most pseudo-modern today and yet simpler in His daily mode of living than the most humble of us. You see, Darling, the failure of our plans to materialize, as <u>we</u> had planned marks merely an incident in our lives together. We have not found Love; we are finding it. We have not reached Love: we are reaching it. Love is a process of <u>becoming</u> at-one with someone else. Music and Love evolve from harmony of souls.

It often seems needless to say these things concerning our Love; things that we have said again and again. And yet, like "the old, old story", these are words to be repeated again and again. In the years to come, my Dear, may we never become so involved in living that we cannot take time for the expression of our deeper feelings.

As much as we can say concerning our heartfelt thoughts, as much as we need to say concerning them, we can never fully express that which is in our souls. With all the strength that I pocess, with all that lies within the realm of my being, I love you, My Own. I long to be with you now, I long to hold you close, and whisper my love.

The world, our nation, I have a job to do. That job comes before the planning of any one individual or any group of individuals. Because of that job, our lives are not our own; we can but accept. To whatever extent possible we must look at our plans as objectively as possible. "God loveth his own!" With a deep prayer for His constant presence with you, I close with

> Our Love,
> Bushy,

P.S. Am greatly encouraged about the help that Jack is giving me for a position.

Plan to visit Helen Saturday and Sunday, and will find out about your letters. I do know that she has been stranded in Pasadena for sometime. Travel very bad out here.

March 2, 1944, Diary

It is interesting to note the birth pangs of World Union which are beginning to be felt. Thinking men see the necessity, and several carefully worked out plans have been proposed. Many there are—a large majority in fact—who think that a World Union will never work.

"UNITED FOR VICTORY"

UNITED STATES ARMY

Stanford University, Calif.
March 3, 1944
Friday Night

My Dearest Heart,

Another letter with the hiccups. You don't mind a great deal, do you? I had wanted so much to call you tonight, and I made an unsuccessful attempt to get the call through. No luuk! I felt sure that last night or tonight you must have received the news that came with my letter of Sunday last.

Just tonight I received your letter of Monday night. It bore the news of Helen's plans for us, and it hurts a bit to know that so much must be thought of as something that might have been. Helen is wonderful and I will tell her how much we appreciate all that she was planning when I see her tomorrow.

We maintain a status quo here. Men are leaving at frequent intervals, but we have heard nothing concerning our situation. Jack, Ted and I have not had time to get results from our plans, but I am encouraged to think that the thing may work out. Jack is planning tomorrow to get a couple of names to whom Sgt. can write, and we will send them by wire to Dad. Jack also has a Major friend in Washington who is working in our favor. Keep your fingers crossed and your faith high.

It is interesting to note the birth pangs of a world union beginning to be felt. There still are many who doubt the practicality of such a plan - probably the majority of the people throughout the world have no belief whatever in such a plan. Others think that the time is in some far distant future. I fear, Darling, that if we who will be making the future allow ourselves to be pushed aside from the consolidation of world power into a path that leads again to war that civilization itself will be destroyed. Mankind cannot risk the horror and destruction that we will be capable of next time. In early history, man found the/the former city state which had proven so useful for so long outmoded. National states had to be organized to cope with more complex society. We too have reached a crossroad in our advancement. The only logical thing to do is to form a World Union after this struggle ends. If we do not, I fear the results.

Another thing that will bare watching is the political field on the home front. Men in uniform are getting fed with the old, old story in Washington of our "representatives" playing politics with our lives. Instead of the welfare of the nation, in fact of the world, these men seem to think only of their own petty prides and prejudices. I intend to vote next election if I have to fill out hundreds of forms to do it. Most of us realize that these politicians in Washington can ruin all that we fight for. We don't like, and I think that ten million men will do something

March 3, 1944, Letter from Art to Dotty, pg. 1

353

about t he situatio n.

T ed and Jack moved over to Branner Hall on We dnesday, an d I of
course was very gla d. Now we are xix abl e to see mu ch more of each other,
and we are able to get much m ore done in the way of learning t o be
"Classi fication in xxii Specia lists". We are learni ng, and Jac k is
a grand teacher. The ma teria l that we a re learning is not dif ficult,
and my experience of several months of o ffice work with Dad wi ll be
invalua ble. It se ems that cl assificatio n work in t he office i s sort
of a cl osed shop, and so it i sn't likely to be over crowded. W e could
never b reak in wit hout t he he lp of someo ne like Jac k who does know the
ropes.

L etter from Bob Schwart zwalder ton ight. The first time that I
have he ard from hi m in some t ime, altho?h I did hav e a long le tter
from Ar lene. He i s in the Me dical Corp in training in Indiana , and
seems t o liking it as well as one could e xpect. He is learning to be
a Surgi cal Technic ian, and wi ll be there until the early part of May.
He says "My persona l ambition as far as t he Army goe s is to be the
first man mustered out after t he emergenc y." I fear that his a mbition
is one shared b y ten million of us in u niform .

O ne of my u tch teacher s, Mrs Heym ans, came f rom Europe just
eight m onths ago. She spent an hour toda y recountin g some of h er
experie nces from t he time of the invasio n of the Lo w Countries (when
she was in Antwerp), her evac uation with her boy, a seventy-ei ght
year ol d grandmoth er, and fiv e others, t hrough Pari s and south . She
told us something of the horr or of the c oncentratio n camps tha t she
worked in. It was n't pleasan t, Darling, and I hope and pray t hat
we in A merica will never have to suffer t he things t hat Europe has
known a nd will yet see.

I have t o w o rk now for awhile with Jack and T ed. Ted an d I
leave t omorrow aft er three-th irty for He len's. Car d from her tonight
says th at she is h oping to ge t the Evaul 's and Astl es over als o. Oh
joy!

W ith a praye r for the l ove that we cherish on my lips, I say
Goodnig ht

My Love,

March 3, 1944, Letter from Art to Dotty, pg. 2

354

March 4, 1944, Diary

Mina (my roommate) had a twelve o'clock pass which he didn't care to use. By a bit of extraordinary luck Ted managed a similar one, and we left here at twelve-thirty. By one-thirty we were in the Pratt home. A couple of policemen picked us up and took us right to the door. Van Cise arrived about seven-thirty followed by Phil 'n family. Leaving the baby with Mrs. Pratt we went out to the Ice Bowl, a few miles away. Enjoyed my first evening on ice skates. Some fun and no spills. Returned to hot chocolate and pie. Talked and planned for a big reunion at San Anselmo next week. To bed late but very happy. Mrs. Pratt sad that Ted Pratt not home on his furlough.

March 5, 1944, Diary

Slept late and up for a good breakfast with Mrs. Pratt. Very beautiful day in contrast with the rainy days past. To Church for good service. Bus late and we got home for late dinner. I was honored by being asked to act as head of the table. Took pictures and enjoying relaxing. 'S wonderful to be able to act as though one were at home. Brought back in '27 Packard [an American luxury car] used by Ex. Pres. Hoover. Driven by famous old colored man, here at Stanford since 1903. Drove us around to see Mr. Hoover's home, etc. Interesting character.

March 7, 1944, Diary

Jack Feldman is doing all that he can to assure some security for our positions if and when A.S.T.P. folds. He has a friend in Washington (a Major) who is working on something for the three of us. In fact, he had a position already opened for Ted and Jack when he received Jack's telegram to include me. That meant that he must start all over again. What a friend!

Jack gave me permission to copy part of what he says concerning ASTP: "I don't know how that ASTP stands... Here in Washington it is a complete orphan. They are throwing it from office to office and no one particularly wants to handle it. That OSS (Office of Strategic Service) deal is a lot of baloney. They may swing a deal for a few men but as for appointments all around you can stop dreaming right now. The A.S.T.P. is somebody's baby, but even I don't know who. I can't give you any dope on the standing of the A.S.T.P. as I told you because nobody here knows what it's all about. Let's hope nobody wants anything to do with it. (Personally, I think nobody does—too much explaining will be necessary)".

Letter from Art to Dotty
Stanford University
March 7, 1944
Tuesday afternoon

My Dearest Dotty,

Your letter of the 2nd came last night, and I was more than happy to find that you maintain strong fortitude in the face of our disappointment. I knew that you would do so, and yet you are wonderfully human. I know it is hard to see how fortunate others have been, and yet there are perhaps many more less fortunate then we. Our plans have only been belayed, our Love remains the stronger for the waiting. You are very wonderful, Darling!

As for how definite the situation is, I think we must reconcile ourselves to the fact that it will be quite impossible to plan now for you to come to California. I found out only yesterday that thirty of the advanced Dutch have left. Many of our group have left and are leaving. It is more than a possibility that we will not be here April 1st, and even if we are here then that we will not remain long thereafter.

You see, Dotty, is some respects it is though I were burning the bridges behind me in regard to ASTP. As I mentioned before, Jack is doing everything in his power to get us pulled out of here as soon as possible. The letter or letters that Sgt. [Sergeant Alvin C. York] writes for us are intended for the same purpose. Ted and I are working every night to learn all that we can concerning classification work. In case we leave before some of our contacts come through, we have still an excellent chance of getting into the work from our reclassification center. There were three factors involved in my decision to leave the sinking ship as it were.

In the first place, I do not believe that there remains the slightest hope of Dutch staying in the program. Second, if it perchance did, there is no assurance that we would be given the opportunity to complete the scheduled course of nine months. In the third place, in case we did remain, did complete the work, the possibilities of getting a decent job seem none to certain. You see, Dear, it was the type of crossroad that we will constantly be meeting. However, other decisions may not be so

356

easy to make. I would have liked to have talked the entire thing over with you, but there is so little time. I prayed for guidance, attempted to see the varied angles of the situation, and then went ahead on my conviction.

In classification there is opportunity for advancement, and for some of sort of permancy perhaps. It may mean that we can delay our plans now, only to have more time with each other later on.

I am telling no one else about these plans. If and when I am placed in a good position, I intend to appear as though it were merely luck that came to my rescue. Outside the family let us say nothing. Jack is going far out of his way to assist a couple of lowly Pfc's. I just a few moments ago received a letter from Mother. They are doing what they can to get a letter for the three of us from Sergeant [Sergeant Alvin C. York].

She also tells me that she received a very nice letter from you, and hopes to answer immediately. Mother and Dad are doing a tremendous job with the Draft work, and I wish there were something that I could do to help. I hope you understand why they have so little time even to write me.

Last week-end was perhaps the most wonderful that I have enjoyed since I entered the Service. By happy chance I was able to make use of a 12:00 o'clock pass which my roommate didn't care to use. By pure luck, Ted also managed the same thing, and we were able to leave by 12:30. By 1:30 we were in the Pratt home in San Jose. Our rides down were marked by being picked up by the cops. To our surprise that took us right to the door. (Helen lives about two miles from the center of town.)

We set around, talked, and I wrote a letter to Hargrave in the afternoon. Van came about seven-thirty, followed in a few minutes by Phil 'n family. We talked for awhile, but soon left the baby with Mrs. Pratt to go to a nearby ice rink. Phil and Ted had skated before, but for the rest it was a new experience. We must indulge again sometime, Darling. It was grand. We returned about eleven to enjoy a pie made for Phil's scouts, and hot chocolate provided by the thoughtful Mrs. Pratt. The Evaul's managed to get away finally, and we made our way to bed.

It was rainy all last week, but Sunday morning dawned a beautiful Sabbath. We ate a hearty breakfast, and attended Church. Again at noon we had a wonderful meal, and then just relaxed. Helen and Mrs. Pratt make us feeling just as though we were at home, and it is a grand feeling. We took a number of pictures which should turn out well.

Our return trip proved fitting climax to the grand thime which we have enjoyed. The three of us were picked up by an old negro

357

gentleman in a 1926 Packard. To our joy we found that he was going right to Stanford, where he has worked since 1903. The car in which we rode was the car which President Hoover had used when he made his inaugural speech here in the Stanford Stadium. This old fellow has a road here on the campus named in his honor, and he worked for Mrs. Hoover at their home here on the campus. Since Van had never seen the campus he insisted in driving us all around, showing us the stadium, the baseball diamond, Mr. Hoover's home, the frat houses, etc. The whole thing was rather exciting.

As I mentioned last week, Ted and Jack are living in Branner Hall with me now, and we are able to [see] each other frequently. We are working hard on classification.

I must close and hasten to class, but will write again soon. Mother's letter came last night and I hope to write her some time soon. Tell her that I don't mean to neglect her, but I just don't have time to write you or anyone y else.

With all the power than [that is] in me is, I hope and work and pray for

    Our Love,
    Bushy

March 8, 1944, Diary

Much to my pleasurable surprise Mr. Pratt, Helen, and Mrs. Pratt stopped by to see Ted and me. They were on their way home from S.F. First time we have seen Mr. Pratt since we came out here. Very nice man. We talked for more than an hour. Their Ted is on a furlough but he didn't have time to come out here. I wish that he could have for their sakes.

Letter from Art to Dotty
Stanford
March 9, 1944 (Thurs.)

My Darling,

Only a few moments before class, but perhaps time to tell you the progress of events here. Tomorrow I have a big area exam so last night I was deeply involved in review in the day room. The cadet officer of my platoon came in calling my name about nine o'clock, and told me that a gentleman was looking for me. Throwing down my work, I dashed out to find Mr. Pratt awaiting. I, of course, was overjoyed to see him, since he has been away each time that we have visited in San Jose. He asked if I could find Ted, so I immediately went upstairs to get him. It turned out that the Pratt's had been visiting in S.F., and all three of them had stopped by on the way home. We went out in the car and talked for almost an hour. The night was well nigh perfect; the company exhilarating. It was grand! We had a good visit and made further plans for the big reunion Sat. in San Anselmo.

Dotty Dear, I wish you could be here so very, very much. The weather is absolutely ideal, the kind I always dreamed about when I thought of Calif. I can only compare the day to the perfect ones which we knew at Maryville in May and June. Nor does the presence of all the nice co-eds help in the least.

Actually you don't need to worry; I see the co-eds only occasionally on the campus. Nevertheless, I am reminded of gayer days when the clouds were as dark and hearts were lighter. By the way, Darling, I miss you a very great deal!

I have some news concerning A.S.T.P. and stuff that I will have to detail later. Jack has a grand letter from Major in Washington, promising to do everything possible for the three of us. He also commented on the general mess in which A.S.T.P. seems to be. That later.

As I mentioned, we plan to visit Phil & Johnny Astler in San Anselmo Sat. & Sun. Helen coming up also. Van to be there. Must study now, if possible, while Spring fills me anew with thoughts of

> Our Love,
> Bushy

P.S. Hope you can send papers with engagement announcement to Mother & Dad.

March 11, 1944, Diary

Good conduct ribbons awarded today in big parade. Good luck in getting to Frisco and took bus to San Anselmo. Helen, Johnny & Jane Astles, Phil and Peggy there. Van unable to come. Before supper we went up to the Seminary to look around. Something of a Maryville atmosphere. Big supper. Took car part way up old Baldy—a nearby hill. Grand view of San Anselmo, Bay, Bay Bridge, Sand Quentin, and even Hamilton Field. Beautiful moonlit night. Back down to play ?

battleships, etc. until 2 a.m. Ted and I slept with the Astles. The little cottages furnished by this Seminary have swell arrangements.

March 12, 1944, Diary

Good sleep until 9:30. Big waffle breakfast. After breakfast packed two cars for Muir Woods, Nat'l Park. Wonderful place fair with all the trees, a stream, etc. Ate a tremendous picnic lunch prepared by the girls. Played flag game and acted in general like children. Strolled around and took pictures. To Muir Beach. They took us to highway head. Ing. South. Seven rides to get to Stanford.

Letter from Art to Dotty
Stanford University, Calif.
March 12, 1944
Sunday Night. [typed]

My Dearest,

I had almost a full page typed to you yesterday afternoon, but we had to fall out for a parade before it was finished. I took it along with me to Phil's, but was unable to finish it there. It became so soiled that I will have to write it over now, but that should n't be too much trouble. On Friday night I was overjoyed to receive two big letters from you: one of Tuesday and one of last Sunday. The announcement of our engagement made me feel good all over, and I have been showing it to every one since it came. The picture is one that I like very much, and I am glad you used it.

Perhaps I should reveal a deep dark secret that I have failed to mention. The much discussed mustache no longer exists. Last week before going down to San Jose I performed the operation without too much misgiving. I promise not to grow another on this side of the Atlantic or Pacific without your permission.

I want to catch up on a bit of back news if I can, and then bring the story up do date with a description of my wonderful week-end at San Anselmo. As I already mentioned before, Jack has a Major friend who is doing all that he can for us in Washington. In fact, Jack didn't tell me, but Ted revealed last night that this Major had already found positions for the two of them when he received Jack's telegram telling him to include me in the deal. This meant that the whole procedure had to be started over again. We of course hope for the same good fortune for the three of us, but that remains for the future to decide. My request to Sgt. [Sergeant Alvin C. York] for a letter for the three of us was at first met with hesitation. I have written again to describe the situation further, and hope that the last letter will have better results. It really seems that something should break for us before too very long.

I was very much interested in what the boy in Washington had to say about the status of ASTP. Jack gave me permission to quote the letter, but of course this is restricted.

He begins. "I don't know how that ASTP stands....Here in Washington it is a complete orphan. They are throwing it from office to office and no one particularly wants to handle it. That OSS (Office of Strategic Service) deals is a lot of baloney. They may swing a deal for a few men but as for appointments all around you can stop dreaming right now. The ASTP is somebody's baby but even I don't know who.....I can't give you any dope on the standing of the ASTP as I told you because nobody here knows what anything to do with it. (Personally— still in quotes—I think nobody does—too much explainin will be necessary.)"

I think that is an interesting sidelight on the situation. I repeat again, that this is for your ears alone, but I thought that it would be something to explain how uncertain even Washington.

We pulled out yesterday afternoon and had excellent luck in getting to San Anselmo (16 miles north of S. F.). Helen had arrived earlier by bus, and we arrived in time to see the Seminary before supper. The buildings (two) set on a high hill looking over the little. The entire section is surrounded by hills, and looks very much like a little valley tucked away in the Smokies. We looked through the library, the dorm, etc., and returned in time for a big meal. Van was unable to come for which we were very sorry, but Johnny Astles and Jane, Phil and Peggy, Ted, Helen, and I made a grand reunion. We didn't get through the dishes until about nine-thirty, and then had to convince the girls that they should go with us on a moonlight hike up a nearby peak (Old Baldy). We finally pulled out, driving part way up. From the top of the hill, we could see the town-twinkled valley, the Bay in the distance, San Quinten, Hamilton Field (big air field), the Bay Bridge, and a thousand stars overhead. Before we left the hill, the moon came coyly from behind the curtain of clouds to make me very lonesome.

We slept late, and arose to enjoy all the waffles that we could down. Since we had a long way to go, we had to omit Church, and pulled out about eleven o'clock for Muir Woods. Climbing over high hills and going down steep inclines, we arrived about noon. I can't adequately describe the majesty of the Red Woods, My Darling. Rising three and four hundred feet, they stand as monuments to time. There is something of an epic grandeur about the trees that makes one stand in awe to wonder what God hath wrought. I will not soon forget the first moment of wonder that I felt as I gazed on them. We wandered about a bit, and enjoyed a delicious picnic lunch. Later we played about like a bunch of kids, sang, and in general felt the exuberance of being alive, together, and in God's presence. Leaving Muir Woods (by the way, it is a National Park), we drove down to the beach, and looked around a bit. Ted and I had to leave about four much to our regret. It was a grand time that we enjoyed.

As so often happens, the hour passes. I must show, study and try to catch up on a bit of lost sleep. (We played pit last night until after one' o'clock. Some fun!

Friendship with the grand friends we made at Maryville should be cherished and maintained throughout the years. We shall find few people as grand as our Maryville friends. Ever and again am I reminded of the kindness of God in giving me the most wonderful of all those I knew at Maryville. Darling, we shall find Heaven as we find

Our Love,
Bushy

Letter from Art to Dotty
Stanford University
March 16, 1944
Thursday Night

My Dearest,

Yesterday I enjoyed a rare experience, and one in which you shared to a large degree. For several days we have had Mr. Chang on the campus—Mr. Chang who teaches Art in the National University in Nanking China. He had given previous demonstrations, but yesterday was my first chance to see him. The demonstrations are in connection with a collection of his work on exhibit in the Art Gallery here.

I find, Darling, that I am more and more influenced by the philosophy and culture of the Chinese. It first began I think when Dad obtained a Translation From Chinese Poetry. I read a book on Chinese philosophy in Roberts as something of a follow up of tidbits I had gathered at Maryville. Last week I heard a lecture on Chinese Art and yesterday I absorbed some of it for two hours. It was here to that I had the opportunity to further introduce myself to the mind of the Orient through reading, lectures, and the seeing of Chinese pictures ("Song of

China"—full Chinese production last night.) So, my experiences are increasing, and I find many things in common with their thought.

One of the interesting things to note concerning the philosophy of the Chinese is their conservative attitude. Invariably they take a middle road. It is this conservative attitude that has enabled the people of China to maintain their culture over a period of almost five thousand years. They have moved slowly but steadily, and have absorbed changes rather than been absorbed. Compare by contrast our cultural history extending over a period less than three hundred and fifty years, and the culture of Europe covering a span of less than a thousand years. Without question the Chinese are stable, even though their lamp burns low at the present moment.

I like the philosophic approach and the attitudes of these people. I think that their approach to the problems of living holds a unique lesson for us of the Western world. The shallowness of our thought may prove inadequate to cope with the problems that confront us in the post-war world. (I wish you could read Bernard De Voto's "Easy Chair" in this month's Harpers.) We could gain much by turning to these people for insight.

So, it was with intense interest that I went to the Art Gallery on Wednesday to see Mr. Chang paint and to look at his work. Perhaps the two most amazing things about his demonstration was his deftness of stroke (he makes no preliminary markings with pencil) and his remarkable technique for blending two colors. In regard to the former, his strokes are made with great precision and without hesitation.

Friday Night

Darling,

The big news has at last come. Rumors have been flying thick and fast for the last couple or three days. An order is on our bulletin board tonight telling the story. Fifty Dutch men are to remain for the 6–L term. Since there are only about thirty-five men in 5–L now who graduate for the advanced term, that means that a few of the group which I am in will be shoved into the advanced group. However, suffer no illusion, My Love, I will not be included in the grouping. Out of a group of about fifty-five, I stand in the lower half, and it is almost certain that selection will be made on a basis of scholastic standing. The notice on the board says that we will be shipped the last week in March. That doesn't give much time as you can see.

I just got the news and haven't had time to collect my thoughts. Of course, I expected it, but I had hoped for a wee bit more time. Jack has a call through tonight to Washington. It will come tomorrow morning. Everything depends on the element of time. If Jack's friend can work fast enough—if he can't there is still, of course, a good chance to work something when I am interviewed by a classification officer. Keep your fingers crossed, but for more than that pray for His will to be done—not ours, but His. The events of the next two weeks, my Love, will determine our future to a very large extent.

Had a wonderful letter from Mother & Dad tonight. I think they are at last happy—completely so—with our plans. I am happy beyond words. You don't know how happy I am that you might consider going to them to help. We shall see. You're wonderful, Darling!

Must get this in the mail now, but will write again Sunday. We're seeing "Blossom Time" tomorrow night.

May God be Merciful and Bless

     Our Love,
     Bushy

March 17, 1944, Diary

Jack and Ted are certain that they are not to remain for 7-L course. News tonight indicates that only 50 Dutch will go into S-L program. There are 35—5-L's now. That leaves me out in the cold.

March 18, 1944, Diary

Jack called major in Washington last night. Call came through this morning. "Sit tight and wait," he says. Priority of this program only catch. To S.F. this afternoon. Wanted to see zoo but it closed. Went instead to see Mission Dolores and Church of St. Vincent De Paul. Back to town to Curran and "Blossom Time." Gallery seats. Life of Schubert with much of his best music. Most of the singing good—orchestra poor. After this saw "Great Am. Broadcast." I arrived in P.A. late—to bed about 4:30. Rather tired.

Letter from Art to Dotty
Stanford U, Calif.
March 22, 1944 Wed night [typed]

My Dearest Own,

'Tis strange how the mood of the passing moment is so transitory, and changes mayhap with a breath of wind from an unexpected quarter. From a height of feeling where one can see the expanse of things good and beautiful and hopeful, we may often be plunged into the depths of despondency. Actually I seldom find myself in such a mood, and I try never to write when my thoughts are shadowed by clouds. However, I must write tonight, and I hope that you will recognize and take into account my pessimism. Darling, you do understand me as no one else does. Many was the night at Maryville [Maryville College] that you cooled my teaming brain with a soft touch of your hand, with softer words, with merely your presence. Please do so tonight, because I need you.

Monday I received two letters from you, and yesterday the same. It's wonderful, Bud! I hope I can respond in part. There are many things that I want to say in regard to the little story, your very fine speech. I may not have time tonight, however, some new developments have arisen in regard to ASTP that I want to take up first.

I will not attempt to recount some of the steps through which the situation has gone in the last couple of days, but will attempt to tell you just where things stand now. The Dutch who are to stay have been chosen, and the number is more than was originally planned for. About sixty will be taking the 6-L work. We will not be told before Saturday who are to stay, so I don't know what the set-up is as yet. Much more has been taken into account than merely scholastic rating, here—Army General Classification Test, Army record, past experience, etc, etc. On the whole I think I have a chance of staying.

Now for the bombshell—I haven't fully decided that I want to remain! Crazy, niet waar?(Dutch) Writing without having had time to chrystalize my thoughts, it seems that our plans would be further by my leaving; and yet perhaps that is wrong. Actually I do want to stay. At least until our friend in Washington can do something. I can always hold my knowledge of classification in reserve and use it when the need arises. The thing that makes me feel so low is to know that no matter what is decided, our plans cannot go through for April 1st. Even if I remain in Dutch after Sat., I may be pulled out at any moment. That makes for uncertainty to say the least. If I find that I am leaving after

Sat., I still have the chance—probably a better one—of getting a good position in classification. Boy, am I in a dither!

No, Darling, you misunderstood me on the telephone when you thought that I didn't approve of your resignation. The fact was that I didn't quite understand what you said that night with all the fading etc. I am glad for I think that you need the vacation. I am more confused than ever as to how soon we can go ahead with our marriage, but I share your belief that something will work out. I am building up our bank account as much as possible, but this month I had to hold back in case I ship before next payday. Should send a fat moneyorder next month, however, Dad told me of the letter he wrote, and I am overjoyed. As to your generous proposal to go help Mother and Dad. I think it is wonderful of you, but first you need a rest. I have had a couple of notes from Muriel and will answer when things settle down one way or another. Happy to hear about all the showers 'n stuff. Some fun and wish I were there for more reasons than one.

Ted and Jack feel certain that they will leave shortly. Am certainly going to miss Ted when we are separated, but that is just one of those things. Hope we can visit with Helen this week, or perhaps go to Centerville. If I am to leave, will get a pass until nine o'clock Monday morning rather than seven Sun night.

I must go up now to work on Classification with Jack and Ted. Meanwhile, My Dearest Heart, I think of you every day and every hour. I love you with a love that transcends the human and approaches the divine. Unfolding like a vast and glorious dream is

Our Love,
   Thine Own
    Bushy

P.S. Just received pictures tonight. Only copies Helen sent, so send one of the apron pictures to Mother & Dad please.

Letter from Art to Dotty
Stanford University
March 23, 1944
Thursday Night

My Dearest Own,

On the very end of my birthday I received the most precious of all gifts that you could have sent—except yourself. Darling, it's absolutely wonderful, the very best I have ever seen of you including the former favorite on the trail with Jenks. Truthfully, I had almost forgotten that the 24th was on important day for, but the fact was vividly brought to my mind. As soon as I opened the package I began jumping up and down practically and then rushed upstairs to show it to Ted & Jack. Boy, am I proud! You are never from me, and yet your picture brings you even closer to my heart. This I shall treasure always and especially will it provide immeasurable comfort and solace while we are separated. Oh, Darling, I love you so very much and yet words can never tell you.

I was much impressed by the little story which you sent me—<u>And Her Name Was Mary</u>. I was impressed because I knew what was meant. You see, I too knew that my "Mary" was somewhere. Through high school I had little interest in dating, but I knew a lot of girls. I enjoyed their conversation, but none held special interest. While others dated, I spent my evenings at home. Far back in the recesses of my mind I knew that somewhere, someday I would find My Love. I knew it as well as I know anything in the world. I would find my Love!

I went to Maryville, I dated a number of girls, I knew many more— All were nice. Still I looked for the day when the girl, the wisp of a dream sent from Heaven, would cross my path. Then I became interested in a certain little girl that rushed by my table in the dining hall (Pearsons, I think they called it). I didn't know her, but I was interested. The story is an old one; we met. There was a sparkle in your eye that still glows with all the power that a heavenly star can possess. I was perfectly satisfied to look no more. Four years ago tomorrow, I sent my first flowers—"Love, Bushy," they said. I was beginning to experience a new something.

I knew that "My Mary" my Love had been found, that my search was ended. Within my breast I knew the feeling that Marco Polo experienced when his eyes opened for the first time on the richness, the splendor of the orient. I knew the feeling that Columbus knew, that scientists throughout the ages have known. A long search ended, I had found My Love.

The story did not end there. Remember the "raspberry bush". An intended joke became an intensely serious matter. I did set myself to the task of making myself worthy you [of] you and of your love. That remains my goal, Darling. I have long since dedicated my life first to Him as He will use me, but second have I dedicated my life to the joyful task of being worthy of the love of one so truly wonderful.

Our lives are still before us; we have everything to look forward to —marriage, home, children. Our Love is deep, and yet it is only a beginning. Not even Death itself will halt the union of our souls together and our soul with God.

Merciful, Father, we thank thee that we have found the greatest of all Thy bounteous gifts—the gift of Love. We pray for Thy continued blessing upon our plans, upon our future. If it be Thy will, may our lives be joined in the holy bonds of marriage; and may the home that will be ours know only Thy Headship. Bless us, use us as Thou wilt—we are Thine. May our path never stray from the way that Christ our Savior gone to us, for it is in His Holy name we offer this supplication. Amen.

> Thine Own,
> Bushy

March 24, 1944, Diary

My birthday passed as pleasantly—even more so—as one could expect in the Army. Last night I was overjoyed by do getting a wonderful portrait of Dotty. It is by far the best I have ever seen. Tonight Ted and Jack gave me <u>Literary</u> England, a grand book containing fifty pictures of literary spots in England. I have seen it often and have often wanted it. Friendship—it's wonderful! I celebrated this afternoon by swimming twenty-two laps in a sixty-foot pool. Tonight I'm feeling the effects. Yes, it was a very nice birthday, but very different from proceeding ones. Still no news as to who is to stay or who will ship. Should find out tomorrow.

March 25, 1944, Diary

Hear Duncan! "There is the bell That summons Thee to Heaven or to Hell!"

After a Dutch test and the lecture this morning, I returned to Branner to find out my fate. As I more or less expected my name was among twenty-six who are to leave. However, when I saw the grades which were posted at noon I have a <u>B</u> in Dutch & <u>C</u> in Area. Others with less are staying. Dr. Sokol sent me to Classification. If Mrs. Heymans recommends I may stay. Ted, Jack, and I bought Easter flowers tonight and later saw "Above Suspicion." [An American spy film starring Joan Crawford and Fred MacMurray.]

March 26, 1944, Diary

Left early for Centerville. Longest [bridge] in country/world being seven and a quarter miles. Reached Phil's Church in time for good sermon. Helen there. After Phil 'n Peggy had dinner out, we rode up Niles Canyon. Very much like Smokies. Said goodbye to Evaul's and took bus from San Jose. Arrived in time for Vespers and C.E. Rev. Pratt home. We talked until very late. Read 3rd Ch. of Proverbs and knelt in prayer before we left. Good luck coming back.

March 27, 1944, Diary

The deep experiences of Christian fellowship such as we enjoyed yesterday and last night hold real meaning for me. Certainly for Ted and perhaps for me it was the last time for us to enjoy their company for a while. Always they have made us feel as though we were their own. Mrs. Pratt is like a mother to us, and Helen like a sister. I can never forget how much our association together has meant to me.

Ted's orders came through today. Camp Roberts—71st Light Division. Poor fellow—it is the last place he expected to go. He had really counted on going East too. Well such is Army life! Order in for all but six of the Dutch who are leaving. I'm one of the lucky ones. Talked to Mrs. Heymans this morning. She says she will do what she can, but promises of course nothing. Graduation parade this afternoon. We got late passes and went to last show. Saw a "Destination Tokyo" with Cary Grant, also miserable show with Laurel and Hardy. Any hope of a break from Washington seems distant now.

Letter from Art to Dotty
Stanford University
March 27, 1944
Monday Night

Dearest Heart,

The plot continues to thinken, and I still don't know where I stand. I saw Mrs. Heymans this morning and she is anxious to do anything possible to assist me. She was to see the director of the F.E.A.L. (Far Eastern Area & Language) at eleven this morning to see what could be done. I shall check early tomorrow morning to find out what has happened.

369

Saturday night we (Ted, Jack & I) wandered a bit around some of the residential sections of Palo Alto. It is really a wonderful little town, and lovely flowers are everywhere. Later we saw "Above Suspicion" a rather exciting spy story. Sunday morning we arose early and Ted and I left for Centerville. As a result of a mistake in our route we crossed the longest bridge in the world. It is the San Mateo Bridge—seven and a quarter miles across the S.F. Bay With good luck we arrived at Phil's Church in time for the morning service. Helen was there, having gotten there earlier in the morning. As per usual, Phil had good sermon.

Tues Night

I missed parts of what he said as a result of the flirtatious eyes of a "babe" sitting near. With many a coy look and many a winning smile, she succeeding in taking my attentions from the pulpit much of the time—But, Darling, you really shouldn't be so jealous of little Phyllis. She is terrifically cute, and loves the attention of her soldier sweetheart. She actually knows me by this time. Phil & Peg were invited out to dinner so we (Helen, Ted, and I) ate in a restaurant. After dinner Phil took us for a ride in nearby hills. I could easily imagine myself riding up the trail toward the Park back in the dear ol' Smokies.

With some degree of sadness we said goodbye about 4:30 and boarded the bus for San Jose. We arrived just in time for Vespers and Young People's Meeting. It was grand to be in CE again. For the first time, Rev. Pratt was at home when we were there. We went home about eight o'clock and stuffed ourselves thoroughly with waffles. Although our pass was good until nine o'clock Monday morning, we decided that we should return Sunday night since Ted had a test on Monday. We sat around and talked, attempting to put off the thought of leaving. Both realizing that it might well be some time before we would be in a "home" again. The Pratt's really treated us as though we were their own, and being able to visit with them has helped some as I try to rationalize twenty-five hundred miles. Before we left Mr. Pratt read a chapter from Proverbs and we knelt in prayer. <u>Darling</u>, our home will be centered from its very beginning around the family altar. It brought a lump to my throat to leave these grand people.

Well I wanted to finish up my account of the week-end, but there have been new developments in my situation which are worth mentioning. This morning I went over to see Mrs. Heymans and learn the results of her efforts. (I couldn't see her yesterday because of the graduation parade in the afternoon.) With a sad face she told me that she had done everything possible but led me to believe that it was to no avail. I was not surprised.

By noon today more orders were posted on the bulletin board, but strangely enough my name was not listed. Only two of us originally listed for shipment have not had orders. Three fellows who were at first to stay are on orders. It may mean that a reshuffling has taken place in my favor, but I don't know. I wait patiently hoping and praying for the best (what ever that is).

Ted is leaving tomorrow for the 71st (Light Infantry) Division which is now on maneuvers near Camp Roberts. Two or three large shipments are going down there. Jack is going to the 89th Division which is on the same maneuver opposing the 71st (Brother against brother, n' stuff!)

We are still counting on something from Washington. Tonight Jack heard of the return of Gen. Woodward from England. He knows him and also his aide is a close friend of Jack. Mmmm! We shall see what we shall see.

Dearest, I did understand what you meant when you said that you felt... "as if you were suspended between the past and the future in a future with no time and little meaning." Very expressive. The feeling was quite similar to the one I recorded in "The Lovely Heart". I think you have a copy.

> "Between a distant
> Star – Haven
> And
> The long. dark moon
> Some where,
> Lost,
> Forgotten
> on an etherless cloud
> Where dark chills
> Shroud,
> and fit full dreams
> Of Hearth stones
> Tantalize."

Yes, Dear, I know very well how you feel.

Heard from Sis tonight. Poor girl sounds a bit lonely too for letters. You should write her more often perhaps. I hope I don't intimidate my own position when I say that. It is a real thrill to get your frequent letters during these days.

I must say Goodnight and very sweetest dreams. May the morrow bring good news that will greatly further plans for

Our Heavenly Love,

Bushy

(Over)

P.S. I forgot to mention that Phil had a call to be Asst. Pastor at New Providence. He turned it down because of work already begun out here. Hope he made the best choice, although I question it a bit.

March 28, 1944, Diary

One formation per day now—Nine o'clock to see that we are back from overnight passes. Up late this morning. After formation over to see Mrs. Heymans to get the results of her efforts. Very apologetic and said she did all that she could for me. Gave no direct word, but led me to believe that I am out. More orders came today and all except two of us who are to leave have their orders. New orders are for 89th Division, Camp Roberts. Poor guys! Rumors circulating tonight that I am staying, but I don't know. Jack's scheduled for the 89th. Rather a blow because Jack and Ted thought that surely they would go together. We wrote letters tonight, and about nine o'clock when out for a long walk. Through "Frat Row" and by President's home to Lagunita Lake. Very beautiful in the light of a new moon. I still a bit of difficulty keeping step with Ted. This involves an old theory of my that I developed at Maryville in some of my long walks there. Nevertheless, Ted is a very grand guy and I shall miss him greatly. We have fought this war together so far.

March 29, 1944, Diary

Telegram to Dotty: "Am staying. How soon can you leave for Frisco? Send schedule. Will have furlough until April 10th. Bring test. Making plans with Helen."

The first event of the day came this morning when Jack received wire that his mother is dying. He, of course, is rather broken up about it. Later he called and found that he can wait to come until Monday. The

second event came when I requested that Sgt. Sullivan call Classification and find my status. There was some delay, but about 1:30 I found that I am to stay. I immediately began to think of sending for Dotty. Ted was quick to strongly advise me to do so. The decision was not long in coming. I am sure of being here three months now, and three months together here will be a veritable paradise. Weather, surroundings, friends—everything one could ask for to start life together—except a bit nearer home. I sincerely believe that a Higher Power than the Army planned that I should stay. He is guiding and protecting His own. With strong faith in Him, I sent wire to Dotty to come at once. Also wired home. "He who hesitates is lost"—we must act with firmness and faith.

Said goodbye to Ted about 7 o'clock tonight. Poor Jack so broken up about the turn of events his mother, Ted leaving, etc. that he broke down completely. I comforted him as best I could and we prayed. Later Mr. Glayd came over to see him and took the two of us to his home. Good friend of Jack's and extremely nice. Although I only met them tonight, they insist that if Dotty and I are stranded for a room we can always have an extra bedroom which they have. Jack had very bad headache and so spent night with the Glayds. This closed a day full of implications for my future. I shall miss Ted a great deal, but Dotty's presence will dissolve my other sorrows. God could not have granted a finer helpmate.

March 30, 1944, Diary

Attended classes again and a fine feeling it was. The fellows who are leaving are little sad, and I can't blame them. Called Helen today and she is very much excited about the wedding. Jack's nerves are rather shot and he had another telegram telling him to come at once. He leaves by a plane 2:30 a.m. tomorrow. Glayds came up tonight with Jack and we drove out by the Lagunita. Very beautiful there. Wire from Dotty. She's coming!

March 31, 1944, Diary

I fear that Jack may be near a nervous breakdown. He is very emotional anyway, and he seemed very unstable last night. Poor fellow became very much attached to Ted and he misses him a great deal. Last classes for the quarter today. I got a pass after the last one to take Jack's radio to town, get blood test, and begin search for a room. *Registered with A.W.V.S. [American Women's Voluntary Services] but they say that they have twenty names for every one room or apartment which they have. Doesn't look too good. Perhaps Dotty can stay in a hotel until something turns up. Passes for the very few left tonight. Mena went to library—typical!—and I wrote a letter home are [and] began to get ready to move. Am beginning to get interested in this wedding I hear about. Hmm!*

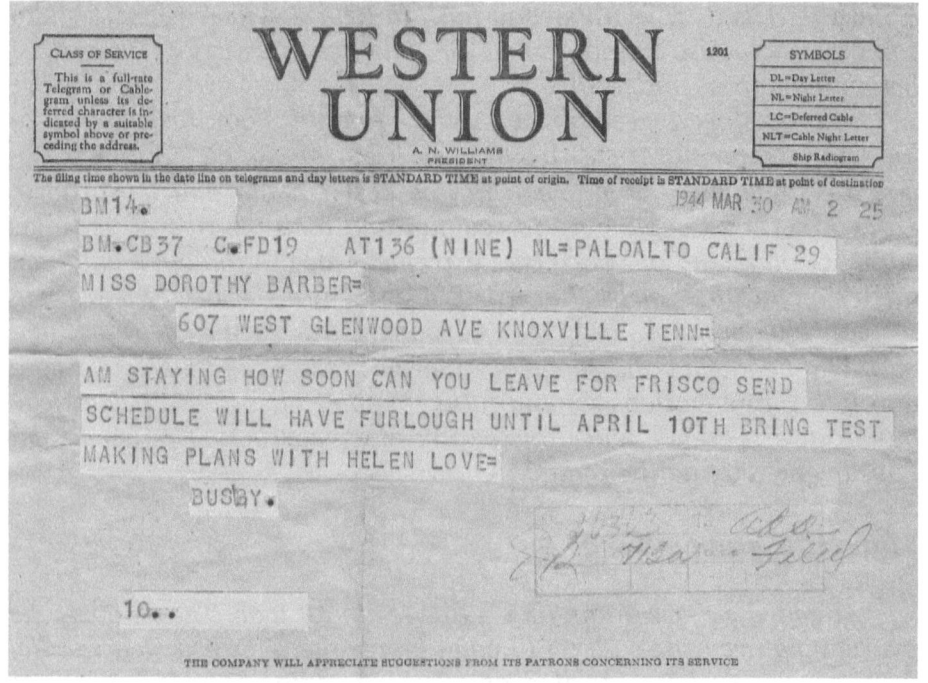

Telegram from Art to Dotty, March 30, 1944

April 1, 1944, Diary

Spent the morning moving over to Encina. Wasted a couple of hours waiting on someone to do something. Was reminded of the Army. (Hurry and wait.) Only about five hundred men left here and we shall stay in Encina. Amid much confusion furloughs were at last given out an hour or so late. Mine was to begin tomorrow morning but I was able to get it about five. Leib (another Dutchman) came around to tell me that he is leaving the rooms which he has. I went down to look at it and decided to take it on the spot. Paid rent in advance. Left about eight o'clock for San Jose and the Pratt's.

April 2, 1944, Diary

Arose late and just in time to attend Sun. S. and church with Helen and Mrs. Pratt. No young people's class, so Helen and I attended older group. Good discussion. Phil called this afternoon and I made arrangements to meet him in Centerville and go to San Anselmo. Working on plans with Helen for the wedding, but can't be too sure until know time of Dotty's arrival. Met Phil at nine. San Anselmo very late via Ferry. Popcorn and bed by 1 a.m.

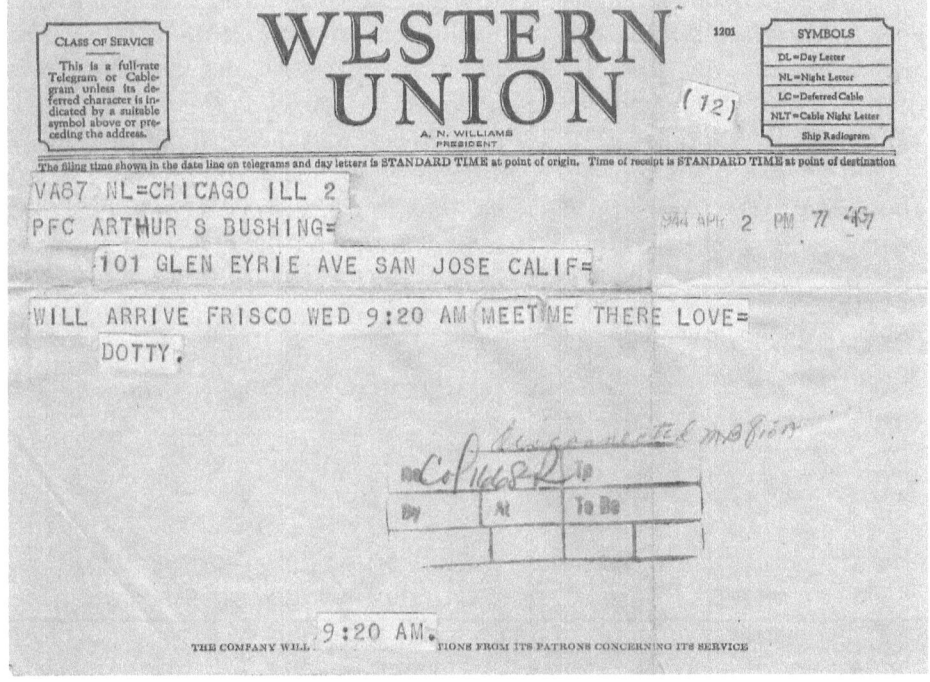

Telegram from Dotty to Art, April 2, 1944

April 3, 1944, Diary

Slept late and after breakfast to the Hill with Phil. I like the little town of San Anselmo very much. Tucked away among the hills, it reminds me of the "hills of home." The protective foliage of the myriad of trees seems to offer complete seculsion [seclusion] from the world around.

April 5, 1944, Diary

Arose at 6:30 in order to get off to early start to meet Dotty. Very interesting ride from Moffat Field into city with a New York lawyer— or I deduced the profession. He knows Thomas Dewey but thinks he made his position from breaks. Doesn't think he has world viewpoint and neither do I. Difficult to figure out how Dewey's popularity continues to grow even though he makes no statement of policy. [On November 7, 1944, President Franklin Roosevelt defeated Thomas E. Dewey to win his fourth term.] Willikie came in last in Wis. election yesterday of rep. to convention. This a severe loss since he has stumped that state. He seems to be loosing ground all the way around. Chased Dotty all over S.F. but found her at last. I was lost in a sort of seventh heaven to be able to be with her again. She came by coach and thus extremely tired. Saw Hal and Dick in Chicago. We came down to San Jose as soon as possible. It seems as though the events of the past ten months were merely a dream and that we have suddenly awakened to find ourselves together again. I feel humble and deeply grateful that I should have the love of one so truly wonderful and good. Dotty will lead me to new heights of achievement because of her inspiration.

* April 6, 1944, Diary

My day of days! We arose late in order that Dotty could get as much rest as possible. She slept well and very much refreshed after the long trip. After a good breakfast, we went to town to take care of last minute details—license, flowers, ring for me, etc. This afternoon she had to get her hair fixed. Phil, Peggy, and Phyllis arrived, but Johnny and Jane Astles couldn't make it. However, I was happy that Van Cise and "Tally" (his "beroemde red head") could be present. 6:30 was to be the fatal hour. 6:30 came; we were still rushing around. A photographer wanted $35 to come to the Church. Pfe.s [?] have to use

(Top row: Helen Tapp, Art Bushing, Dotty Bushing, Van Cise
Bottom row: Peggy, Phil Evaul, Tally—Van's girl.)

a box camera! Catching the last rays of the evening sun, we snapped a few pictures just before leaving for the Church. We rushed down. Peggy, Phyllis, and Mrs. Pratt came down by bus and arrived only in time to see us walk down the aisle. It was Phil's first ceremony and he was a bit nervous. Dotty and I too were new at the business, but our part was carried on with out serious mishap. I started a merry go round with Dotty's ring, but we finally got it on her finger. She had a bit of difficulty with mine and Van couldn't repress a laugh. It was best man by the way, and a good one he was. Phil was able to perform the entire ceremony with the exception of pronouncing us man and wife. That Dr. Saunders did. Although I listened to music my heart was singing, we did have organ numbers and a soloist. Our favorite "Through the Years" was played and "Because" was soloed. The ceremony was filled with meaning and I have never seen Dotty more beautiful. Her radiance filled me with inner warmth and joy. As I stood at the alter waiting for her to come down the aisle, my mind was not filled with a multitude of racing memories. I knew only one

Peggy & Phil, Art & Dotty, and Ted Kidder

thing, my mind was filled completely with the overwhelming love that exists between us. Much was added to the ceremony by the fact that we remained for the Easter Communion Service. It was our first act as man and wife. Dr. Saunders mentioned our presence and after the service was concluded we were made to feel completely at home. Congrats and congrats! After this we went out to the Pratt's again for a little party—food, cake, etc. Here we received some very nice presents. The whole gang was very wonderful to us. Amid a shower of rice we left and Phil, Peggy, Helen, Van & Tally bringing us to our "HOME" on Waverley. Phil showered remaining rice on Van & Tally at the bus.

Sunday, April 9, 1944, Diary

As per usual we slept late this morning but arose in time to get to a very find Easter Service at the First Presbyterian. Dr. Everett Clay Thomson, the minister. He seems to combine the sounding thinking of Dr. Orr, the effective presentation of Dr. Lloyd with more power than anyone I have heard in a long while. Broke all tradition by seeing

"[The] Song of Bernadette" with Jennifer Jones (Academy Award Winner this yr.) Excellent show. [Dotty explained in an interview, February 2020, that it was not acceptable to go the movies on the Sabbath. But the two of them felt that because this was a movie about the life of a Saint, that it was all right, especially this being their honeymoon.]

```
Knoxville News Sentinel, Living Department
WWII Wedding Stories
P. O. 59038
Knoxville, TN 37902

June 1944, a soldier in the Army Specialized Training Program
(ASTP) at Stanford University writes to his fiancee in Knoxville to
ask if she can come West for their long-planned wedding.   He
expects to be in training for another six months. The bride-to-be
and her mother make hasty preparations and secure a Pullman
reservation.   A few days before departure, word comes that the
soldier's name has appeared on a list to ship out.  Plans canceled.
     Shortly before his one-week break, orders change, and the
soldier is to stay for at least one more quarter.  Telephone calls,
telegrams, and she boards a train San Francisco via Chicago--no
Pullman reservation this time.
     Two trains from Chicago to SF, one via LA, one direct.  Which
train station?   Confusion regarding timetable.   Soldier calls
mutual friend in San Jose; so does the weary traveler.  Meet at the
Greyhound station for the ride to San Jose.  Again, two stations.
Again, soldier picks the wrong one, More telephone calls to mutual
friend; soldier and handful of flowers are in a state of wilt.  The
long day is Wednesday.
     Next day the downtown Presbyterian Church in San Jose is
decorated for 7:00 P. M. Maundy Thursday service.  Six o'clock a
small party appears.   A young minister, graduate of Maryville
College, addresses questions to bride and groom--both MC graduates.
Matron of honor, MC, classmate of bride.   Another soldier and
classmate of groom is best man.  One of three people attending is
likewise a Maryville College graduate.
     Four children, seven grandchildren, and fifty-one years later,
we laugh at those confusing hours and days.  Not so in June 1944.

Dorothy Barber Bushing
Arthur S. Bushing

713 Jones Avenue
Maryville, TN  37804

982-2787
```

[An article submitted by them about their wedding, possibly misdated.]

379

[As you'll notice, Art and Dotty are now together so they have little need to write all those letters. Dotty encourages him to continue with his writing though, so the diary entries increase.]

April 10, 1944, Diary

Furlough ended and back to work. Arrived in time for reville [reveille] and found out later that I was due last night. No one seemed to know the difference. Am rooming with Lillywhite and Kreisler. Before class someone came to tell me of a swell offer here on the campus for Dotty—room board, $80 per month for part time work. Didn't know details but called lady and then called Dotty. She visited the place (Gerona Rd.) and decided to take it, moving this afternoon. Fast work! I don't like to leave our little place on Waverley St. but this seems like a good opportunity. Three small children (one, two, and three years of age) in the home of Prof. Guerrard (?sp) Great advantage to be here on campus. Went over for a few minutes tonight to see Dotty. Not to save that I find Mrs. Guerrard completely to my liking. She is the type that wants things done her way. Honey-dripped words.

May 11, 1944, Diary

Aunt Emma sent $10 money order as wedding gift today. Certainly wonderful of her. I am getting a picture made for her which I shall send shortly.

May 12, 1944, Diary

My ego given a boost today when I received mention in The Stanford Daily for a recent physical efficiency test. I ranked seventh it seems. Letter from Bill (Hargrave) today. Still in Portland, he has been assigned to his ship "USS Alpine." Seems to like it and expects to leave at any time. Up to his old tricks of finding nice girls that he "really falls for." To put it mildly, he's fickle, but solid gold nonetheless.

Dotty went down to Helen's this morning to stay with her while her mother is away.

May 13, 1944, Diary

Parade today with our '03's Asked for early pass and was excused from inspection. Left for San Jose at 3:30 and arrived at the Pratt's before 5. Road with sailor on way to L.A. to see Mother he hadn't seen in two years. Pratt's have a wonderful little home six miles out of town in the foothills. Read some good stuff that Roland has written. I had no hope that Ted would be able to get away, but the lucky guy did. Arrived about 11:30. We talked, sang etc. until 2 a.m. He picked up iron for us from same fellow going to P.O.E. Grand to see him once more. He leaves the 20th for Benning. Jack F. May get in cryptography. Air Corp taken out of Inf. and sent back. Ted thinks something cooking for us.

May 14, 1944, Dairy

Up late and good breakfast (a la wife) with Dotty and Ted. Rain began about noon. We prepared picnic anyway and Phil & Peggy brought food. Ate on the floor before glowing fire. Later drove up a couple of miles to Alum Rock Park. Very nice place. Rushed Ted to five o'clock bus and I said goodbye to Phil & Peggy and hitchhiked back to school. Dotty staying with Helen next week. Hated to say so long for last time to these folks. Had lots of fun with them.

May 20, 1944, Diary

Speech this morning in Dutch class. We prepared papers and read them, but this not to Mrs. Heyman's liking. Drilled this afternoon with '03's is good old Camp Roberts style with lots of "gold brickking." Nominal inspection and off by 3:40. Hitchhiked down to San Jose with usual good luck. Got a big kick out of mowing Pratt's lawn tonight. It took me back to days when I had my own lawn to mow and also of the days ahead. Spent evening studying Dutch while Dotty made a skirt and Helen packed.

May 21, 1944, Diary

Helen arose early to get to Sunday school. Dotty and I got up in time to get to Church. We ate in town and then returned home. Had but little time to get our things together and go back to town for bus. Helen going to Centerville tonight and then leaves tomorrow with Phil 'n family for East. Letter from Van Cise tonight. He's in Newport News, Va., but misses Calif. and "Tally" I think. Able to write long letter home tonight.

May 22, 1944, Diary

No place like the Army for juicy rumors. Wing, one of the Dutchmen, is the son of a high ranking officer in the Ninth Service Com. in Utah. His mother writes that we are to be used in "radio teams"—what that involves I have no idea. She is supposed to have known about the number staying after April 1st long before it became official. This, of course, adds prestige to the rumor. Today marks the beginning of the second half of the quarter so we should know something within a few weeks.

Dotty came up tonight for supper and we studied in the Ed. Lib. The elevator in that building has proven interesting to us. Two page letter from Dad that made us happy to receive. Luther York reported to Army within recent weeks. 15 day auditing job just completed on S.S.S. [Selective Service System] work in the office. Still the work piles up for Mother and Dad. [Luther York was the son of Joseph Marion York, Sgt. Alvin C. York's brother.]

Again assigned job of section leader. No particular joy in that but neither is there too much work. No "C.2." and that's something.

May 23, 1944, Diary

Cpl. MacMillan, a former Dutchman, returned to the campus today to tell us of Dutch radio teams being trained in Camp Crowder. This follows along same lines as rumor that started yesterday. Learned from a 7-L Chinese student that men were called out last July for the same work and some are still in Crowder—others are in Italy with mobile broadcasting units. The plot thickens.

Dutch assignments lately have been utterly impossible—100 word vocal to learn, five stron [possibly "strong"] verbs with myriad of uses, prepositions, long translation, Washington lessons, etc. Mrs. Heymen's joining the Dutch WACS and leaves soon for Georgia.

May 24, 1944, Diary

Big Dutch test today—two hours of sentences and story to write. Not as difficult as I expected. Relief to have it done. Now we can begin *to worry about Area exam Friday. Parade this evening for those getting good conduct ribbons. We get of at 1:30 on Sat. Dotty came up and we studied in the library tonight.*

May 25, 1944, Diary

Worked 3 hours this afternoon on Area. Dotty had supper with me but returned home. Didn't go home tonight but stayed here to study. Working very hard to get a decent grade in area for a change.

May 26, 1944, Diary

I came away from the Area test with the feeling that I had given the teachers what they wanted. Material largely on Fejos lectures and probably the best test that we have had. A great relief to be through with it. Rather inspired to be asked to pitch for the Dutch team in our softball game with Chinese today. We won. Dotty up for supper. Through study at 7:30 under the new system. We went home and I got back for bed-check. Lucky boys with class "A" passes off from 7:30 until tomorrow morning.

My old trouble is back. Constant headaches for past six weeks. I hesitate to go to doctor but if it keeps up I suppose I should. Am beginning to have difficulty with sleep again, and study is seriously hampered. Jack says I'll get a C.D.D. [Certificate of Disability for Discharge] but I don't want that. I have a lot of pride and it would hard to stomach a discharge.

May 27, 1944, Diary

Had a couple of hours of Dutch from a Dutchman connected with broadcasting from S.F. Off at 1:30 as a result of Wed. parade. Met Dotty at the station and we took 1:45 bus for Frisco. Upon arrival we went out to Golden Gate Park and hurried through Young's Museum and the Chinese Tea Garden. The latter has the greatest variety of flora found in the country I am told. Back in town we killed an hour in a hotel lobby before eating. After supper to the Opera House [War Memorial Opera House] for the Ballet—"Chopinade," (classic), "The Triumph of Hope" (premiere By Jean de Botton) and "Winter Carnival." The modernistic "Triumph" was impressive but it left a bad taste in the mouth. The Hades scene was rather raw. However, as a whole the program was very fine. Lighting effects (rainbow, smoke rising, etc.) very well done in "Triumph." Missed bus at 11:30 and had to wait until 12:40. Home by 2:30. I was so tired that I slept on Dotty's shoulder most of the way. We didn't get up until 1:30 in the afternoon. Tch, Tch.

May 29, 1944, Diary

After six weeks of difficulty with my head, I decided to go on sick call today. The doctor offered little help. Said I had right to go to hospital but probably no help to be gained. Intimate C.D.D. and in general made me feel like a heel. Hang it all, I have the trouble! My memory is hampered and my study is seriously restricted. I intend to hold on as long as possible before going to the hospital—if it comes to that. Time this week reports that the Army has turned down 1,340,000 men for neuropsychiatric causes and given 216,000 discharges. "Psychoneurotics are high-strung, nervous people who are not crazy but who cannot face certain difficulties without developing bothersome (you said it!) symptoms such as headaches, tiredness, weakness, tremors, fears, insomnia, depression, obsessions, feelings of guilt."

June 2, 1944, Diary

Pitched again today in our last softball game. We won easy victory from ERC's. Rainy with clouds, reminding me of fickle E. Tenn [East Tennessee] weather. Off at seven-thirty tonight. Off at seven-thirty, and to Waverley. Surprised Dotty at 10 o'clock by telling her that I was staying home. My roommate C.P. and a good-egg as O.D. Studied for a bit of instruction in extended order drill tomorrow. I'm reminded of the dear old infantry days.

Far more important for me was a test in Dutch today. Three of us were called into [Mrs.]... Heymen's office one at a time. The entire Dutch faculty was there and I was given a short article to read. After five minutes I was asked to tell the story in Dutch in my own words. Not too difficult but I naturally made mistakes. I find that in such a spot I speak from my reflexes—not by clear thought processes. No explanation was given but perhaps another elimination contest is taking place. I think I am doing almost as much as I can. One can do little more.

June 3, 1944, Diary

I was asked yesterday to help with instruction in extended order drill. Enjoyed it very much and avoided a march which my platoon made. Off at three-thirty. Went directly home for quiet evening.

* June 6, 1944, Diary

D-DAY!

Shouting awakened me before reveille this morning. I opened one eye, looked at my watch and turned over. "Darn those guys," I thought. Reveille sounded and I arose. Fog over the Bay cut off the sunlight and I shivered a bit. I crossed the room and closed the windows. More noise in the hall—I felt a tension in the air that foretold important news. I heard the word "Invasion"! D-Day was here.

Great moments in history cannot be felt with their full import by those experiencing them. The entire world holds its breath while our men storm the beaches of France; the very earth's core will shake with the onslaught against fortress Europe. We wait and pray.

Directed by "Ike" Eisenhower and lead by "Monty" Montgomery, our forces struck in the early hours of the morning against the beaches between Le Harve and Cherbug [Cherbourg]. 11,500 planes blanketed the attack and only 50 Nazi planes seen in first 24 hrs. 4,000 ships used and only two destroyers and 1 PT boat reported lost. Germans surprised and driven inland. Paratroops (30,000 reported) landed around Caen. It was revealed tonight that invasion plans delayed 24 hrs. due to bad weather in channel. Capt. Brown has recommended 35 of us for OCS—4 from my Dutch section.

D-DAY!

CLEAR
CLOUDY
RAIN
SNOW

Shouting awakened me before reveille this morning. I opened one eye, looked at my watch and turned over. "Darn those guys," I thought. Reveille sounded and I arose. Leguen the Kay put off the sunlight and I shivered a bit. I crossed the room and closed the windows. More noise in the hall — I felt a tension in the air that foretold important news. I heard the word "Invasion." D-Day was here.

Great moments in history can not be felt with their full import by those experiencing them. The entire world holds its breath while our men storm the beaches of France; the very earths core will shake with the onslaught against fortress Europe. We wait and pray.

Directed by "Ike" Eisenhower and led by "Monty" Montgomery, our forces struck in the early hours of the morning against the beachs between Le Havre and Cherbourg. 11,000 planes launched the attack and only 50 Nazi planes seen in first 24 hrs. 4,000 ships used and only two destroyers and 1 PT boat reported lost. Germans surprised and driven inland. Para troops (30,000 reported) landed around Caen. It was revealed tonight that invasion been delayed 24 hrs. due to bad weather in channel. Capt. Brown has recommended 35 of us for OCS & from my Dutch section.

Art's actual entry into his diary, June 6, 1944

June 8, 1944, Diary

Almost no news of specific sort is being released concerning the invasion. It is becoming evident that the first reports were rather overdone. Although our bombers have done a tremendous job in softing up the enemy positions, stiff enemy resistance met our landings. In some cases the first wave was completely wiped out. There is tough fighting ahead, but I think it entirely within the realm of possibility that we can crush the bleeding Nazi machine in twelve to fifteen weeks. Russia has amassed tremendous strength to the East. Air Power will be decisive now as we destroy the armies of the Reich one by one. Most news so far has been from German sources, and most of it amazingly accurate—interspersed, however, with highly spiced propaganda punches. Seems to be new technique.

Dotty up tonight. We went home at 9:30. She's beginning work on my Army scrapbook. Samarriet and "Mac" at home on vacation.

* June 9, 1944, Diary

Joel Lillywhite, my roommate, represents an extremely complex character. Brilliant in mind, very nervous, highly emotional, his ideas, opinions, and feelings change as constantly and as rapidly as the famous E. Tenn. weather in spring time. He has a beautiful wife whom he professes to love very much. I think he does. Yet a couple of days ago he broached an acquaintance with a Stanford girl. The first day or two he spoke of "beautiful friendship." His feelings were whipped into passion and the girl seems to have felt likewise. She, being somewhat leveled-headed put a stop to the whole affair, but it was against his wishes and desires. The fellow is so highly impulsive and emotional, that he refuses to consider in a rational manner the results of impetuous action. I have a new insight into the lives of such men as Byron, Keats, Poe and others. [Lord Byron, John Keats, & Edgar Allan Poe.] Here is a man who finds love (his sort) as an ultimate worth any price.

June 14, 1944, Diary

Large forces of the new B-29's, (a super-super bomber) bombed Japan proper from bases in China. Almost no details given as yet. Supposed to be twice the size of the Fortress, the new bomber has a range which enables it to make a trip from N.Y. to Europe and return.

This mission marks merely the first in a long series of raids which will crush Japan to her knees.

June 15, 1944, Diary

Our forces in the Pacific have scored a great blow against the Japs with a landing on Saipan—1,449 miles from Japan itself. From Guadalcanal we began our long drive back. At first it was island by island but soon we began island hopping. Hollandia, a hundred miles up the New Guinea coast; Byak, three hundred and fifty, now Saipan, another thousand miles. From this base we can cut off Southern Asia and the wealth of supplies which it affords. From there we can take the Philippines and begin intensive operations against Japan proper.

June 16, 1944, Diary

Big area exam today. As usual the fellows griping about it. It was a rather difficult test and I felt that I did extremely poorly on it. Upon my return to Encina I went to the P.X. for cup of coffee. One of the fellows called me out saying that someone was looking for me. Imagine my surprise when I found Miss Katherine Davies outside. She is visiting with her sister-in-law in Santa Cruz and came to Palo Alto this afternoon. Luckily I had a free hour and we talked Maryville at a rapid rate. Cadets are leaving soon and I guess "The Hill" will become a girl's school. Later Miss Davies went down to see Dotty. Certainly wonderful to see someone directly from Maryville.

Finished up Physical Fitness test today with improvements in almost everything. Total of 625 points out of 700 possible. With anything above 585 we can choose our own sport next term. Hope I can play tennis.

June 17, 1944, Diary

I bought a bond in the Fifth Drive and thus got an early pass lasting until Monday morning. Col. Eden at first rejected the idea, but finally came through. Dotty and I did our first entertaining tonight. Invited Earl and Betty Russell to come down for the evening. Earl is 6-A Dutch and leaves at the end of the term. He's a crazy combination between Schwarzwalder and Hargrave, but lots of fun. We had a enjoyable evening looking at pictures, playing the player piano, etc. They missed the last bus and had to take a taxi.

June 18, 1944, Diary

Slept late as usual on Sun morning. However, we did get up to the Stanford Chapel for Church Service. The head of the Dept. of religion here, Dr. _____ [Art left this blank.] gave the sermon. Very good.

June 20, 1944, Diary

Rather simple Dutch test today—six sentences and a letter to write. This winds up my exams for the quarter and I have decided to go to the hospital with my headaches. This marks ten weeks of daily headaches. If the psychiatrists and Jack are correct, I may as well face facts and accept them. If they are wrong, I also want to know and find the course if possible. I still can't convince myself that the difficulty is neuroses. I have every reason to be happy and completely adjusted to Army life. However, if the case is mental, I am certainly better adjusted to the idea psychologically.

June 21, 1944, Diary

Great naval engagement reported off the Philippines. Supposed to have been in progress since Monday, but almost no details released as yet. Our fleet has been trying for months to boot the Japs out. Perhaps this is the big battle we've been waiting for. If so it may be all important. To loose [lose] could lengthen the war by many months; to win would likewise shorten it. Fighting continues on Saipan and we are making progress.

Spent the morning in the dispensary. My headaches have continued for ten weeks and I must get something done. The doctor was extremely nice and made several attempts to find my trouble. Decided to send me to Dibble for Consultation. At Dibble was sent to EENT [Eye, Ear, Nose and Throat]. My classes are too strong, but Dr. Very vague and told me to return next week. Think we may get to the bottom of my trouble. 'Twould be a wonderful relief to find physical cause and then the remedy. Truck left me and I hitch-hiked back to eat supper with Dotty.

June 22, 1944, Diary

Progress is being made in Normandy with the Germans putting up stiff resistance in Cherbourg. We have been fighting in and around the city for a couple of days. In Italy the Nazis retreat in a near-rout. They are expected to make a stand on a line running through Florence, but the Allied forces are chewing them to bits as the [they] retreat.

June 23, 1944, Diary

My very good friend Lt. McCoy gave me an overnight pass tonight off at seven-thirty. All fellows filling out new allotments get 12 o'clock passes tomorrow and those buying a bond get both early and late passes. This means that I will not have to report until Monday morning 6:30. It also means that I will have four nights in a row at home. Not bad. Dotty heard lately from a couple in Texas. Man is a cadet and gets week-ends off sometimes. I'm extremely lucky even if I don't have class A pass.

Lt. McCoy by the way is to be C.O. next quarter. Most of the fellows are going to be terribly disappointed, but he's been swell to me.

Dotty went to S.F. today in an attempt to get reservations in Yosemite for our furlough. Everything taken through August. At least we are lucky to have an invitation to spend the week near Santa Cruz.

June 24, 1944, Diary

Early pass again as a result of bond purchase. Both Dotty and I had to go to Doctor with a very bad throat. I realize how much I get from the Army when her bill was about $7.00—mine nothing. Had supper in Chinese restaurant with Earl and Betty Russell. Afterward we went to the place on the campus. Spent most of the evening listening to them play—they are almost as good as Carl and Floty. Our throats still bad and we left early.

Interviewed today by Major from O.S.S. He's finding our various qualifications. I'm a possible cryptographer he says.

June 25, 1944, Diary

We decided it wise to spend the day at home to doctor our throats. Spent the entire day eating, sleeping, and reading a little. Dotty can prepare a wonderful meal with our two hot plates and a toaster, and so we eat royally.

June 26, 1944, Diary

Republican convention opened in Chicago this morning. There seems to be few questions to settle. Bricker still fighting hard, but Dewey seems a sure bet. (The band wagon is rolling.) Gov. Warren of Calif. who will make the welcoming address will probably be nominated for Dewey's running-mate.

June 28, 1944, Diary

Thomas Dewey was nominated in Chicago by the Rep. Conventions on the first ballot—one vote dissenting and that for MacArthur. Gov. Bricker nominated as running mate by unanimous vote after his withdrawal from the presidential race. Gov. Warren stopped a move to draft him for the second post by affirming his duty to his job in Calif.

July 1, 1944, Diary

Didn't have to return to school till 8:00 and so had breakfast at home. Finished my packing and stored my bags. After inspection stopped by Earl Russell's to pick up some food they sold us. Said goodbye to them and then went home to get our things ready for vacation. Planned to leave on 2:40 bus, but it was filled. No more standing room allowed. Had to wait until almost 5:00. Arrived at Mt. Hermon about 7:30. Mrs. Boyd brought us to our cabin, high above the road, secluded, an almost perfect view. We are carried away with the spot. We are sleeping in the open air on the porch.

July 4, 1944, Diary

Beautiful day and we decided to visit "Big Trees" only a short distance from our cabin. We arose relatively early—any time before 9 o'clock is early this week—and had breakfast. We then prepared a *lunch and put it in the knapsack. Making our own trail we went over the ridge back of our cabin and down to the railroad track.*

July 9, 1944, Diary

Up in time to clean up cabin completely. It was very hard to leave our first vacation home, but we took our things down to the Boyd's before noon and enjoyed our Sunday dinner with them. They have certainly been very nice to us. At bus stop more than twenty people. Two seats and no standing. We got the seats by luck. Got back to Stanford late but supply job awaiting me.

July 14, 1944, Diary

The great Russia drive now 22 days old—has reached a point only 12 milers from East Prussia. Last Sunday when we returned from Mt. Herman the Germans were more than 100 miles away. This all out drive is to be the last offensive needed to crack the German machine it seems.

Today Joe Kaelber and Jean Ziemer were married in First Presby. Church. Dotty was attendant and Bob Youngblood best man. After ceremony we went out to supper with Mr. and Mrs. Tolley.

July 18, 1944, Diary

Two ammunition ships blew up at Port Chicago last night at 10:19. The port is in the Bay Area North of S.F. About 350 reported dead. This is by far the greatest catastrophe of the war on the home front. The force of the explosion felt in Palo Alto. [Port Chicago Disaster]

July 19, 1944, Diary

Russians in East Prussia tonight.

July 20, 1944, Diary

After several days of heavy bombing and shelling of Guam, our forces landed on the island today. No details as yet fourth coming. On Monday it was learned that Tojo [Tōjō Hideki] had stepped down from his position of Prime Minister. This was to be expected following the long succession of reverses. Today the entire cabinet resigned. This is in conformity with Japanese politics, but it does show the strain of our continued victories. The startling news came from Germany. An attempt was made today on the life of Adolf Hitler. Internal dissention [dissension] was merely rumor up to now.

July 25, 1944, Diary

Events are moving at ever increasing rate. Germany is making an all out attempt to mobilize every available bit power to try to halt the rising tide of the Allied forces. 3000 planes proceeded to a limited attack in Normandy. The Russians open up new fronts almost daily. Today along the the entire 1000 mi. front the battle rages. 500,000 men of the Nazi machine have been lost to the red armies. They are within 50 miles of Warsaw. This city is being evacuated it is reported. The last German has been driven from Russian soil. It is becoming evident that the cleavage within Ger. is far wider than it was supposed. The attempt on Hitler's life is supposed to have been known for two weeks by the Gestapo. A violent blood purge is being carried on with many top military men being shot before the familiar firing squad.

July 28, 1944, Diary

Russians are within 20 miles of Warsaw tonight and driving on.

August 28, 1944, Diary

In Age of Reason, Paine says, "That which is now called natural philosophy, embracing the whole circle of science... is the study of the works of God, and of the power and wisdom of God in his works, and is the true theology." While I cannot go all the way with his thoughts, I do think that Paine is striking at a theory which I have long held. For centuries science and religion have appeared to be diametrically opposed to each other. It is my belief that these two are both in possession of partial truth. Like my story of the three blind men and the elephant; like the two legs of the triangle both leading upward to the apex. There is but one Truth and it is all inclusive.

August 2, 1944, Diary

For the first time in Dutch class I gave this speech without first writing it out in Dutch and using notes in Dutch. Just cast Harper of Macassar from paper written by 7-L men last quarter. Other fellows have been doing this for several weeks. Malay test back. Very poor test as attested by several perfect papers and many with only 1 or 2. I made 3 and had a B for my efforts. Wish very much it could have been an A. my helpful roommates (Phil Katz and Joe Kaelber) removed my two month old mustache by force. Dotty likes it much better gone. As for me—! Spent three hours on salvage and exchange. Good helpers.

Our forces have advance 30 miles in the last 24 hrs. No resistance being met. Russia drives ever closer to Germany. Germans reported evacuating southern Finland. 4,735 Britons killed by robot bombs. 1 million evacuated from London. Turkey breaks diplomatic relations w. Ger. [with Germany]

August 5, 1944, Diary

Big news from Ted Kidder today. He's working as file clerk in reg. hq. in Ft. Benning. Good job with evenings free. He's planning to be married about the middle of the month. I'm very happy for him. Already has a room, and his Dad, on vacation in Knoxville, can perform the ceremony. Oh joy!

Am. [American] tanks swept 75 miles today to reach Brest and our troops have swept S. on the Brittany peninsula to reach the Loire R. [river]

August 6, 1944, Diary

To church this morning to hear Dr. Beard, Pres. of St. Theological Sem. Very fine sermon. After a quick lunch we took train to So. S.F. and Tally's (Van Cise girl friend). Had swell dinner cooked by Tally. Her parents certainly are crazy about Van. I think that she is also. The three of us we [went] to the Ice Follies. Very beautiful. Returned home by bus very late. (By buying $7.50 in stamps I had Sun. night pass.

August 7, 1944, Diary

Taken completely by surprise today when Gaston Garrett (S/Sgt.) stopped by to see me on his way back to Santa Maria air base. He is *the first home towner that I have seen since I left. Certainly wonderful to see and talk to him.*

August 12, 1944, Diary

"Tally" Betten court (Van Cise's "red head") came down for the week-end. We saw "Going My Way" with Bing Crosby tonight. Picture fair. Tally our first overnight guest. I slept with great comfort on mattress on floor.

August 13, 1944, Diary

After big breakfast took Tally up to Stanford. Walked up to Ex-Pres. Hoover's home, and around the quad. Returned for dinner in the mid-afternoon. Later relaxed in backyard and talked.

Art & Dotty

August 16, 1944, Diary

Good game of tennis with a freshman who is trying to decide whether to major in English or science. I can sympathize with him. I played him once before and in one 6-0. Today 7-5 in his favor. My game is improving.

Had terrific stomach [ache] after supper tonight, but soon passed away. Went to Eda Bldg. to work in Dotty's office. Terrific pain in right side dvl-ped [developed]. I got to Encina slowly and sent Dotty home. Phil called doctor and Joe got ice-pack. Capt. McCoy came in to see me & Maria Flowerman stayed around. Doctor assured me that I didn't have appendecitus. He didn't know what the trouble was.

August 17, 1944, Diary

Slept well last night and got up for reveille. After classes were finished at three o'clock, I went over to dispensary for a check. Queer feeling in my side all day. Found that I was supposed to be confined to quarters all day.
Blood count taken and found high (11,200) Rushed to Dibble. Just time to see Dotty before I left. She rushed over from work. Shoved in Ward 8 and another blood count taken. Rushed to operating room, and everything done by 9:30. Had spinal anthestic [anesthetic] and awake during entire operation. Some fun!

August 18, 1944, Diary

Feeling fine today.

August 20, 1944, Diary

Eddie Cantor here today. I was rolled to the adjoining ward where I observed the little show he put. His famous eyes remind me of those of a cow. [Eddie Cantor was a comedian and singer performing on stage, radio, and film.]

August 21, 1944, Diary

Allied forces toys before Paris waiting into an instance notice to take the city. Revolts are breaking out in Paris and it may be that the French can take their capital without help. The avowed purpose of the

Allied forces is to destroy the German Army—that it is doing. Thousands upon thousands of Germans are dying before the mighty onslaught. France is being severed and thousands more Germans are being trapped. Leval is fleeing and reported to be attempting to gain safety within Switzerland. Montgomary said today that the end is in sight. B-29's blasted Yzwatz twice yesterday.

Dotty and Jean to see me today. Gee, it's wonderful to see Dotty each day while I'm getting well. She gets more beautiful each passing day.

Ninth Sen. Com, is supposed to be making plans to use our Dutch training.

August 23, 1944, Diary

Aug 23rd may go down as second only in importance thus far to D-Day. 50 thousand French patriots liberated Paris today (report time clocked 6:30 am EST) French Police Force assisted in final defeat of Nazi forces. The Tri-Color again makes Paris a free city. Marsailles also was liberated today and the Allied forces have driven 140 north from the beach heads in S. France. Today Roumania signed a peace treaty with Russia and the Allied govts. Bulgaria will follow suit momentarily. Tito holds most of Yugoslavia and thus the Balkans are virtually freed. Roumanian troops are already reported clashing with the former Nazi "friends." The road is opened for Rus to drive against Hungary. I predict that German [Germany] will fall within two weeks.

At home plans are going full speed ahead at Dumbarton Oaks to map a world organization that will provide a firm basis for world cooperation. Dulles, who will likely be Sec. of State under Dewey, is confirming with Cordell Hull on Foreign matters. Ted Pratt in OCS. Very happy. Today Dotty & I called Helen and Phil from my bed—new service of Telephone Co.

August 24, 1944, Diary

The situation in France seems to be very much confused. The Germans did not honor the armistice and today are fighting again. Gen. Bradley has sent forces in to help the French, but the exact situation is not known. Rumania is reported to be fighting the Nazis in the Balkans. Bulgaria is moving to reach a peace agreement with Rus [Russia], and Hungary is suffering "political cramps." Indications are that Rus will give Transylvania to Rumania and take Bessarabia. At home Vice-Ch. Wilson of WPB resigned today—this resulted from squabble with Production Chief Nelson.

Talked with Sgt. back from N. Guiena [Guinea]. He says we have had troops in Philippines since April. "Alamo Rangers" or some such name. [Alamo Scouts—the Sixth Army Special Reconnaissance Unit.] Big secret. Aussies, Am, Japanese & Melanesiens [Melanesians] go in to map the territory.

I got up for the first time today. Spent most of my time in the "Kamar Kechil [kamar kecil means the bathroom or toilet]." Used wheelchair a bit. Dotty comes every day.

August 25, 1944, Diary

Big news today is that the Germans are retreating from the Calais coastal area from where wanton damage has been done on London by robot bombs. At least 3 1/2 million had been evacuated from London as a result of these bombings. The big drive against German herself seems to be in the offing Tri-part: treaty signed by U. S., Br., and free Fr. recognizing De Gaulle as civil administrator. Big blow in Pacific against Philippines expected soon. Army expects defeat of Ger. by Oct 1st but Navy expects war in Pacific to last until end of 1945.

Dotty and Jean out to see me today. They had x-ray fearing a contact from Mr. De Fine who is in hospital with very bad T.B. So far I am getting to keep my private room with a private bath included. This irregular but head nurse wise. Walked around a bit today, but still feel a bit weak. We have fewer than 20 patients in this ward and everything very lax. Some big-time band here today—Jan Graeba (?) [Jan Garber] & Merrimacs.

August 26, 1944, Diary

Time reports on book by Dr. Trueblood of Stanford—The Predicament of Modern Man. "The world is sick and the disease is skepticism. But now, unlike the Victorian era, it...man's skepticism of man... A group of 50 really devoted Christians who are not in the least bit apologetic and who are willing to make the spread of the gospel their first interest would affect mightily any campus in the country... The same can be said of an average town." (See Special Data Page at end of month.

Helen, Phil Katz and Dotty to see me today. Helen up for the week-end. I was up almost all day feeling fine.

August 27, 1944, Diary

To church this morning with my Filippino friend. Bored with sermon by sincere but satisfied Chaplin. Went to first chow in the mess hall. Phil, Peggy, and Phyllis came over and had lunch with Dotty and Helen. All came out to the hospital about three bringing a big watermelon. We went out under the trees to eat it. Kleenix very scarce but I was able to get it here in the PX for the girls.

August 28, 1944, Diary

As a follow-up for renewed thought concerning religion (see Sat. & Sun. comments, I began tonight to read The Age of Reason by Tom Paine. Breaking away from orthodox belief, he expresses his disbelief in any church that he knows. "My own mind is my own church." He quotes Addison paraphrasing of the 19th Ps. which ends... "The hand that made us is divine." What more does man want to know than this, he asks. (cf. Whitman later). In many ways I find fault with Paine's "reason", but it is highly interesting and thought provoking. This thought was brought to my mind: The church is not an end in itself, but should be only an instrument which aids the individual in finding a satisfactory answer to the impinging hail of relig. and moral questions. Every man to have a firm religious faith, must find that faith through a never ending search for moral truth and religious conviction.

Good to see Dotty-alone-today. To library tonight; read and typed letter home.

August 29, 1944, Diary

Got a pass today at 13:00. Dressed a [and] caught Stanford truck. Saw a number of the fellows back at school. Capt. McCoy kindly brought Dotty and me home. Wonderful to be home. Dotty cooked delicious meal for the two of us. Had a lot of mail for the two of us. Long letter from Bill Hargrave. My last letter took from June 23 to Aug. 10th to reach him. He's Lt. (j.g.) [?] now. Still having girl trouble. Got back to hospital 11:45 feeling far better than when I left. My strength is returning.

August 30, 1944, Diary

Am doing far too little study and am getting to the point where I enjoy a bit too much my life of relative inactivity. Am going to occupational therapy daily as required, but doing little of value. It is actually a place where when can find many things to occupy the time —constructive things at that. I'm getting quite well although I foolishly jumped tonight to turn on a light. Hope there 's no repercussions. Dotty and I are out this afternoon. I spent two hours and a half typing seven pages to Bill Hargrave.

We should be making a landing on Philippines any day now. Probably shortly thereafter a landing on Formosa. Bulgaria trying to negotiate peace. We have drive across Marne, one nearing Belgium border, and one into Pas-de-Calais robot bomb area. Germany will fold suddenly. Ploiesti fields taken by Rus. today.

August 31, 1944, Diary

Today it was reported that we have suffered casualties amounting to 343,491 thus far. However, Russia has suffered 5 million, China 5 to 9 million, Gr. Britain 800,000. Reports today indicate that German may collapse at any moment. Eisenhower says she will fall this year—this now seems very mild indeed. Rus. rushed into Bucharest today. Br. captured Amiens, isolating 100 mi. of robot bomb coast. 400,000 Ger. casualties in north Fr. since invasion, and drive five days ahead of schedule. Almost all of Slovakia reported in hands of Czech patriots. Robot bombs continue. Robt. Murphy [Robert Daniel Murphy], who handled diplomatic relations in N. Africa with Vichy, has been sent to London as special envoy to plan gov't for defeated Ger. It is wondered if he has the experience. Why not Winant [John Winant]? If we muddle our peace negotiations, heaven help us. Surely we will not be so blind as last time.

Palo Alto Community players gave a very good English drama entitled "Inquest" tonight.

This idea of small groups of activated Christians is essential. The seed of Frank Brink's thought aroused at Maryville five or six years ago. The idea of the Brotherhood as was evolved by frequent and lengthy discussion between Bob Swartzwalder, Dick Boyd, myself and others was this. I think after of those discussions, and wonder how the others feel after being away from M.C. [Maryville College] For myself my conviction has grown. Although fraught with certain difficulties, our ideas were sound.

September 1, 1944, Diary

George Kahin of our Dutch group at hospital today and I had a chance to talk with him for an half hour. He and someone else are planning to see Dr. Eurich (?) at Stanford concerning the Dutchmen. This fellow was or is head of Navy V-12, and George thinks there is a chance of our being transferred to the Navy. It is supposed to have happened once before. 'Twould be logical since Navy is administrating the Pacific islands thus for taken. Certainly far more chance of getting a rating because of our training.

My pass began at 1:00 o'clock today. I came home to find Joe & Jean Kaelber preparing to move. Mrs. De Fine, our landlady, has made no reasonable accusations against them, taking away cooking privileges. Locking telephone room etc. She's very sweet to us. We ate in town tonight and then went to show with Joe and Jean. Saw "Address Unknown" (w/ Paul Lukas) & "Show Business" (w/ Eddie Cantor). Without thinking, I ran down the stairs tonight which didn't help my side.

September 2, 1944, Diary

Slept until 10:45 this morning. Jean and Joe moved this afternoon to a room on campus. I fear that we shall miss them. Dotty particularly will miss Jean. We visited them in their new room on campus. Very nice place indeed.... Yesterday I bought Dr. Trueblood's new book The Predicament of Modern Man. As I begin, it appears to be clearly thought through, concise, and deep in its insight.... Tonight radio Atlantic (anti-Nazi located within Ger.) reports Allied tanks fighting on sacred Reich soil.

September 3, 1944, Diary

To Church this morning, hearing very fine Labor Day Sermon. "Let no man put asunder." —economics and religion, ending with a eulogy for labor and unions. Sounded in the first part as though he had just read Dr. Trueblood's book, op. cit. Wonderful to be home for almost three days. After an afternoon siesta, Dotty played the piano awhile for me. Wrote letters homes tonight. Dotty had touch of appendicitis. Its chronic and I'm worried about it.

September 4, 1944, Diary

Another red letter day. Today we are reported to be fighting on Germany soil. Belgium capital of Brussels taken and the great part of Antwerp fell intact. 100,000 Germans are reported trapped along the coast of Dunkirk. History is to be repeated with shoe on the other front. Germany is throwing up everything to get all possible forces within the inner fortress. She is pulling out of Greece and Finland, and we are forcing in on the famed Gothic Line. Finland pulled out of 3 1/2 yr war with Rus. today. Hungary smolders and the Czechs fight openly. German forces strong only in Poland in and around Poland. It would appear that the Germans have made another fatal strategic error.

A great three day attack is reported on the Bonin 2nd Volcano Island. Many of us would be surprised if our next strike was here (on 600 mi. from Japan). Bad news is that Japanese drive southward in China toward Canton.

Wrote letters tonight in Library and the studied a little—not enough! Ward almost empty and I retain my private room.

September 5, 1944, Diary

Unable to get complete digest of war news tonight, but everything indicates that Germany will be unable to make a strong stand against the onslaught of Allied might. One report has our forces fighting in the Rhine Valley.

Questions are arising as to whether or not post-war peace planning will but lead again to power politics and international animosity. F.D.R. Blueprint contains nothing new and seems but a rehashing of the League of Nations. The Big Four would have their "sphere" of influence which would logically lead to rivalry in overlapping areas. It will be fatal to western civilization—all civilization, in fact—if we allow the seeds of another world war to germinate in the coming peace conference. I fear that Mr. Roosevelt has become an ultra-conservative as a result of political stagnation. His dilly-dallying in dozens of vital matters tend to support this. Innumerable squables [squabbles] in Wash. (Jones & Wallace, Byrnes

& WLB, Nelson & Wilson etc, etc ad infinitum indicates faulty administration in the personage of the president.

Left at 1:00 o'clock on pass. Sun bathed until Dotty came home. Dad has decided not to go to Brooklyn on vacation.

September 6, 1944, Diary

A few of the rumors concerning the situation in Europe have been dispelled, but the black out on news remains. Patton's sixth has been stalled for a week in Loraine awaiting supplies. Patrols have crossed into Germany, but fighting on German soil seems uncertain. Full agreement has been reached at Dumbarton Oaks with a plan similar to the one presented by US-Council, Assembly, and World Court. Wash. announced plans for demobilization when Ger. falls. Overseas men w. [with] dependents first. Probably no Navy or Air Corp out until Japan defeated. Everything in Europe to go to S.W. Pacific

Was moved into ward today because of crowded room situation. Lucky to have stayed so long, but hated to leave my privacy. Guess I'm not the gregarious type, but I don't care to play "Cassino" all day. Getting a lot of letters written and some studying done. Learned today that I am supposed to be here until Sept. 20th. Perhaps I will get special consideration because of being at Stanford.

September 7, 1944, Diary

U.S. First Army drove deep in Ardennes Forest in Belgium while Third Army drove slowly ahead in Metz-Nancy area. Patton meeting stiff resistance against the Siegfried Line. Army reports landing in northern Yugoslavia a week ago. Dewey opened political campaign in Philadelphia tonight, blasting the Admin. "Afraid of the future; afraid of peace; no foresight." He quoted Hershey as saying that it will be cheaper to keep the soldiers in service than to set up bureau and pay them after discharge. Dewey has fine voice and made a telling speech. Gallup poll yesterday showed 50% of voters for Dewey; 49% for FDR. Those who probably will not vote show tendency to FDR. Trend in Rep. direction.

I made up an excuse and kept Dotty home today. Wanted to finish a silk rug for her. Worked all afternoon and almost finished. Still writing and reading. Don't bother with entertainment here.

September 8, 1944, Diary

Three Allied Armies within twenty-five miles of Ger. tonight. One within 18 mi. Germany in full retreat in low countries, but resistance stiffening in Moselle Valley. More than a 100 B-29's have hit an imp. Jap ind. target in Manchuria. Jap air force reported to be driven out of S. Philippines.

This morning I finished up my rug for Dotty just before lunch. Complete surprise to her. My pass began at 1:00 and I went up to the campus to meet Dotty and get some clothing from my room. All of the fellows think I'm crazy to try to get out of the hospital. They are gold-bricking [appearing to work, but in truth, doing less work than one is able] at every turn. We shopped in town for a gift for the Evaul's and then saw "Hairy Ape" with Wm. Bendix [William Bendix] and "Marine Raiders" [RKO war film]. The latter, a lousy war show; the former a fair reproduction of O'Neill's play. The original sociological implications were much simplified. Extremely warm today and our room like an oven. Late supper and to bed.

September 9, 1944, Diary

We arose late and had to rush around to catch 1:00 o'clock bus for Centerville. Arrived in time to see Phil off to furlough in San Jose. We played a hilarious game called "Contact" until very late. For several weeks Dotty has been very desirous of planning for our future family while I have been desisting. The immediate months ahead are very uncertain. However, after much thought and a talk with Phil tonight, I was about won over. When we talked about it again, I found that Dotty has jumped the fence also.

September 10, 1944, Diary

Heard Phil preach at Newark and Centerville. Same sermon, but good. Dotty sang a beautiful solo at each place. She has a very fine quality of tone and I wish she could get more training. Helen came up and we went up Cove Canyon for a delightful picnic. Roland has been grounded and may be sent home. Helen naturally a bit worried. Probably our last visit to Centerville. We've had fellowship of the unique M.C. [Maryville College] variety since last Jan. 1st.

September 11, 1944, Diary

Yanks are fighting in full force on holy Gen. soil and large sections of the Maginot Line have fallen. About 150 Ger. planes destroyed today but 48 bombers lost. (Supposedly unconfirmed Ger. has new rocket plane so fast our gunners can't draw bead on it.) We destroyed 52 Jap ships in one great task force raid on So. Philippines and 18 in another. A gigantic blow to their shipping. Attack on Philippines is imminent. Doctor told me today that my papers will be cleared by Wed. Certainly glad to hear that, although I fear I have lost a great deal by 25 days' absence. Had teeth cleaned and two filled this afternoon, but have to return tomorrow for five more. Lucky to get work done here—in many camps only emergency work is done. Spent the night finishing _Age of Reason_ and studying.

I realize anew from time to time that I suffer from an inferiority complex which I should try to overcome. It can lead to no good as time goes by, and I do believe that I can get rid of the trouble, at least in part.

September 12, 1944, Diary

After 29 days I was released from Dibble today.

September 13, 1944, Diary

Yanks have landed on Halmahera [largest island in the Maluku Islands] tonight. This the last stepping stone before the Philippines. Seven columns drive into Ger. tonight slow but sure advances are being made. The conference at Quebec between FDR & Churchill continues. Overall Pacific Commander selected and it is reported to be Navy man. Probably Nimitz. Russia about to capture Warsaw.

September 14, 1944, Diary

I had an interesting ride home today. While waiting on the bus, I gave a Naval Officer standing on the corner a sloppy salute—(I had better begin to improve that salute!), and then began talking with a couple of Dutchmen [regarding] their recent three day passes. Before the bus came we were picked up by a nice Buick and a pleasant doctor of about seventy years. Seeing Dr. Trueblood's _Predicament of Mod. Man_ on the floor in the rear of the car, I broached the subject of the book and found him interested. Before he let me out on University Ave. I had heard also his theory on war marriages and babies. As I walked on toward home I caught up with a little fellow not more than six years old. We exchanged theories on the making of sling shots and I found that present-day sling shots like everything else are suffering from the war. Now it takes 16 rubber bands instead of the two strips of inner tubing that I used. This little fellow didn't even know what an inner tube was. Tch! Tch!

September 15, 1944, Diary

The Pacific theater has opened a new act in the drama beginning enacted there. The attack on Halmahera was on the island of Morotai rather than the main island. Heavy bombing of the main installation put the Japs off guard. The airfield is already being put in shape for our use. Palau Island group has also been invaded as a preview to taking over the Philippines. Siegfried Line is being pierced with Yanks 10-12 miles inside Ger. territory. Germans seem to be holding off Rus. at expense of their West Wall.

Dotty copying my area notes for friend Keesing. Tonight we went to the Little Theater for a Jaranera ballet—or rather exhibitions of various types of dance. Mr. Dolmanto, of royal Jaranera blood, whom I have seen before, gave a court dance and a friend of his gave one of the more popular dances. Samples of batek were also shown and the process described. Glad Dotty had a chance to see all of this and I certainly enjoyed it.

September 16, 1944, Diary

See Page for Sept 14. Finland fighting for her former Ally, German. West Wall continues to be found weak. War in Pacific continues successfully.

October 1, 1944, Diary

Up just in time to attend World Wide Communion at the Presbyterian Church. Had to be back at school by one o'clock to scrub floors, so we ate dinner in the dinning hall. Home early. Finished packing one barracks bag and Mrs. Glathe took them to the station for me. Mr. Glathe leaving again on trip South. Phil and Peggy called up from Centerville and said goodbye.

WESTERN FRONT—Arrows locate main Allied drives including the crossing of the Waal Rhine River at Nijmegen. These troops are driving north to save the airborne garrison pocketed at Arnhem and turn the German right flank. Heavy battles also are under way on the First and Third Army sectors.

Map of the Western Front, September 22, 1944

October 4, 1944, Diary

At last the day dawned for which I have waited almost sixteen months. I ate breakfast at home and then went up to school to wind up the supply job. Got through by about ten, gathered my papers, bade a fond goodbye to Stanford, and got my last ride down Palm Drive. Met Dotty in town to buy a few things for our trip after stopping by Palo Alto Hospital to say hello and goodbye to Billy Glathe. We rushed around at 940 trying to get our last minute packing done. Missed the train we had planned to take, but caught a bus. Mrs. De Fine kindly took us with all our baggage to the station. We wanted to make 5 PM Ferry and had to pick "Tally" Betten court up. Barely made it by taxi. Joe and Jean, Bob Youngblood, Bob Wiche, and MacIntosh all on board. We waited three hours on Oakland Pier and then failed to get in a decent car. At least four of us were together. It was an exhilarating feeling to be leaving Calif. for home after sixteen months here.

October 5, 1944, Diary

Dotty and Jean Kaelber spent an almost sleepless night, but I managed 5 1/2 to 6 hrs. We watched the sun peak out of the hills west of Reno and spent most of the day speeding across the Nev. plains.

October 11, 1944, Diary

Arrived in Chicago about noon—about three hours late. Dick and Hal were on hand to greet us and we had lunch in town with them. Both seem to be doing well and are certainly happy in their work. We called Muriel and enjoyed talking with her. We caught our train just at 2 o'clock and luckily found good seats. Our car was a very nice one and the sudden influx of southern accents resounding on our ears was greatly appreciated. (Almost no view of Chicago) I managed to sleep soundly as we whirled southward and homeward.

October 8, 1944, Diary

Arrived in Chattanooga again after sixteen months away. How well I remember our last night walking the platform, waiting. We left our bagage [baggage] in the bus station and found that our bus didn't leave until 8:45. Went to the Reid House and had breakfast. Called the folks at Knoxville and then I called Harold Bates. The Cumberlands never looked sweeter as we rode toward Crossville. By a lucky break a Norman girl was there and took us home. What a wonderful feeling to see Mother and Dad.

October 15, 1944, Diary

To church this morning with Dad to hear the new Methodist minister. Mother remained at home to cook dinner, much against my desires. Wonderful dinner though it proved to be. Good sermon by Rev. Brooks. Sounds like a good man for the post. Met a number of people that we hadn't seen. Visited Mr. Crooks and also Mrs. Goss tonight.

October 19, 1944, Diary

We arose early and left by seven o'clock for the "hills of home." Dr. Peyton, Mr. Barber, Dotty, and I drove up to the parking spot near Alum Cave. In all my life I have never seen beauty to compare with that of the Smokies dressed in their autumn leaf. The colors are near their height and are beyond the possibility of expression. We stood with awe looking out over canopy after canopy of blazing beauty. We marked the varying appearance of the Chimneys as we look up, out, and down on them. We decided that its all in the point of view. After climbing a way beyond the Cave, we returned to the car much against our will. We met Mom, Aunt Carol and Florence and ate lunch beside the road. Dr. Peyton, Dad, and Floty had to return, and the rest of us stopped at Gatlinburg on the way to the cabin. Day cloudy but I tried to get some pictures of molasses making. Later I helped make when it begin to get dark and they were far behind.

October 20, 1944, Diary

Arose about four o'clock to fix the fire. A steady rain was falling and it continued until the time we left at noon. Wonderful to see a steady E. Tenn drizzle in contrast to the long dry seasons of Calif. We ate a late breakfast with plenty of hot biscuit, fried apples, and molasses. I drove back to Knoxville—the longest drive for me since I entered the service. When we arrived at home, I had letters from Tom J. & Ted K. Ted has a discouraging note from the 71st. The outfit is frozen as far as ratings are concerned and it is getting "hot." (Army jargon for "ready to go overseas"). I have to go on the range and take a 5, 9, & 25 mile marches. T.L. will be in the hospital when I go thru Atlanta.

October 21, 1944, Diary

Arose early this morning and made an attempt to reach Maryville in time for chapel. Uncle West kindly let us have his car. We arrived just after chapel was out and found Dr. Hunter and Lloyd on the steps to greet us. For the next two hours we talked with Dr. Hunter in his office. It was an exciting moment to return again to the campus. There were many new faces among the student body, but the faculty was much the same. We had to tear ourselves away to get back. Stopped by Uncle Charlie's place but didn't see anyone. Again at Uncle Ben's. Big traffic jam coming from UT 'Bama game. Brought Mary Ruth home.

October 22, 1944, Diary

To Church to hear Dr. Peyton deliver an excellent sermon on "The Challenge of Change" using our hike last Thurs. as the basis. After a hasty lunch we found that the train was an hour and a half late. Florence took us down to the train. Met Dave Hall and we managed to get good seats together. Dave is doing well at U. of Ala. in Navy med sch. There is always a strange feeling that accompanies leave taking and especially when the future is so uncertain.

October 23, 1944, Diary

Although the train was late, we reached Birmingham just at 10 o'clock. I rushed to find the Central of Ga, finding it just as the train man yelled "All Aboard!" I made it by only a few seconds. I was able to sleep for about three hours before arriving in Columbus about 2:30. From there I took a taxi to the 71st. After much delay and after disturbing the sleep of a captain on duty at Dir Hdg., I finally was told to go to bed and sleep in the 14th. I awoke some time after eleven to find myself in a "casual" barrack. I spent most of the afternoon being assigned to Co. K. 14th. 1st platoon, third squad, ammunition carrier for the B.A.R. (Browning Automatic Rifle.) So far no chance to see any of the other Stanford men. It isn't hard to realize how the wind is blowing and to know what Ted meant by saying the outfit is "hot".

Hdg. Is trying to finish up records, supply rooms are making up packing boxes. Many men are new and there could be little co-operative technique for combat. Some think that we are to get an MP training for Army of occupation. United Nations to recognize De Gaulle gov't in Fr.

October 24, 1944, Diary

As I wrote Dotty tonight, I seem to have come in during the lull before the proverbial storm. We fell out this morning about 9:30 and marched out about 2 miles for a dry-run on a combined tank-infantry problem. We were back by 11:30. The leaves have a bronze hue that offers a reserved beauty somewhat in contrast to the brilliant colors of the Smokies. I enjoyed the walk very much. This afternoon about eighteen beds were filled in the platoon. I slept from one to almost three. I had planned to go into town to see Ted & Cordy tonight but we were restricted to sign forms and incidentally the payroll. We were released about eight but my pass has not been made out. I went down to the PX for a haircut. Found that MacIntosh (Stanford man) is in Co L. just next door. He is the only one of the ten Dutchmen that I have seen. Met a sgt. tonight who like me is disgusted with the violent language that fills the air around us. He has a deep religious faith and doesn't hesitate to tell others what he thinks. Think he will be interesting to know.

Letter from Art to Dotty
Co K 14th Inf.
APO 360, Ft. Benning
Oct. 24, '44 (Tues.)

My Darling,

There is a quiet hush around the barracks—fifteen fellows are still enjoying the sequesterd sp(?) haunts of a land of dreams, three of us have just awakened. It is but a few minutes passed three and we have slept since one o'clock.

No, this doesn't seem to fit into my picture of the army. Well, it is only a distorted picture. The men say that this lull has been in effect for more than a week, but it must be merely the lull before the proverbial storm. The order has been given to get rid of all cars by Nov. 6th. The consensus of opinion is that this means we are to move by about Nov. 15th. It may be later because it takes a long time to move 15,000 men.

I should not conjecture too much until I talk to Ted. He should have some indication of "what's cookin".

This morning we went out a couple of miles for a problem involving tank and infantry tactics, but were there and back in two hours. I was called in to complete my records on firing the M-1, cartime, [?] etc. (Just as a side light, the corporal from the orderly room just came and had to awake all the non-coms in the platform—about five or six.)

As yet, I have no equipment. The supply room I suppose is very busy, and I hope they remain that way as far as my equipment is concerned. There is a slight possibility that I will not receive any equipment here, but I suppose the possibility is very slight.

My plans to see Cordy & Ted are slightly changed since we are restricted tonight. It seems that we have to sign the payroll and initial certain forms. It is possible that we may get through in time for me to go into town anyway. I hope so. I wrote Ted today, just in case I don't get to see him.

Did I mention that I am to send home all of my suntana? [?] At any rate, the fellows here have turned them all in, and the first sgt. told me to ship mine home. Suits me! Maybe Dad can use a pair.

I just met an interesting fellow: a sgt. who was in the 82 Bn. in Camp Roberts. He seemed very nice during the last couple of days, and I found him talking a bit about religion to some of the fellows tonight. He, like myself, is absolutely disgusted with some of the language that goes on in our outfit. I have never heard anything as filthy. The sgt. says he may preach them a sermon sometime. I think that his acquaintance may prove very interesting as time goes on.

If I had had a pass made out I would have been able to go to town after eight o'clock. However, it was so late & since I couldn't get one anyway I came down to the Barber shop to get a hair cut. I hope I can get it before the shop closes at nine. Guess I'll have to try again tomorrow night to see Ted & Cordy.

By the way, I ran into MacIntosh tonight. I knew that he was in 14th Regt., and tonight I saw him standing in line to get his pay book fixed up. He came with Wiche, but doesn't know where anyone else is located. He is in the company next door and I guess we will see a great deal of him. Ted isn't far away and I hope he will drop around tomorrow.

Lights are going out in a few minutes. I did get my haircut.

Goodnight & sweetest dreams, My own.

I love you, Bushy

412

71st Inf. Div.
Ft. Benning Ga.
Mon. Oct. 23, 1944

My Dearest,

My mind is beginning to whirl at a rapid rate, and I suppose that it will continue at this rate for some time. The platoon that I am in is filled with men like myself doing nothing! Many of the fellows have just come from the paratroopers having flunked out, and there are a few odds & ends like myself from other outfits. Rumors fly back & forth. Probably no one knows anything but nevertheless they talk.

Although the train was late in Knoxville as you know, we made up a great deal of time. When I arrived in Birmingham, the clock showed that ten o'clock was bistary [?] by two minutes. Dave opened a door for me and I jumped out. I rushed up to two or three onlookers and ask about the Central of Ga. No one knew. I dashed toward the station and ask someone else. He pointed out the track and I ran toward it. "All aboard," I heard. A door was open and I dashed in. The kindly conductor, seeing that I had made my train by only a very few seconds, allowed me to pay for my ticket on the train.

To my utter surprise, the Central of Ga., was a far nicer train then the Southern. In fact it was as nice as our streamlined coach coming into Chicago. I found a comfortable spot in the observation car and stretched out to sleep. We arrived in Columbus on time and from their [there] I shared a cab with a Lt. and another enlisted man to the 71st Div. Hdg. There I awoke a man on duty, who later prove to be a captain. He gave me a number to call for a jeep. The wait was a lengthy one but finally a truck arrived and I was brought to the 14th Reg.

Here I found a very nice staff Sgt. who asked if I had had any sleep. When I told him "very little," he sent me to the barracks in which I began this letter. There I curled up on a duty mattress (the time being about 5:00 or 5:30) and fell immediately to sleep. I heard almost nothing until about eleven o'clock this morning. No one seem to care what happened to any one. The amazing thing has been so far that I have seen nothing of any of the other fellows from Stanford.

I was called out for lunch shortly after I started this; and, after eating, I came back to 14th Regt. Hdg. where I first reported last night. I was told that someone had been looking for me to give me my assignment but I must have been asleep. At least, I heard or saw nothing. I am now awaiting being shown some where.

Of course, first impressions are seldom valid. I am sure that a few days will change some of my first ideas. However, I was immediately impressed by the tremendous size of the place, and second I suppose was the pleasant experience of seeing Gowga pines everywhere.

There are a whole flock of men just arriving from Camp Roberts, Camp Hood, Texas, and to Camp Robinson, Ark. I see a lot of sgts. , & corporals in the groups. Hmm! If the 71st was over strength before, it will certainly be over flowing now.

Later

A guide came and I was finally assigned to Co K, 1st platoon, 3rd squad, ammunition carrier for the BAR (Browning Automatic Rifle). Hmm!

I'm catching on to a lot of things. I think, and I sense the way the wind is whistling. I hope to get a pass tomorrow night and get down to see Ted & Cordy. I'm going to make every effort to find a place as soon as possible. Darling, the cold truth seems to be that I can expect to move again soon. No one knows where, why, or when. But things are definitely moving. Perhaps I can get a reservation in the guest house & then you can find a place after you arrive in case I can't find something. I understand that a marriage license is necessary at the guest house so better bring that along. Also better get that examination out of the way as soon as possible. I may send a telegram any time I find something.

All suntana have you been turned in and the 1st Sgt. told me to send mine home as soon as possible.

I'll write more as soon as possible, but I want to get this letter out.

Darling, no matter what comes in the ensuing days, nothing can shake the faith and strength that comes from

Our love,

Bushy

Still later—

I have a room reserved in the guest house for next Monday night. Hope to see Cordy & Ted tomorrow and plan with them to find a place. The guest house is good for three days. Will write more tomorrow.

Love

Bushy

Don't forget alarm clock. Send about 3 or $4 in your letter. I think it will come thru all right to send bills. You might register it if it isn't too much trouble.

414

October 25, 1944, Diary

Morning was taken up by one hour of close order drill; afternoon in getting very pre functory physical exam and three shots. I couldn't get my pass until 6 o'clock, but left as quickly as possible without supper. Arrived at Ted's shortly before seven. He and Cordy have a rather nice room and good location. It was wonderful to see and talk with them again. From all we can gather, we may learn anytime from two weeks to two months. More likely the former. Things are confused because Ted says trucks were redrawn again today. However, we're told tonight that we are to leave for P.O.E. very shortly. Twenty-five mile hike next week. Regt. rec'd info on N.Y. Harbor. Looks like Europe is our direction. Ted thinks that we will go over for three months training and then maneuvers. It would seem that Army of Occupation is a safe bet. Ran into Bill Kinsey who is just a few companies away in the 14th. Hear that three of the fellows at Riche we're kicked out of Military Intelligence. Met a Sgt. tonight who was at Stanford first 3 mo. Was made Asst. BAR man today.

Letter from Art to Dotty
Co K 14th Inf APO
Ft Benning.
Oct. 25, 44 (Wed Noon

Darling,

Of necessity it seems that my letters at this time must be poorly written, both in construction and in content. I usually write now on my knee and with poor lighting. At any moment I can expect something to arise which will interrupt my train of thought and my writing.

The one unifying thought behind all that I write is my deep and devoted love for you, my wife. My entire thought, my entire being is filled by the ever present strength that comes from the knowledge that we are one in soul and spirit. I love you.

As yet I have still not seen Ted; but, as far as I now know, I will be able to go into town tonight. I will take my suntans down and leave them there until I can ship them. Perhaps you can take them back. I think he can tell me what's going on, but I think that maneuvers is the best bet. Whether it will be in this country or not is another question. I am sure that it will not be Ft. Benning however. For that reason, and until I find out more, I think it wise for you to travel light. Bring clothes etc. that will necessary for about a week unless I write otherwise.

Later

It is very late & I just returned from Ted's & Cordy's. More about that later. Unless I write to the contrary, go to their address at 510 Broad St. in Columbus when you arrive. Hope you get there some time during the day on Monday. Cordy works until 4:30. They live in the third door on the right of the hallway. I'll try to meet you there in the evening unless otherwise prevented. Might be on bivouac, and if so will wire, if I find out in time. Expect to leave here by Nov. 5th or before. Don't think we can plan for you to stay much longer than 3 days in guest house. Buy round trip. 'Scuse rush. I love you very dearly,
Thine own Bushy

October 26, 1944, Diary

Put on detail this morning. Sgt. in charge didn't know where to go. We ended up at 2nd Bn. Hdg. We came back to the 1st. We returned to the 2nd. There a detail was just leaving and we were told that we weren't supposed to be there. However, we had to go along to the railway siding where we unloaded 15 boxcars that had been loaded the day before. About 30 flat cars were being unloaded of 75 mm & 105 mm guns. Oh, this Army! Efficiency etc. I hurt my side and didn't go out this afternoon. 2nd Army came around for gas inspection. Asst. non-com took nine of us and drilled us for a half hour on gas. We passed the inspection with flying colors. Saw Kinsey and Oelbaum tonight. OCS open for two hours today and Kinsey applied. Goes before board tomorrow. I intend to inquire about it. From the looks of things, I can see absolutely no future in the 71st for me. Everything is filled and I don't think that I will have an opportunity to use my language.

October 28, 1944, Diary

Luckily I got off about 3 o'clock and went to town to see Martha and Scotty (1st Lt. Honaker. She had told Cordy of the possibility of finding a room. We visited Mrs. Grimes just across the street. At first she refused but I talked her into it. Very lucky considering the room shortage. Returned to eat with Ted and Cordelia. Harold K. on sick leave and stopped by to visit. He has a Barber-Bushing type of humor that is amazingly similar. We "rioted" until a late hour and then he and I returned to camp where he stayed in Ted's bed.

October 29, 1944, Diary

Able to get a pass this morning after some difficulty with a young lieutenant who was too absorbed in the funny paper to know what the score was. Rode in with Sgt. Soderstrom and later to church with him. Met the Kidders there. Good sermon by Dr. Reid. (1st. Presby) and solo by Osie (?) Hawkins, Metropolitan Opera star. Ate Sun. dinner with Kidders. Cordy an excellent cook. Enjoyed a swell M.C. bull session. Difficult to pull away.

October 30, 1944, Diary

Dotty arrived today! For the first time since I came a week ago we went out into the field all day. Also for the first time in my Army life, I rode a truck to work. We went out about twelve or fourteen miles for a squad problem. Gee, we are rusty! After some confusion concerning my class "A" pass, I was able to get away. Ted kindly waited for me and we rushed home post hast. Dotty had gone there upon arrival. She was dressed in her corduroy dress with a blue blouse. Very becoming. The week that we had been a part had seemed very long and I fear the succeeding months will be for longer. We left Ted's and took bus to our new "home." Stopped by to see Martha Honakey before going to our room. Our room is extremely nice with half bath, etc. etc. No cooking facilities, but for our short time it will suffice. Dotty tells me that Tom Jones stopped by to see her on Sat. I've been trying to get him to do that for months. Awfully glad he did. Have decided to investigate the possibility of becoming a chaplain's assistant.

November 3, 1944, Diary

Wed. Nov. 8
Today we were given a list of things to be turned in for storage. One suit of O.D.'s, combat boots, new shoes, 1 pr. leggings, gloves, new fatigues etc. I had one pair of O.D.'s in the cleaners and have never

417

had but one pair of fatigues. I explained my position to the supply room. "You have to turn in 1 pr of fatigues," I was told. But I will have absolutely nothing to wear, I told them. "Well, you have to turn them in." Wait a system! I didn't turn them in, but I thought of how often such illogical orders are given.

November 4, 1944, Diary

Big news came down officially today. We are to stay at least another month. Perhaps longer. (Two according to Ted's Colonel.) Almost everything had been packed and some stuff had been sent already. What a system! Full field inspection on bunks today and orientation. Off after lunch with pass until Mon morning. Ted luckily got off at noon also. Slept this afternoon and then went into town for supper with Kidders in cafeteria. Afterward we went out to our room and played rummy until a late hour. Our land lady Kindly brought in cookies for us.

November 5, 1944, Diary

Eleven full hours of sleep. Up and to church just in time to meet Ted & Cordy going in. Good sermon by Dr. Reid, but only two points. 3rd missing. Met Ted Pratt after church. Awfully good to see him. A friend of Kidder's from the 5th came along and we had quite a party. Poor Cordy! Ted P has dvlped [developed] a rather pessimistic view pt. of the Army, as well he might. However, thinks OCS a breeze and advises me to take it. I'm torn between "vice and versa." I'm not sure.

November 6, 1944, Diary

Have a case of poison ivy developing on my knee and so went on sick call this morning. Everyone rushing around to prepare for IG (inspector general) inspection.

A fact that is becoming more and more evident to me as I continue here is that the present adjustment to the Army is far harder than the initial one which I made. I suppose that several factors may account for this. The type of fellow with whom I have daily contact is of a far rougher variety than any I have here to fore known. In Roberts all the men were potential ASTP'ers. Many had had college work. Here every type is represented from old Army men to fresh recruits just out of basic. The usual standard, represent a new low in my experience. Thus the contacts have been something of a barrier to me. * Another difficulty to overcome is the contrast of Stanford with Dotty being there and Ft. Benning. The married man does have adjustments to make that a single man doesn't have. Stanford was very close to civilian life and it is almost as though I were entering the Army for the first time. A third factor in my adjustment has been a certain dissolutionment concerning the Army. The fervor which I had during my basic is gone. Perhaps I was kidding myself, but I sincerely thought that I liked basic. I regret to say it but I fear that I have lost the old fire that I had to make the very best of anything and everything I try. It hasn't been lost entirely, but at least my attitude toward the Army is somewhat different. Another issue comes to mind and that is the partial let down of being back in a rifle company—a mere rifleman. Of course, I only came a few days ago. Many things can happen. Before I left Stanford I steeled myself to expect nothing from my training. Subconsciously I suppose that I never gave up thinking that I would get a break. Well, even though I seem to have a fatalistic strain, I do believe that a break will be coming my way. Meanwhile I must make the best adjustment that I can. "...Leave to labor and to wait."

* I must hasten to add that at least two in my platoon have very high standards. Boul Root and Carl Soderstrom.

November 8, 1944, Diary

I wrote Tom Jones on Monday that although I felt in my proverbial bones that FDR would be reelected, I was encouraged by a bit of wishful thinking here and a little logical thought there. Some of these: Rep trend, Dewey's campaign, and Fortune's finding of many secret voters for Dewey. Of course, it was but wishful thinking. The final results will not be known for some time but Roosevelt has the election by a comfortable margin. My first reaction was to think that the millions who elected him would regret it. That was a hasty thought and one thoroughly unjustified. Many mistakes have been evident throughout, but he has done a great job. We are winning the war, peace plans are in the making, many snags can be straightened out now with the election out-of-the-way. I think that the nation is almost unanimous in hoping that Roosevelt will not have to pass his post on Truman. The latter has no large popular following.

On KP all day yesterday until 10:30 last night. Cook unhappy at way we got the work done. I.G. inspection a farce but it did create a great deal of confusion. (See page for Fri. Nov. 3)

November 13, 1944, Diary

Nov. 20   See Page for that date [Art's note]
Started out this morning on 50 mile map problem. Just a platoon at a time. I started out as first scout. Rainy and cold. We carried full field packs with two blankets. Rather heavy. Problem involved following a aerial photo. We made our first food point by three o'clock, and spent the rest of the afternoon sitting around. Boul Root and I bunked together and we made a very comfortable sleeping bag with overhead shelter. I felt very much conscience-striken tonight. I detailing men for guard, my squad leader (S/Sgt O'Connell) put down numbers. Without intending to see, I saw one of the numbers. I guessed last, but avoided guard. That which I would, I do not; and that which I would not, I do. Oh, the weakness of the human flesh.

Letter from Dave to Art
13 Nov 44

Dear Arthur:

Your letter of 30 Aug. was a real treat, and my tardiness in answering should not be considered an indication that I did not appreciate it. First let me say that I hope you are entirely recovered from your ordeal, and that you are better off than ever without your "appendix vermiformis." By now you have no doubt graduated and been transferred to another station, but after the usual 2 weeks delay in the the mailroom of SCU3905, this will no doubt be forwarded to you. When I received your letter in mid-September I was preparing to go on furlough, & figured on answering when I returned. I started on Sept 27th & with my wife, who was in Atlanta, I went to East Orange, N.J. & visited some friends for about a week, during which time we pretty thoroly took in New York and adjacent territory, all of which was new to both of us. On the return we stopped briefly in Washington & saw the important sights, then to Atlanta where we spent the last 4 days of my furlough.

Shortly after reaching East Orange I received a telegram ordering me back to duty on Oct 11th (3 days before my furlough was supposed to end) in ordered to attend QM-OCs, for which I had applied last June. I reported here on Oct 14th, and am now in the 5th week of the 17 weeks course, which is really a honey. It is really something to sink your teeth in, and very interesting. It is much more concentrated than the course at Stanford, and more difficult because there are many more subjects, and because of the rigorous military training that is concurrent with the academic work. It seems as tho they pile stuff on you for the express purpose of trying to break you down under the strain, and if you crack, even a little,—out you go. The casualties usually run from 20% to 35% of each class, with most of the eliminations at the end of the 6th, 11th & 14th weeks. A fellow has to be a very good soldier in every respect, as well as a good student to make the grade, and if I can do it, I will be a better man then I thought I was, or else it will [be] a miracle,—probably the latter.

My wife is living in Petersburg nearby & spend Sat nites & Sundays with her when not on K.P., C.Q., Interior Guard duty, fire duty, spel police duty, etc. etc. Yesterday we went to Richmond and got our bearings for a future trip which will include most points of historic interest, of which there are a great many. I like Virginia better than any Southern State I've seen so far. Camp Lee is very clean & well administered. The food is excellent, and we get 2 day service in the QM laundry, believe it or not. I'm learning a lot of new things about the army & developing a new respect for it, even tho I still don't like it very well. I have little time for correspondence, but please write again, and I will try to answer promptly. Sincerely yours, Dave.

* November 16, 1944, Diary

Nov. 27
[Art's handwritten
date]

As I ride into Columbus each evening, the bus brings me through the "Jim Crow" section of town. This is actually my first contact with the deep South and it is revealing to say the least.

Often for half a city block, one sees houses only a few feet apart, exactly alike. Unpainted, wind and rain swept, they stand in an out-of-season bleakness. Doors stand half open, revealing meagerly furnished rooms; a bed, a straight chair, a ragged rocker. Outside one may see a $1500 car appearing strangely out of place, perhaps an old "T" Model sits on the curb or a bicycle adorns the front. Usually, of course, there is nothing. Hard packed earth, a curb, the street—that is all. At more than one corner one sees a young buck lean against one side of a telephone pole while a beguiling negress supports the other side. Two little boys play marbles for keeps in a circle drawn in the wet sand. A buxom middle aged woman carries a basket of laundry across the street and passes the time of day with a white-haired grandfather tearing a packing box apart for kindling. Down the street an M.P. Sgt. marches proudly along, his white belt, and MP arm band brightening up the twilight shadows.

This could almost be "Tobacco Road," but Tobacco Road with the impetus of a war economy. There's lots of money in the country now. Even here it has reached. After the war—who knows? Too likely it seems that Tobacco Road will return. The curse that fell upon this land following the Civil War has not been lifted. It lingers on in hundreds of such towns as Columbus.

November 19, 1944, Diary

Spent almost the entire day in bed in an attempt to throw off a cold. Over to the Honakers tonight for another reunion supper. Lt. "Chuck" Foreman, Ted & Cordy. Dotty and myself were guests. Lovely evening with much of Maryville to discuss. Chuck has recently transfered from AA and is now taking an 8 wk. blitz to make an infantry officer.

November 23, 1944, Diary

Slept until 6:15 this morning. What a nice feeling to awaken at 3:45, turn over, and go back to sleep. Returned to camp and fell out at 10 o'clock for map reading etc. We gold bricked through until 12:30 when the C.O. released us to go to the Protestant services if we so desired. I attended with Root and a couple of other fellows. Chaplain Hail spoke but I fail to fully appreciate the message. He pulled me aside after the service and told me of an opening in the 66th for a chaplain's assistant. After a full dress turkey dinner in the mess hall, I hastened to the 66th and tracked down the chaplain. He was very nice, but left this situation very much up in the air. Several others are trying hard for the same job. My lack of musical ability is a decided disadvantage. Got to bus station by 3:30. Two bus came and filled up. I was still standing in line. Finally made it home by 5 o'clock. We went down to Ted's and Cordy & Dotty prepared a Thanksgiving supper.

Very fine meal with the real home touch. Home late but I can sleep late in the morning. "'Tis colder now."

November 25, 1944, Diary

To K.D. (Known Distance) Range this morning to find zero of rifle. Spent morning firing five shots. Very cold these mornings. Back by 11:30 (On trucks both ways. About 12 miles.) Cleaned rifle up and left for home about one o'clock. Dotty had just moved to 510 Broadway. Who could have imagined a year ago that Ted and I would be not only be together but both married and living next door to each other. Big shopping spree to get essentials. Rainy and cold. Swell to have cooking at home again.

November 26, 1944, Diary

Up about ten and to church with Ted & Cordy. Good sermon by Dr. Miller—a visiting minister from Ohio. Met Ted Pratt, Martha & Scott Honaker, and a friend of Cordy's. Ted P. & the friend came home with us and we had a wonderful meal. Ted missed a big order to Fort Meade. POE. He gets his commission on Wed. Probably a delay en route. Spent a pleasant afternoon reading, writing, and talking.

November 27, 1944, Diary

We fell out this morning in the rain and slogged through the slimy Ga. [Georgia] mud to our area for a problem in attack & withdrawal. The overcast sky seemed to close in about us. Fog rolled up the hill and then came the rain. It had [?]

For the first time in my Army life I heard my CO. apologize to the company. I could hardly believe my ears. We had marched out about a mile from camp to our assembly area for a problem. The order to stand arms was given but the response was sloppy. The order was repeated. Still sloppy. Capt. Long [?] gave the platoon leader five minutes to give instruction in standing arms. After this we tried some more. Someone dropped a rifle in the mud & the "old man" did a lot of fancy cursing. I have often heard much worse and certainly wasn't surprised. After giving a demonstration with a couple of sgts, the CO. held a conference w. [with] the leader. Stepping out from the conference, he made a nice speech apologizing for blowing up. Now I have seen almost everything!

423

November 28, 1944, Diary

Political unrest permeates the European scene as the clouds of war clear around the edges. The forces of communism oppose the parties in power which are supported by Britain and the U.S. These leftist forces are struggling to hold arms—this is one bone of contention. There are many others. This situation is most advanced in France, Belgium, and Greece. The following summary is an excerpt from Time, *Nov. 27, page 33.*

"Scarcely anywhere did Britain and the U.S., hampered by the vast job of waging war, and alarmed by the threats of social violence, offer a political leadership intelligent or tough enough to counter-act the Communists or sufficient economic aid to quiet the popular unrest.

"To most Europeans democracy, U.S. style, was a new experience. Many, perhaps most of them, emerging from facist [fascism, simply put, is a one-party dictatorship] domination, had been eager for it. But there were in a mood to judge it strictly by its deeds. Because its deeds were falling far short of their hopes, they were in a mood to judge it harshly. Unless the U.S. and Britain acted quickly to retrieve the ground they had lost, they might win the war but lose Europe. For Europeans were faced with a historic choice—between the fumbling X of democracy as represented by the western Allies, and the untried Y of Communism backed by the thunderous prestige of the Red Army and the swift-sure strokes of Soviet foreign policy. Their choice might extend the area of human freedom to the center of Europe or it might roll democracy back to the Western Hemisphere. For Europe, and for the world, this was a winter of decision, a winter of crisis—and the crisis was already at hand."

* November 30, 1944, Diary

Problem this afternoon and tonight. About 12 miles out. Cold but bearable. First time that we have worked with another company. M in support: Returned by 2300. Ted had brought my OCS papers back and left a note to the effect that it is closed. During the past four weeks, my papers were returned three times. Every possible delay seems to have put in my way. Six or eight days were taken to send them back for very minor corrections. Perhaps it is for the best, but at the moment it is a bit hard to take. We waste so much time. I get very much disgusted with my surroundings—not only personnel but also activity. Paid today and the "crap" games are rampant. How and why guys can and do lose a month's wages in a very few minutes is beyond me. I suppose the excitement of the moment is their reward. Perhaps that is what all of us seek. Even in peace time I suppose there are a relatively small percentage who truly enjoy the work the [they] do. People live and work with the thought of the pleasure past or to come. Sometimes it is derived from music, sometimes books or art. Often too the pleasure is from wine and women. What is the answer? Will the great majorities ever learn the sources of true and complete happiness? Yes, of course, goodness and truth will eventually triumph; but the road is long and arduous.

In recent weeks I have been attempting to analyze the reasons why the moral and ethical standards of so many men are lowered so much after contact with Army life for a short time. Boys who never drank before learn to drink; boys who never smoked before learn to smoke. Men who had been true to wives or loved ones break all bounds. Why should men break away from all ideals that they have clung to for years?

I think that one reason for this is the fact that so many men feel that they are being unfairly treated by the very fact that they are in the Army. They were drafted; they didn't want to come to the Army. In other words, they turn a bit sour on the world. With this attitude, it is only a step to self pity and only another to the place where standards are dropped. Once the snowball begins to roll, it is difficult to stop.

Another reason for the changing attitudes, and action results, I think from the topsy-turvy world in which the soldier finds himself. Often-times his entire system of values must be shifted. In civilian life, virtue was rewarded as was hard work. Initiative was to be cultivated and was recognized for its true north. In the Army, no one cares about one's private life. "Gold-bricking" (Army slang for doing as little work as possible) is looked upon almost as an ideal. At least almost everyone practices it to a greater or lesser degree. It is rare for real initiative to be noticed or taken account of. Thus when a young man comes to Army, he finds his whole set of standards and values are swept away at one stroke. If he is firm enough and mature enough, perhaps the individual can withstand the chaotic storm around him. Many times, however, the poor G.I. emerges from his first phase of confusion off balance and striking about wildly for a new tact. In such a state, he is wide open and unprotected from the germs of lower standards—profane language, strong drink, etc.

December 2, 1944, Diary

Drew guard for tonight and Sun. [Sunday, which is tomorrow] Went on at 18:00. Two hours on and four off for 24 hrs. I had relatively easy post. On my tour from 0600 - 0800 Sun. morning I found fires in boiler rooms which I felt I should investigate. I did—for many minutes. Drunks brought in to guard house in wee hours caused a bit of disturbance.

* December 7, 1944, Diary

Dec. 7th—3 years ago today I spent the day in good Maryville fashion: to church; after lunch in Pearsons, down town to visit Floyd Loperfide with some of the fellows; back early to Messiah practice. As I passed behind Carnegie, the news flashed over the radio—Pearl Harbor Bombed! On that day our country plunged into a long struggle. My day's work seemed symbolic, in part, of that three-year period.

When I arrived in camp, the rain had begun to fall. By the time we fell out, it was raining hard. We rode out in open trucks about twelve miles and began a tactical cross country march with full field packs. The rain poured; it was cold. No one, not even the officers knew what was going on. Sometime in the afternoon we arrived at area P-2 only about 3 miles from camp. There we dug in defensive positions. The rain stopped but a cold wind continued to blow. We ate chow somewhere in the rear area where it was necessary to cross a ravine in pitch darkness. At nine we were told to pitch tents. We (four of us) we ready for bed by 9:30. At 10 we were told to roll full field packs and prepare to withdraw. Barracks by 12:30.

Perspective is one of the hardest things for the ordinary GI to retain. In the first place, the man on the line is told almost nothing concerning overall planning. He knows what his squad, his platoon is doing; but more than that he doesn't know. In the second place, he would not be likely to understand completely the strategy of large scale movements unless given detailed instruction. In the third place, GI Joe does not have enough interest in strategy to try to understand even if details were provided.

Yesterday, I think I suffered more than in any other 18 hr. period in my Army life. The rain, the cold, the seeming lack of purpose in our activity—these things made it extremely difficult to rain a rational viewpoint.

December 10, 1944, Diary

We slept late this morning in order to get ahead for next week. Stayed home from church with a guilty feeling. Prepared dinner for Beul and Dorcas Root. (Swell couple from Wis.) Spent most of afternoon eating and cleaning up. Went to an organ concert at Presbyterian Church. Very fine. Poor Dotty's soul is thirsting for music as is mine.

December 11, 1944, Diary

Arose out of every warm and comfortable bed at 3:20. With much misgiving I left, after kissing Dotty goodbye for a week. Outside it had just begun to rain and I caught a taxi to camp, arriving just in time for reville. We ate breakfast at 4:30 and pulled out about 5:40. Someone had misplaced my raincoat and I rushed around at the last minute trying to find it. For four hours we marched in a steady downpour of rain. Occasionally when the rain slacked a bit, the cold wind cut with icy fingers through our clothing. One becomes a bit deadened to intense and extended cold, but the process is hard. We arrived at our area and dug in to keep warm. Orders came to pitch tents, but no fire allowed. We made three man tents where possible, piled wet pine needles in to lie on, and removed wet socks. I managed to get four or five hours sleep. Chow very mediocre with only sandwiches for lunch. Field stove brought out by supper, which at least gives hot coffee and hot water in which to wash mess kits. Early guard and to sleep by eleven.

December 17, 1944, Diary

Both Ted and I had to return to camp this morning for a clothing inspection. Tried to go to church out there, but unable to do so.

December 20, 1944, Diary

To hospital today for final heat treatment on my arm. Much improved by treatments. Able to get a couple of presents [Christmas] in main PX but for the most part everything is gone. Brought back by Harvard, a Stanford Dutchman who left in April. Marked time this afternoon by doing a cross country compass problem. To my complete surprise, I was included in a list for good conduct medal. It is hardly on honor however. One fellow has just returned from "over the hill" and another fellow who received the award was over the hill at the time. How can one take pride in such a medal.

December 22, 1944, Diary

Most of the fellows on guard last night and the rest on detail this morning. I did nothing. Passes for a very few of us this afternoon for Christmas shopping. I bought a pair of gloves for Dotty and then went home to sleep for three hours. We were scheduled to have a clothing inspection on Sunday morning. Ted brought the news tonight that we are to have the inspection tomorrow. I intend to try to get home with a fellow in Hdg. Plat. who lives in Murfesboro [Murfreesboro].

We bought a tree but no decorations were to be found. We bought aluminum paint, picked up pine and sycamore cones, and painted them. With cellophane, we made icicles; and with crape paper made streamers for the tree. Dotty has done a beautiful job on the mantle.

December 23, 1944, Diary

For the seventh or eight time we had clothing check today. A complete farce. Weekend passes finally given to 50% of company. I just missed a ride all the way to Knoxville. Left camp about 3:30 expecting my ride to pick Dotty and me up when he completed inspection. We packed and were ready to leave. The ride never came. We wired homes that we could not come. Played bridge with Ted and Cordy until a late hour. Certainly disappointing to have a pass to go home and then not be able to make the trip. Travel conditions are terrible.

December 24, 1944, Diary

We arose late, just in time to get to church. Very nice service at Presb. with sermon by Dr. Reid. We ate in town with Ted & Cordy. A wonderful day, warm with a delightful sun shining. Walked down by the Chattahoochee R., took pictures and gathered mistletoe. Tonight we went to Communion Service on our first Xmas Eve together. Ted and Cordy ate supper with us by candle light.

December 25, 1944, Diary

Arose about nine-thirty. We took down our stockings down before breakfast. Dotty had mine fired up very nicely. We ate a hasty breakfast and then fell upon our packages. I gave Dotty a couple of pairs of 51 gauge hose, and perfume in addition to a raincoat some weeks ago. Mary Ruth sent her a lovely blouse. I bought her a pair of gloves as a gift from Mother. "Mom" & Dad Barber gave me a subscription to Time and a copy of The Ages of Man, a Shakespeare Anthology [maybe The Seven Ages of Man]. Dotty gave me a beautiful pair of blue rayon pajamas, a photo folder suitable to take with me, an a copy of Lend-Lease by Stettinius.

December 27, 1944, Diary

I was knocked completely off my feet by news which we received in two Christmas letters today. The letters, mailed the same day oddly enough, were from Hal Lloyd and Muriel Geisler. Last Christmas they became engaged (unofficially). In early Oct. when Hal met us in Chicago, everything was perfect. Later in the month it seems that Muriel broke the engagement and at once became engaged to a Baptist minister in Manitowoc, Wis. where she had been working.

Hal is terribly hurt and I can easily understand. I feel very badly about the break up also because I developed a personal interest and knowledge of their relationship during my senior year in college. At that time, Hal was very uncertain of his position. Muriel loved him very much and suffered much as a result of his uncertainty. She did everything but actually cry on my shoulder as I listened to her difficulties. After a very long time, it seemed that everything had been straightened out.

December 28, 1944, Diary

Germany offensive in Belgium seems to have developed into serious threat to our impending winter campaign. Two major weaknesses seem to have been revealed by the Germany successes: (1) our intelligence failed completely to give warning of a German preparations, and (2) our plans had been wholly offensive with no defensive positions having been prepared.

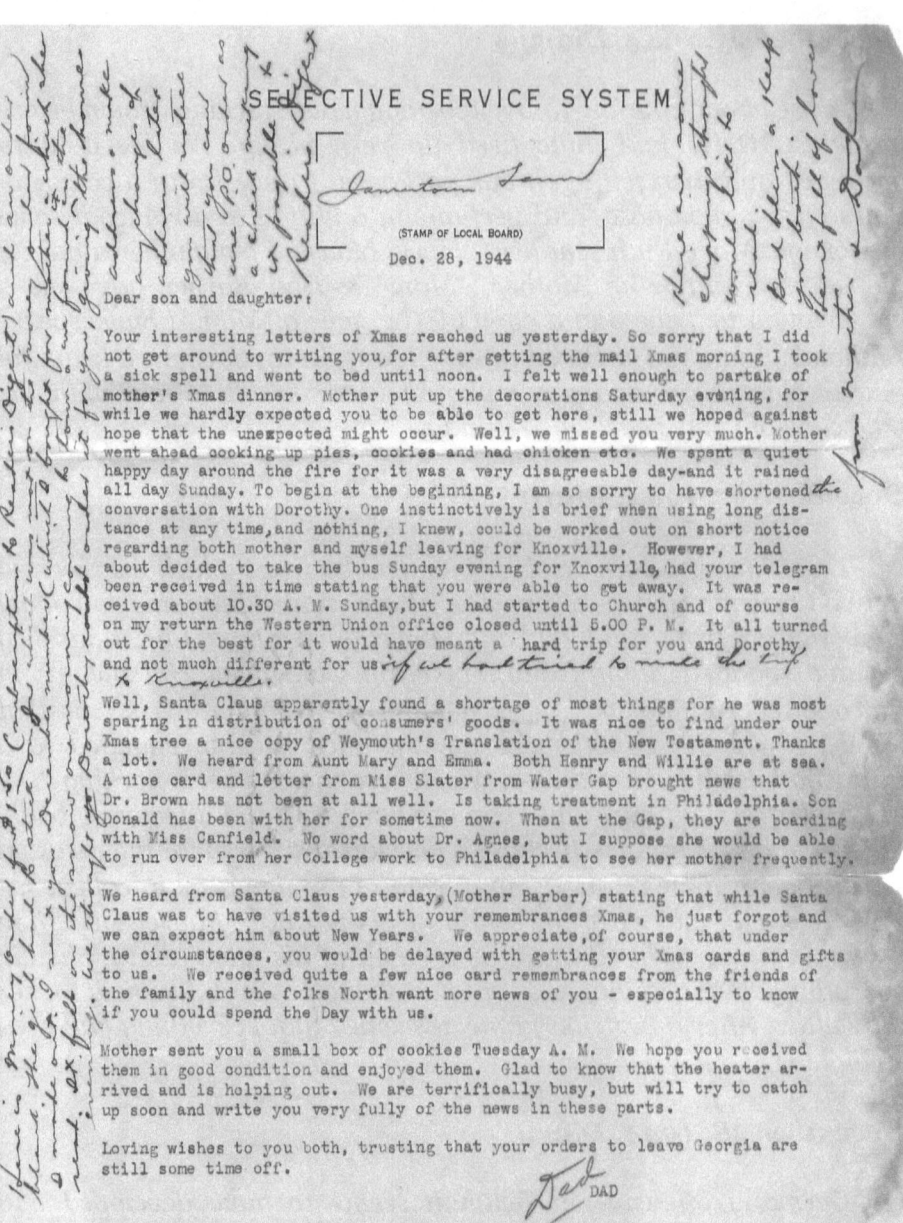

SELECTIVE SERVICE SYSTEM

(STAMP OF LOCAL BOARD)

Dec. 28, 1944

Dear son and daughter:

Your interesting letters of Xmas reached us yesterday. So sorry that I did not get around to writing you, for after getting the mail Xmas morning I took a sick spell and went to bed until noon. I felt well enough to partake of mother's Xmas dinner. Mother put up the decorations Saturday evening, for while we hardly expected you to be able to get here, still we hoped against hope that the unexpected might occur. Well, we missed you very much. Mother went ahead cooking up pies, cookies and had chicken etc. We spent a quiet happy day around the fire for it was a very disagreeable day-and it rained all day Sunday. To begin at the beginning, I am so sorry to have shortened the conversation with Dorothy. One instinctively is brief when using long distance at any time, and nothing, I knew, could be worked out on short notice regarding both mother and myself leaving for Knoxville. However, I had about decided to take the bus Sunday evening for Knoxville, had your telegram been received in time stating that you were able to get away. It was received about 10.30 A. M. Sunday, but I had started to Church and of course on my return the Western Union office closed until 5.00 P. M. It all turned out for the best for it would have meant a hard trip for you and Dorothy, and not much different for us *if we had tried to make the trip to Knoxville.*

Well, Santa Claus apparently found a shortage of most things for he was most sparing in distribution of consumers' goods. It was nice to find under our Xmas tree a nice copy of Weymouth's Translation of the New Testament. Thanks a lot. We heard from Aunt Mary and Emma. Both Henry and Willie are at sea. A nice card and letter from Miss Slater from Water Gap brought news that Dr. Brown has not been at all well. Is taking treatment in Philadelphia. Son Donald has been with her for sometime now. When at the Gap, they are boarding with Miss Canfield. No word about Dr. Agnes, but I suppose she would be able to run over from her College work to Philadelphia to see her mother frequently.

We heard from Santa Claus yesterday, (Mother Barber) stating that while Santa Claus was to have visited us with your remembrances Xmas, he just forgot and we can expect him about New Years. We appreciate, of course, that under the circumstances, you would be delayed with getting your Xmas cards and gifts to us. We received quite a few nice card remembrances from the friends of the family and the folks North want more news of you - especially to know if you could spend the Day with us.

Mother sent you a small box of cookies Tuesday A. M. We hope you received them in good condition and enjoyed them. Glad to know that the heater arrived and is helping out. We are terrifically busy, but will try to catch up soon and write you very fully of the news in these parts.

Loving wishes to you both, trusting that your orders to leave Georgia are still some time off.

DAD

December 28, 1944, Letter from Art's dad to Art

430

December 29, 1944, Diary

A small scandal is developing at the post regarding GI equipment. During recent weeks, clothing has been passed out with a Santa Claus freedom. Shoes, shirts, pants, in short almost everything. At long last the Army is getting wise to this waste. The post office has found package being shipped out containing GI material. Now all packages must be accompanied by a note from the C.O. or an officer certified that no government property is contained. MP's check all cars leaving the post and even board the buses to make a nominal check. The general attitude seems to be to get by with as much as possible. One fellow in my platoon has taken home l pr. combat boots, 1 pr. service shoes, 3 prs. OD pants that I know about.

Within recent weeks, has come news of a big Blackmarket wing in France involving 180 GI's (including officers) and another in Burma. Gasoline and cigarettes are the principal items.

December 30, 1944, Diary

Prolonged clothing check again (for the tenth time). This afternoon I was just hoping that I would be able to spend the weekend in town. Sgt. Utrupt knocked me over with the announcement that he could give 3 3-day passes if a good reason was given. I told him that I had had 8 days at home in 19 months. I had no idea that I might get it, but after going then Capt. Long (my C.O.) to Lt. Col Guthrie, Bu, C.O. I rec'd my pass. I rushed home and Dotty was ready very quickly. We luckily made an Atlanta bus by mere minutes, even finding seats. Bus from there for Chattanooga at 11:30.

December 31, 1944, Diary

Arrived in Chattanooga about 3:30. Found a hotel room and slept about 4 hrs. In Crossville found Ike Conaster going to Jamestown and he took us over. How very wonderful to be home! Mother and Dad received my telegram only a short time before we arrived. We stayed up until a late hour talking. Both Mother and Dad seem to be looking much better then when I saw them last.

American Landscape

SOMEONE asked me "What is
America?"
 Is it the face on the stamp, the
 bright words
Whispered like a litany through the
 slums
Of cities and shrieked by the refugees
Crowding from the boats? Is it the
 glare
On the face of the cop, the smile of
 demagogues?
Is it the siren screaming through the
 streets?
Is it the fresh blue grass of Kentucky,
Or the sweet clean pine of North
 Carolina?
Is it the trim white houses of New
 England,
The lilacs pushing at the curtain or
 rain?
Those from Missouri, the long prairies,
 say,
"Show me! What is this land
 America?
I want to know the road there, I
 want to know
Where it ends." West, east, up and
 down the coasts,
Someone is asking the way back, the
 way forward
To America. Asking, asking—the
 women
Wearing jeweled flags above their
 hearts.
Could there be America without these
 women,
The fierce morning flame of pride
 within their breasts?
The hunter in the virgin forest says,
"Is this my land, staked by the rising
 sun,
My hearth-fire, the green flame of the
 tall trees?
Is it, is it, is it?" O keep asking,
Young America! A word is what
 you make it.
A land is the way all the rivers run
In so many counties, the way the men
Look from their eyes in Utah, Maine,
 Georgia!
It is the way they feel at daybreak
 when the sun
Falls upon their fields. Keep asking,
 O youth!
The quest, the seeking in your
 thoughtful eyes,
Is the meaning of the nation. While
 this lives,
The winds of the land withhold their
 requiem,
And the shining oceans hold back
 the shadows.

Charles Edward Eaton in "The Best
Poems of 1942," Selected by Thomas
Moult. (Harcourt, Brace).
 * * *

Charles Edward Eaton in "The Best Poems of 1942"
selected by Thomas Moult.
[Exchanged in letters between Art and Dotty.]

Dotty & Art

Lisa Soland and Dotty Bushing

EDITOR'S NOTE
AND ACKNOWLEDGMENTS

J had the pleasure of first meeting Dotty Bushing during the technical week of my new one-man play *Sergeant York*, which opened in Knoxville on April 20, 2018. My friend, Mary Bogart, arranged the meeting because Dotty knew Alvin York, and Mary thought that Dotty might offer some personal insight into the WWI hero. It was during that initial meeting that Dotty informed me of her late husband's WWII diary and her unfulfilled desire to have his diary published.

Our initial approach to the publication began only with Art's diary of Army life from January 1945 to April of 1946, but because of their fine collection of artifacts, it was difficult to be content with this well-told, but partial story. As Art writes in the author's preface, "The big job would be to choose and delete." Well, the "big job" was mine, and Art wasn't kidding! The two lovebirds were prolific to say the least, setting the goal of writing to each other every day they were apart. Over three and a half years, that is a lot of letters! Though I tried to be ruthless in my editing responsibilities, it was an impossible task because, through their letters, I had quickly fallen in love with them both, as I know you will too.

The history buffs will enjoy a few references to Sgt. Alvin York as told from the viewpoint of Art's father, who worked as Sgt. York's personal secretary. Art and Dotty attended Maryville College together, and throughout this two-volume set, there are countless references to their alma mater as well as to their friendships forged there.

Volume I: 1943 to 1944 covers Art's experience in the Army prior to leaving for the European Theatre. Volume II: 1945-1946 covers Art's time overseas, before and after his four months in actual combat. I find the time following combat most compelling, while Art waits patiently (and sometimes not so patiently) for his redeployment and his return home to Dotty's arms. Though this time period appears to be less action-packed, it is an aspect of WWII not adequately explored in other history books or non-fiction art forms.

Enormous gratitude must be paid to Martha Hess and Dotty for their original work editing Art's diary entries from January 1945 through April of 1946. Throughout these writings, the capitalizations in the brackets are Art's later added notations. All the chapter divisions and titles are his as well. Chapter 1 has been published in Volume I, and Chapters 1 through 9 in Volume II. As editor, I did not have access to the original diary—only Dotty's and Martha's fine revision.

I also cannot emphasize enough how grateful I am for my assistant, Tonya Hobbs, who joyfully participated in transcribing the letters. Without her supportive spirit and willingness to serve, this collection would have taken much longer to complete. Also, it was wonderful to work alongside Dotty's daughter, Jennifer, as well as all the other Bushing children who have been very kind and accommodating in every way. I would also like to personally thank writer Darnell Arnoult who made herself available to me as a friend and consultant.

Think about publishing a two-volume set, totaling about 1200 pages, and asking busy folks to read them and write promotional quotes. That was tough to do—to ask. But I was completely surprised at the enthusiasm. Not one person declined. Their response alone warmed my heart to such an extent, that it made the entire two years of working on the books worth it. This had everything to do with Art and Dotty Bushing's legacy, of course. But still, 1200 pages?! Here are their precious names: Sam Venable, Michael F. Dilley, Gerald York, Dave Tabler, Tom Bogart, Gerald W. Gibson, Douglas Mastriano, Joanie Latorre, and Charles Hubbard. I'm very grateful. But I am especially grateful to Dotty who entrusted me with her late husband's writings.

The 1943 and 1944 diary entries have been transcribed in their entirety and without revision. Like all the letters, no errors in spelling or punctuation have been fixed. Those diaries and every letter have been presented as close to how they were originally written or typed as possible. I especially enjoyed reading the letters Art typed on a faulty typewriter as we have the privilege to watch his frustration grow in battle with two obstinate typewriter keys! Capturing the language as it was originally executed offers a clearer portrayal of the writer's personality, mindset, and environment. Even under the conditions in which they were living, with all their challenges—the war, and separation from each other—the reader can clearly see how intelligent, kind, loving, and expressive they both were, as also were their family and friends. These volumes capture the sweetest of exchanges on every front, and I have been honored to play a role in bringing these values back to the forefront of whatever public is drawn to them.

The diary, letters, and photographs have been arranged chronologically. The diary entries are italicized and justified; the letters are not, with a page divider placed between them. When "Maryville" is mentioned, the writers are referring to either Maryville College located in Maryville, Tennessee, or the town of Maryville. When Art Bushing returned from Europe, he taught at Maryville College for 50 years, so one can understand the impact that institution had on the two of them.

We were in the deepest throes of transcribing the letters when COVID-19 hit our world of publishing and the world at large. Up to this point, I had been trying to visit with Dotty regularly, but on March 12, 2020, that all came to a screeching halt. I could not help but find it all so profound how each of the letters, the struggles, the fears, and the unknowns that Art and Dotty were facing, we too were now experiencing to some degree.

In the letter dated February 25, 1945, Art wrote to Dotty: "I am trying to keep up with my notes reflecting something of the life of the G.I., my surroundings, and my own thoughts and feelings regarding these things.... I hope that I shall be able to return with my little black book filled to the brim. The squad already expects me to publish what I am writing and they are extremely curious as to what I put down. I hope that it will prove of interest to our little ones." It is to these "little ones," Art and Dotty's descendants, that I dedicate my part in bringing these two books—their story—into your hands. And to Art, who "hitched his wagon to a star" when he married you, Dotty. May these books honor your husband, your children, and the generations to come, creating the lasting legacy for Art your heart desired. Another "dream" of his complete.

Lisa Soland, Senior Editor
Climbing Angel Publishing
June 2020
Knoxville, Tennessee

AUTHOR'S BIOGRAPHY

Dr. Arthur Story Bushing (March 24, 1922 – October 29, 2008) was born in Oroville, Washington, but spent much of his childhood in Jamestown, Tennessee. His father, Arthur Samuel Bushing, was personal secretary to WWI hero Sgt. Alvin C. York and in 1939 Art "Junior" graduated from the Alvin C. York Institute. Art began his teaching career in 1943 as instructor of physics at Maryville College, where he had received his undergraduate degree and met his wife, Dorothy "Dotty" Bushing. During WWII, he served in the United States Army in the European Theatre and earned the Bronze Star, the Battle of the Rhineland, and the Battle of Central Europe medals. In 1947, he returned to his alma mater as an assistant professor of English, while completing his master's degree from the University of Tennessee. Over the fifty years of teaching at Maryville College, countless students were taught from his *Manual of Outlining and Research*, and he enjoyed touring and lecturing on the life of Sgt. Alvin C. York. Dr. Bushing retired from teaching in 1996, but he and Dotty continued to be active in the life of the College, which included serving as historians. Dr. Bushing was also an active member of Highland Presbyterian Church, serving as Elder and Sunday School teacher for many years. In 1991 Art was recognized by the College with an honorary doctor of letters degree and in 2000 he was presented the Maryville College Medallion, the highest honor bestowed by the College. Art and Dotty enjoyed 64 years of marriage and were the proud parents of four children: Stuart, Barbera, Kathryn, and Jennifer.

ABOUT CLIMBING ANGEL
PUBLISHING

Climbing Angel Publishing exists for the purpose of sharing stories of hope and encouragement, aiding in the gathering together of community, and supporting the process of betterment. The following books are available at ClimbingAngel.com and major bookstores.

Adult Books: *(Romans 8:28-30)*

In His Image
By Faith
My Birthday Gift to Jesus
Without Ceasing
SonLight
Corona Victus: Conquering the Virus of Fear
Art Bushing: His Diary, Letters, & Photographs of WWII
Art & Dotty: His Diary, Their Letters & Photographs of WWII

Children's Books: *(Philippians 4:8)*

The Christmas Tree Angel
The Unmade Moose
Thump
Somebunny To Love

www.ingramcontent.com/pod-product-compliance
Lightning Source LLC
Chambersburg PA
CBHW021951120726
47898CB00001BA/56